Paul A. Schutz · Michalinos Zembylas

Advances in Teacher Emotion Research

The Impact on Teachers' Lives

 Springer

Editors
Paul A. Schutz
Department of Educational Psychology
University of Texas at San Antonio
USA
paul.schutz@utsa.edu

Michalinos Zembylas
Program of Educational Studies
Open University of Cyprus
Cyprus
m.zembylas@ouc.ac.cy

ISBN 978-1-4419-0563-5   e-ISBN 978-1-4419-0564-2
DOI 10.1007/978-1-4419-0564-2
Springer Dordrecht Heidelberg London New York

Library of Congress Control Number: 2009927723

Printed on acid-free paper

Springer is part of Springer Science+Business Media (www.springer.com)

Foreword: Performance, Pedagogy and Emotionality

Norman K. Denzin

A few years ago, one could hardly find any research on emotions in education and teaching. The roots of this neglect are not unrelated to the dominance of epistemo-logical and methodological traditions that has sought to establish clear dichotomies between personal/public, emotion/reason, and quantitative/qualitative issues. Fortunately, this is changing and the authors in this fine collection of chapters, drawn from a wide range of epistemological and methodological traditions, show the complexity in thinking and doing research on emotions in teaching.

Instead of outlining the contribution of each of these traditions, I want to promote a direction that a number of the authors in this book discuss in a variety of different ways. As such, this is essentially a call for a *critical pedagogy and performance approach* to the study of teacher emotion research, that is, an approach, which places criticality and sociality at the center of our investigations on emotions.

Emotions are felt as lived-performances, staged in classrooms, hallways, play-grounds. In these spaces teachers and students, as moral agents, enact the felt emo-tions of rage, love, shame, desire, despair, empowerment. These moral performances define the public and private faces of the schooling experience.

The interpretive study of teachers and students emotionality, the place and impact of emotions, performance and public pedagogies on teachers' and students' lives is at a crossroads. As this unique point in history, we live in a surveillance world. More than ever before, the politics of democracy and critical pedagogy require educators and students bring passion and commitment to social justice to the learning process. Critical pedagogy cultivates human potential, honors the selves, identities, and emotional experiences of teachers and students. It becomes the cornerstone of democracy itself (Giroux 2007, p. 3). Numerous chapters in this collection raise such issues either at the center of their investigation or at the back-ground. What is important is that even the research that is seemingly unconnected to its sociological terrain – it is unavoidably contextualized in ways that are not immediately recognized.

N.K. Denzin
University of Illinois at Urbana-Champaign, Urbana, IL, USA

Building on the incisive arguments of the editors and contributors to this volume, I am therefore calling for critical inquiry that is sensitive to the multiple contexts of teacher emotion research, from teacher's emotions, to emotion management, and display, to commercialization, to student illness, learning, diversity, reform, gender, class, religion, and social inequality. This research is grounded in the *performance tradition* (Denzin 2003, 2009; Bagley 2008) in the widest possible sense. This tradition is located on a global stage. Madison and Hamers (2006) convincingly argue that performance and globality are intertwined – that is, performances become the enactment of stories that literally bleed across different kinds of borders. Being, for example, a student or teacher of color is to be "enmeshed in the facts of … foreign policy, world trade, civil society and war" (p. xx). Regardless of the methodology utilized, the investigation conducted and its implications are performances embedded in certain socio-political contexts and assumptions.

In this globalized world, race and the staging and performance of racialized identities, within the popular culture marketplace of fashion and consumption, remain, as W.E.B. Du Bois (1978) would remind us "the problem of the twenty-first century" (Du Bois 1978 [1901], pp. 281, 288). Schooling in this new century cannot succeed "unless peoples of different races and religions are also integrated into the democratic whole" (Du Bois 1978 [1901], pp. 281, 288). Postmodern democracy cannot succeed unless educators, policy makers, politicians, and critical scholars are able to adopt methodologies that transcend the limitations and constraints of a lingering, politically and racially conservative postpositivism. This framework attaches itself to state organized auditing systems and regulatory laws (like No Child Left Behind in the United States, for instance). These links and these historical educational connections must be broken. Never before has there been a greater need for a utopianism, which will help us imagine a world free of conflict, terror and death, a world that is caring, loving, truly compassionate, a world that honors healing.

Critical pedagogy and performance approach does not limit itself to one set of methodologies and epistemologies but utilizes a variety of tools to highlight criticality and sociality. To these ends, I locate the performance approach within a racialized, spectacle pedagogy, that is – pedagogy that critiques power relations and new surveillance techniques either at the macrosociological or the microsociological level. The most important events of the last decade include several wars and conflicts (e.g. Iraq, Afghanistan, Darfur, Middle East), terrorist attacks, and an institutionalization of a new surveillance in many countries (Garoian and Gaudelius 2008). A critical performance approach must locate itself in these historical spaces, which now encompass surveillance regimes in virtually every educational setting – school, college and daycares.

The editors and contributors to this important and most timely volume offer indispensable guidelines and models for engaging these issues both at the macro (societal) and the micro (pedagogical) level, explicitly or implicitly. We owe them a great debt.

References

Bagley C (2008) Educational ethnography as performance art: towards a sensuous feeling and knowing. Qual Res 8(1):53–72

Denzin NK (2009) Qualitative inquiry under fire: toward a new paradigm dialogue. Left Coast Press, Walnut Creek

Denzin NK (2003) Performance ethnography. Sage, Thousand Oaks

Du Bois WEB (1978 [1901]) The problem of the twentieth century is the problem of the color line. In: Green DS, Driver E (eds) On sociology and the black community. University of Chicago Press, Chicago, pp 281–289

Garoian CR, Gaudelius YM (2008) Spectacle pedagogy: art, politics and visual culture. SUNY Press, Albany

Giroux H (2007) Democracy, education and the politics of critical pedagogy. In: McLaren P, Kincheloe JL (eds) Critical padagogy: Where are we now? Peter Lang, New York, pp 1–8

Madison DS, Hamera J (2006) Performance studies at the intersection. In Madison DS, Hamera J (eds) The sage handbook of performance studies. Thousand Oaks: Sage Publications, pp xi–xxv

Contents

Contributors

Lori Price Aultman
Department of Teacher Education, Spring Hill College, USA,
laultman@shc.edu

Katrijn Ballet
Center for Educational Policy and Innovation, Catholic University of Leuven,
Belgium
katrijn.ballet@ped.kuleuven.be

Ronald A. Beghetto
Department of Teacher Education, University of Oregon, USA
beghetto@uoregon.edu

Robert V. Bullough
Jr. Center for the Improvement of Teacher Education and Schooling (CITES)
and Department of Teacher Education, Brigham Young University, Provo,
Utah, USA
bob_bullough@byu.edu

Mei-Lin Chang
Department of Educational Policy and Leadership, Emory University, USA
chang.616@osu.edu

Sharon Chubbuck
Department of Educational and Policy Leadership, Marquette University, USA
sharon.chubbuck@marquette.edu

Dionne I. Cross
Mathematics Education, Indiana University, USA
dicross@indiana.edu

Heather A. Davis
Department of Curriculum and Instruction, North Carolina State University, USA
heather_davis@ncsu.edu

Christopher Day
Director, Teacher and Leadership Research Centre, School of Education,
University of Nottingham, England
christopher.day@nottingham.ac.uk

Jessica T. DeCuir-Gunby
Department of Curriculum & Instruction, North Carolina State University, USA
jessica_decuir@ncsu.edu

Norman Denzin
Department of Advertising, University of Illinois, Urbana-Champaign, USA
n-denzin@uiuc.edu

Eileen Estes
Department of Educational & Counseling Psychology, University
of Louisville, USA
eoeste01@louisville.edu

Anne C. Frenzel
Department of Psychology, University of Munich, Germany
frenzel@psy.lmu.de

Thomas Goetz
Department of Psychology, University of Konstanz,
Germany & Thurgau University of Teacher Education, Switzerland
thomas.goetz@uni-konstanz.de

Christine S. Grant
Department of Chemical and Biomolecular Engineering, North Carolina State
University, USA
grant@ncsu.edu

Crissie M. Grove
National Center For Education Statistics/Association For Institutional
Research, USA
cgrove@airweb2.org

Qing Gu
Senior Research Fellow, School of Education, University of Nottingham,
England
qing.gu@nottingham.ac.uk

Ji Y. Hong
Department of Educational Psychology, Instructional Psychology
and Technology, University of Oklahoma, USA
jyhong@ou.edu

Barbara Jacob
Department of Psychology, University of Munich, Germany
bjacob@edupsy.uni-muenchen.de

Geert Kelchtermans
Center for Educational Policy and Innovation, Catholic University of Leuven,
Belgium
geert.kelchtermans@ped.kuleuven.be

Sue Lasky
Department of Leadership, Foundations & Human Resource, University of
Louisville, USA
sue.lasky@louisville.edu

Linda A. Long-Mitchell
School of Social Work, University of Georgia, USA
lalong@uga.edu

Debra K. Meyer
Department of Education, Elmhurst College, USA
debram@elmhurst.edu

Izhar Oplatka
Department of Policy and Administration in Education, Tel Aviv University, Israel
oplatka@post.tau.ac.il

Liesbeth Piot
Center for Educational Policy and Innovation, Catholic University of Leuven,
Belgium
liesbeth.piot@ped.kuleuven.be

Jerry Rosiek
Department of Teacher Education, University of Oregon, USA
jrosiek@uoregon.edu

Paul A. Schutz
Department of Educational Psychology, University of Texas at San Antonio, USA
paul.schutz@utsa.edu

Peter Sleegers
Educational Organization & Management, University of Twente, The Netherlands
p.j.c.sleegers@gw.utwente.nl

Elizabeth J. Stephens
Department of Psychology, University of Munich, Germany
stephens@psy.lmu.de

Jessica J. Summers
Department of Educational Psychology, University of Arizona, USA
jsummers@email.arizona.edu

Jeannine E. Turner
Department of Educational Psychology and Learning Systems, USA,
Florida State University
turner@mail.coe.fsu.edu

Klaas van Veen
ICLON, Leiden University, Netherlands
kveen@iclon.leidenuniv.nl

Ralph M. Waugh
Department of Educational Psychology, The University of Texas, USA
ralphmwaugh@yahoo.com

Meca Williams-Johnson
Department of Curriculum, Foundations and Reading, Georgia Southern
University, USA
mecawilliams@georgiasouthern.edu

Ken Winograd
Teacher and Counselor Education, Oregon State University, USA
winograk@oregonstate.edu

Michalinos Zembylas
Program of Educational Studies, Open University of Cyprus, Cyprus
m.zembylas@ouc.ac.cy

Part I
Introduction

Chapter 1
Introduction to Advances in Teacher Emotion Research: The Impact on Teachers' Lives

Paul A. Schutz and Michalinos Zembylas

Abstract In this chapter we discuss the importance of this edit volume and begin the discussion of issues related to inquiry on teacher emotion. In addition we set the stage for the remainder of the book by providing a brief introduction to the different sections of the book and the chapters those sections contain.

Keywords Teacher emotion · Emotional labor · Burnout

Some reports estimate that nearly 50% of teachers entering the profession leave within the first 5 years (Alliance for Excellent Education 2004; Ingersoll 2003). One explanation of why teachers leave the profession so early in their career might be related to the emotional nature of the teaching profession. For example, teaching is an occupation that involves considerable emotional labor. Emotional labor involves the effort, planning, and control teachers need to express organizationally desired emotions during interpersonal transactions. As such, emotional labor has been associated with job dissatisfaction, health symptoms and emotional exhaustion, which are key components of burnout and related to teachers who drop out of the profession (Jackson et al. 1986; Maslach 1982; Morris and Feldman 1996; Schaubroeck and Jones 2000). Research into emotional labor in teaching and other aspects of teachers' emotions is becoming increasingly important not only because of the growing number of teachers leaving the profession, but also because unpleasant classroom emotions have considerable implications for student learning, school climate and the quality of education in general.

Over the last few years, educational researchers have made progress towards identifying the role of emotions in education (e.g., Boler 1999; Linnenbrink 2006; Nias 1996; Schutz and Pekrun 2007; Schutz and Lanehart 2002; van Veen and Lasky 2005).

P.A. Schutz (✉) and M. Zembylas
Department of Educational Psychology, University of Texas at San Antonio, San Antonio, TX, USA
e-mail: paul.schutz@utsa.edu

P.A. Schutz and M. Zembylas (eds.), *Advances in Teacher Emotion Research:*
The Impact on Teachers' Lives,
DOI 10.1007/978-1-4419-0564-2_1, © Springer Science+Business Media, LLC 2009

Currently, there are a number of researchers investigating teachers' emotions in a variety of educational contexts; these researchers highlight how emotions are inextricably linked to teachers' work, development and identity (e.g., Hargreaves 2005), and how those emotions impact teachers' lives (e.g., Liston and Garrison 2004; Zembylas 2005). Yet, to date, there has been no systematic effort to critically synthesize how or what aspects of teacher emotion should be studied and theorized. In fact, researchers are only beginning to examine various manifestations of the transactions among teaching and emotions, which suggests that additional research and theorization on teachers' emotions is urgently needed as it will help the educational researcher garner a better understanding of how emotions influence teaching, learning and teachers' lives.

The authors in this edited volume, entitled *Advances in Teacher Emotion Research: The Impact on Teachers' Lives*, use a variety of different methodological and theoretical approaches to provide a systematic overview of our current understandings of the role of emotions in teachers' professional lives and work. More specifically, the authors discuss inquiry related to teachers' emotions in educational reform, teacher identity, student involvement, race/class/gender issues, school administration and inspection, emotional labor, teacher burnout and several other related issues. This volume, then, represents the accumulation of many different epistemological and theoretical positions related to inquiry on teachers' emotions, acknowledging that emotions are core components of teachers' lives.

In general, our objectives for this edited volume are to examine the philosophical, psychological, social, political, and cultural backgrounds and contexts that are constitutive of contemporary research on the role of emotions in teaching around the world; to appreciate the contextual and international dimensions of teacher emotions in education; and to contribute to on-going efforts to analyze the implications for teaching, teachers' lives, teacher attrition, and educational reform.

To do so, this volume features a number of important scholars from around the world (e.g., Belgium, Cyprus, Germany, Israel, the Netherlands, UK and USA) who represent a variety of disciplines (e.g., Educational Psychology, Cultural Psychology, Sociology, Philosophy, Cultural Studies, Gender Studies, Multicultural Education, and Teacher Education), scientific paradigms (e.g., experimental research, non-experimental field studies, phenomenological approaches, pragmatism, constructivism, critical race theory, post-structural, feminist, and post-positivist perspectives), and inquiry methods (e.g., quantitative, qualitative, ethnographic, philosophical, historical, autobiographical, and multimethod approaches). In addition, the edited volume deals with a variety of populations (e.g., school, university students) and educational activity settings (e.g., classrooms, independent study).

As such, *Advances in Teacher Emotion Research* takes an eclectic look at teacher emotions, presenting current research from diverse perspectives, thereby making this volume a significant contribution to the field. This combination of variety, timeliness, potential for transformation of the field, and uniqueness makes this a very important edited book.

The book is organized into *six sections*. In this chapter "Introduction to Advances in Teacher Emotion Research: The Impact on Teachers' Lives" we begin the discussion of issues related to inquiry on teacher emotion and set the stage for the remainder of the book. In the second section the authors focuses on "Teacher Emotions in the Context of Teaching and Teacher Education." This section features such scholars as Christopher Day and Qing Gu; Robert V. Bullough; Izhar Oplatka; and, Debra K. Meyer. The work of this group of international authors focuses on inquiries of teacher emotions in relation to issues of mentoring, emotion management and regulation, and student–teacher relationships.

In Chap. 2, Day and Gu, explore the nature of teachers' emotions and emotional identities within the context of their own desires to achieve a sense of well being and their desire to promote that sense of well being among the pupils they teach. In this chapter they consider the conditions that promote or fail to promote teachers' emotional well being (a more encompassing and, potentially a more accurate way of depicting teachers' aims than "job satisfaction").

In Chap. 3 Robert Bullough explores aspects of the emotional life of beginning teachers and the experienced teachers who mentor them. First, he briefly describes the institutional context within which teachers and mentors conduct their work, a context increasingly shaped by the pressures of high-stakes student testing and punitive approaches to accountability. Drawing primarily on the work of the late philosopher, Robert Solomon, he then describes the appraisal theory of the emotions that ground the analysis, noting how, unlike moods, emotions are intentional and have an object to which they refer. This theoretical framework is used in the context of reviewing beginning teachers and mentors. Through presenting and analyzing two case studies, Bullough illustrates various aspects of the connections existing among emotion, identity, and expectations in the lives and work of a beginning teacher and a new mentor. Particular attention is given to the effects of achieving or failing to achieve a productive professional identity.

In Chap. 4 Izhar Oplatka reviews the research on emotion management in teaching since the 1990s, including the theoretical knowledge underlying this research, to display its contribution to our knowledge base about emotional displays and their determinants in school teaching. Oplatka discusses emotion management at work and then focuses on forms of emotion management in teaching. Oplatka also reviews and analyzes factors affecting emotion management in teaching – such as the culture of teaching, gender, seniority, and the principal. Finally, Oplatka discusses the implications of emotion management in teaching.

In Chap. 5 Debra Meyer discusses teaching as emotional practice and how that practice is tied in with teacher identities. Her focus in this chapter is on the first stage of professional induction – the student-teaching experience and how teachers communicate emotions. In other words, she explores the question: what emotions are "appropriate," and when they should be expressed? Meyer argues that it not unusual for college supervisors and cooperating teachers to empathize with student–teachers' emotions, but assume their emotions can be adjusted with reason or easily ignored. Attempts to separate emotions from or to join them with teaching practice have implications for teacher identity and development. Through a synthesis of these related bodies of literature with examples from her own research on student teachers' emotional experiences, Meyer examines some of the possible trajectories for new teachers as they enter the emotional practice of teaching.

The third section addresses issues related to the role of emotions in the context of "Student and Teacher Involvement." This section features chapters by Mei-Lin Chang and Heather Davis; Anne Frenzel, Thomas Goetz, Elizabeth J. Stephens and Barbara Jacob; Susan Lasky and Eileen Estes; Jerry Rosiek and Ronald A. Beghetto; and, Paul A. Schutz, Lori P. Aultman, and Meca R. Williams-Johnson. This group of scholars focuses their chapters on issues of teacher emotional experiences, the emotion dynamics in student–teacher relationships, emotional scaffolding and dealing with student or student family illness.

In Chap. 6 Chang and Davis examine the emotional by-products of developing relationships with students. They begin the chapter by reviewing the power of student–teacher relationships in promoting adaptive student outcomes including enhanced motivation and achievement. They examine the pleasant and unpleasant emotional by-products of being involved with students and the role repeatedly experiencing unpleasant emotions may play in teacher burnout. They tackle the emotional life of "challenging relationships" specifically with regard to the judgments teachers may make about student behavior that can lead to emotional exhaustion and compassion fatigue. Their central question is: When things don't "feel good," what are adaptive strategies for reframing, rethinking, and reinvesting in relationships?

In Chap. 7, Anne Frenzel, Thomas Goetz, Elizabeth J. Stephens, and Barbara Jacob focus on teacher emotions resulting from appraisals of success or failure (i.e., teachers' achievement emotions) with respect to achieving instructional goals. Frenzel and colleagues present theoretical assumptions and empirical findings regarding the antecedents and effects of achievement emotions more generally, and specify those for the context of teaching. Based on deliberations that teachers' emotions simultaneously impact their instructional behavior and are affected by their appraisals regarding succeeding or failing during instruction, the authors propose a model depicting the interplay between teachers' emotions, their instructional behavior and student outcomes. They present results from both qualitative and quantitative studies testing assumptions brought forward by the model.

In Chap. 8 Sue Lasky and Eileen Estes propose that that schools have a particular place in the lives of students living with cancer, and that many teachers are largely unprepared to understand the ongoing psychosocial and physical challenges they can face. They suggest that for teachers who educate students living with cancer there may be emotional stress or satisfaction unique to their experiences that are largely uninvestigated. They also outline a phased line of research that will investigate how to develop school-based, yet community wide networks of support to provide resources than can sustain teachers through the emotionality inherent in walking with students through their cancer journeys.

In Chap. 9 Jerry Rosiek and Ronald Beghetto suggests that teachers regularly think about how to scaffold students' emotional response to the subject matter they teach. They further makes the case that when teachers think deeply about how students emotionally encounter their subject matter they are inevitably led to reflection on the social and cultural context of their students' lives. Thinking about students' emotions thus becomes one of the primary ways through which the specifics of a given subject matter and the broader sociocultural influences on student learning become intertwined in teacher thinking. This connection is illustrated with several case vignettes. In examining these cases, a second point is made: Teacher reflection on students' emotional response to the subject matter frequently elicits emotional responses from the teachers. These emotional responses, he argues, are not excessive, but are necessary components of teachers' pedagogical content knowledge.

In the final chapter in this section, Paul Schutz, Lori Aultman and Meca Williams-Johnson focus on teacher emotion from an educational psychology lens. In doing so, they explicate some of the current theories related to the nature of emotion. In recent years, there has been renewed interest in the debates about the nature and structure of emotion in psychology and educational psychology. In other words, are there distinct categories of the emotions (e.g., anger, fear) or is it more useful to conceptualize emotion with a dimensional model (e.g., pleasant vs. unpleasant, active vs. inactive)? Schutz, Aultman and Williams-Johnson will use those perspectives to help us understand teachers' emotions and discuss research related to how teachers negotiate relationship boundaries with their students, how teachers develop useful emotional climates in their classrooms, and how teachers attempt to deal with the emotional labor needed in negotiating their role as a teacher.

The fourth section addresses issues related to "Teachers' Emotions in Times of Change." This section will feature chapters that represent the programs of research of Geert Kelchtermans, Katrijn Ballet and Liesbeth Piot; Klaas van Veen and Peter Sleegers; Jeannine Turner, Ralph Waugh, Jessica Summers, and Crissie Grove; and Dionne Cross and Ji Hong. An important area where emotions come into play in education is related to educational reform. This group of scholars will focus their chapters on teachers and their emotions in relation to issues of reform efforts and political changes.

In Chap. 11, Geert Kelchtermans, Katrijn Ballet and Liesbeth Piot focus on the way teachers experience their job and their professional identity. Their narrative and biographical approach allows for an in-depth reconstruction of the political and moral tensions teachers experience; the pressure to reconceptualise their "selves"; and as a consequence the emotional quality of their work lives. They argue that the changes in the working conditions deeply affect teachers both in their professional actions and the emotional experience of the job. Teachers experience intense emotional conflicts as they struggle to cope with conflicting identity scenarios, the web of (conflicting) loyalties they find themselves in, etc. Their findings confirm, exemplify and deepen their earlier work on vulnerability as a structural characteristic of the teaching job.

In Chap. 12 Klaas van Veen and Peter Sleegers begin by reviewing studies of teachers' emotions in relation to reforms. They examine different theoretical perspectives and methods and elaborate on the strengths and weaknesses of this relatively new field of research, adopting a social-psychological approach to emotions. They argue that this field is still in need of a coherent conceptual framework for adequately understanding teachers' emotions. Their central assumption is that reforms strongly affect teachers' emotions due to divergent reasons, varying from feeling insecure and threatened, to feeling reinforced and enthusiastic. What those studies into teachers' emotions show in general is that most reforms affect teachers' professional sense of self or identity; teachers feel their core beliefs and assumptions are at stake. At a deeper level, teachers often feel that they are not recognized as professionals, rather as employees or executors of the ideas of others. They also attempt to provide an overview of the potential issues at stake for teachers in the contexts of reforms, referring to the content, process of implementation, and teachers' agency

In Chap. 13 Jeannine Turner, Ralph Waugh, Jessica Summers, and Crissie Grove suggest that professional-development is often used as catalysts for transforming research-based theories and findings into best-teaching-practices and increased student-achievement within whole-school reform efforts. Their investigation of educational reform is informed by three theories: Self-Determination Theory, Control-Value Theory and circumplex models of interpersonal relationships. From a Self-Determination Theory perspective, individuals' intrinsic motivation is facilitated through environmental supports of three personally relevant elements: autonomy, competence, and relatedness. From a Control-Value Theory perspective individuals' motivations and emotional correspondents are due to personal judgments regarding relevant-issues of control (e.g., agency/self-efficacy) and personal values (e.g., goals). Finally, a circumplex model is then used to describe two primary dimensions of principals' interactional behaviors that provide overt and covert messages about their support (or lack of support) for teachers' autonomy and competence. They propose that emotional foundations developed through teachers' interpersonal interactions with principals merge with teachers' values and perceptions of control to shape their motivations for implementing high-quality professional development.

In the final chapter is this section, Dionne Cross, and Ji Hong, examine the effects of both nationwide and local efforts to improve the state of our educational system in the areas of Mathematics and Science. Although these mandates are designed at the federal level, the grueling task of implementation is often bestowed on the local school districts and, ultimately, on teachers who are most closely connected to learning. Reform in these domains often involves teachers transitioning from a traditional, didactic teaching approach to one that is student-centered and inquiry-based. Changing teaching practice is an emotionally laborious and challenging process, as it often involves modifying teachers' existing beliefs about the domain, teaching and learning, and also reshaping their professional identity as a teacher. In this chapter Cross and Hong will discuss the influence of teachers' domain-specific beliefs and professional identity on their emotional experiences as teachers attempt to incorporate reform-oriented practices in their mathematics and science classrooms. Their discussion will also include findings from empirical studies related to these issues with descriptions of teachers' experiences from emic perspectives.

The fifth section will focus on teachers' emotions in relation to issues of "Race, Gender and Power Relationships." This section will feature chapters that represent the programs of research of Ken Winograd; Jessica T. DeCuir-Gunby, Linda A.

Long-Mitchell, and Christine Grant; and, Michalinos Zembylas and Sharon Chubbuck. This group of scholars focus their chapters on issues of race, gender and emotion in teaching, the role of power and affect, and the emotions of teaching in the context of citizenship education.

In Chap. 15 Ken Winograd, examines non-white discourses for emotion as it relates to the work of teachers, particularly those voices of African Americans, Native Americans and Latino/a Americans. The existing literature on emotion rules and teachers' emotions is referenced and critiqued as it (mis)represents non-dominant discourses in relation to emotions. It appears that non-white workers, including teachers, think differently about emotions, especially how they use emotions in the classroom to manage their professional identities as well as the behavior of students. Winograd re-examines data previously collected by himself in a self-study of his own emotions as a teacher; in addition, there is new data describing the emotional experience of teachers of color. While the work of (white researchers like) Hochschild and others is still useful in the study of work-related emotions, the chapter *centralizes* (as opposed to marginalize) the non-dominant discourses and, in the end, suggests how emotions (the experience of emotions and their display) serve both the personal and political interests of teachers of color.

In Chap. 16, Jessica T. DeCuir-Gunby, Linda A. Long-Mitchell, and Christine S. Grant, suggest that although the number of African American and Latina professors of engineering has increased in the last decade, engineering faculty and engineering student populations remain grossly overrepresented by White men. Because of this, African American and Latina women professors often experience unique difficulties that stem from their race, gender, and the intersection of their race and gender. The purpose of this chapter is to use a Critical Race Theory (CRT) and Critical Race Feminism (CRF) framework to explore the emotions associated with being underrepresented women professors of color in engineering. In doing so, the authors focus on CRT's tenet of Whiteness as Property, particularly the elements of the right of use and enjoyment and the right to exclude. Also, DeCuir-Gunby and her colleagues utilize intersectionality theory from CRF to examine the interaction of race and gender in the experiences of the participants (Crenshaw 1989). Their analysis concentrates on the emotions involved in interacting with faculty and students. Finally, they discuss strategies for coping with race and gender-related stress in academia.

In Chap. 17 Michalinos Zembylas and Sharon Chubbuck focus on the interplay of emotions with social justice education, with particular attention to how emotions and social justice education can be mutually engaged as both critical and transformational forces to produce better teaching and learning opportunities for marginalized students. They discuss the relevance and complexity of emotions in relation to social justice, through sustaining or remedying social inequalities. They then describe an example of teaching for/about social justice, showing how reflecting on and interrogating emotions can help perpetuate or disrupt historical and local practices that that reproduce inequity. This example is grounded in empirical data taken from a case study of a white novice teacher who attempted to teach for/about social justice in an urban school in Midwestern United States. In the last part of the chapter, Zembylas and Chubbuck argue for the urgent need to reconceptualize the interplay between emotions and social justice education in order to capitalize on the possibilities that lie therein. In particular, they build upon a previous analysis of the notion of *critical emotional praxis* – that is, critical praxis informed by emotion that resists unjust systems and practices as well as emotion that helps create a more fair and just world in our classrooms and our everyday lives – to show how inclusive this notion can be in addressing issues of social justice education.

In the final section, "A Future Agenda for Research on Teachers' Emotions in Education," we synthesize the themes that emerge from the other chapters. Additionally, we discuss future directions for inquiry on teachers' emotions are discussed, as well as implications for classroom instruction, intervention, teachers' professional development, teachers' lives, and educational policy and leadership. In this section, we use the content of the chapters to discuss the variety, timeliness, and potential for transformation of the field, and the unique contributions of the chapters to our understanding of teachers' emotions in education.

As indicated, there has been a tremendous concern for teacher attrition in recent years. One of the areas that have not been adequately investigated in relation to this problem is teacher emotion. In the coming years, it will be valuable to further examine the emotional impact on teachers' lives and work, especially in the context of recent and forceful efforts emphasizing the need for accountability in schools and the rapid increase of high-stakes testing. In addition, there is often an underestimation of the complexity of teaching: teaching is often perceived as a rational activity, but the emotional complexity of teaching is neglected. This edited book addresses all of those concerns. Considering the importance of education, it is crucial to not only understand the causes or antecedents of teacher emotions, but also to better understand how these experiences influence students' and teachers' success in the classroom. This edited book helps us move in that direction.

References

Alliance for Excellent Education. (2004). Tapping the potential: Retaining and developing high-quality new teachers. (Report). Washington, DC

Boler M (1999) Feeling power: emotions and education. Routledge, New York

Crenshaw K (1989) Demarginalizing the intersection of race and sex: A Black feminist critique of antidiscrimination doctrine, feminist theory and antiracist politics. University of Chicago Legal Foru 139–167.

Hargreaves A (2005) Educational change takes ages: life, career and generational factors in teachers' emotional responses to educational change. Teach Teach Educ 21:967–983

Ingersoll RM (2003) Who controls teachers' work? Cambridge, Massachusetts: Harvard University Press

Jackson SE, Schwab RI, Schuler RS (1986) Toward an understanding of the burnout phenomenon. J Appl Psychol 71:630–640

Linnenbrink L (2006) Emotion research in education [Special issue]. Educ Psychol Rev 18(4): 307–314

Liston D, Garrison J (2004) Teaching, learning, and loving. Routledge Falmer, New York

Maslach C (1982) Burnout: the cost of caring. Prentice Hall, Englewood Cliffs, NJ

Morris JA, Feldman DC (1996) The dimensions, antecedents, and consequences of emotional labor. Acad Manage Rev 21(4):986–1010

Nias J (1996) Thinking about feeling: the emotions in teaching (Introduction to special issue on teachers' emotions). Cambridge J Educ 26(3):293–306

Schaubroeck J, Jones JR (2000) Antecedents of workplace emotional labor dimensions and moderators of their effects on physical symptoms. J Organ Behav 21:163–183

Schutz PA, Lanehart S (2002) Introduction: emotions in education [Special issue]. Educ Psychol 37(2):67–68

Schutz P, Pekrun R (eds) (2007) Emotion in education. Academic, Boston

van Veen K, Lasky S (2005) Emotions as a lens to explore teacher identity and change: different theoretical approaches. (Introduction to special issue on emotion, teacher identity and change). Teach Teach Educ 21(8):895–898

Zembylas M (2005) Teaching with emotion: a postmodern enactment. Information Age Publishing, Greenwich, CT

Part II
Teacher Emotions in the Context
of Teaching and Teacher Education

Chapter 2
Teacher Emotions: Well Being and Effectiveness

Christopher Day and Gu Qing

Abstract In this chapter we explore the nature of teachers' emotions and emotional identities within the context of their own desires to achieve a sense of well being and effectiveness and their desire to promote that sense of well being and achievement among the pupils they teach. We consider the conditions that promote or fail to promote teachers' emotional wellbeing (a more encompassing and, potentially a more accurate way of depicting teachers' aims than "job satisfaction").

Keywords Well-being • Effectiveness • Teacher emotion

This chapter will endeavour to contribute to knowledge of variations in the influences on teachers' emotions in the belief that, in this century seems especially, more demands are being made teachers to contribute to the academic, social and emotional well being of pupils. Thus it is important that policy makers, teacher educators and school principals attend to teachers' own sense of well-being. We will explore the nature of teachers' emotional well being as a necessary condition for teachers' sense of effectiveness. We define "well being" as both a psychological and social construct:

> … a dynamic state, in which the individual is able to develop their potential, work productively and creatively, build strong and positive relationships with others, and contribute to their community. (Foresight Mental Capital and Wellbeing Project 2008: 10)

We use this term, rather than "job satisfaction" (Evans 1998, 2001) because it encompasses the personal as well as the professional and because it is the combination of these two elements that illustrates teaching at its best (Csikszentmihalyi 1990; Palmer 1998; Fried 2001).

C. Day (✉)
Teacher and Leadership Research Centre, School of Education, University of Nottingham, Nottingham, England
e-mail: christopher.day@nottingham.ac.uk

P.A. Schutz and M. Zembylas (eds.), *Advances in Teacher Emotion Research:*   15
The Impact on Teachers' Lives,
DOI 10.1007/978-1-4419-0564-2_2, © Springer Science+Business Media, LLC 2009

There is now a considerable body of research internationally which attests to the importance of emotion in teachers' management of teaching and learning in classrooms (Hargreaves 2004, 2005; Nias 1996; Schutz and Pekrun 2007; van Veen and Lasky 2005; Zembylas 2005). Much of this relates to the positive and negative effects on teachers' motivation, self-efficacy, professional identities and job satisfaction of pupil behavior (Hargreaves 2000), leadership, classroom and school climate (Leithwood 2007) and centrally initiated policy initiatives which have changed the conditions under which teachers work, and in some cases, how they teach (Troman and Woods 2001). Recent studies have also identified statistically significant associations between teacher commitment and pupil attainment (Day et al. 2007), and the importance of resilience (Gu and Day 2007; Henderson and Milstein 2003), emotional understanding and care to effective teachers (Denzin 1984; Goleman 1996; Noddings 1992).

At this particular time in history many teachers work in environments that are hostile to their well-being. Schools contain children and young people who are more likely than at any time previously to live uncertain emotional lives, in homes in which there is a single parent or in homes where both parents are working and, so, are unable to be present at times of real and unanticipated need (Layard and Dunn 2009; New Economics Foundation 2009). In addition, at least in so-called "developed" nations, pupils are likely to be familiar with information and communications technology and, as a result, more aware of the limitations of school and classroom learning and, by extension, those of their teachers. Alongside these challenges are those that emanate from results driven "performativity" agendas of governments, in which teachers' abilities to improve student attainment results are scrutinized and judged to a greater extent than previously. This cocktail of challenges affects teachers in all countries. It means that there is more bureaucratic accountability, that the work of teachers is more intensive and that, in general, their work has become more demanding.

There is an abundance of evidence that one consequence of these changes has been a lowering of morale (Dinham and Scott 2000; Guardian 2003; Ingersoll 2003). Associated with such lowering of morale has been a sense of "vulnerability" (Kelchtermans 1996) and uncertainty of professional identity. We note this not in order to judge but rather to examine the felt consequences upon teachers in order to associate such challenges with the urgent need to attend to their emotional as well as cognitive health as factors which are of equal importance in their effectiveness. Researchers have observed that teacher identities are constructed not only from the technical and emotional aspects of teaching (i.e. classroom management, subject knowledge and pupil test results) and their personal lives, but also "as the result of interaction between the personal experiences of teachers and the social, cultural, and institutional environments in which they function on a daily basis" (Sleegers and Kelchtermans 1999: 379). Emotions thus play a key role in the construction of identity (Zembylas 2003). They are the necessary link between the social structures in which teachers work and the ways they act:

> The connection is never mechanical because emotions are normally not compelling but inclining. But without the emotions category, accounts of situated actions would be fragmented and incomplete. Emotion is provoked by circumstance and is experienced a transformation of dispositions to act. It is through the subject's active exchange with others that emotional experience is both stimulated in the actor and orienting of their conduct. Emotion is directly implicated in the actor's transformation of their circumstances, as well as circumstances' transformation of the actor's disposition to act. (Barbalet 2002: 4)

It follows that how teachers feel about their professional identity will be associated with their sense of well-being and that this is likely to relate to their sense of effectiveness. The complexities of achieving change and sustaining effectiveness are illustrated in Fig. 2.1, which maps the inter-connected relationships between teachers' professional life phases, their professional identities and their well being, commitment and effectiveness both perceived and in terms of measures of pupils' progress and attainment (Day et al. 2007: 238):

Research representing the affective dimensions of teaching is, therefore, important, both because these dimensions reinforce the association between cognition and emotion and because they act as reminders to policy makers, teacher educators and school principals that "teacher effectiveness" is the product of the preparation and continuing support of both the head (cognition) and the heart (emotion). Such a reminder must, however, provide more than a means of understanding and awareness raising. For it to be useful to the business of improving teaching and learning,

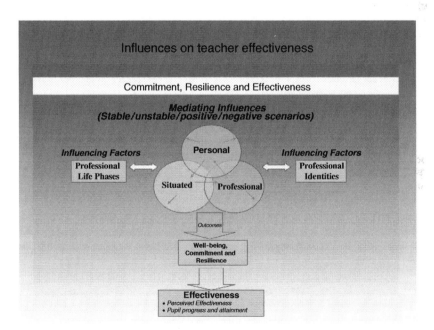

Fig. 2.1 Teachers' well being, commitment and effectiveness

it must also be able to be applied within the broader as well as the narrower contexts in which teachers' work is conducted and evaluated. At a time when teaching in the twenty-first century is rated as one of the most stressful professions (Kyriacou 2000; PWC 2001; Nash 2005), there is a particularly urgent need to focus more on the role of positive emotions in sustaining teachers' positive qualities and strengths, their care about/for the children, their motivation, commitment and ability to continue to give their best in the profession – despite challenges and setbacks – and thus their sense of well being and effectiveness.

Teacher Emotions and Well Being

There are three truths about teachers' emotional worlds: (1) their observable behavior (their emotions) may mask their feelings. In other words, it is impossible for others, however much "emotional intelligence" (Goleman 1996) they may have, to manage teachers' feelings. However, they may create conditions which either help or hinder in managing these by the organizational structures which they establish in schools and through the relationships which they promote; (2) the emotional content of their lives in schools and classrooms may have short and longer term consequences for how they feel about themselves and others and how they behave (i.e. their experiences of interactions with pupils, colleagues, parents and, more vicariously, policy agendas from within or without the school, may affect their self-efficacy, sense of professional identity and, ultimately their commitment and effectiveness); and (3) like the vast majority of human beings, teachers' goals in life and work are to experience pleasure rather than pain as part of a continuing process of seeking adjustment to changing contexts or scenarios rather than attempting to maintain a fixed point of balance.

Any attempt to understand teachers' emotional well-being must recognise it as a relational process. At the heart of this is the dynamic interaction between the circumstances and activities in which teachers are engaged and their psychological, cognitive and emotional resources (see also NEF 2009). Fredrickson's (2001, 2004) recent development of a "broaden-and-build" theory of positive emotions suggests that a subset of positive emotions – joy, interest, contentment and love – serve to build individuals' personal resources which, in turn, contribute to their sense of well being. Ranging from physical and intellectual to social and psychological resources, they "function as reserves that can be drawn on later to improve the odds of successful coping and survival" (Fredrickson 2004: 1367). More importantly, by focusing and building upon positive emotions, individuals may "transform themselves, becoming more creative, knowledgeable, resilient, socially integrated and healthy individuals" (2004: 1369). Transformation occurs in and is influenced positively and negatively by the different contexts in which people live and work and the effectiveness they are able to bring to the management of these.

Damasio (2004a) identifies three emotional "tiers" or "settings" that are key to teachers' work: (1) background emotions (not moods), (2) primary emotions and

(3) social emotions (ibid: 43). It is reasonable to suggest that teachers' capacities to apply these are likely to affect and be affected by their sense of well-being. For example, where well-being is negatively affected, so would be teachers' ability to read others' background emotions. Although these are not especially observable in behavior, they are important indicators of teachers' capacities to be effective in, for example, detecting energy or enthusiasm or diagnosing subtle malaise or excitement, edginess or tranquillity in pupils and colleagues. As Damasio observes, "If you are really good, you can do the diagnostic job without a single word being uttered…" (Damasio 2004a: 43). Primary emotions include fear, anxiety, anger, disgust, surprise, sadness and happiness. Any or all of these are likely to be present in teachers' work, but if negative emotions persist they may result in the loss of a sense of well being by teachers in their ability to succeed. Social emotions are more context related than primary emotions. They would include "sympathy, embarrassment, shame, guilt, pride, jealousy, envy, gratitude, admiration, indignation and contempt" (Damasio 2004a: 45). For example, teachers may experience shame and guilt when they feel that they have fallen short of their own or others' moral standards in a fundamental way (Hargreaves 1994, 1998). Pupils, also, have spoken of sympathy and praise (related to gratitude and admiration) as being associated with "good" teachers and embarrassment, shame and contempt as being associated with "bad" teachers.

Where teachers' well being is threatened or not supported, it is likely that their ability to identify, work with and, where appropriate, moderate background, primary and social emotions is impaired. Conversely, teachers' felt improved ability to monitor and manage the three tiers of their emotions is likely to strengthen the opportunity of achieving a sense of personal and social well being. In the next part of this chapter we will, through stories of three early, middle and later years teachers, focus upon the conditions which promote or act against the primary and social emotional well being of teachers which, we have suggested, is essential to their sense of success.

Stories of Three Teachers

These stories are drawn from a 4-year large scale mixed methods research project involving 300 teachers in 100 primary and secondary schools in England (Day et al. 2006, 2007). They illustrate how teachers' sense of emotional well being, in particular their primary and social emotions, may be affected by different conditions in different phases of their professional lives. The examples themselves provide "broad brush" illustrations of the emotional responses of teachers of different teaching experience to positive and negative influences in the contexts in which they work and live. However, it is reasonable to infer that as they experience and respond to influences, their sense of emotional well-being will increase or decrease and that alongside these variations their capacities to be effective may also be affected.

Story 1: Stchel – An Early Years Teacher

Stchel, 27 years old, a Year 6 teacher in a highly disadvantaged urban primary school, saw his vulnerable professional life trajectory become more positive as a result of his promotion and increased self-efficacy and confidence in the profession.

Declining Well Being in an Unsupportive Environment

Stchel had worked in his current school for five years, originally taking the job because of his ideological commitment to the school's poor socio-economic context. However, having experienced some unpleasant incidents with parents, he admitted that he felt a little depressed. This primary emotion, together with a felt lack of support from the school leadership team, negatively impacted upon his work as a teacher and state of well-being. He was also "getting fed up" doing things that others really ought to be doing and felt that there was some unfairness in the school. This was largely because of a lack of recognition of achievement of Stchel and his colleagues by the leadership. Colleagues did not always pull their weight. Thus, the social emotional was one of contempt:

> When I started this school I was expecting to be told I'd done something good or bad and I wasn't praised or told off for doing things, so I didn't really know where I was. I've been here a little bit now so I don't expect praise or to be told off unless you do something really bad. It is just lack of communication.

Nevertheless, Stchel enjoyed interacting with other members of staff and the social aspects of working in his school, and this was a major element in his decision to stay at the school. He enjoyed teaching and the intrinsic rewards from working with children. He had no behavioral problems with pupils, but noticed that he did not have as much free time as his friends in other professions. He often did not leave school until 7pm and then did more work at home. Saturdays were spent catching up on jobs at home – shopping, washing, etc. and then he spent Sunday working. He was happy for work to dominate at this early stage of his career but felt that, "I don't know if I can take many more years of doing what I am doing. While I am young I'm fine. But as I get older, I don't know, as other commitments take over. I just want a bit of life really". Professionally, his sense of well-being was in decline. Ill health was, at the time, also a critical issue challenging his personal well-being. He had time off for several hospital operations.

Career Advancement and Increased Sense of Well Being: Conditions and Outcomes of Positive Adaptations

In May 2005, however, life changed with the appointment of a new deputy head. Stchel was given more responsibility in the school. He was pleased to have the extra responsibilities and saw taking these on as a good move in terms of promotion and professional life development. This greatly improved his motivation and sense of well-being. The new Deputy Head had taken the school "out of the comfort zone," which Stchel thought was positive, although a little challenging. Nevertheless, he was keen to prove himself. Generally he felt more comfortable, more confident and positive about his ability to make a difference in the school.

Story 2: Abi – A Mid Years Teacher

Abi's professional life phase 4–7 was characterized by her efforts to settle in her current secondary school, her struggle with a lack of work-life balance and her deep resentment towards the performativity agenda. As a result, her sense of well-being was at stake and she was considering leaving teaching. This downward trajectory had, however, changed radically for the better at the beginning of her current professional life phase (8–15). Contributing influences were her new job (with promotion), her increased confidence in working with the performativity agenda, the prospect of an improved work-life balance, and her decision to return to New Zealand to teach. Abi ultimately regained her high levels of motivation, commitment and sense of efficacy in teaching. The marked increase in her state of well being at work and in her personal life played an integral part in her positive professional identity and feeling of effectiveness in the classroom.

Abi was 30 years old and had taught English for 9 years. She had taught in Australia for 4 years before coming to England, where she worked in other schools. Abi had always wanted to be a teacher and entered teaching with a sense of vocation. This still applied although she felt that she had lost "some rose-colored ideas" that she had had when she first became a teacher.

Abi taught Key Stage 3 (13–14-year-old pupils) mixed ability classes of 23–25 pupils in her school – a large, 11–16, rural, moderate socio-economic Beacon Community College that had Key Stage 4 [1](14–16-year-old pupils) results well above similar schools. The sourcing of pupils from "council estates" was new and she had been shocked by the adverse home conditions for learning that some of the pupils faced.

Well Being Eroded

Abi's school provided strong professional and personal support, but the department was less supportive. She liked the nice working environment at her school and got on well with her colleagues. Having been in the school for a year, Abi felt "a lot

---

[1]Key Stage 4 is 'the legal term for the last two years of compulsory schooling in maintained schools in England, Wales and Northern Ireland – normally known as Year 10 and year 11 in England and Wales, and Year 11 and Year 12 in Northern Ireland' (Wikipedia).

more at ease." She knew her students better and had established rapport with them. She found it difficult to "switch off" easily. Her personal drive to enable students to succeed was the cause of her high self-efficacy. When she arrived home she still had more work to do and spent half a day at weekends doing schoolwork. She described herself as sometimes being in trouble at home for being "in teacher mode". She could not imagine, "not being in teaching". Abi's partner was living in a different city. They had been separated for over a year, and this had negatively affected both her work and personal life. She felt tired and less well organized in her work because of her weekend traveling to visit her partner.

The results driven agenda in English schools had had the greatest negative impact on her morale and motivation to teach because it ran counter to her personal philosophy of teaching. She felt that testing and marking seemed to be more important than fostering pupils' independent learning. There had been a fall in her motivation as she began to feel increasingly that she had "less control over what I teach and how I teach it". The accompanying pressure meant that she "had less time to build relationships". She spent a lot of time "marking, reading, filling in results, feeling under pressure to teach something well and quickly". This had led to a feeling of being "overwhelmed" and "more grumpy at work", with "no time to teach fun, creative lessons" that would help with social skills as well as learning. With few positive cognitive and emotional resources to draw upon, she spoke of a considerable decline in her state of well-being. She was not sure whether she would remain in teaching long term as she found it "emotionally draining" and "mentally tiring".

Support and Recognition: Well Being Restored

The beginning of Abi's new professional life phase, however, also meant a new beginning in her professional and personal life. In this new phase, Abi was more settled in her current school and began to get on well with her Head of Department. Although she found the overall pupil behavior "challenging," nevertheless, "the rapport with the children" in the classroom continued to motivate her as a teacher. She still enjoyed seeing the children progress. Support and recognition from the school and departmental leadership, coupled with staff collegiality, contributed to her high levels of social well-being. Mentoring pre-service teachers had made her think more about her own teaching and had also positively impacted her perceived professional identity and effectiveness. The target driven culture remained a negative influence on her work, but Abi did not feel as strongly about this as before. She had found ways to get around the rules, tests and targets and learned to inject her own interests into her teaching.

Her increased job and life satisfaction and fulfilment, enjoyment of her positive relationships with others in the school and feelings of being able to realise her educational values and goals in the classroom contributed significantly to her sense of well being, which provided her with strengths and energy to manage negative emotions and circumstances in pursuit of a more satisfying personal and profession life. Abi was moving to another school with a promotion in the new academic year.

She looked forward to her new job because it also meant her reunion with her partner and improved work-life balance. She did not want to leave her current school, but felt that her personal relationship was equally important.

Sadie, 47 years old, was head teacher in a small, rural, high socio-economic Church

Story 3: Sadie – A Late Years Teacher

Sadie suffered from relentless pressure as a consequence of adverse personal events and heavy workload. Nevertheless, she had managed to sustain high levels of motivation, commitment and sense of effectiveness both as a teacher and as a principal. Her high levels of self-efficacy and agency, together with support from her school colleagues, made a major contribution to her positive professional outlook and her ability to sustain a sense of well being in the face of setbacks and challenges.

of England primary school. She came from a teaching family and had always wanted to be a teacher. She had taught for 26 years and still enjoyed working with children.

Sustaining a Sense of Well Being Against the Odds

When she first joined the school, Sadie found that there was "a competitiveness [in the school], to a degree that it became destructive in the classroom and between parents and staff, so the whole picture was grim." Pupil behavior was appalling too. She appointed a new highly committed and enthusiastic teaching staff, created a positive teaching culture, and turned the school around. For Sadie, the professional and personal support from the staff and the governors had had the greatest positive impact on her emotional well-being.

During the week, Sadie often worked late in the office so that she could spend most of the weekends with her family.

> I think the teaching profession, if you're not careful it can totally destroy your home life – I think the hardest thing for people to do is to find the balance – I've only realistically found the balance in the last five to six years … I also live away from school now – I travel 100 miles a day. That has actually helped because without living so close to school I can't pop in during the holidays or weekends – and it's good reflection time sitting in the car with nobody hassling.

Personal events had had a detrimental effect on her work. Sadie's husband was suffering from severe depression, which coupled with an Ofsted[2] inspection, put her under tremendous pressure. Coming to work became a relief and remedy for her at

---

[2]The Office for Standards in Education, Children's Service and Skills which inspects and regulates the quality of work in schools in England and Wales.

the time. In the end she had become ill. Nevertheless, she insisted that she always had the ability to manage tensions and bring back her work-life balance.

Despite the negative factors, Sadie continued to enjoy working with children and maintained high levels of motivation and commitment in her job. "Seeing children enjoy learning" had been the main source of her motivation and job satisfaction.

> I enjoy being a teacher. I love being a teacher. I'm very enthusiastic about my job. If I wasn't I wouldn't stay in the job. I do feel there are expectations that are unfair from the government and from parents and I do feel that there is a cultural element of parental responsibility being passed to our shoulder by the government as well as parents.

As her husband's condition gradually improved, Sadie found herself more relaxed at home. Sadie was highly confident in her ability to be an effective teacher and an effective principal and enjoyed a high level of job satisfaction. She disapproved of the target-driven culture and believed that exam results were only a snapshot of her pupils' achievements. Although she derived great pleasure from her pupils' good academic results, she did not think that the results had affected her approach to teaching at all. She was proud that her school was not driven by government initiatives and tests because she saw herself as being now well placed, with her enhanced experience and confidence, to implement the actions that she believed were best for her children's learning. She commented that she felt confident in many ways:

> Confident about what the statistical data shows me, also confident because I have feedback verbally and written from children, parents and staff. We did a questionnaire on the effectiveness of the school for the parents and it was the most incredibly positive response you could imagine. Things have moved forward and the school has become a community.

Having experienced various setbacks and challenges in her personal and professional lives, Sadie was pleased that she managed to sustain her feelings of effectiveness. Her sense of agency and resilience had played an important part in her capacity to build upon positive experiences and emotions in the face of negative circumstances and restore her "inner balance" (Krone and Morgan 2000: 92). In addition, her success in establishing rapport, collective trust and sense of belonging at her school and in pursuing her values and philosophy of education had contributed considerably to her job satisfaction and state of well being at work.

Managing Teacher Well Being: The Call to Teach, The Management of Change and Organizational Identity

These teachers' stories are illustrations of the emotional peaks and troughs that they experienced in their primary and social emotions in response to a range of personal, professional and situated influences in their work and lives. For example, all teachers shared happiness, enjoyment (primary emotion) and pride (social emotion) as a result of their contributions to their pupils' progress. Abi's resentment towards the performativity agenda, mental and physical tiredness from a lack of work life balance, produced a sense of guilt for not being able to teach creative lessons for her pupils. Schtel's initial disenchantment with the leadership in the school changed when a newly appointed leader provided him with new opportunities to develop. Sadie's success in detecting and transforming the "grim" nature of "a competitiveness" in her school and in appointing enthusiastic teaching staff had, to some extent at least, relied upon her ability to observe "background" emotions of her colleagues, pupils and parents. Taken together, the stories of the three teachers and the trajectories of their professional lives in particular, suggest that teacher emotions are psychologically and socially constructed in "social relationships and systems of values in their families, cultures, and school situations" which "profoundly influence how and when particular emotions are constructed, expressed, and communicated" (Zembylas 2003: 216). They also highlight the importance to effectiveness of teachers' ability to exercise three emotional tiers – background, primary and social – in three settings: individual (their own sense of vocation), relational (with their colleagues), and organisational (the broader policy and micropolitical contexts of their work)(See Gu and Day, forthcoming).

The professional and personal experiences of each of these three teachers within particular contexts or scenarios that variously threatened or supported their sense of well being may be characterized as journeys of emotional self-adjustment and professional growth. That such growth occurred was a testament to three factors that were essentially emotional:

1. Their "inner motivation to serve" (Hanson 1995: 6) had called them into teaching and it had been this which had provided an emotional baseline which fueled their capacity to withstand the negative challenges of the changing environments in which they worked
2. Their emotional management of change
3. Their sense of social and organizational identity

The Call to Teach

The embodiment of a sense of vocation and sense of self-efficacy in the teacher self provides a favorable antecedent condition for teachers' positive emotions. Their sense of vocation, especially, provides a sense of purpose for their actions, and their management of their experiences, feelings and emotions. It fuels teachers' personal resources with "determination, courage, and flexibility, qualities that are in turn buoyed by the disposition to regard teaching as something more than a job, to which one has something significant to offer" (Hanson 1995: 12). For many teachers, becoming a teacher is a proactive and positive response to an inner emotional call. They may have been drawn to teaching in a challenging school because they wanted to make a difference to students from socio-economically deprived backgrounds – as in the case of Stchel. For Abi and Sadie, their inclination to teach had been driven by a strong calling since childhood and they continued to enjoy the pleasure of working with children in their current schools. Children's progress and achievement stayed always at the heart of their job fulfilment and sense of well-being.

Like many other teachers in the profession, these three teachers' "missionary zeal" and "moral values" (Nias 1999: 225) had functioned as internal psychological and emotional supports for them, encouraged them to be "vocationally and professionally committed" (Nias 1999: 225), and helped them to find strength and power (i.e. sense of agency) to achieve "personal autonomy and personal significance" (Hanson 1995: 6). Their care and love for their pupils, and enthusiasm and passion for their teaching, formed an important part of their professional identities and resulted in a strong sense of purpose, professional aspirations, agency and resilience.

However, a sense of vocation is insufficient in itself for teachers to teach well and to sustain their well being. Self-efficacy is a vital part of well being which may affect their self-motivation and personal and professional life trajectories (Bandura 2000: 120). Bandura (1997) suggests that "perceived self-efficacy is concerned not with the number of skills you have, but with what you believe you can do with what you have under a variety of circumstances" (1997: 31). In the context of teaching, teachers' sense of efficacy is their judgement about their capability to promote students' learning and "bring about desired outcomes of student engagement and learning, even among those students who may be difficult or unmotivated" (Tschannen-Moran et al. 1998: 202, cited in Hoy and Spero 2005: 822). Hoy and Spero (2005) argue that these self-judgments and beliefs "affect the effort teachers invest in teaching, their level of aspiration, the goals they set" (2005: 345). Goal relevance and congruence, as Sutton and Wheatley (2003) observe in their review of the literature on teachers' emotions and teaching, are essential for experiencing well being: "positive emotions arise from goal congruence whereas negative emotions arise from goal incongruence" (2003: 330). Teachers experience growth in self-esteem, confidence, hope and optimism when they feel that their actions are consistent with their values and beliefs (Nias 1996) and that they can make a difference in the academic performance of students (Hoy and Spero 2005). Conversely, limits to teachers' efficacy are seen as a source of their feelings of vulnerability, powerlessness, frustration, disappointment and disillusionment (Kelchtermans 1996). Research has found that in-school support has a significant impact upon early years teachers' self-efficacy as they are in a phase of gaining experience and establishing their professional identity in the classroom as well as in the profession (Day and Gu 2007).

For Stchel, Abi and Sadie, their sense of well being made differing contributions to their endeavours to manage primary and social emotions. As an early years teacher, Stchel suffered from the inadequacy of management support, which he greatly regretted. New career opportunities had greatly improved Stchel's motivation, efficacy and sense of well-being, and he was no longer considering leaving teaching.

In common with Stchel, Abi had also experienced a period of developing her sense of efficacy. However, in contrast with Stchel, Abi had prior teaching experience in Australia. The source of her stress and struggle was the mechanism and structure of the English education system. Nias's (1999) research suggests that, "guilt and loss of self-esteem through the betrayal of deeply held values can be emotionally damaging as appropriating or resistance" (1999: 225). Her observation explains the emotional strain that Abi had experienced. Abi found that her personal interests and professional values were out of line with the government target-driven initiatives and regretted that she no longer had the time and energy to provide care for her pupils. The recovery of her self-efficacy had benefited from improved support from the departmental leadership, her successful self-adjustment to her department and school and her improved work-life balance. Her recovery not only reflected her high level of personal efficacy. It was also the result of a process of her persistently mediating between structural (macro), situated (meso), professional and personal (micro) factors in pursuit of her educational values and a sense that she had a made a difference to the growth of her pupils.

For all three teachers, an immediate consequence of their exercise of self-efficacy was their feelings of regaining control, self-esteem, confidence and, ultimately, motivation, commitment and sense of effectiveness in the profession – all of which recharged their abilities to manage their social and primary emotions which were at the heart of their emotional well being.

The Emotional Management of Change

Teaching involves "intensive personal interactions, often in crowded conditions, with large numbers of pupils who are frequently energetic, spontaneous, immature and preoccupied with their own interests" (Nias 1996: 296) together with a continuing focus upon promoting a sense of individual and collective well being through the management of internal and external change. Within such a living reality, teachers' abilities to manage complex background, social and primary emotions with students, parents and colleagues are of vital importance to the construction of their well-being.

For teachers working in schools in socio-economically challenging circumstances, as in the case of Schtel, staff collegiality plays a particularly critical role. Schools, in this sense, represent a network of dynamic social and emotional relationships. Teachers' capacity to work and engage with others and "to offer support to and ask for support from others" (Edwards and Mackenzie 2005: 294) affects the quality of learning of their pupils. Edwards' (2005, 2007) recent development of "relational agency" (i.e. "a capacity to align one's thought and actions with those of others in order to interpret problems of practice and to respond to those interpretations" (Edwards 2005: 169–170) provides a useful lens to interpret and understand how teachers manage (or do not manage) different emotions, well being and commitment in the emotional context of educational change.

The contemporary landscape of teaching is littered with successive and persisting government policy reforms that have increased teachers' external accountabilities, work complexity and emotional workload. As the stories of these three teachers show, positive relationships with colleagues and pupils function as an emotional resource which enable them to manage external change initiatives, to continue to develop in emotionally demanding teaching and learning contexts and to derive joy, pride and fulfilment from "those components of the job which… [they]… value" (Evans 1998: 11).

Organizational Identity

In their study of teacher turnover, wastage and movements between schools, Smithers and Robinson (2005) found that:

> Teachers are more likely to stay in schools where there is a clear sense of purpose, where the teachers are valued and supported, and where appropriate appointments have been made. The impact of good leadership could be outweighed, however, by factors largely outside a school's control such as location, cost of living, demographics and teachers' personal plans. (2005: i)

Schools are the primary venue where teachers' professional identity is constructed and transformed. Teachers' identity formation in the social, cultural and political context of schools is shaped by and shapes certain organizational structures and power relations and is dependent upon teachers' exercise of their agency (Zembylas 2003, 2005). The emotional components of teacher identity provide meaning to their experiences (Haviland and Kahlbaugh 1993).

In the case of Sadie, the pride, joy, enjoyment and commitment that she derived from the school ethos that she created, the progress and achievement of her pupils, and above all, her ability to successfully connect her values, beliefs and actions in leading her school, constituted the key characteristics of her professional identity – both as a teacher and as a manager. These positive emotions functioned as the "glue" of her identity (Haviland and Kahlbaugh 1993), which mirrored key features of the power relations and the social structure within the organization in which she worked and which she led.

Creating schools as organizations which care for teachers as well as pupils is no longer an option, but a necessity in the contemporary contexts of teaching. Nias (1996) reminds us – teachers' emotions, "though individually experienced, are a matter of collective concern" and "their consequences affect everyone involved in the educational process" (1996: 294). School leadership plays a critical role in bringing together this "collective concern", in establishing meaningful relationships, and in encouraging, enabling and engendering a culture of trust and care and a sense of belonging in schools. Teachers' professional identities and emotions, thus, carry the characteristics of the school in which they work. The experiences of Stchel and Abi illustrate that they would have been lost to the teaching profession if there had not been positive changes in the organizational cultures of their schools.

Conclusion

The importance of teachers' capacities to manage their emotional lives in different settings is now becoming widely recognized and accepted. It is "indispensable for survival" (Damasio 2004b: 49) and, some would argue, to their capacities to be effective (Day et al. 2007). There is as yet too little research in education, which has sought to analyze the relational and organizational conditions which influence teachers' capacities to manage their emotions in ways that enable them to manage their well being and to sustain their effectiveness.

The stories of the three teachers in this chapter reveal that to be effective, the state of teacher emotional well-being matters. However, to achieve and sustain a healthy state of well being, teachers need to manage successfully the cognitive and emotional challenges of working in different, sometimes difficult scenarios which vary according to life experiences and events, the strength of relationships with colleagues, pupils and parents, the conviction of educational ideals, sense of efficacy and agency and the support of colleagues and school leadership. Moore Johnson (2004) reminds us that,

> ... anyone familiar with schools knows that stories about the easy job of teaching are sheer fiction. Good teaching is demanding and exhausting work, even in the best of work places... (2004: 10)

In the early years of teaching the importance of in-school support predominates. Stchel's enhanced confidence and desire to "broaden horizons" in the teaching profession had greatly benefited from the positive effects of supportive school leadership and "appropriate collegial relations" (Nias 1999: 223). His experience is typical of early years teachers (Sikes et al. 1985; Bullough and Baughman 1997; Hoy and Spero 2005). For both Abi and Sadie, staff collegiality was a contributing influence on their positive professional outlook. Nieto (2003) suggests that to retain teachers' commitment in the profession, schools need to become places where teachers find community and engage in intellectual work. In addition to supportive leaders and colleagues, good teacher–pupil relationships had had a positive effect on these three teachers' positive professional life trajectories.

Many teachers enter the profession with a sense of vocation and with a passion to give their best to the learning and growth of their pupils. For some, these become eroded with the passage of time, changing external and internal working conditions and contexts and unanticipated personal events. They lose their sense of purpose and well being which are so intimately connected with their professional identities, self efficacy and agency, their belief that they can and do make a difference to the progress and achievement of their pupils. The evidence in this chapter is unequivocal in its conclusions that such a sense of well being is a necessary condition which enables them to draw upon, deploy and manage the inherently dynamic background, primary and social emotional contexts in which they teach and in which their pupils learn.

References

Bandura A (1997) Self-efficacy: the exercise of control. WH Freeman, New York
Bandura A (2000) Cultivate self-efficacy for personal and organisational effectiveness. In: Locke EA (ed) Handbook of principles of organisation behavior. Blackwell, Oxford
Barbalet J (2002) Introduction: why emotions are crucial. In: Barbalet J (ed) Emotional sociology. Blackwell, London, pp 1–9

Bullough RV, Baughman K (1997) First-year teacher, eight years later. Teachers College Press, New York

Csikszentmihalyi M (1990) Flow and the psychology of discovery and invention. Harper and Row, New York

Damasio A (2004a) Looking for Spinoza: joy, sorrow and the feeling Brian. Vintage, London

Damasio A (2004b) Emotions and feelings. In: Manstead A, Frijda N, Fischer A (eds) Feelings and emotions: the Amsterdam symposium. Cambridge University Press, Cambridge, pp 49–57

Day C, Gu Q (2007) Variations in the conditions for teachers' professional learning and development: sustaining commitment and effectiveness over a career. Oxford Rev Educ 33(4):423–443

Day CW, Stobart G, Sammons P, Kington A, Gu Q, Smees R, Mujtaba T (2006) Variations in teachers' work, lives and effectiveness. Research Report 743, DfES, Nottingham

Day C, Sammons S, Stobart G, Kington A, Gu Q (2007) Teachers matter. Open University Press, Maidenhead, Berks

Denzin NK (1984) On understanding emotion. Jossey-Bass, San Francisco, CA

Dinham S, Scott C (2000) Moving into the third, outer domain of teacher satisfaction. J Educ Adm 38(4):379–396

Edwards A (2005) Relational agency: learning to be a resourceful practitioner. Int J Educ Res 43:168–182

Edwards A (2007) Relational agency in professional practice: A CHAT analysis. ACTIO Int J Hum Act Theory 1:1–17

Edwards A, Mackenzie L (2005) Steps towards participation: the social support of learning trajectories. Int J Lifelong Educ 24(4):287–302

Evans L (1998) Teacher morale, job satisfaction and motivation. Paul Chapman Publishing Ltd, London

Evans L (2001) Delving deeper into morale, job satisfaction and motivation among education professionals. Educ Manage Adm Leadersh 29(3):291–306

Foresight Mental Capital and Wellbeing Project (2008) Final project report. The Government Office for Science, London

Fredrickson BL (2001) The role of positive emotions in positive psychology: the broaden-and-build theory of positive emotions. Am Psychol 56(3):218–226

Fredrickson BL (2004) The broaden-and-build theory of positive emotions. R Soc 359:1367–1377

Fried R (2001) The passionate teacher: a practical guide, 2nd edn. Beacon Press, Boston, MA

Goleman D (1996) Emotional intelligence. Bloomsbury Publishing, London

Gu Q, Day C (2007) Teachers resilience: a necessary condition for effectiveness. Teach Teach Educ 23:1302–1316

Guardian (2003) Workload hits teacher morale. Report on General Teaching Council/Guardian/Mori Teacher Survey. 7 Jan 2008

Hanson DT (1995) The call to teach. Teachers College Press, New York

Hargreaves A (1994) Changing teachers, changing times. Cassell/Teachers College Press, London/New York

Hargreaves A (1998) The emotional practice of teaching. Teach Teach Educ 14(8):835–854

Hargreaves A (2000) Mixed emotions: teachers' perceptions of their interactions with students. Teach Teach Educ 16:811–826

Hargreaves A (2004) Inclusive and exclusive educational change: emotional responses of teachers and implications for leadership. Sch Improv Manage 24(2):288–309

Hargreaves A (2005) Education change teaks ages: life, career and generational factors in teachers' emotional responses to educational change. Teach Teach Educ 21(8):967–983

Haviland JM, Kahlbaugh P (1993) Emotion and identity. In: Lewis M, Haviland JM (eds) Handbook of emotions. Guilford Press, New York, pp 327–339

Henderson N, Milstein M (2003) Resiliency in schools: making it happen for students and educators. Corwin Press, Thousand Oaks, CA

Hoy AW, Spero RB (2005) Changes in teacher efficacy during the early years of teaching: a comparison of four measures. Teach Teach Educ 21:343–356

Ingersoll RM (2003) Who controls teachers' work?. Harvard University Press, Cambridge, MA

Kelchtermans G (1996) Teacher vulnerability: understanding its moral and political roots. Cambridge J Educ 26(3):307–323

Krone K, Morgan JM (2000) Emotion in organisations. In: Fineman S (ed) Emotion metaphors in management: the Chinese experience, 2nd edn. Sage, London

Kyriacou C (2000) Stress busting for teachers. Stanley Thornes Ltd, Cheltenham

Layard R, Dunn J (2009) A good childhood: searching for values in a competitive age. The Children's Society, London

Leithwood K (2007) The emotional side of school improvement: a leadership perspective. In: Townsend T (ed) The International handbook on school effectiveness and improvement. Springer, Dordrecht, The Netherlands, pp 615–634

Moore Johnson S (2004) Finders and keepers: helping new teachers survive and thrive in our schools. Jossey-Bass, San Francisco, CA

Nash P (2005) Speech to worklife support conference. London Well being conference, London, 21 Apr 2005

New Economics Foundation (2009) National accounts of well-being: bringing real wealth onto the balance sheet. New Economics Foundation, London

Nias J (1996) Thinking about feeling: the emotions in teaching. Cambridge J Educ 26(3):293–306

Nias J (1999) Teachers' moral purposes: stress, vulnerability, and strength. In: Vandenberghe R, Huberman AM (eds) Understanding and preventing teacher burnout: a sourcebook of international research and practice. Cambridge University Press, Cambridge, pp 223–237

Nieto S (2003) What keeps teachers going?. Teachers College Press, New York

Noddings N (1992) The challenge to care in schools: an alternative approach to education. Teachers College Press, New York

Palmer PJ (1998) The courage to teach: exploring the inner landscapes of a teacher's life. Jossey-Bass, San Francisco, CA

PricewaterhouseCoopers (2001) Teacher workload study. DfES, London

Schutz PA, Pekrun R (2007) Emotion in education. Academic, San Diego, CA

Sikes P, Measor L, Woods P (1985) Teacher careers: crises and continuities. Falmer, London

Sleegers P, Kelchtermans G (1999) Inleiding op het themanummer: professionele identiteit van leraren (Professional identity of teachers). Pedagogish Tijdschrift 24:369–374

Smithers A, Robinson P (2005) Teacher turnover, wastage and movements between schools. DfES Research Report: No. 640

Sutton R, Wheatley K (2003) Teachers' emotions and teaching: a review of the literature and directions for future research. Educ Psychol Rev 15(4):327–357

Troman G, Woods P (2001) Primary teachers' stress. Routledge, London

Tschannen-Moran M, Woolfolk Hoy A, Hoy WK (1998) Teacher efficacy: its meaning and measure. Rev Educ Res 68:202–248

van Veen K, Lasky S (2005) Emotions as a lens to explore teacher identity and change: different theoretical approaches. Teach Teach Educ 21(8):895–898

Zembylas M (2003) Emotions and teacher identity: a poststructural perspective. Teach Teach Theory Pract 9(3):213–238

Zembylas M (2005) Beyond teacher cognition and teacher beliefs: the value of the ethnography of emotions in teaching. Int J Qual Stud Educ 18(4):465–487

Chapter 3
Seeking Eudaimonia: The Emotions in Learning to Teach and to Mentor

Robert V. Bullough Jr.

Abstract In this chapter I explore aspects of the emotional life of beginning teachers and the experienced teachers who mentor them. First, I briefly describe the institutional context within which teachers and mentors conduct their work, a context increasingly shaped by the pressures of high-stakes student testing and punitive approaches to accountability. Drawing on the work of the late philosopher, Robert Solomon, I then describe the appraisal theory of the emotions that grounds the analysis of two cases. Various models of teacher development are described and issues associated with mentoring discussed. The cases illustrate various aspects of the connections existing among emotion, identity, self-narratives, and expectations in the lives and work of a beginning second career teacher and a new teacher mentor.

Keywords Mentor · Eudaimonia · Affective appraisals · Teachers emotion

Emotions are dynamic parts of ourselves, and whether they are positive or negative, all organizations, especially schools, are full of them (Hargreaves and Fullan 1998, pp. 55–56).

Teaching has always been intensely emotional work, but the nature of that work is changing in the face of a new managerialism that relies upon fear, embarrassment and teacher guilt to gain improved student performance (as demonstrated by rising standardized student test scores). The result, as Valli and Buese (2007) argue, is that teaching is becoming ever more stressful, intense, much less personal and the curriculum less flexible and more focused on "disciplining the teachers" (p. 545). Facing such conditions, Bottery (2003) suggests that schools increasingly evidence a "culture of unhappiness," where trust is unnecessary because work is so highly controlled and micro-managed.

R.V. Bullough (✉)
Center for the Improvement of Teacher Education and Schooling (CITES)
and Department of Teacher Education, Brigham Young University, Provo, UT, USA
e-mail: bob_bullough@byu.edu

P.A. Schutz and M. Zembylas (eds.), *Advances in Teacher Emotion Research:*
The Impact on Teachers' Lives,
DOI 10.1007/978-1-4419-0564-2_3, © Springer Science+Business Media, LLC 2009

Nichols and Berliner (2007) detail the ways in which the use of high stakes standardized student testing in the US is undermining the ethical foundations of schooling. Cheating, they observe, is now commonplace – states, school districts, schools, and teachers feel justified in cheating to produce high test score results, evidence of student learning. Feeling the pressures of "performativity" (Ball 2003) and being pressed to produce predictable outcomes, educators increasingly find themselves needing to engage in "fabrications" – producing "versions of an organization (or person) which [do] not exist...in order 'to be accountable'" (p. 224). "Judgmental relations" alter how teachers and students interact and increasingly teachers find it necessary to be other than themselves when teaching, a major source of unhappiness in work. Jeffrey and Woods (1996) observed similar developments in England with Ofsted-sponsored (Office for Standards in Education) school inspections. Based on a study of five primary schools, they noted a "deprofessionalization" of teachers, and that increasingly teachers felt "fear, anguish, anger, despair, depression, humiliation, grief and guilt – emotions produced by the mismatch between the power of the critical event [of being inspected and having test scores published] and the cultural resources provided by their beliefs and past experiences" (p. 340). As one teacher remarked: "Ofsted's completely there all the time now, no matter what I'm doing. I forgot to take the National Curriculum booklet home at the weekend to write down, at the side of this week's plans, exactly where it fits in and it wrecked my weekend" (p. 329).

These are harsh realities, leading to a disturbing conclusion – reform efforts of these kinds are harmful to teachers and likely undermine the well-being of those they teach. Yet, as Gu and Day (2007) argue, "most teachers adapt, at least survive, and do not leave the profession. Whether their work is more closely prescribed as a result of reform or not, they continue to do the best they can for the students they teach under changed and challenging circumstances, usually with their beliefs about their core purposes and values intact" (p. 1303). Adapting and surviving under such conditions are emotionally demanding tasks, however, and energy invested in these ways could better be used in support of quality education for young people.

This chapter seeks to open for consideration aspects of the emotional life of beginning teachers and the experienced teachers who mentor them. Mentoring, of course, is a form of teaching and like all teaching, it too is emotionally loaded, characterized by delightful highs and distressing lows. Since mentors play such a prominent role in beginning teacher development, discussing mentors and beginning teachers together seems appropriate, promising to illuminate the emotional lives of both parties. Among the assumptions underpinning the analysis, one particular set bears special mention up front. To teach well is an expression of profound hopefulness. Despite how physically, cognitively, and emotionally demanding teaching is, on the whole teachers are resilient people who care deeply about those they teach and the work of teaching. Caring, however, involves both "*negative* and *positive* emotional labor" (Isenbarger and Zembylas 2006, p. 124). It is in their relationships with those they teach and with those with whom they work that teachers find their greatest satisfactions and deepest disappointments.

The argument presented here is straightforward: (1) Policy makers have paid far too little attention to teacher well-being; (2) greater efforts are required within schools to foster conditions supportive of teacher happiness as an essential condition for quality teaching and student learning; and (3) locating these conditions necessitates a much better understanding of the work-life and emotions of teachers and mentors.

A Word on Happiness

Here happiness is conceived as eudaimonia – often translated as "flourishing" – an ancient Greek concept of increasing importance in studies of well-being (see Averill and More 2004). Happiness is an odd emotion. Often lacking an object, it is more like a mood than an emotion. Other times it has a clear object – a break-through of a child who has struggled with reading or having taught an engaging science lesson and being confirmed by one's students as an inquiry teacher as a result (on this more will be said shortly). Generally, happiness is "the emotional state associated with full engagement or optimal performance in meaningful activity" (Averill and More 2004, p. 664); and as such, like hope, happiness is infectious (McDermott and Hastings 2000). The result is confidence building and self-confirming, which implies achievement of a worthy standard or goal. Speaking directly to the ethical issues raised by Nichols and Berliner, the aim, as Aristotle argued, is "virtuous activity, it must be the activity of the highest virtue, or in other words, of the best part of our nature" (Aristotle 1943, p. 233). On this view, happiness is closely related to meeting expectations and to how large a gap exists between what a person hopes to achieve and what is actually being achieved, which leads toward questions of identity, of what sort of person the teacher is thought to be and takes him or herself to be. The strong link between emotion, including happiness, and identity is one reason why current reform efforts are so disturbing to many teachers. As Day et al. (2006) conclude from their study of 300 English educators: "The majority linked 'being a teacher' with 'being yourself' in the classroom and school" (p. 604). Being other than self is alienating, frustrating and a source of anger (Fisher 2002).

Emotion as Judgment

The view of emotion offered draws heavily on the work of the late philosopher, Robert Solomon, and his appraisal theory of the emotions, most especially his argument that unlike moods, emotions are intentional and have an object to which they refer. Knowing the object of an emotion opens that emotion for discussion and reveals the underpinning basis for the judgment made. Here Peter Goldie (2004) provides a helpful insight suggesting that "listening" to one's emotions is a "Good

Thing" (p. 98). Listening is a good thing for many reasons, among them that "emotions or lack of them... speak the truth about if and how much something matters to us" (Baier 2004, p. 207). They are self revealing. Anger, joy, delight, and frustration each speak to what is important to us. Hence, Solomon (1993) argues, "An emotion is a judgment which constitutes our world, our surreality, and its 'intentional objects.' An emotion is a basic judgment about our Selves and our place in our world, the project of values and ideals, structures and mythologies, according to which we live and through which we experience our lives" (pp. 125–126).

Later, Solomon (2004) expanded on this insight: "An emotion is rather a complex of judgments and, sometimes, quite sophisticated judgments, such as judgments of responsibility (in shame, anger, and embarrassment) or judgments of comparative status (as in contempt and resentment)" (p. 83). Hence, emotions – affective appraisals – have intentionality; they are about something, some object, that "is seen as *important* for some role it plays in the person's own life" (Nussbaum 2004, p. 189). The judgments made are often "of the body" (Solomon 2004, p. 87), prelinguistic, inarticulate and unconscious but nevertheless powerful, moving. In them "we acknowledge our neediness and incompleteness before those elements that we do not fully control" (Nussbaum 2004, p. 184). Such judgments are not merely reactions to the world, but subjective forms of engagement with it. Emotions are, therefore, embedded in history, logical and purposeful, bearing our intentions for the future and what we take to be living well. They speak to what sort of person we are, to our identity, and so intertwined within them are our hopes, expectations, and desires.

For the purposes of this chapter, Solomon (1993) makes a helpful distinction, already mentioned, between emotion and mood: "There are passions which need not even begin with a particular incident or object, which need not be *about* anything in particular; these are *moods*" (p. 112). And mood is a factor in determining one's emotional response to a situation or event, making some responses more rather than less likely. Being in a "bad mood" I might snap at a student for doing something that his friend did earlier in the day without my comment. Conversely, being in a "good mood", in the afternoon I might warmly compliment a student for work done that I would have ignored had someone else done it that very morning. But, there is another and more significant sense in which mood is important. Over time, as work cultures form and evolve, intentionally or unintentionally, those cultures come to embody "structures of feeling" that shape emotion and normalize experience (Zembylas 2002). Hoy et al. (2008) note, for example, that interest is growing in how to build optimistic cultures in schools, with norms that "reinforce individual tendencies to be optimistic just as a pessimistic faculty would dampen individual teacher's optimism" (p. 832). Here, optimism is a mood.

This second sense, mood as a characteristic of an organizational culture, underscores not only how cognition is distributed across persons who share situations (Moore 2007) but also their affect. Put differently, sharing a work context also means sharing a way of acting, talking, thinking, and to a degree feeling about and within that context.

In teaching, vulnerability is widely thought to be a dominating mood (Kelchtermans 1996). There is no question but that working within a demanding and unpredictable environment (Helsing 2007) and within an institutional and political context obsessed with accountability leads to often nagging feelings among teachers of being exposed, open to easy wounding by students, parents, administrators and politicians (Kelchtermans 2005). Over time, emotional exhaustion, depersonalization, and reduced personal accomplishment, the signs of burnout, may appear (Maslach 1999). Given this situation, the temptation is to conclude, as so many studies of teacher stress and burnout do, that vulnerability is an aspect of teaching that needs correction if not removal. But, teachers experience and respond to challenging work conditions differently: Some withdraw and become cautious and timid, some push back (Kelchtermans 2005), and others become more teachable displaying the heightened sense of the need to grow and develop that underpins what Van Eekelen et al. (2006) describe as the "will to learn" (p. 411). The will to learn might be grounded either negatively or positively – on one hand the desire is to strengthen one's ability to control the classroom for self-protective reasons while on the other the intent is to better learn how to effectively engage children. Clearly, many teachers, perhaps most, enjoy the unpredictability of children and accept the uneasiness of teaching as the price they pay for the delight (a positive emotion) of being surprised. For these teachers openness to wounding is experienced mostly as readiness to learn, a much-desired state.

Feeling vulnerable and using a regressive coping strategy, some teachers certainly do seek to flatten the classroom, make it more secure, predictable, and less emotionally volatile. They do so by employing high levels of routinization and carefully managing problems. As they do so, however, their range of attentiveness shrinks, ever so slightly; and what they already are able to do and to feel sets the boundaries of their teaching expertise which then recede (see Bereiter and Scardamalia 1993). This, of course, is the danger when vulnerability becomes a heavy mood, one that prompts resistance to any and all suggested program changes, even good ones. Yet, it is also readily apparent that just as teachers differ so do teaching contexts, and these differences contribute to how teachers experience and respond to their work and its emotional intensity – for some, teaching becomes impossible because so little is predictable and so much is threatening; for others teaching becomes a form of energizing improvisation made possible by a culture that supports and celebrates the miracle of learning.

For thinking about teaching and learning to teach, a major virtue of appraisal theories of the emotions like Solomon's is that they acknowledge "the possibility of choice and responsibility but also [allow for] that ambiguity between willfully engaging and 'getting caught up in' that captures the fundamental ambiguity of the emotions themselves" (2004, p. 84). Such theories give place to human agency and variability, and thereby balance tendencies toward an over-determining structuralism. In short, they are hopeful. By locating the intentions driving emotion, such theories provide a helpful means for sense making. Recognizing that emotions have objects, reveals how each emotion "serves distinct functions in the way it *organizes* perception, cognition, and actions (behavior) for coping and creative endeavors, and in the way it contributes to personality and behavior development" (Izard and Ackerman 2004, p. 253). Thus, threats to the self or blockages to self-realization, which undermine happiness, are marked by what Fisher (2002) describes as the "vehement passions." Additionally, such theories acknowledge the general stability of the emotional patterns that underpin the self and how these support action tendencies – characteristic ways of thinking and behaving (Sutton and Wheatley 2003). Clearly, efforts to change the self – to change unproductive action tendencies – and work contexts inevitably involve work on and through the emotions (this point finds strong empirical support in studies of hope) (see Snyder et al. 2005).

Models of Becoming a Teacher

A good deal of research has been done on the early phases of learning to teach, and in most of these some place is given to emotion, particularly as emotion is related to what are characterized as common crises or turning points in development. Although criticized for its linearity (Bullough 1997), the stage model proposed by Kevin Ryan proved influential. Drawing on insights from the research of Frances Fuller (Fuller and Bown 1975), Ryan argued that beginning teachers go through four emotion-laden stages, each underscoring a particular developmental challenge: "fantasy," "survival," "mastery" and "impact." In the fantasy stage the novice imagines what teaching will be like and embraces images of teaching like the best teachers she ever knew and of being loved and confirmed by students. This is a period characterized by "unrealistic optimism" (Weinstein 1989). The survival stage signals a struggle for the beginning teacher's professional life as discipline and management problems overwhelm skill and understanding; the mood is one of profound vulnerability coupled with both fear and hope, passions of the "imminent future" (Fisher 2002, p. 79). Surviving, the developing neophyte enters the mastery stage of teaching, the "craft stage, where the new teacher begins to learn the craft of teaching in a step-by-step fashion" (Ryan 1986, p. 14). Self-confidence grows, and the teacher is able to see that her actions have positive effects, which strengthens the resolve to teach and encourages hope. Eventually, with increased experience and ongoing reflection on that experience, a teacher enters the impact stage, which corresponds roughly to Berliner's (1988) "proficient" stage in the development of teaching expertise. Here declarative and procedural knowledge combine, such that the teacher knows who she is and what to do and does it with an eye toward furthering student learning. From the perspective of Fuller's work, as a teacher moves through the stages self concerns, worries about being liked, for instance, give way to concerns about student learning.

In the years following publication of Fuller and Ryan's research it has become increasingly evident that teacher development can be understood only very loosely as linear, and that for many teachers teaching remains emotionally taxing – characterized by dramatic highs and lows, often tied to student lives and performance (see Isenbarger and Zembylas 2006). As documented in *First-Year Teacher Eight Years Later* (Bullough and Baughman 1997) individual teachers' trajectories of development are in varying degrees idiosyncratic, often spilling outside of even the most carefully crafted models, and that differences in temperament as well as context help account for these variations. Using Huberman's (1989) career cycles as a framework for speaking about Kerrie Baughman's development as a teacher over a period of 8 years, we concluded that "Kerrie's career path seems less linear than circular; she spins outside the expected pathways... She seemed to go through spirals – sometimes very tightly wound and compressed – of stabilization-experimentation-reassessment" (Bullough and Baughman 1997, p. 58). Each transition involved intensive emotional labor – stabilization indicating a settling – sometimes stimulated by personal decisions, such as to discard an established instructional routine or program in favor of another approach, and sometimes prompted by contextual changes, a difficult child being assigned to her classroom or a change in assignment (see ibid, Chapter 7). As was true for Kerrie, evidence increasingly suggests that beginning teachers' thinking is much more complicated and far richer than often thought and that impact concerns prominently shape the decisions made (see Bullough et al. 2004; Watzke 2007).

Among the virtues of the various stage theories is that they began to open for systematic study the difficulties of learning to teach, many of which are widely shared. Beginning teachers often report that learning to teach is exhausting, emotionally and intellectually challenging, and sometimes even threatening to the self, producing contradictory feelings of fear and hope. As one beginning teacher remarked:

> Daily stress! It's all the little things like phone calls home, dealing with parents, administrative duties, constant meetings... This is all new to me... I have no experience to [draw upon] if a child is having difficulty. I have to use my best judgment. I feel like some parents look down on me and wish that their child had the other kindergarten teacher because of my inexperience. (Goddard and Foster 2001, p. 359)

Ryan's "Fantasy" and "Survival" stages pointed in this direction. So did Fuller's focus on the self-concerns of beginning teachers. In turn, when describing teacher career cycles, Huberman (1989) concluded that the teachers he studied had either "easy" or "painful" beginnings, and as their careers unfolded teachers moved in different directions, some toward affirming the decision to teach and engaging eventually in new forms of self-discovery, reinvestment and experimentation, while others moved toward monotony and disenchantment. Use of these terms, "easy" and "painful" beginnings, underscores the emotional nature of the experience of learning to teach. Along the way, as noted, Huberman's model helps locate a set of common decision points, sometimes experienced as crises, often precipitated by disappointment, self-doubt, and frustration, particularly with work conditions (Liu and Ramsey 2008).

The emotional volatility of learning to teach is well illustrated by the adjectives used by two beginning teachers to portray their experience of teaching over the course of their year as interns (Bullough and Young 2002, p. 421). Each week they responded to an email questionnaire. Early in the year, Jossey, a 23 year-old, married, beginning teacher working in an urban school wrote: "[Teaching is] rewarding, good, eventful, stressful, interesting, improving." In January teaching was still "eventful" and "rewarding" but it was also now "hard, frustrating." In April, she wrote: "rewarding, difficult, beneficial, disappointing, busy." Cheryl, single, and also working in a low-income school, used the following adjectives to describe her experience early in the year: "[Teaching is] exhilarating, fun, exhausting, challenging." In January she wrote: "fun, long, exhausting, nerve-wracking, busy, lucky, exciting." Then in April, a shift took place, indicating dramatic changes in Cheryl's experience of teaching. She wrote: "boring, tiring, nerve-wracking, frustrating." From this random sample study of 16 of 100 interns, the authors concluded: "In the same week, even on the same day, interns would swing from [hopefulness] inspired from a single successful lesson or an unexpected thank-you note from a struggling student to self-doubt and discouragement following a student's outburst or a lone activity that fell flat" (Bullough and Young 2002, p. 422). The authors continue by noting that while the swings were dramatic, they need to be seen "within the overall trajectory of development over the course of the year... [The] emotional trajectory apparent in the data...was one of growing confidence, grounded in increasing instructional competence... and a growing richness and depth of relationship with mentors, students, and other teachers" (Bullough and Young 2002, p. 422). These data support the conclusion of Flores and Day (2006): "Teaching calls for and, at its best, involves daily, intensive and extensive use of both emotional labor (e.g. smiling on the outside whilst feeling anything but happy on the inside) and emotional work which enables teachers to manage the challenges of teaching classes which contain students with a range of diverse motivations, personal histories and learning capacities" (p. 221).

Mentors and Mentoring

With increasing appreciation of the difficulties of learning to teach and of the inherent complexities of teaching, coupled with growing understanding that school improvement is heavily dependent on teacher learning, there slowly came recognition that beginning teachers need assistance of various kinds if they are to grow and to succeed professionally. The importance of such efforts is underscored by the career-long lingering influence of the first year of teaching (Gratch 1998). Mentoring has been embraced as a solution to this and other related problems such that, as Colley (2002) writes, mentoring is now "the 'in' thing" (p. 257). Mostly, the literature on mentoring has been celebratory, including studies that find in mentoring a solution to problems of teacher retention (Kelley 2004; Smith and Ingersoll 2004) and development (Marable and Raimondi 2007), and studies indicating that mentors as well as beginning teachers find mentoring valuable (Clinard and Ariav 1998). "[Mentors] learn by developing new insights into their own and others' teaching styles and approaches and by cultivating new relationships, and they often experience a renewal of enthusiasm and commitment to their craft and career" (Templeton 2003, pp. 163–164).

There are, however, exceptions. Mentoring does not always produce such desirable outcomes, as many beginning teachers and mentors attest. While participants generally deem mentoring relationships successful, a conclusion reached by

Kilburg and Hancock (2006), problems often arise, as they did for about one-fourth of the 149 teams they studied. A variety of difficulties are reported, each leading to increased work-related stress. One of the more significant is that the mentoring role often is not well understood (Sundli 2007) and role conflict and ambiguity have been linked to burnout among teachers. Tension between the support and assessment responsibilities of mentors may produce confusion and uneasiness and heighten feelings of vulnerability for both mentors and mentees (Rippon and Martin 2006; Williams and Prestage 2002, p. 42). In the move from teaching to mentoring mentors discover that a new professional identity must be forged. Of this, and the uncertainty that follows, more will be said shortly. Suffice it here to say that when becoming a mentor, teachers rely heavily upon what they know when enacting the role (see Orland-Barak 2005). The result is that, absent specific and focused mentor education, which is relatively rare, they often rely on insights gained from how they, themselves, were taught (Rajuan et al. 2007), how they teach (Martin 1997) and how they were mentored, if at all (Bullough 2005).

Mostly, not wishing to complicate or add to a beginning teacher's self-doubts, mentors understand their role as centering on support and avoiding being intrusive, directive, or critical (Young et al. 2005). The result is that novice learning is truncated, as Feiman-Nemser (2001) argues: "Norms of politeness and the desire for harmony create barriers to productive mentoring interactions" (p. 1033). The value of mentors being supportive, polite, and generally avoiding challenge or criticism is bolstered by a view widely shared that learning to teach is primarily a matter of discovering one's own teaching style and that "good teachers work things out for themselves" (Feiman-Nemser 2001, p. 1033). One result of this belief and strategy is that the emotional volatility of the mentor-mentee relationship is leveled at least on the surface, yet for some mentors guilt may arise, a feeling of not having done all they could do to assist the beginning teacher to develop. This same strategy and supporting viewpoint justifies and encourages the quite common practice among mentors of withdrawing from active involvement with mentees in favor of "checking in" once they are convinced that the mentee can survive in the classroom and will do no harm. For mentees, however, withdrawal frequently is experienced as abandonment and the resulting relational uncertainty deepens vulnerability.

For mentors, mentoring often is merely an added responsibility in addition to teaching. Busy teaching, mentors find themselves engaged in an ongoing and emotionally taxing triage, responding as they can to what are often insistent and contradictory demands with too little time to do what they believe needs to be done. They juggle priorities, especially between family and work responsibilities and, having difficulty establishing balance, once again guilt may follow, just as it does for teachers (Bullough and Baughman 1997). Additionally, as Hobson (2002) found, internally mentors often feel torn between their dual roles, to teach students and to mentor. Facing a choice, mentoring may be subordinated to teaching.

Matters are made more difficult for mentors when, as Zeichner (2002) notes, the work of mentoring frequently is not valued by universities or schools. "I had a fellow teacher make a comment to me about two days ago. He said mentoring must be a nice break for you" (Bullough and Draper 2004, p. 283). As identities change or expand, serving as a mentor may lead to separation from other teachers and a sense of not belonging. Moreover, speaking with colleagues about a mentee's problems can lead others to conclude that the mentor is not up to standard, which leads to self-doubt and sometimes fear. Worse, there is the frightful possibility that in soliciting advice from teachers or administrators on how to help a struggling mentee that something will be said that would hurt future employment opportunities. Under such conditions a strategic disengagement may seem wise.

Structural issues contribute significantly to the difficulty of building sustainable and supportive relationships between beginning teachers and their mentors, and add to the list of commonly expressed frustrations. Lack of time for planning and for ongoing conversation about teaching is a pressing issue (Athanases 2006; Kilburg and Hancock 2006). Often, mentors and mentees do not have the same planning periods, teach the same subjects or grade levels, or even work in the same schools. Mentor-mentee relationships are inevitably complex and fragile (Rippon and Martin 2006, p. 86) and conditions like these make relationship building even more challenging emotionally.

Identities and Emotions

The dramas of learning to teach and learning to mentor play out against the backdrop of forming a professional identity as a teacher and as a teacher-becoming-a-mentor (Bullough 1992; Zembylas 2003). Professional identity is one of the desired outcomes of the various stage models of learning to teach, a result of having been tested physically, intellectually, and emotionally, and of having achieved oneself as a teacher. Once formed, whether as teacher or mentor, identity demands defense; and from it, one acts and expresses agency. Haviland-Jones and Kahlbaugh (2004) present a provocative and helpful view of how identity and emotion connect. In their "dynamic systems approach," emotion "functions as the 'glue' for identity" (Haviland-Jones and Kahlbaugh 2004, p. 294).

> [The] centrality of emotion in identity may seem to clash with a compelling argument that identity is a consciousness of one's memories – that is, one's history – in some organized pattern, often a continuous narrative... At one level, it is indisputable that a sense of one's own identity is constructed from narrative memory.... However, we believe that we are arguing about a motivational process that underlies the very construction of such memories and the motivation for their construction. If people organize their thoughts, memories, and future hopes around happy events, it would be circularly the case that they are most themselves when this organization functions well and should have a sense of not being themselves if it does not function. Moreover, happy people should use particular strategies for thought (including memory construction) that are somewhat different from those of people who feel most themselves when they are excited or exhilarated. (pp. 294–295)

On this view, adult identity includes "sets of rules that are emotionally dense and that offer usable information about life" (p. 295). Moreover, such rule sets are relatively stable and enduring, characterizing a socially embedded and preferred way of coming at and acting upon life and of making sense of experience, making it "normal." Hence, emotional and intellectual preferences are linked to theories of the self, the sort of person we present ourselves as being and take ourselves to be, and these, in turn, invite and are supported by various social forms of recognition such that others can and do characterize us as this or that sort of person and either seek or avoid engagement with us. In turn, as suggested by positioning theory (Harre and van Langenhove 1999), all the while we actively seek self-confirmation. So mentors seek recognition by those they mentor and in turn beginning teachers seek self-confirmation from mentors and students. When either or both fail to receive expected confirmation, disorientation follows, perhaps anger and defensiveness or, in contrast, concern turned to engagement, conversation, and reconsideration.

The social processes of recognition, identification, and membership – roles played, groups to which one belongs – shape identity and make it dynamic, context sensitive, and to a degree fluid and multiple (Zembylas 2003). Indeed, without recognition, being seen by others in certain ways, there is no identity at all (Gee 2000–2001). Of course a teacher or mentor is more than a teacher or mentor and also is a citizen, a father or mother, son or daughter, stamp collector, bibliophile, or, recognizing the dark side of human nature, tax cheat. Each of these many identities have an emotional loading – sometimes producing internal conflict – and a pattern that supports and sustains a cluster of embodied, linked, and evolving narratives. Such narratives are recognized as belonging to the self-as-teacher, as mentor, father or mother. These are stories we tell of ourselves and that others tell of us which display and justify who we are or are thought to be. As judgments, emotions and combinations of emotions underpin, energize, and sustain the narratives we tell. For mentors, beginning teacher narratives of self-as-teacher often make giving feedback extremely difficult especially when what needs to be said challenges what the beginner takes herself to be. When a beginning teacher is certain she is doing a wonderful job in the classroom but is criticized by her mentor, surprise follows, sometimes anger. Perhaps the mentor calms the situation and reaffirms the beginning teacher narratives by saying, "You are doing great, but my job is to push you even further." Conversely, a mentor's remarks may be also overly positive, disconfirming what the beginning teacher believes is true about her teaching, and embarrassment or an uneasy pride follows. That emotions are seldom pure, and, having a temporal trajectory come in combinations, helps explain what might seem to be unpredictable behavior and why when facing contending impulses to act one rather than another tendency finds expression – the desire of a teacher to lash out in anger at a child's defiance is contained by immediate recognition of the shamefulness of such acts. Adults, but most especially teachers, *do not behave in such ways*. One emotion, anger – a threat to the self – is blocked by another and self-conscious emotion and judgment, shame.

Who Am I? Two Case Studies

To deepen and ground the discussion, parts of two case studies follow. These are intended to illustrate the tight link that exists between emotion and identity, and most especially what transpires with serious challenges to professional identity encountered by beginning teachers and mentors. Virtually all beginning-teachers ask and must answer the question: Who am I as teacher? Mentors ask and answer the parallel question: Who am I as mentor? Like beginning teachers, new mentors face the challenge of forming a new professional identity, one different from but complimentary to that formed when teaching but fitting a different context and set of expectations. Like the move from student teacher to teacher, the transition from teacher to mentor is often experienced simultaneously as stressful but also invigorating. As noted, the processes involved in forming new identities for both beginning teachers and new mentors involve serious emotional work and labor, which profoundly affect personal well-being.

The first case study is of Lyle, a 37-year-old married, father of two children, and biology graduate who had worked many years as a laboratory technician specializing in the study of viruses (Bullough and Knowles 1990). This case is presented because it is one of the early studies of second-career teachers, individuals who have an especially high stake in career success, and offers a particularly revealing portrait of the emotional life of a beginning teacher as well as of the problems of identity formation within a hostile work environment. Prior to entering a teacher education program Lyle said that in the lab he had been "unhappy for a long time" (p. 102). He desperately needed a change in vocation and he thought teaching offered an opportunity to continue working in biology in interesting ways.

The second case study is of Barbara, a new high school mentor of two beginning English teachers (Bullough 2005). Barbara was widely considered an extraordinary teacher who approached both teaching and mentoring through her core personal identity as mother and nurturer. "Mentoring is a mom thing, I feel like a mom," she said (p. 148). Her mentees recognized her as a nurturer and responded positively to her enactment. Released from two periods a day for mentoring, Barbara actively sought opportunities to help her mentees, trying, as she said, "to do a little more than they ask for because they are afraid to ask" (p. 149). This contrasts sharply with the common mentoring practice of waiting to be asked before offering assistance (Young et al. 2005) but reveals issues associated with the challenges of caring as a dominating teaching expectation and professional identity (Isenbarger and Zembylas 2006).

Lyle, a Beginning Teacher

Lyle student taught for 5 months half-time in a junior high school. Teaching half-time provided opportunities to plan instruction and to visit classrooms other than those of his two cooperating teachers. Based on his experience, "Initially, Lyle thought of teachers as experts who possessed specialized knowledge to be passed along and down to students" (p. 103). This poorly fitting conception of teaching lead to problems in student teaching where he had difficulty pitching lessons at an appropriate level for student understanding and was puzzled by the lack of student interest in science. He remarked: "I realized that there's a hell of a lot more to [teaching] than subject matter... [Realizing] that has been very difficult for me"

(p. 103). Discovering that his view of teaching as imparting expert knowledge to students was unproductive, he began to embrace his cooperating teachers' emphasis on science as process. He was impressed by what each of these teachers could do and agreed with their views that "Science is doing things with your hands and your mind." His understanding broadened: "now, I think what teachers do is try to arrange and design an experience for a child to maximize understanding [of the content]...they're thinking about what they're doing; they're learning from it... In other words, inquiry" (p. 104). Lyle completed student teaching intending to become an inquiry teacher.

Anxious about employment, Lyle accepted the first job offered. The offer came from the principal of a large junior high school, whose population of 1,100 students was generally poor, mobile, and, according to Lyle, not very interested in school. His seven-period schedule included no biology classes – four periods of low-ability mathematics in a highly structured and prescriptive program, two of eighth-grade physical science and, for extra pay, one monitoring ISS (In School Suspension). He had no planning period. Hence, five of Lyle's class periods required working with groups of students who were among the least engaged in school. Worse, Lyle had virtually no depth of experience in the subjects he would teach. The prescriptive curriculum of the mathematics classes required virtually no planning, but it also inspired little or no personal investment. Lacking content area knowledge, he found it necessary in the physical science classes to rely heavily upon the textbook, which downplayed the value of learning science as process – the view he hoped would drive his teaching. Still, he began the year committed to designing lab experiences for the students. Soon he discovered there were few lab materials available in the department and that textbooks dominated virtually every science teacher's curriculum.

Lyle found himself struggling to survive in a hostile and lonely work environment, just those sorts of struggles that prompted Ryan (1986) to conclude there is a "survival stage" when learning to teach. From Huberman's (1989) model, Lyle's was a "painful" beginning. "For a person used to being respected [and trying] to define himself as an inquiry teacher who would stimulate students to explore problems, student challenges to his authority were sharp and painful blows to his already fragile sense of self" (p. 106). Early in the year he wrote in his journal: "the whole day [was] so traumatic! I wasn't ready for eighth graders in general... Third period remedial Math is the worst combination of defiant and mouthy boys I've ever seen... These guys took me to the cleaners immediately" (p. 106). Suggesting the survival stage of learning to teach, classroom control became a first priority. Lyle was uncertain how to respond to student misbehavior and soon fell into the only role that presented itself, policeman. Within the school this was the preferred relationship between teachers and students, one well understood by both parties. Yet, Lyle felt uncomfortable, not quite able to play the part even as he felt he must. "I just don't have that hard edge yet that is needed...to come down IMMEDIATELY and kick ass!" He moved, haltingly between desires of becoming an inquiry teacher or the tough authority figure that he thought the situation demanded, and he was miserable.

Frustration grew. While angry with the students, he was hardest on himself: "During my instructions for a lab there came a time [when] I should've retracted the [activity] and put them to work writing or [doing] other seatwork, but I didn't! Damn it, what's wrong with me?!" (p. 106). Lyle was torn, buffeted by extreme emotions, and an object of self-loathing. He was disgusted with himself and his lack of ability to motivate students, angry, shamed by his ineffective lessons, and after the fact guilt ridden when arbitrarily singling out one student over others for disciplining. Each day he left school wondering if teaching was "beyond" him. Gradually, the desire to become an inquiry teacher became a distant dream, a fantasy.

Obsessed with establishing classroom control and ever fearful, by mid-year the standard for lesson planning was whether or not an activity would invite misbehavior. As the months passed, Lyle became increasingly irritable and negative toward the students. The students, he concluded, were mostly to blame for his unhappiness. The narratives he generated supported this conclusion:

> Deep down, sometimes, I still can't accept that some of [the students] just have a meanness about them or a dishonest and out-of-control nature... And yet this is the nature of the beast. I still grapple with this. A day like today makes me feel incredibly inadequate and incompetent, no matter who I am or what kind of person I am. (p. 108)

The "beasts", he concluded, disliked authority, a dislike he took personally. "It almost seems to be my role to be their target." Fisher (2002) argues that anger is "related to informal moments of seeking justice" (p. 66), and Lyle wanted justice.

Over time, anger turned to resignation as Lyle engaged in the disturbing task of trying to distance himself mentally from the problems of teaching.

> I'm [working] mentally on not letting the kids and things that happen at school get to me too much... I've also been listening and thinking about other teachers' suggestions [about how] to...distance myself from the students. (p. 108)

Apparently, the other teachers shared his conclusions about the students, which raises disturbing questions about the nature of the influence a formal mentor might have had on Lyle had one been assigned. Numbed and self-concerned, Lyle stopped planning ahead, and lowered his expectations, a coping mechanism harmful to both himself and the students. What remained was the hope of establishing a "truce" with the students – a bargain that if they would behave he would make certain class was not unpleasant.

Lyle thought he could become a kind and friendly "policeman," even though he found no pleasure in relating to students in such ways. Here it is important to note that it seems likely the students did not recognize Lyle as a teacher nor did he so recognize himself, and as previously noted, recognition is essential to forming then sustaining identity. After all, by his own admission Lyle was an ineffective policeman. Policing left him feeling "empty," and, just as Erikson (1968) suggests, lacking identity there is "no feeling of being alive." The scientist and man who had taken such pleasure in the "whole process of learning science" gave up any pretense that teaching had anything to do with content or inquiry, at least not in his school and department, and he gave up on this possible self.

The storylines Lyle created to explain and justify his behavior to himself and to others grew out of his judgment of the students as threatening, dangerous, and mean. As objects of his emotions, and despite many of their life situations, ultimately he thought some students deserving of his anger. In principle, he might have generated a very different story, one that made the school system or the principal who set his schedule the object of anger, but he did not. Some emotions, however, turned inward, toward the badly divided man he had become. As Fisher (2002) shows, vehement emotions like anger and fear force "an almost painfully pressing awareness of self" (p. 60), and in such moments the self is revealed for what it is. Lyle's fragile identity as an inquiry teacher, fractured leaving him unable to act consistently in the classroom. He did not know the emotional rules of the policeman professional identity although apparently the students and his colleagues did. Moreover, he lacked the skills of enactment; Lyle did not know how to get the students to recognize him as a policeman, let alone a scientist.

While extreme, among beginning teachers the pattern although not necessarily the intensity of Lyle's experience is not unusual nor are the emotions associated with it rare. As Flores and Day (2006) write of the teachers in their study: "When they described the teachers' role and good teaching, issues of flexibility, care, responsiveness to students' learning needs, and the use of a variety of methods were recurring features. However, the way they taught went against their initial (ideal) beliefs. Embedded in their practices and in their understanding of their job was a permanent dilemma" (p. 230). The dilemma is between what is required by the social order, as Erikson (1968) suggests, and how this requirement conflicts with the integrity of the somatic and personal orders. The result is alienation, inauthenticity, and for Lyle, a profound and deep unhappiness and lingering anger.

Barbara, a New Mentor

In teaching, caring and nurturing call forth intense pleasant and unpleasant emotions (Isenbarger and Zembylas 2006). Having formed a professional identity as a teacher centered on caring and nurturing, Barbara brought these same values and commitments to mentoring; it was through teaching and her identity as a teacher that she first thought about mentoring the two beginning English teachers to which she was assigned. As she discovered, the transfer was neither easily nor smoothly accomplished.

Centering one's sense of self as teacher on caring and nurturing presents a wide range of complex challenges. In addition to how caring and nurturing expectations often conflict with a range of professional and social order responsibilities, most especially including classroom management, teachers consistently struggle to set limitations (Bullough and Knowles 1991). Boundary setting encloses responsiveness, which may produce guilt, where the emotional object is the failure to meet an internalized and valued standard of performance and expectation, and fear of disappointing or not measuring up. But without setting limits mentee requests may become excessive; and Barbara set no boundaries.

> [Barbara] worked with me in the library as a co-teacher while the students worked for days on research. She was so awesome! I have 32 rambunctious students in that period, and I

literally would NOT have made it without her... She knew this and sacrificed an hour and twenty minutes every other day last week to help me get through the library work-days for research. Yet, she offered it willingly. I didn't even have to ask. (p. 149)

Mostly, the interns appreciated Barbara's efforts, but both occasionally complained she was not doing enough.

Behind the scenes, Barbara was feeling her way along as mentor. Because role expectations were unclear, for guidance she drew upon her teaching experience and her own experience of being mentored as a beginning teacher. She felt insecure, but did not let on. Instead, engaging in intense emotional labor, she worked to appear confident and self-assured even when she was not. For example, she worried about being observed by the mentees and labored to control her fears of modeling before them. Like many beginning mentors, she feared deeply that she would not have the answers her mentees needed and wanted (see Gless 2006). Also, she was concerned that she was not doing what the university-based teacher educators expected of her.

Over the year a strong emotional bond developed between Barbara and the two beginning teachers as she continued to protect, support, and provide for them. Seeming like children, Barbara loved them, as she said, and felt deeply invested in their success. They, however, did not see themselves as children. In an e-mail, one mentee wrote: "I really love my mentor. We have become friends, and I feel like I can go to her for help, that she will help me in a practical and kind way" (p. 151). The second mentee did not feel quite so close to Barbara, which troubled Barbara (although not the mentee) even though the relationship was reportedly very productive and positive. Structural issues – conflicting teaching schedules – interfered with building the sort of intimate relationship – mother and daughter – Barbara desired, and she felt guilt and disappointment at having been unable to care for this mentee as she thought she should have.

Neither mentee, Barbara remarked, had any idea of what she was doing for them. She did not want them to know. Nor did they fully realize the extent of Barbara's other commitments as teacher, school PTA representative, and cheer advisor, among others. By hiding how busy she was and not limiting their requests, she made certain the mentees continued to come to her for assistance like children. Had they ceased to ask for help, Barbara may have lost the recognition she so badly desired as a nurturer and mother. The cost of such recognition, however, was high. Barbara especially struggled with knowing the kind of feedback she should give to the mentees and how or even if she should evaluate their teaching performance. These were, after all, her children. "I don't want to offend them, [make it] so they won't come to me. But I want to make them better teachers. Relationships are important, way too important [to risk]" (p. 152). Yet, she felt compelled to do some evaluating because her other professional identity as teacher required her to protect students from harm. The teacher nurturer and mentor nurturer professional identities conflicted, a tension Barbara managed but did not resolve.

Barbara delighted in being helpful and supportive and watching the mentees grow and develop as teachers. While her personal identity as mother brought with it a requirement that the mentees be children and in some sense needy, it was not necessary for them to think of themselves that way just so long as they continued to want assistance. Barbara needed to be needed and, unfortunately, this expectation made it impossible for her to fully meet her own expectations: No matter how much she did for her mentees, they still required more. Such an identity is probably impossible to sustain, inevitably promising disappointment. Moreover, nurturing can sustain neediness and prevent growth, a danger that, although slight, was evident in Barbara's hesitancy to correct or criticize the mentees. Growth requires both support and challenge (Reiman and Thies-Sprinthall 1998); and Barbara could support, but she could not challenge.

Considerations

Both cases, of Lyle and Barbara, well represent how emotions and narratives are linked, with narratives offering explanations and justifications for action. The heavy emotional labor involved in forming and then sustaining a professional identity, particularly when that identity challenges aspects of the established social orders, is also apparent. This is most evident for Lyle, but nonetheless true also for Barbara, for whom unbounded nurturing offered an identity but one that required extraordinary emotional labor to sustain. After all, Barbara felt compelled to hide the high personal cost of meeting the mentees ever growing demands. On this view, the object of Lyle's emotions was self-preservation, indicative of the survival stage of teaching discussed earlier. Lyle could not engage fully in his work; his performance was but an unpleasant role-play lacking in the virtue associated with eudaimonia. Had he succeeded in becoming an effective policemen his unhappiness would have remained unless, of course, he could become other than himself by forming and then maintaining a new professional identity. As an ineffective policeman, his professional life was often miserable, certainly joyless.

Ironically, even if Lyle had been able to enact an identity as an inquiry teacher, difficulties may have remained. Within the school, inquiry was not recognized as appropriate for teaching the "beasts." Had he succeeded in becoming an inquiry teacher Lyle may not have been treated by other teachers as being one of "them". As it happens, not only skills and understanding would have been required to enact an inquiry identity but also courage. To some degree the happiness of eudaimonia is dependent upon recognition that one has acted appropriately, skillfully, and wisely, and this may require looking outside of the school, perhaps to a science educator association supportive of inquiry approaches to teaching.

Mostly, although often tired, Barbara flourished, enjoyed mentoring, and thought she was performing an important and valued professional service. For the most part she achieved the identity she sought, that of nurturer and mother, although at a significant cost. But, can her actions be characterized as virtuous? To be sure, she worked hard and acted with generosity. She was not, however, quite certain what represented excellent mentoring generally or for her two younger colleagues specifically. Barbara's standard for skilled and helpful mentoring grew out of her experience as a teacher and as a mentee, which, as remembered, she transferred wholly to what was a new situation. At several points she sensed, although did not articulate, that these experiences were not quite adequate for guiding her actions as a mentor. She had doubts and a few regrets. She had not been educated as a mentor; and to engage in virtuous activity the "good" must be an object of continuous study and review. There was a hidden problem: Barbara's need to be confirmed as a nurturer was in some ways more important to her than her mentees' need to grow as teachers. Barbara's professional identity enabled her to act supportively but not critically toward her mentees, and she wondered and doubted if her actions were as helpful as they should have been. By learning more about mentoring and about herself as teacher and mentor a deeper happiness could await Barbara. There is, as Bereiter and Scardamalia (1993) argue, something wondrous about surpassing ourselves, and that is the call for eudaimonia.

Conclusion

The implications of embracing eudaimonia as a central goal for mentoring and teaching are far reaching. As earlier noted, very little attention is given to teacher well-being in the current school reform discourse, generally quite the opposite is the case (Valli and Buese 2007). Teachers and those who teach them are consistently told they are ineffective and underperforming. Yet, positive affect is transformative – being one's best, teaching consistently with what one knows best helps the young to learn in ways that strengthen and deepen the quality of human relationships is essential to the happiness of teachers and mentors. Consider: the emotional state of teachers influences their thinking about teaching in numerous ways, both positively and negatively (Sutton and Wheatley 2003), as the two cases illustrate. Speaking of humans generally, Isen (2004) notes that: "Positive affect has...been found to promote creativity and flexibility in problem solving and negotiation, as well as both efficiency and thoroughness in decision making, and other indicators of improved thinking" (p. 417). Furthermore, "there is evidence that positive affect promotes stimulation seeking – that is, enjoyment of variety and of a wider range of possibilities – but only when the situation does not promote the person to think of unpleasant outcomes" (Isen 2004, p. 423). Drawing on laboratory studies, Peterson (2006) confirms these conclusions: induced pleasant emotions prompt "broader attention, greater working memory, enhanced verbal fluency, and increased openness to information" (p. 58). Happy people – understood in the sense suggested here – are more open to information and likely more accepting of difference. Hence, more interesting curriculum and instruction probably result. Motivation is affected by how teachers feel about their work as is goal setting and the expectations held of teachers, points especially evident in the case study of Lyle. Similarly, teacher commitment is affected, as is resilience, by how well or how quickly teachers bounce back from disappointment (Gu and Day 2007).

This brief foray into the emotions associated with becoming and being a teacher and a mentor points toward a wide range of questions. None is of greater importance in a time of rising managerialism and performativity than those associated with better understanding the institutional conditions necessary for educators to flourish. Happy educators – in the sense of eudaimonia – are crucially important to forming schools that are better able to provide for the well-being of children. The link should be obvious, but sadly it is not.

References

Aristotle (1943). On man in the universe. Walter J. Black, Inc., Roslyn, NY

Athanases SZ (2006) Adopt, adapt, invent: induction leaders designing mentor curriculum. In: Achinstein B, Athanases SZ (eds) Mentors in the making. Teachers College Press, New York, pp 83–95

Averill JR, More TA (2004) Happiness. In: Lewis M, Haviland-Jones JM (eds) Handbook of emotions, 3rd edn. The Guilford Press, New York, pp 663–676

Baier A (2004) Feelings that matter. In: Solomon RC (ed) Thinking about feeling: contemporary philosophers on emotion. Oxford University Press, New York, pp 200–213

Ball SJ (2003) The teachers' soul and the terrors of performativity. J Educ Policy 18(2): 215–228

Bereiter C, Scardamalia M (1993) Surpassing ourselves: an inquiry into the nature and implications of expertise. Open Court, Chicago

Berliner DC (1988) Implications of expertise in pedagogy for teacher education and evaluation. New directions for teacher assessment: proceedings of the 1988 ETS Invitational Conference. Educational Testing Service, Princeton, NJ, pp 39–67

Bottery M (2003) The leadership of learning communities in a culture of unhappiness. Sch Leadersh Manage 23(2):187–207

Bullough RV Jr (1992) Beginning teacher curriculum decision making, personal teaching metaphors, and teacher education. Teach Teach Educ 8(3):239–252

Bullough RV Jr (1997) "First-year teacher" eight years later: an inquiry into teacher development. Teachers College Press, New York

Bullough RV Jr (2005) Being and becoming a mentor: school-based teacher educators and teacher educator identity. Teach Teach Educ 21(2):143–155

Bullough RV Jr, Baughman K (1997) First year teacher – eight years later: an inquiry into teacher development. Teachers College Press, New York

Bullough RV Jr, Draper RJ (2004) Mentoring and the emotions. J Educ Teach 30(3):271–288

Bullough RV Jr, Knowles JG (1990) Becoming a teacher: struggles of a second-career beginning teacher. Qual Stud Educ 3(2):101–112

Bullough RV Jr, Knowles JG (1991) Teaching and nurturing: changing conceptions of self as teacher in a case study of becoming a teacher. Qual Stud Educ 4(2):121–140

Bullough RV Jr, Young J (2002) Learning to teach as an intern: the emotions and the self. Teach Dev 6(3):417–432

Bullough RV Jr, Young JR, Draper RJ (2004) One-year teaching internships and the dimensions of beginning teacher development. Teach Teach Theory Pract 10(4):365–394

Clinard LM, Ariav T (1998) What mentoring does for mentors: a cross-cultural perspective. Eur J Teach Educ 21(1):91–108

Colley H (2002) A "rough guide" to the history of mentoring from a Marxist feminist perspective. J Educ Teach 28(3):257–273

Day C, Kington A, Stobart G, Sammons P (2006) The personal and professional selves of teachers: stable and unstable identities. Br Educ Res J 32(4):601–616

Erikson EH (1968) Identity: youth and crisis. W.W. Norton & Company, New York

Feiman-Nemser S (2001) From preparation to practice: designing a continuum to strengthen and sustain teaching. Teach Coll Rec 103(6):1012–1055

Fisher P (2002) The vehement passions. Princeton University Press, Princeton

Flores MA, Day C (2006) Contexts which shape and reshape new teachers' identities: a multiperspective study. Teach Teach Educ 22(2):219–232

Fuller FF, Bown OH (1975) Becoming a teacher. In: Ryan K (ed) Teacher education. University of Chicago Press, Chicago, pp 25–52

Gee JP (2000–2001) Identity as an analytic lens for research in education. In: Secada WG (ed) Review of research in education, vol 25. American Educational Research Association, Washington, DC, pp 99–125.

Gless J (2006) Designing mentoring programs to transform school cultures. In: Achinstein B, Athanases SZ (eds) Mentors in the making. Teachers College Press, New York, pp 165–175

Goddard JT, Foster RY (2001) The experiences of neophyte teachers: a critical constructivist assessment. Teach Teach Educ 17(3):349–365

Goldie P (2004) Emotion, feeling, and knowledge of the world. In: Solomon RC (ed) Thinking about feeling: contemporary philosophers on emotions. Oxford University Press, New York, pp 91–106

Gratch A (1998) Teacher and mentor relationships. J Teach Educ 49(3):220–227

Gu Q, Day C (2007) Teachers resilience: a necessary condition for effectiveness. Teach Teach Educ 23(8):1302–1316

Hargreaves A, Fullan M (1998) What's worth fighting for in education?. Open University Press/ Ontario Public School Teachers' Federation, Buckingham/Philadelphia

Harre R, van Langenhove L (eds) (1999) Positioning theory. Blackwell, Oxford, UK

Haviland-Jones JM, Kahlbaugh P (2004) Emotion and identity. In: Lewis M, Haviland-Jones JM (eds) Handbook of emotions, 3rd edn. The Guilford Press, New York, pp 293–305

Helsing D (2007) Regarding uncertainty in teachers and teaching. Teach Teach Educ 23(8):1317–1333

Hobson AJ (2002) Student teachers' perceptions of school-based mentoring in initial teacher training. Mentoring Tutoring 10(1):5–20

Hoy AW, Hoy WK, Kurz NM (2008) Teacher's academic optimism: the development and test of a new construct. Teach Teach Educ 24(4):821–835

Huberman M (1989) The professional life cycle of teachers. Teach Coll Rec 91(1):31–57

Isen AM (2004) Positive affect and decision making. In: Lewis M, Haviland-Jones JM (eds) Handbook of emotions, 3rd edn. The Guilford Press, New York, pp 417–435

Isenbarger L, Zembylas M (2006) The emotional labour of caring in teaching. Teach Teach Educ 22(1):120–134

Izard CE, Ackerman BP (2004) Motivational, organizational, and regulatory functions of discrete emotions. In: Lewis M, Haviland-Jones JM (eds) Handbook of emotions, 3rd edn. The Guilford Press, New York, pp 253–264

Jeffrey B, Woods P (1996) Feeling deprofessionalized: the social construction of emotions during an OFSTED inspection. Cambridge J Educ 26(3):325–343

Kelchtermans G (1996) Teacher vulnerability: understanding its moral and political roots. Cambridge J Educ 26(3):307–324

Kelchtermans G (2005) Teachers' emotions in educational reforms: self-understanding, vulnerable commitment and micropolitical literacy. Teach Teach Educ 21(8):995–1006

Kelley LM (2004) Why induction matters. J Teach Educ 55(5):438–448

Kilburg GM, Hancock T (2006) Addressing sources of collateral damage in four mentoring programs. Teach Coll Rec 108(7):1321–1338

Liu XS, Ramsey J (2008) Teachers' job satisfaction: analyses of the teacher follow-up survey in the United States for 2000–2001. Teach Teach Educ 24(5):1173–1184

Marable MA, Raimondi SL (2007) Teachers perception of what was most (and least) supportive during their first year of teaching. Mentoring Tutoring 15(1):25–37

Martin D (1997) Mentoring in one's own classroom: an exploratory study of contexts. Teach Teach Educ 13(2):183–197

Maslach C (1999) Progress in understanding teacher burnout. In: Vandenberghe R, Huberman AM (eds) Understanding and preventing teacher burnout. Cambridge University Press, New York, pp 211–222

McDermott D, Hastings S (2000) Children: raising future hopes. In: Snyder CR (ed) Handbook of hope: theory, measures and applications. Academic, San Diego, pp 185–199

Moore DT (2007) Analyzing learning at work: an interdisciplinary framework. Learn Inq 1:175–188

Nichols SL, Berliner DC (2007) Collateral damage: how high-stakes testing corrupts America's Schools. Harvard Education Press, Cambridge, MA

Nussbaum M (2004) Emotions as judgments of value and importance. In: Solomon RC (ed) Thinking about feeling: contemporary philosophers on emotion. Oxford University Press, New York, pp 183–199

Orland-Barak L (2005) Lost in translation: mentors learning to participate in competing discourses of practice. J Teach Educ 56(4):355–366

Peterson C (2006) A primer of positive psychology. Oxford University Press, New York

Rajuan M, Beijaard D, Verloop N (2007) The role of the cooperating teacher: bridging the gap between expectations of cooperating teachers and student teachers. Mentoring Tutoring 15(3):223–242

Reiman AJ, Thies-Sprinthall L (1998) Mentoring and supervision for teacher development. Longman, New York

Rippon JH, Martin M (2006) What makes a good induction supporter? Teach Teach Educ 22(1):84–99

Ryan K (1986) The induction of new teachers. Phi Delta Kappa Educational Foundation, Bloomington, IN

Smith TM, Ingersoll RM (2004) What are the effects of induction and mentoring on beginning teacher turnover? Am Educ Res J 41(3):681–714

Snyder CR, Rand KL, Sigmon DR (2005) Hope theory. In: Snyder CR, Lopez SJ (eds) Handbook of positive psychology. Oxford University Press, New York, pp 257–312

Solomon RC (1993) The passions: emotions and the meaning of life. Hacket Publishing Company, Indianapolis

Solomon RC (2004) Emotions, thoughts, and feelings: emotions as engagements with the world. In: Solomon RC (ed) Thinking about feeling: contemporary philosophers on emotion. Oxford University Press, New York, pp 76–88

Sundli L (2007) Mentoring – a new mantra for education? Teach Teach Educ 23(2):201–214

Sutton RE, Wheatley KF (2003) Teachers' emotions and teaching: a review of the literature and directions for future research. Educ Psychol Rev 15(4):327–358

Templeton L (2003) Into the fray on the very first day: lessons from an unconventional mentor. Mentoring Tutoring 11(2):163–175

Valli L, Buese D (2007) The changing roles of teachers in an era of high-stakes accountability. Am Educ Res J 44(3):519–558

Van Eekelen IM, Vermunt JD, Boshuizen HPA (2006) Exploring teachers' will to learn. Teach Teach Educ 22(4):408–413

Watzke JL (2007) Longitudinal research on beginning teacher development: complexity as a challenge to concerns-based stage theory. Teach Teach Educ 23(1):106–122

Weinstein CS (1989) Teacher education students' preconceptions of teaching. J Teach Educ 40(2):53–60

Williams A, Prestage S (2002) The induction tutor: mentor, manager or both? Mentoring Tutoring 10(1):35–46

Young JR, Bullough RV Jr, Draper RJ, Smith LK, Erickson LB (2005) Novice teacher growth and personal models of mentoring: choosing compassion over inquiry. Mentoring Tutoring 13(2):169–188

Zeichner K (2002) Beyond traditional structures of student teaching. Teach Educ Q 29(2):59–64

Zembylas M (2002) 'Structures of feeling' in curriculum and teaching: theorizing the emotional rules. Educ Theory 52(2):187–208

Zembylas M (2003) Emotions and teacher identity: a poststructural perspective. Teach Teach Theory Pract 9(3):213–238

Chapter 4
Emotion Management and Display in Teaching: Some Ethical and Moral Considerations in the Era of Marketization and Commercialization

Izhar Oplatka

Abstract I review the research on emotion management in teaching since the 1990s, including the theoretical knowledge underlying this research. My focus will be on describing its contribution to our knowledge base about emotional displays and their determinants in school teaching. I also discuss emotion management at work and then focuses on forms of emotion management in teaching. I also review and analyze factors affecting emotion management in teaching – such as the culture of teaching, gender, seniority, and the principal. Finally, I discuss the implications of emotion management in teaching.

Keywords Emotion management · Marketization · Teaching

The modern labor organization is usually thought of as cold and rational, as no place for the experience and display of emotions, a conjecture that for many scholars no longer represents the "real" day-to-day life of employees (e.g., Ashkanasy et al. 2002; Fineman 2000), including teachers (Oplatka et al. 2002; Zembylas 2005). It is widely held, nowadays, that employees in almost all kinds of work organizations and occupations are engaged in emotions explicitly and implicitly, including schools and teaching.

Thus, much research has sought to investigate emotions and forms of emotion management among teachers worldwide providing more knowledge about the connection between educational change and teacher emotion (Hargreaves 1994, 2000); the link between teacher emotion and teacher beliefs (e.g., Zembylas 2005); and the expressions of emotions in teaching, such as guilt (Hargreaves 1994), anger and frustration (Sutton 2002), enthusiasm (Oplatka 2004, 2005) and the like. The teaching occupation is commonly seen as a practice that is deeply embedded in emotional experiences (Hargreaves 1998; Nias 1999).

I. Oplatka (✉)
Department of Policy and Administration in Education,
Constantiner School of Education, Tel Aviv University, Israel
e-mail: oplatka@post.tau.ac.il

P.A. Schutz and M. Zembylas (eds.), *Advances in Teacher Emotion Research:* *The Impact on Teachers' Lives*,
DOI 10.1007/978-1-4419-0564-2_4, © Springer Science+Business Media, LLC 2009

Interestingly, however, many education reforms introduced into educational systems of many western countries during the 1990s have consistently ignored the emotional aspects of teaching, calling to intensify its "rational", measurable aspects. This was accompanied by a re-conceptualization of the teacher's role in terms of collegiality, accountability, assessment, competition and responsiveness (Helsby 1999; Oplatka et al. 2002). Above all, the reforms emphasized the need to adopt concepts developed in business organizations as a means to improve the schooling process and its outcomes (e.g., standardization, assessment), and the terminology of "pupils as clients" penetrated the education systems (Day 2002; Goodson 1997; Levin 2001; Oplatka et al. 2002)

In light of the proliferation and dominance of business-like ideologies and concepts in the educational discourse, I would like to reflect in this chapter upon the concepts of emotion management and display as they have been explored in largely non-education organizations and are implicitly and indirectly favored by those who conceptualize teaching as service occupation rather than a moral and emotional engagement.

This kind of reflection, I believe, may help sharpen the need to remain committed to the emotional aspects of teaching in any reform initiative concerning the role of teachers and teaching. In addition, the discussion in this chapter is intended to shed light on the emotional complexities embedded in teaching, which in turn, are unlikely to enable rationalization and standardization of teaching as many reformers have long strived for.

Briefly, following a review of both the literature on emotion management (including emotional labor) both in non-education organizations and in schools, it is argued here that emotion management that is aimed at the achievement of external benefits (e.g., organizational success, impressive management) is incompatible with the ethical and moral aspects of teaching and may result in negative effects on those involved in the schooling process. This conjecture, in passing, may account for the shortage of studies about emotion management in educational arenas. The chapter ends with some empirical suggestions for future research.

The Research on Emotion Management in Service Organizations

Emotion and its display are critical and fundamental to human activity in all organizations (Schutz and DeCuir 2002). It is defined as "an awareness of four elements that we usually experience at the same time: appraisal of a situation, changes in bodily sensations, the free or inhibited display of expressive gestures and a cultural label applied to specific constellations of the first three elements" (Hochschild 1990, pp. 118–119). Yet, emotions are generally of short duration and are associated with a specific stimulus, as opposed to "mood" which is more enduring, more diffuse and less related to specific stimuli (Frijda 1993).

Most theories of emotions acknowledge the relationship between specific emotions and specific types of behaviors (Fredrickson 1998). As such, emotions may have an impact on important social processes, such as trust in others, perceptions of honesty, interpersonal attraction and group commitment (Lord and Kanfer 2002). Thus, pleasant emotions are assumed to engender a number of important organizational processes, such as skill building, creativity, effective social relations, organizational commitment, collective orientations, and prosocial behaviors (Fredrickson 1998).

For many years, emotional reactions at work were seen as disruptive, weak and a deviation from the sacred rationality in the organization (Zembylas 2005). But, during the last two decades, a greater legitimacy has been given in many western countries to emotion management and displays in the workplace (Lewis and Stearns 1998), and the research on emotions in organizations began to deal with the question of why and how employees may display or manage particular emotions, including emotions that differ from how they feel (e.g., Ashkanasy et al. 2002). Management of emotions has also been termed "emotional labor" (Hochschild 1983), although Zembylas (2005) distinguishes between the two terms, indicating that "emotion management emphasizes the process of regulating one's emotions while emotional labor focuses more on the consequences of this process" (p. 50).

Service employees have a special duty to ensure customer retention and satisfaction through appropriate emotion management (Ashkanasy et al. 2002) (i.e., through "the process by which individuals influence which emotions they have, when they have them, and how they experience and express these emotions") (Gross 1998, p. 275). In other words, many service employees have to shape the perceived "right" (that is, managerial prescribed) emotional displays to the customer, which means the involvement of real labor on the employees' part (Hochschild 1979). Emotion management at work can take many forms, including suppressing emotional reactions, exaggerating them, or modulating their expression (Zembylas 2005). It focuses on conscious efforts to shape emotional expression according to what is "appropriate" in a certain organization or society (Hochschild 1979).

Emotion management can occur through the regulation of the precursors of emotions such as how one appraises the situation or inhibits emotion displays, and through conscious modification of the physiological or observable signs of emotions (Gross 1998; Hochschild 1983). In this sense, emotion management involves modifying the emotions one has by reappraising an event or modifying expression by faking or enhancing facial and bodily signs of emotion (Zembylas 2005). Note, however, that employees can attempt to modify their outward appearance without genuinely altering how they actually feel (i.e., faking), or they can express the desired emotion and try to summon those emotions (i.e., to express true emotions). The first strategy has been referred to as "surface acting" and the second one "deep acting" (Hochschild 1990; Groth et al. 2006), but one should look at these strategies as edges of a continuum rather than an absolute binary.

A well-known distinction has been made in the literature between two terms – "emotional labor" and "emotion work." The first concept, "emotional labor", is used by Hochschild (1983) to capture a very specific meaning associated with the management of emotions, namely being paid to manifest a specific emotional state as part of one's job. It refers to a situation in which employees are required to display particular emotional states as a part of their job (Hochschild 1983), displays for which they receive remuneration and which are controlled by others (Wharton 1993). Morris and Feldman (1996) suggest that emotional labor is the "effort, planning, and control needed to express organizationally desired emotions during interpersonal transactions" (p. 987). Organizations usually have certain explicit or implicit "display rules" (Rafaeli and Sutton 1989), that is, norms and standards of behavior which indicate which emotions are appropriate and should be publicly expressed and which emotions should be suppressed. These rules, termed also "emotional rules" (Zembylas 2005), may determine how employees are obliged to feel and to express emotions in occupational sectors characterized by emotional labor.

Thus, emotional labor involves selling the emotional self for the purposes and profits of the organization – a smile for sale, for example. The grocery store clerk whose manager instructs her to smile when dealing with customers is being paid not only to manage her emotions as part of her job, but also for manifesting specific emotions (Callahan and McCollum 2002).

The second concept, "emotion work", in contrast, refers to a state where the individual is autonomous in managing his/her emotions in the workplace, is not paid for doing so, and emotion management of any kind is not enforced (Hochschild 1983). Callahan and McCollum (2002) clarified this concept by distinguishing it from "emotional labor":

> We argue that the term emotion work is appropriate for situations in which individuals are personally choosing to manage their emotions for their own non-compensated benefit. The term emotional labor, on the other hand, is appropriate only when emotion work is exchanged for something such as a wage or some other type of valued compensation (p. 282).

Thus according to Callahan and McCollum (2002) emotion work is controlled by the individual, while emotional labor is controlled by the organization (Wharton 1993).

A further distinction between the concepts is suggested by Strazdins (2002). Whereas, emotion labor (emotion management in her words) refers to the management of emotions in the self in order to display a particular feeling, emotional work refers to behaviors used by individuals to alter other people's feelings. It is the "behaviors enacted to meet emotional role demands and improve the well-being of others at work and in the family" (p. 232).

It is worth noting, however, that the distinction is not sufficiently evident and there are many exceptional cases. For example, if employees are not paid to go to festivities as part of their actual position in the organization, yet are expected by superiors to attend and to be cheerful about it, according to Callahan and McCollum (2002), there is the potential for "indirect emotional labor" rather than "emotion work". In addition, when service workers display niceness, warmth, or friendliness, they intend to affect customers' feelings (make them feel welcomed, care for, etc.). In doing so, service workers may manage their own emotions, appraise the other person's feelings, and behave accordingly (i.e., speak warmly, listen). Yet, I would like to use this distinction as a conceptual framework to analyze recent reforms and policies in education worldwide and their possible implications for the teacher's role in terms of ethics, morality, and the like. The reader should look at this distinction a theoretical conceptualization that may help analyze the reality rather than the reality itself.

The research thus far has pointed to a wide variety of antecedents of emotion management at work, including local norms (Plas and Hoover-Dempsey 1988), affective requirement (Ashforth and Tomiuk 2000), professional and organizational norms (Fineman 2000), culture and emotional cultures (Hochschild 1990). Rafaeli and Sutton (1989) showed that service employees' displays of pleasant emotions were directly related to positive customer reactions and organizational effectiveness. Emotional responses can be intensified by reactions such as panic in others, or they can be reduced by the reassuring calm responses of others, particularly formal leaders (Lord and Kanfer 2002). These and other factors underpin what people in service roles should and should not display or feel, what they should feel and try to feel, and how they should attend to, codify, appraise, manage and express feelings.

Similarly, a great deal of research examined the effects of emotion management (e.g., Ashkanasy et al. 2002; Grandey 2003; Pugh 2001) assuming that emotion work has use-value while emotional labor has exchange-value (Callahan and McCollum 2002). Links have been shown to exist between emotional labor and emotional exhaustion, job dissatisfaction, and lack of organizational identity (Grandey 2003; Morris and Feldman 1996). The strain of emotional labor can even lead to employee burnout (Ashkanasy et al. 2002).

In contrast, some authors have pointed to a correlation between pleasant displays of emotions, job satisfaction (Wharton 1993), and ratings of service quality (Pugh 2001). Grandey (2003) explained this contradiction by the strategies employed; whereas "surface acting" has a number of negative effects on employees, "deep acting" may be beneficial to their well-being. In other words, there is nothing good or bad with emotion management unless it is used for instrumental purposes (e.g., for making the client buy a product he does not need). Along the same lines, Strazdins (2002) claimed that the effect of emotion management is determined by the degree to which the emotional labor involves pleasant or unpleasant emotions – only the latter may lead to health costs.

A thorough discussion about emotional dissonance, arising from the last point, appears in the literature about emotion management in the workplace. Emotional dissonance occurs when one's displayed emotions differ from one's actual emotions (i.e., when one is behaving against his personal values and beliefs) (Abraham 1998), or in other words, when one's beliefs and values are compromised or consumed under certain emotion management work regimes (Fineman 2000). These situations are intensified when the organization expects service agents to not only display prescribed emotions but to actually feel them as they are interested in creating a work context that routinely evokes the desired emotions (Ashforth and Tomiuk 2000). In addition, some tensions could be expected where gender expectations about workers are in contrast with job expectations in respect to emotion displays and management (Fineman 2000).

It is commonly held that emotional dissonance is an aversive state that one typically seeks to avoid or escape (Ashforth and Tomiuk 2000). It was positively associated with emotional exhaustion and job dissatisfaction among customer service representatives from a variety of industries (Abraham 1998), and was found to exact a health cost and low job control (Strazdins 2002). A typically suggested remedy is to redesign the job in ways to permit more personal expression (Fineman 2000), or to display emotions closer to the employees' feelings, even if this represents deviance from organizational norms (Ashkanasy et al. 2002).

To sum up, the research on emotion management and displays in non-education organizations provides some insights into the place of emotions in teaching as well as evokes some questions about teaching as an emotional engagement. For example, how do social norms and emotional cultures mold work behavior of teachers? What are the emotion-rules that are rooted in school culture? What are the "right" emotion displays for schoolteachers? How do teacher learn the "appropriate" emotion management in their workplace? Why do teachers suppress some sorts of emotion displays? And so forth.

The next section describes the research on emotion management and displays in teaching and analyzes its major directions. It is based on the conjectures that (a) the intensity and complexity of emotion displays and the degree of control over the emotion management differ (Zembylas 2005) and (b) that different work organizations will inherit the wider emotion rules of the society of which they are part, but they also adapt them to create their own codes of emotion property (Fineman 2000).

Forms of Emotion Management in Teaching

Each occupation has patterns of emotions and emotional display that are somewhat distinctive and related to cultural, historical and societal practices that convey meanings and affects to members of that culture (Oatley 1993), and teaching is no exception. In this occupation, emotion management is an integral part of the teacher's job, especially when he or she is engaged in interactions with pupils (Hargreaves 1998; Nias 1989; Oplatka 2004). This is discussed by Zembylas (2005):

> Emotion management strategies are often used as a natural aspect of teaching and learning without problematizing them in any way. Thus, emotion management over time becomes part of a teacher's habitus… that is so embedded in one's practices that no interrogation is involved (p. 209).

It is worth noting, however, that teachers' work also consists of what Forrester (2005, p. 274) terms "non-work" in the sense that there is no direct economic benefit for caring. Israeli school-teachers shared the assumption that emotional understanding, caring and emotion displays in teaching are actually discretionary, non-obligatory role elements. Display of emotion in teaching was not perceived as a mandatory task, or as part of the teacher's role description. A failure to display emotion cannot lead to any formal sanction and teachers are not necessarily trained to employ them (Oplatka 2007a). In this sense, emotion management is underpinned by ethical and humanistic dimensions underlying teaching occupation, which frequently act as a source of intrinsic motivation for individual teachers (O'Connor 2008).

Thus, many teacher emotions, including warmth, love, amazement, excitement, human nurturance, anger, embracement, sorrow, or enjoyment are a result of cultural, social, institutional and political relations (Hargreaves 1998; Oplatka and Eizenberg 2007; Zembylas 2005). These and related emotions may be considered to underpin the work of many elementary teachers much more than principles of pedagogy or learning (Hargreaves 1994), for good teaching is about passionate commitment and feeling positively towards children (Blackmore 1999; Oplatka 2004; Prosser 1999).

For the purpose of this chapter, a deeper look at the forms of emotion management in teaching as they have been unearthed in the research is warranted. Teaching, like many other professions, requires active emotional labor for the benefit of the child. It is evident that teachers may "pretend" to be disappointed or surprised at a student's question (Hargreaves 1998; Sutton 2002), are commonly expected to "smile" and appear cheerful on days even when they are not quite up to it (Jackson 1986), or to communicate with students in a more relational, personal and moral manner under most conditions (Klaassen 2002). Most teachers in Sutton's (2002) study said they displayed their pleasant emotions publicly, and middle school teachers who felt tense during anger or frustration often reacted with a teacher stare, a frown, or by talking more or less than they did when not frustrated or angry (Sutton and Conway 2002). New Israeli kindergarten teachers expressed frustration, distress or disappointment when having to negotiate with parents (Oplatka and Eizenberg 2007)

Additionally, teachers manage their emotions when they are enthusiastic about a new initiative (Oplatka 2005), show patience with a frustrating colleague, or are calm in the face of parents' complains (Hargreaves 2000). In this sense, Sutton (2002) wrote: …Other ways teachers regulated their positive emotions were to 'get themselves up' before school and to prepare themselves to be 'enthusiastic and energetic' (p. 9).

Although some of them may be tired and feeling down, still they may manage their emotion in order to appear enthusiastic so their students will be excited about the learning process (Sutton 2002). For instance, the teacher, Michael, felt that his work often involved "creating a sense of belonging with kids you don't really know" (O'Connor 2008, p. 122). Yet, there are teachers who have learned to regulate emotions because it was more effective to do so (Sutton 2002). Sometimes, the preferred manner in cases of unpleasant emotions was repression, as a school-teacher confessed in his paper:

> Often I felt embarrassment, anger, fear and anxiety as it related to my teaching performance but I tended to keep these feelings to myself and engaged in self-accusatory and self-blaming behavior… (Winograd 2003, p. 1668).

Having said that, he specified his emotion management in interactions with superiors:

> When my emotion (anger, disgust) was directed toward the hierarchy, administrators or others, my emotional expressions never developed into anything more than a grumble, which is the most benign form of political resistance. Mine and my colleagues' anger at the hierarchy was always restrained and guarded, reflecting the women/teacher ideal as kind, gentle and nurturing (Winograd 2003, p. 1669).

The last point brings up the potential gender difference in emotion management. Although Hargreaves (1998) claimed there were no great emotional differences between male and female teachers, it is likely that emotion management in teaching corroborates, to a certain extent, gender stereotypes. Thus, women teachers might be expected to display self-restraint, patience, non-aggressiveness, caring, and nurturing, all of which features attached stereotypically to women in our society (Winograd 2003). Yet, when women display these and related emotions they may be dismissed as out of control and this is considered to be inappropriate for a male (Campbell 1994).

The concept of emotional labor, according to Hargreaves (1998), puts care and caring into context, because it shows that care is not only a personal choice or moral imperative to an act of work, but depends also on the context in which the work is performed. Thus, the context of teaching, and especially the nature of teacher–pupil interactions, often highlights the moral importance and centrality of caring or concern in the teacher's work (Goldstein and Lake 2000; Nias 1999; Noddings 1984). Elementary school teachers regard their relationship with their pupils as a personal rather than an impersonal, bureaucratic one (Prosser 1999).

For Noddings (1984), caring involves the establishment of meaningful relationships, the ability to sustain connections and the commitment to respond to others with sensitivity and flexibility. In classroom teaching, caring takes, among other things, the shape of encouraging dialogue, exhibiting sensitivity and flexibility to students' needs and interests (Rogers and Webb 1991), providing a place of comfort and safe environment (Hargreaves 1998), expressing love towards pupils (Nias 1989), and making children feel happy and cared for (Prosser 1999). Educators in Beck and Kooser's (2004) study, for example, felt that caring required attention to the personal and that it couldn't be exercised merely through policies or programs.

Care and caring for can be operated through emotion management, mainly when the "care" has external expressions such as those depicted above. Thus, caring can be regulated and managed just like any other emotion display in the classroom.

The Determinants of Emotion Management and Display in Teaching

One's experience and display of emotions reflects the totality of a person's experience, which includes organizational culture, gender, race, class, education and personality (Winograd 2003). Thus, four categories of determinants of emotion management in teaching have been identified in the literature about teacher emotion.

The Culture of Teaching

Congruent with the "constructive approach" (Oatley 1993), the cultural and ideological basis of the teaching occupation seems to guide where, when and how teachers are supposed to display particular emotions in different contexts (Lasky 2000; Winograd 2003; Zembylas 2005). Cornelius (1996) explains this approach:

> The experience and expression of emotions is dependent on learned convictions or rules and that, to the extent that cultures differ in the way they talk about and conceptualize emotions, how they are experienced and expressed will differ in different cultures as well (p. 188).

Underlying this emergent research on teaching and emotions are two interrelated assumptions: Firstly, the capacity of teachers to display a certain emotion in their work is not just a matter of personal disposition, but also of cultural influences (Hargreaves 2000; Nias 1999; Zembylas 2003). For example, Lasky (2000) found that the emotions teachers experienced in their interactions with parents were a mélange of personal and cultural beliefs, largely shaped by the professional norm-based discourses and moral values they appropriate within the culture of teaching.

Secondly, and arising from the first assumption, the culture of teaching is likely to exert much influence on teachers' management of emotions at work (Nias 1999). When elementary education is concerned, this kind of culture is premised to be a culture of care, love, concern, affection and other possible emotion displays towards children (Hargreaves 2000; Nias 1989, 1999; Noddings 1984).

Cultural-professional scripts, leading to strong feelings of commitment and responsibility over young children, are argued to result in teachers' investment of enormous amounts of time and energy in their caring relationship with their students (Nias 1999). Hence, the three teachers in O'Connor's (2008) study viewed the kindness and caring they showed to others as both professional choice and as a necessary part of their work. Their caring attitudes seem to be influenced both by their need to sustain positive professional relationships with their student and by their individual beliefs about their role as teachers.

The culture of teaching which encourages some kinds of emotion displays in the classroom is also related to historical reasons. Teachers are expected to care for a wide variety of historical reasons including religious origins, parental images of teachers, and a broad definition of teaching (Prosser 1999). Note, however, that emotion displays serve to defend social norms and systems of belief. The ways we respond to emotions are "tied to values, to conditions that involve one's identity" (Sarbin 1986, p. 91).

Emotion Rules

The research on emotion management discussed in the previous section has pointed to the key role of emotional rules (i.e., of cultural, social and institutional norms, regulations and standards), in employees' emotion displays in varied work contexts. In teaching nowadays emotional rules have become less rigid and formal implying that emotional labor in teaching became more subtle, varied and complex, as Zembylas (2005) made out, although it does not mean complete relaxation in this kind of rules or a lessening in a teacher's emotional labor. In many places, including the USA and the UK accountability policies and high standardization of the teacher's role may, in contrast, regulate some "preferred" forms of emotion management for the sake of student high achievements.

Note that every school has its own emotional rules, either informally or formally, guiding what kinds of emotions are legitimized to display and which are not in the classroom. For example, O'Connor (2008) found that schools that seek to define their teachers as service providers whose job is to promote the needs and values of the institutions have overlooked the personal and individual nature of teachers' work.

Some scholars suggest that teachers' identities have a stronger influence on their emotion management then prescribed rules (e.g., Hargreaves 1998; Winograd 2003). Thus, Winograd (2003) confessed that he controlled much of his emotional labor, resulting in a sense of job satisfaction. Hargreaves (1998) indicated that becoming a tactful, caring, or passionate teacher is also related to personal disposition. The decrease in strict emotional rules in many education systems of western countries further empowers the place of the teacher him/herself in the emotion management (Oplatka 2007a, b), as this process is negotiated and modified in the explicit and implicit emotional rules (Zembylas 2005). Additionally, when teachers become emotionally burdened, their caring feelings may be transformed into emotional labor (i.e., the publicly observable management of feelings sold solely for a wage) (Goldstein and Lake 2000).

Gender

How emotion is viewed and managed is also highly gendered (Blackmore 1999). In this sense, the rules for the expression of emotions for female elementary teachers historically reflect expectations that women show emotional restraint and self-control (Boler 1999), albeit women are mythologized to be the carriers of emotions (Blackmore 1999). Interestingly, as most teachers in many education systems are women, the gender expectations in respect to emotions are also "transmitted" to male teachers, as Winograd (2003) maintained:

> Given the dominance of elementary school faculty by women and the historical position of women in society and organizations, the culture of elementary schools and the rules for emotional expression tend to apply to both male and female teachers. As a male teacher, I felt subject to many of the same rules for my emotion display as my colleagues, most of whom were women (p. 1646).

Various Determinants

Other determinants of emotion management in teaching that have been identified related to expected pupil outcomes, organizational climate and structure, seniority and the principal's leadership. Thus, some teachers expressed their belief that children who feel secure in an adult's affection can concentrate on learning (Prosser

1999, p. 68), and others saw providing a good and complete education as a caring act (Beck and Kooser 2004).

The organizational structure and climate of the school also enjoins teachers' emotional management and molds their perception of appropriate emotional displays (Hargreaves 1998; Zembylas 2003). For instance, the teacher, Christina, believed that the private school she currently worked in expected her to care for her students in order to show the parents they are getting value to money, even though her original motivation for teaching was to effect change in her students' behavior through building personal relationships with them (O'Connor 2008).

Researchers have also suggested that seniority was also related to teachers' emotion displays and management. Thus, novice teachers have to go through socialization processes to acquire "appropriate" emotional displays in cases of frustration (Roulston et al. 2003), and Sutton (2002) found that teachers' control over emotional displays might change over time. In this respect, Hargreaves (2005) showed that early career teachers tend to be energetic, enthusiastic and intense while some late-career teachers feel emotionally drained.

Finally, Israeli teachers felt that positive displays of emotion, attentiveness to teachers' needs and individual consideration by principals help replenish teachers' supplies of emotion displays and care giving. Attentiveness to and interest in a teacher's life and work seem to generate an emotional bond between principals and teachers, which in turn encourages teachers to display positive emotions towards their own pupils (Oplatka 2007a)

The Potential Effects of Emotion Management in Teaching

Understanding the effect that emotion management has on teachers provides useful information. However, although Hargreaves' (1998) has made assertions about the key aspect of emotions in the teacher's role, we know very little about the effects of emotion management on teaching, learning and schools. Broadly speaking, there are potentially positive and negative effects.

To begin with, the positive effects of emotion management were related to effective instruction and interesting lessons (Hargreaves 1998, 2000). For example, some teachers in Sutton's (2002) study provided a variety of reasons for regulating their emotions, the most common of which were related to effectiveness or positive outcome expectancies. Put simply, teachers believed that regulating their unpleasant emotions made them more effective in the classroom (e.g., manage their anger so it will not interfere with their lesson). Furthermore, teachers' explicit efforts to care seemed to be recognized and appreciated by most students (Beck and Kooser 2004), probably due to, teachers' propensity to link between emotion management and students' benefits (Hargreaves 2000).

Most of the studies, nevertheless, have implied a link between emotion management and negative effect in teaching, as managing or masking emotions consumes much energy and involves moral dilemmas and internal conflicts, as the research on emotion management in non-education organization has long indicated. Thus, emotion management (including caring, repression and the like) may make teachers vulnerable in times of excessive demands (Hargreaves 1998), exhausted due to the inherently unequal nature of a caring teacher–students relationships (Rogers and Webb 1991), or create tension due to a contradiction between their professional roles and personal commitments to care (Beck and Kooser 2004). Likewise, the more central the care is to a teacher, the more emotionally devastating is the experience of failing to provide it (Hargreaves 1994).

Concluding Remarks: Teaching Cannot Be Emotionally Labored

The discussion to this point highlights, in my view, the stark distinction between the principles of emotion management as an emotional labor in for-profit organizations and the moral, ethical aspects inherent in teaching as an emotional practice. Let's begin by discussing the section about the research on emotion management in non-education organizations. For Hochschild (1983) and others, emotional labor is a largely negative phenomenon, which involves trading in part of the self for the reward that people get from their employers, or for the profitable rewards that accrue from commercial encounters (i.e., for the benefit of the organization and not necessarily the client). Thus, if we construct the teacher–pupils relations in terms of service agents versus clients, as some advocates of market forces in education postulated, we may evoke several moral dilemmas for our teachers, mainly because emotions play a key role in this kind of relations, as scholars in education showed (e.g., Nias 1989; Zembylas 2005).

These dilemmas can be succinctly formulated as questions: do we want our teachers to manage their emotions with the intention of improving their school's national or international rating? Can we imagine a teacher who expresses sensitivity toward her pupils just because she wants their parents to keep supporting the school financially? Is it moral and ethical to request teachers to develop a caring attitude just in order to make the pupils and their parents good ambassadors in the marketing process of the school? Can school management institutionalize emotional rules according to which teachers must express excitement and amazement in class just to promote the school's image as a caring school? Can principals request their teachers to repress unpleasant emotions such as anger and frustration in class for image purposes although these unpleasant emotions could be part of the pupils' socialization process? And finally, shall we expect teachers to repress their emotions in their meeting with parents even in cases where they feel the parents are hurting their child's development?

I assume the answer to these and similar questions is no. Although teachers have been observed to experience both pleasant and unpleasant emotions at work (Little 1996; Oplatka 2005), connectedness is deeply inherent in effective teaching to enable the reduction of teaching to technical dimensions only (Palmer 1998).

As long as the teacher regulates and manages emotions for the benefit of the pupils rather than the school or him/herself, the regulation/management is on par with the moral and ethical principles of teaching. But if not, we can look at emotion management in teaching as a moral deception. Put differently, when teachers smile at a child not because they respond to his/her needs in affection and empathy but rather because it may raise the school image as a place with warm atmosphere, this act is a "moral deception" of the pupils.

Moral deception, I believe, may exacerbate the negative results of emotional labor discussed at length in the research on emotion management both for teachers and pupils. In this sense, when teachers manage their emotional displays instrumentally and thereby inconsistently with "the culture of teaching", the extreme emotional dissonance they may experience is likely to engender a large gap between their professional norms and organizational demands in the era of marketization, competition and accountability. For example, in one of my studies about school marketing conducted in the UK (Oplatka et al. 2002), I met a Special Education teacher who was told by her principal she could not market her school to parents of students with special education needs because it might damage her school's image. She confessed feeling personal distress due to the moral dilemma she experienced (Oplatka et al. 2002). In addition, we know that standardization and accountability policies reduced the frequency of teachers' affective interactions with children (Prosser 1999). Dillabough (1999) further argued that institutionalized teacher standards often act to marginalize and repress individual beliefs and experiences by viewing the private sphere as irrelevant and subjugating the aims of the individual to those of the system. I do believe that new policies that will further the construction of pupils as clients will make it very hard for teachers to do their work without paying high personal prices such as chronic stress, burnout and depression.

As most of empirical emotional labor research so far has left the positive or negative effects of emotional labor on customers relatively untouched (Groth et al. 2006), I would like to speculate about the potential negative influences of emotion management on the pupils themselves. These influences can be epitomized as follows: let's imagine that pupils feel that their teacher displays pleasant emotions towards them not because this is what he feels but because the principal expects him or her to do so for instrumental reasons. What would their emotional reaction be then? What are the "moral messages" the teacher transmits to them? What will such emotion regulation do to their "moral development". I can go on with these questions, but I think my own conclusion in this respect is transparent.

There are two further points I want to consider here. First, is there a way to bridge the gap between the rational policies introduced in educational systems during the last decade and the emotional aspects of teaching? To answer this question I bring up Tolich's (1993) concept of "autonomous emotional labor" according to which the employee manages emotions to conform to his/her own standards not only because he/she feels it is right but also because he/she chooses to under the circumstances in which he lives and works. In other words, if emotion management was not under the control of policy-makers or school management but was susceptible to the teacher's discretion many of the negative effects I discussed above could be minimized. Teachers' emotion management should be ruled by external elements to a certain extent only, in order to permit teachers to manage their emotions in conjunction with their professional and moral values, and their authentic self.

The second point, arising partially from the first one, is a sort of reservation. It has long been held that the display and experience of emotion in the workplace vary tremendously across societies (Earley and Francis 2002; Peterson and Smith 1995), although we know of a relatively strong set of core emotions that are identified across cultures, including anger, happiness, sadness and disgust (Ekman 1973). Hochschild (1983) remarked:

> Some cultures may exert more control on the outer surface of behavior, allowing freedom to actual feelings underneath. Such cultures may focus on the expression rules that govern surface acting. Other cultures may exert relatively more social control on the inner emotional experience, focusing on feeling rules that govern deep acting (pp. 56–76).

Thus, my negative attitude towards the incorporation of emotional labor and strict emotional rules into teaching should be constrained by cultural influences. Put another way, cultural contexts defining superior–subordinates relations in school, teacher–pupils relations, and school–environment relations have much impact upon teachers' emotional experience and display in a certain social group. For instance, in a review I conducted about teaching and principalship in developing countries (Oplatka 2004, 2007b) I found out that hierarchy and obedience to superiors and strict organizational and social rules are central elements in a school's life to a point in which the principal is seen as "a king in his/her realm". It is likely, then, that teachers working in these countries may regulate their emotions in accordance with strict social and cultural rules without feeling emotional dissonance or moral dilemmas. This issue, nonetheless, should be explored in future research on emotion management in teaching worldwide.

Suggestions for Future Research

Evidence concerning emotion management in teaching is relatively thin, therefore subsequent research ought to inquire into how teachers manage their emotions in the era of accountability, standardization and marketization that has tended to ignore the caring aspects of teaching (O'Connor 2008) and divested teachers' attention from emotionality to measurable school outputs. This research should also probe into the factors affecting emotion management and regulation in teaching, patterns of emotional rules and emotion management in schools, and the potential effects of teachers' emotion management for the school organization, pupils, parents, and the teachers' colleagues.

Clearly, much research is needed around questions such as, why do teachers display certain emotions and repress others? How do teachers keep pupils satisfied through emotion management? What is considered to be "correct" emotion regulation in teaching and who decides? How do teachers decide which emotions to suppress? Do teachers perceive emotion management as a discretionary action? How do teachers learn to regulate emotions? How do they learn the school's emotional rules? What is the role of principals and policy-makers in teachers' emotion management? And so forth. A comparison of research findings related to these and other questions among nations and social groups is of high significance as it may provide insights into the potential influence of cultural scripts, national arrangements, and historical and social contexts upon emotion management and emotional engagement in teaching.

A second suggestion for subsequent research concerns a cross-cultural perspective to the nature of emotion in the workplace. That is, how might teachers' display and experience of emotions lead to meaningful differences and similarities across cultural boundaries? How do cultural dimensions influence the emotion displays of teachers in varied countries? This sort of research will enable, among other things, the establishment of an international database about emotion management and emotional rules in teaching and its effects on a wide variety of aspects in the school's life.

References

Abraham R (1998) Emotional dissonance in organizations: antecedents, consequences and moderators. Genet Soc Gen Psychol Monogr 124:229–246

Ashforth BE, Tomiuk MA (2000) Emotional labor and authenticity: views from service agents. In: Fineman S (ed) Emotion in organizations. Sage, London, pp 184–203

Ashkanasy NM, Zerbe WJ, Hartel CE (eds) (2002) Managing emotions in the workplace. M.E. Sharpe. Introduction, Armonk, NY

Beck LG, Kooser J (2004) Caring across cultures. Paper presented at the annual meeting of the American Education Research Association, San Diego

Blackmore J (1999) Troubling women: feminism, leadership, and educational change. Open University Press, Buckingham

Boler M (1999) Feeling power: emotions and education. Routledge, New York

Callahan JL, McCollum EE (2002) Obscured variability: the distinction between emotion work and emotional labor. In: Ashkanasy NM, Zerbe WJ, Hartel CE (eds) Managing emotions in the workplace. M.E. Sharpe, Armonk, NY, pp 219–231

Campbell S (1994) Being dismissed: the politics of emotional experience. Hyptia 9:46–66

Cornelius RR (1996) The science of emotion: research and tradition in the psychology of emotion. Prentice Hall, Upper Saddle River, NJ

Day C (2002) School reform and transitions in teacher professionalism and identity. Int J Educ Res 37:677–692

Dillabough JA (1999) Gender politics and conceptions of the modern teachers: women, identity and professionalism. Br J Sociol 20:373–394

Earley PC, Francis CA (2002) International perspectives on emotion and work. In: Lord RG, Klimoskei RJ, Kanfer R (eds) Emotions in the workplace: understanding the structure and role of emotions in organizational behavior. Jossey-Bass, San Francisco, pp 370–399

Ekman P (1973) Darwin and facial expressions: a century of research in review. Academic, Orlando, FL

Fineman S (2000) Emotional arenas revisited. In: Fineman S (ed) Emotion in organizations. Sage, London, pp 1–24

Forrester G (2005) All in a day's work: primary teachers performing and caring. Gend Educ 17(3):271–287

Fredrickson BL (1998) What good are positive emotions? Rev Gen Psychol 2:173–186

Frijda NH (1993) Moods, emotion episodes and emotions. In: Lewis M, Haviland IM (eds) Handbook of emotions. Guilford Press, New York, pp 381–403

Goldstein LS, Lake VE (2000) Love, love and more love for children: exploring preservice teachers' understanding of caring. Teach Teach Educ 16:861–872

Goodson IF (1997) The life and work of teachers. In: Biddle BJ, Good TL, Goodson IF (eds) International Handbook of Teachers and Teaching. Kluwer, Dordrecht, pp 135–152

Grandey AA (2003) When the show must go on: surface acting and deep acting as determinants of emotional exhaustion and peer-rated service delivery. Acad Manage J 46:86–96

Gross JJ (1998) The emerging field of emotion regulation: an integrative review. Rev Gen Psychol 2:271–299

Groth M, Henning-Thurau T, Walsh G (2006) A conceptual model of the effects of emotional labor strategies on customer outcomes. In: Zerbe WJ, Ashkanasy NM, Hartel CEJ (eds) Research on emotion in organizations. Elsevier, Amsterdam, pp 167–193

Hargreaves A (1994) Changing teachers changing times. Cassell, London

Hargreaves A (1998) The emotional practice of teaching. Teach Teach Educ 14(8):835–850

Hargreaves A (2000) Mixed emotions: teachers' perceptions of their interactions with students. Teach Teach Educ 16:811–826

Hargreaves A (2005) Educational change takes ages: life career and generational factors in teachers' emotional responses to educational change. Teach Teach Educ 21:967–983

Helsby G (1999) Changing teachers' work: the 'reform' of secondary schooling. Open University Press, Buckingham

Hochschild A (1979) Emotion work, feeling rules and social structure. Am J Sociol 85:551–575

Hochschild AR (1983) The managed heart: commercialization of human feeling. University of California Press, Berkeley

Hochschild A (1990) Ideology and emotion management: a perspective and path for future research. In: Kemper T (ed) Research agendas in the sociology of emotions. State University of New York State, Albany, NY

Jackson PW (1986) The practice of teaching. Teachers College Press, New York

Klaassen CA (2002) Teacher pedagogical competence and sensibility. Teach Teach Educ 18:151–158

Lasky S (2000) The cultural and emotional politics of teacher–parent interactions. Teach Teach Educ 16(8):843–861

Levin B (2001) Reforming education: from origins to outcomes. Routledge, London

Lewis J, Stearns P (1998) Introduction. In: Stearns P, Lewise J (eds) An emotional history of the united states. New York University Press, New York, pp 1–14

Little JW (1996) The emotional contours and career trajectories of (disappointed) reform enthusiasts. Cambridge J Educ 26:345–359

Lord RG, Kanfer R (2002) Emotions and organizational behavior. In: Lord RG, Klimoskei RJ, Kanfer R (eds) Emotions in the workplace: understanding the structure and role of emotions in organizational behavior. Jossey-Bass, San Francisco

Morris JA, Feldman DC (1996) The dimensions, antecedents, and consequences of emotional labor. Acad Manage Rev 4:986–1010

Nias J (1989) Primary teachers talking. Routledge and Kegan Paul, London

Nias J (1999) Teachers' moral purposes: stress, vulnerability, and strength. In: Vandenberge R, Huberman AM (eds) Understanding and preventing teacher burnout a source-book of international research and practice. Cambridge University Press, New York, pp 223–237

Noddings N (1984) Caring: a feminine approach to ethics and moral education. University of California Press, Berkeley

O'Connor KE (2008) You choose to care: teachers, emotions and professional identity. Teach Teach Educ 24:117–126

Oatley K (1993) Best laid schemes: the psychology of emotion. Cambridge University Press, Cambridge

Oplatka I (2004) Women teachers' emotional commitment and involvement: a universal professional feature and educational policy. Educ Soc 22(2):23–43

Oplatka I (2005) Imposed school change and women teachers' self-renewal: a new insight on successful implementation of changes in schools. Sch Leadersh Manage 25(2):171–190

Oplatka I (2007a) Managing emotions in teaching: towards an understanding of emotion displays and caring as non-prescribed role elements. Teach Coll Record 109(6):1374–1400

Oplatka I (2007b) The context and profile of teachers in developing countries in the last decade: a revealing discussion for further investigations. Int J Educ Manage 21(6):476–490

Oplatka I, Eizenberg M (2007) The perceived significance of the supervisor, the assistant, and parents for career development and survival of beginning kindergarten teachers. Teach Teach Educ 23:339–354

Oplatka I, Hemsley-Brown J, Foskett NH (2002) The voice of teachers in marketing their school: personal perspectives in competitive environments. Sch Leadersh Manage 22(2):177–196

Palmer PJ (1998) The courage to teacher. Jossey-Bass, San Francisco

Peterson MF, Smith PB (1995) Role conflict, ambiguity, and overload: a twenty-one-nation study. Acad Manage J 38:429–452

Plas JM, Hoover-Dempsey KV (1988) Working up a storm: anger, anxiety, joy, and tears on the job. W.W. Norton, New York

Prosser J (1999) School culture. Paul Chapman Publishing, London

Pugh D (2001) Service with a smile: emotional contagion in service encounters. Acad Manage J 44:1018–1027

Rafaeli A, Sutton RI (1989) The expression of emotion in organizational life. In: Cummings LL, Staw BM (eds) Research in organizational behavior. JAI Press, Greenwich, CT, pp 1–42

Rogers DL, Webb J (1991) The ethic of caring in teacher education. J Teach Educ 42(3):173–181

Roulston K, Darby A, Owens A (2003) Beginning teachers' anger. Paper presented at the annual meeting of the American Educational Research Association, Chicago

Sarbin TR (1986) Emotion and act: roles and rhetoric. In: Harre R (ed) The social construction of emotions. Basil Blackwell, Oxford, pp 83–97

Schutz PA, DeCuir JT (2002) Inquiry on emotion in education. Educ Psychol 37(2):125–134

Strazdins L (2002) Emotional work and emotional contagion. In: Ashkanasy NM, Zerbe WJ, Hartel CE (eds) Managing emotions in the workplace. M.E. Sharpe, Armonk, NY, pp 232–250

Sutton RE (2002) Emotional regulation goals and strategies of teachers. Paper presented at the Annual Conference of the American Educational Research Association, New Orleans

Sutton RE, Conway P (2002) Middle school teachers' day-to-day experiences of anger and frustration. Paper presented at the Annual Conference of the American Educational Research Association, New Orleans

Tolich MB (1993) Alienating and liberating emotions at work. J Contemp Ethnogr 22(3):361–383

Wharton A (1993) The affective consequences of service work: managing emotions on the job. Work Occupation 20(2):205–232

Winograd K (2003) The functions of teacher emotions: the good, the bad, and the ugly. Teach Coll Record 105:1641–1673

Zembylas M (2003) Emotions and teacher identity: a post-structural perspective. Teach Teach Educ 9(3):213–238

Zembylas M (2005) Teaching with emotion: a postmodern enactment. Information Age Publishing, Greenwich, CT

Chapter 5
Entering the Emotional Practices of Teaching

Debra K. Meyer

Abstract I discuss teaching as emotional practice and how that practice is tied to teacher identities. My focus in this chapter is on the first stage of professional induction – the student-teaching experience and how teachers communicate emotions. In other words, I explore the question: what emotions are "appropriate," and when should they be expressed? I argue that it not unusual for college supervisors and cooperating teachers to empathize with student teachers' emotions, but assume their emotions can be adjusted with reason or easily ignored. Attempts to separate emotions from or to join them with teaching practice have implications for teacher identity and development. Through a synthesis of these related bodies of literature with examples from my own research on student teachers' emotional experiences, I examine some of the possible trajectories for new teachers as they enter the emotional practice of teaching.

Keywords Student teaching · Emotional practice · Emotional understanding · Emotional labor

Around the world, the teaching profession heralds its emotional rewards while struggling with teacher shortages, high teacher attrition, and teacher "burnout." Since Lortie's (1975) work on teachers' lives in the United States, scholars have reexamined the myriad of changing, and sometimes unchanging, factors that influence teachers' decisions to enter, remain in, return to, or leave the profession (Rinke 2008). Attracting new teachers is vital to every nation's future. Therefore, what attracts and sustains teachers becomes a central question for educational research. Like many professions, what draws and keeps educators in the profession are "working conditions." Although "working conditions" are frequently cited as a major reason for teacher attrition, they vary considerably from nation to nation as well as within nations (Dove 2004; Rinke 2008). However, missing from many discussions

D.K. Meyer (✉)
Department of Education, Elmhurst College, USA
e-mail: debram@elmhurst.edu

of "working conditions" is the emotional labor of teaching. Although the emotional outcomes of teaching have been consistently documented as important to teachers' professional satisfaction (e.g., student success, fulfillment; Hargreaves 2000; Lortie 1975; Rinke 2008), these emotional rewards rarely are considered in relation to the economic or political factors, even though they may be the least expensive and most compelling reasons for teaching.

Fortunately, through the work of scholars from a variety of perspectives, the contexts of teaching that support and undermine emotions from the earliest stages in teachers' careers are being more closely examined, as this volume illustrates. These new perspectives and research studies promote a more nuanced view of teacher development and compel us to re-conceptualize teaching as more than content knowledge and pedagogical skill. These emerging views strongly suggest that we reexamine our educational practices from teacher education through teacher retirement using a lens that includes the emotional practice of teaching.

Research on teacher emotion is relatively new and is least developed regarding preservice teachers' experiences prior to their first year of teaching. Therefore, in this chapter I explore what it means to enter the emotional practice of teaching (Denzin 1984; Hargreaves 2000) and how newly developing teacher identities involve emotions (e.g., Tickle 1991). My focus is on one of the earliest and most common experiences in a teacher's career – the student teaching (i.e., internship) experience. During this period, which may be as brief as several weeks or as long as a year, preservice teachers are expected to participate as teachers and assume responsibility for instruction with support of a mentor. However, during student teaching these prospective teachers are not afforded as many choices as they are held responsible, which evokes a myriad of tensions. Examining emotions during the student teaching experience, therefore, is important because it captures a part of the histories that teachers bring to their careers and classrooms.

Given that the research on teacher emotion is emerging at the preservice stage, in the first part of the chapter I mostly extrapolated from research gathered from novice and experienced teachers about *how* teachers learn to communicate their emotions, *what* emotions are deemed "appropriate," and *when* and *with whom* they should express their emotions. Although scholars have argued that the traditional view of emotions as under a teacher's control is a limiting one (Zembylas 2005), student teachers are introduced to teaching in a highly controlled environment and frequently feel powerless at the same time they are being asked to assume more control. In addition, it is common for student teachers' university supervisors and classroom mentors to sympathize with the myriad of emotions being experienced. At the same time, it is also common for supervisors and mentors to urge student teachers to manage their emotions and conform to professional expectations. These early attempts to separate emotions from or to join them with teaching practice have important implications for teacher identity and development. As Swanson (1989) explained, socio-emotional relationships influence teacher identity by connecting teaching experience and school culture. Two major sets of relationships develop in student teaching: (a) relationships with mentors and (b) relationships with students as their "student" teacher. To illustrate some shared emotional tensions that surround these early experiences of teachers, in the second half of the chapter, I use written reflections from and interviews with student teachers throughout this transition from student to teacher. Finally, I address how the current work in teacher emotion could positively impact teacher education, especially during the time of student teaching.

The Emotional Practice of Teaching

Scholars have argued that teacher emotions are best conceptualized as culturally and socially situated (Boler 1999; Ria et al. 2003; Zembylas 2003). Boler (1999) called for "rethinking emotions as collaboratively constructed and historically situated, rather than simply as individualized phenomena located in the interior self" (p. 6). In this chapter, I use the term *emotional practice* to reference the ways in which teachers are constantly engaged in emotional processes that help them understand themselves, their relationships with others, and guide these interactions. Denzin (1984) defined *emotional practices* as being situated and embedded in interactions with others and described them as occurring at two levels: the practical and the interpretive. This definition readily applies to learning to teach because student teachers are mentored into the acts of teaching as well as the formal and informal rules surrounding their actions. In addition, their actions are subjected to continuous, formal and informal, self- and other evaluation at depths rarely experienced after student teaching. Student teachers are encouraged, and commonly required, to reflect upon their actions in terms of *how*, *when*, and *where* they practice and *who* are their students (i.e., how they are meeting their students' learning needs). In other words, emotional practice is highly visible during student teaching due to the intentional ways in which practice is discussed and assessed.

However, one critical component of emotional practice that seldom occurs during this period of a teacher's career is attention to the situated aspect of teaching. The focus in learning to teach is primarily on prototypical aspects of pedagogy and management and rarely considers the emotional experiences and the ways in which professional culture is constraining or supporting these early experiences. As such, reformulations of teacher identity also are being constrained to concentrate on the technical aspects of teaching, rather than the emotional and motivational. This suggests that many student teachers become members of a professional culture by accepting its practices before they may be aware of its constraints. Oplatka (2007) asserted two assumptions that undergird current work on teacher emotions: (a) emotions are expressed or managed in ways concurrent with cultural standards and (b) the teaching culture of a school influences the ways in which teachers manage their emotions. And yet, these assumptions are seldom explicitly part of any teacher education program or student teaching experience.

Emotional Understanding

Although it is common to recognize the triumvirate of knowing *what* (content or declarative knowledge), knowing *how* (pedagogy or procedural knowledge), and knowing *when* (conditional knowledge) in teacher education, situational understanding is not central in learning to teach. In addition, there is little, if any, explicit instruction in how to establish and negotiate relationships as a preservice teacher. Student teaching is often de-contextualized, and yet, context is continually influencing teaching decisions and experiences. Therefore, student teachers typically participate in emotional practice without evaluating it in any productive way. Instead, they are often encouraged or choose to cope by ignoring or masking their emotions.

Hargreaves (2000) applied Denzin's concept of emotional practice to teaching by describing how teachers create or mask emotions to meet the demands of the changing contexts of teaching:

> As emotional practitioners, teachers can make classrooms exciting or dull and leaders can turn colleagues into risk-takers or cynics. Teaching, learning and leading may not be solely emotional practices, but they are always irretrievably emotional in character, in a good way or a bad way, by design or default. (p. 812)

In defining emotional practice, Hargreaves emphasized Denzin's concept of *emotional understanding* as a core feature in that teachers must comprehend the emotions of their students to make instructional decisions and interact successfully. Such emotional understandings are historical in nature and formed through interpreting current situations in light of past emotional experiences (Hargreaves et al. 2001). Hargreaves et al. (2001) illustrated this concept when they described how the elementary and secondary teachers in their study sought to develop emotional understanding with their students and the ways in which it "was central to how they taught them, how they evaluated them, what kinds of curricula they planned and selected for them, and what kinds of structures they adopted as a context for teaching them" (p. 144). Teachers sought to fulfill their own needs as well as the needs of their students (e.g., choosing teaching strategies based on personal enthusiasm and enjoyment).

In addition, creating emotional understanding simultaneously involves forming relationships. Hargreaves et al. (2001) explained that "emotional engagement and understanding in schools (as elsewhere) require strong, continuous relationships between teachers and students so that they learn to read each other over time" (p. 138). They also made the case that *emotional work* and *emotional goals* are critical in teaching because teachers have "emotional investments" in their relationships and their success and fulfillment depend on these relationships. They illustrated how caring is one way of demonstrating emotional understanding and can have costs (see also Isenbarger and Zembylas 2006), as is the case of the teacher who reported being criticized too much for caring early in her career: "People would say to me in my first few years of teaching, 'You've got to toughen up. You're too soft, you're too sensitive, and you take everything so seriously'" (p. 141). However, she maintained that if she had stopped caring, she would have ceased being a teacher, and she worked to sustain this philosophy throughout her career.

Emotional Work and Emotional Labor

The concepts of emotional practice and emotional understanding are commonly integrated into discussions of the *emotional work* and *emotional labor* of teaching. As a diverse area of scholarship, there appear to be multiple meanings for these terms, based on different theoretical perspectives. For example, Oplatka (2007) distinguished between emotional labor and emotional work by defining *emotional work* as the emotions that teachers freely experienced and self-regulated, in other words they are felt emotions that are not expected (e.g., expressing concern for students) or are not compensated as part of job responsibilities (e.g., "smiling at the customer"). In contrast, *emotional labor* involves the external regulation of emotions by cultural expectations, which displays emotions that are not felt or autonomous. Similarly, Flores and Day (2006) described teaching as involving daily, intensive and extensive use of both emotional labor and emotional work. They asserted that both emotional labor and emotional work help teachers to manage the challenges of teaching, but too much labor may lead to a disengagement, a loss of trust by students, personal vulnerability, feelings of inadequacy, and teacher stress or burnout.

In comparison, Zembylas (2005) proposed a different theoretical perspective for defining emotional labor and emotional work. For Zembylas, emotional work involves the evoking, suppressing, and shaping of an emotion and emotional labor is the outcome of that work. He views emotional labor as managing emotions, which may have either positive or negative outcomes, but at the same time can cause emotional dissonance with serious motivational consequences. In other words, as Boler (1999) argued, emotional management is not simply a set of skills, but it constitutes how we approach, understand, and shape emotional work. Rather than different kinds of emotions that are regulated by different sources, Zembylas' (2005) perspective involves emotional work and emotional labor as active processes that are interrelated, not distinct. Emotional work, then, is as self-regulated as emotional management and both are influenced by emotional rules. Zembylas argued that teachers' emotions help them negotiate roles and relations, but emotional rules may be "disguised as ethical codes, professional techniques, and specialized pedagogical knowledge" (p. 52). In this way emotions can help teachers assess and choose if they want to conform to existing norms and expectations. It is this view of emotional practice – as a continuum of emotional work and labor – that is used in this chapter. When emotional management is present, so is emotional labor.

A compelling way to conceptualize emotional labor is terms of "emotional geographies," a term which Hargreaves (2000) coined to illustrate the idea of proximity to others that all teachers constantly negotiate. These "geographies," which are socio-cultural, moral, professional, physical, and political, are ways of describing teachers' relationships to others (e.g., students, parents, staff, society) and as such involve emotional labor and management. Emotional geographies share similarities and differences when comparing teacher success and satisfaction throughout their careers (Hargreaves et al. 2001). In addition, differences in school organization evoke different geographies, especially when comparing the emotional labor of elementary teachers and high school teachers. For example, Hargreaves (2000) reported that elementary schools evoked different emotional geographies because classrooms allowed for more personal and physical closeness, but the power differences between teachers and students (i.e., the political geography) also could result in more dislike and rejection of particular students (i.e., a lack of emotional understanding). For secondary teachers the physical and professional geographies were the most important threats to emotional understanding because these teachers had shorter amounts of time with students in a day, which is divided into subject-specific periods, and often found their roles as content specialists interrupted by organizational needs and professional expectations. As Hargreaves (2000) cautioned, a focus on cognitive standards and outcomes reinforces the very organizational constraints and professional expectations that undermine emotional understanding, which ironically is needed to sustain the learning of these very standards.

Like their more experienced mentors, preservice teachers appear to quickly become aware of their emotional practices (e.g., Goldstein and Lake 2003). Their experiences at emotional management often remain a source of motivation throughout their careers, even in school cultures that constrain what is appropriate. Similarly, Hargreaves et al. (2001) maintained that caring was one way to demonstrate emotional understanding that involves emotional labor with costs, as they illustrated in the previous example of the teacher who reported being criticized for caring too much early in her career. The tension experienced between the professional culture and the felt experience of learning to teach presents opportunities to conform or resist. Zembylas (2005) asserted that teachers control their emotions, but that the professional culture often promotes the evaluation of what is appropriate professionalism, and even what is a professional identity. The teacher from the Hargreaves et al. (2001) example defined herself through her resistance to accept the emotional rules of her colleagues. She found another path that helped her to define a different possibility and created a teacher identity that supported emotional understanding.

Emotions and Teacher Identity

Teachers' emotional practice and teacher identity are intertwined. As Zembylas (2005) argued, emotion and identity are simultaneously social and individual. Identity becomes reshaped and disciplined through discourses and practices of emotion. However, for the most part, the research literatures on identity and emotions have evolved separately and, as highlighted in the previous section, there are conceptual differences regarding what constitutes *teacher identity*. Whereas most scholars regard teacher identity as constantly evolving, it is typically juxtaposed with teachers' professional roles that are often viewed as stable. Professional roles may be assigned to teachers or described by them, but professional identities emerge through their values and emotions (O'Conner 2008) and are constituted through power relations (Zembylas 2005). As such, teacher identity and professional role are intertwined in that identity as a teacher develops as experienced emotions are connected with or disconnected from professional role expectations. As Zembylas explained, "discourses transmit and produce power, which in turn continuously produces and constitutes the self. The discursive production of self is both liberating and constraining; discourses provide possibilities for and determine the limits of self-understanding. Identity is understood through resistance and domination" (p. 5).

Similarly, Flores and Day (2006) defined identity as "an ongoing and dynamic process which entails the making sense and (re)interpretation of one's own values and experiences" (p. 220). They found that identity is constructed and re-constructed depending on personal history, pre-service education, and school culture. But they reported a relatively weak influence of pre-service programs. Their research suggested that the weak effect of teacher education programs was seen in how new teachers' views of teaching were immediately challenged in schools and their work became more routine (cf. Zembylas' *emotional rules*). Flores and Day concluded that the first years of teaching involve a powerful re-construction of identity as teachers face socializing forces, which Cole and Knowles (1993) have described as teachers' "shattered expectations." Not only are teachers continually reconstructing their identities based on discrepancies between their assumptions and experiences, but also these changes are highly context dependent, and frequently are idiosyncratic (Flores and Day 2006).

We must be careful about comparisons of novice and experienced teachers who teach in very different contexts and bring to teaching different personal histories. No matter how long a teacher's career, we also must be cautious about examining teaching experiences only retrospectively (Rinke 2008) because these individual histories have everything to do with current perspectives. For example, Knowles and Holt-Reynolds (1991) found that student teachers used past experiences as students to assess their instructional approaches. Their responses appeared to illustrate what Hargreaves et al. (2001) described as how experienced teachers fulfilled their own needs by choosing what they would be interested in or what has been successful in the past for them as a student. Moreover, Knowles and Holt-Reynolds (1991) found that a common reason preservice teachers give for entering the profession was to promote what they personally valued as a student: "As preservice teachers talk about and explore their future roles as teachers, they frequently speak of their own experiences as students as if those experiences were prototypical" (p. 93).

Even teachers who share very similar positions in the same school would be expected to have different emotional experiences for different reasons. Teachers' careers come at different times in their lives and take different pathways (Rinke 2008). At the same time, although mentoring programs are prevalent in today's schools, little has changed since Lortie (1975) wrote, "The way most beginners are inducted into teaching leaves them doubly alone; they confront a 'sink-or-swim' situation in physical isolation and get only occasional cultural support in the process" (p. 234). Even today in the United States, Kardos and Johnson (2007) found that new teachers most frequently began their careers in environments in which they were "off-line" or not integrated into a professional community. They reported that more than half of new teachers in the four states surveyed (California, Florida, Massachusetts, and Michigan) did not believe their colleagues were concerned about students who were not in their classes and just under half did not believe their colleagues valued collaboration. Kardos and Johnson (2007) concluded that many new teachers' experiences are isolated and disconnected from any collective effort and this isolation falsely presumed a new teacher's immediate expertise. This is in stark contrast to the highly monitored student teaching experience only months prior, which seems to highlight the student teacher's novice status. The way in which new teachers are inducted into the profession therefore appears to recreate this cycle of expecting the novice to immediately become the expert. Because new teachers "fly solo" to build expertise and assume responsibility for their own students they come to expect future teachers to "make it" alone and do not feel responsible for students who are not in their classroom. Such early experiences appear to explain the complexities among teachers' perceptions of autonomy, competence, and relationships, which are so important to teachers' professional satisfaction (Rinke 2008).

Emotional Practice in Student Teaching

The gateway for most teachers is through a supervised practice or student teaching experience. To this experience they bring not only their formal studies in education, but also their histories as students and in relationships (Knowles and Holt-Reynolds 1991). As Flores and Day (2006) suggested, researchers should focus on how new teachers reconstruct identity as teachers and how they assess early emotional experiences in teaching. If we assume a historical basis for emotions, emotional understanding, and teacher identity, then we need to explore how these are formed at various times and in different contexts of a teacher's life. One important point of transition for examining emotional practice and its relationship to teacher identity is during the student teaching experience.

Student teaching is critical for exploring teacher identity and emotional practice because it represents a period when the new teacher has the potential to be explicitly mentored and monitored into a professional role. Therefore, it presents a unique opportunity to "try on" some of the roles of teaching, to explore what it means to be a teacher, and to submit or resist the status quo. Furthermore, student teaching is a period during which practices are consistently evaluated and dissected, openly available to the student teacher and publicly discussed. This experience, in other words, is one where "others" commonly "look in." As a teacher educator for the last 15 years, I recently focused my qualitative studies on the student teaching period. I followed two groups of student teachers (24 student teachers) through their 15-week student teaching experiences using reflective electronic journals, which were already required by their programs, online surveys about their emotional experiences, and individual "exit" interviews. With this data, I have begun to link the emotional practices of learning to teach to some shared experiences. I have started to examine how emotions and motivations are intertwined with the relationships that new teachers are building with their students, mentors, and others in their school communities. Relationships, therefore, serve as a platform for my analyses of *emotional tensions* that arise and often persist as student teachers assume these early instructional responsibilities under their own and others' scrutiny. I define an *emotional tension* as a reoccurring conflict between unpleasant emotions and pleasant emotions that are juxtaposed around the same reoccurring situation or issue. In this way, I am interested in exploring what student teachers are feeling, resisting, and choosing (Zembylas 2005), and how their induction into the emotional practice of teaching might be influencing their reformation of their teaching identities. As I illustrate using their words, these tensions are examples of emotional practice that are bound to relationships and situated within specific classroom cultures.

Emotional tensions are illustrated using three common themes that have emerged from my research. The first theme is one of finding autonomy in relation to the mentor teacher (a.k.a. cooperating or supervising classroom teacher), which highlights how student teachers commonly experience a tension between independence and support. The second theme is one of competence and fulfillment, which reflects a tension between teaching in ways that promote student learning that is personally interesting and satisfying, but in resistance to teaching in ways that confirm the control and expertise of the mentor teacher. The third theme centers on building relationships with students, a tension that involves both joy and pain in the management of these relationships.

Autonomy: Finding a Space to Teach

A common tension in student teaching is finding a working balance between successfully assuming instructional responsibilities and the gradual release of support by the mentor teacher. Across all data sources student teachers consistently speak of this tension or note its absence. Student teachers commonly reported feeling anxious or frustrated by what they viewed as their mentor teachers' lack of trust because they could not assume instructional responsibility as quickly as they thought was possible. Not being given this opportunity early was interpreted as not being trusted. Even when given the chance to teach, the issue of trust remained. Not feeling trusted was illustrated in Claire's (a first grade student teacher) first journal entry: "[My cooperating teacher] is going to have a hard time letting go – I hope she is able to trust me eventually." Claire responded to her anxiety and nervousness by writing that it influenced how she approached her mentor: "I have a hard time asking her (if I) can do certain things." Even when she began to assume instructional responsibilities, Claire continued to struggle with autonomy and she described feeling anxious about taking on more responsibility. In other words, although she wanted more responsibility, she was anxious about assuming it because she did not feel supported. Claire's decision to not share her feelings with her mentor became an emotional practice that she continued throughout student teaching. Claire's anxiety about the relationship with her mentor teacher reflected her uncertainty about her professional role as a student teacher. Claire struggled with emotional understanding, which she described as influencing the decisions she made about seeking help and how she interacted with the students.

In contrast, Marie (a student teacher in a fifth-grade classroom) was focused on becoming independent even in the face of evidence that her mentor teacher did not fully support her autonomy. Throughout her student teaching, Marie consistently expressed pleasant emotions surrounding experiences that made her feel like it is "my classroom" and unpleasant emotions when she perceived her mentor teacher reclaiming it as "her classroom." In the early weeks of student teaching, Marie wrote that she "loves" the support of the other fifth-grade teachers and assumes full responsibility for instruction. Midway through student teaching, however, she expressed concern as her mentor teacher began to interject herself into Marie's lessons (e.g., raising or waving her hand to intervene in a lesson). When Marie discovered that her mentor teacher was keeping separate grade records, she felt frustrated by what she perceived as distrust. Then, when the mentor teacher insisted on certain types of graded work, Marie viewed this as controlling her instructional choices – making her "a worksheet teacher." Like Claire, there were times when Marie decided to suppress her feelings and not resist the mentor teacher's wishes. But unlike Claire, Marie resisted when she could, noting how sometimes she would go along with her mentor teacher's suggestions when they were not as important, but make her own instructional choices when the opportunity presented itself. Claire and Marie both illustrate how student teachers try to fit into role expectations and also how they resist them. Both student teachers also show how emotional labor (i.e., the managing of their emotions) is connected to the norms of their particular classrooms, mentors, and schools.

Not all student teachers experienced a tension with their mentor teachers and several student teachers reported that they were both surprised and pleased to be given the freedom to assume instructional responsibilities as quickly as they wanted. In other words, the different professional role expectations for student teachers were wide-ranging and the extent to which they were explicitly negotiated varied by context. In many ways, their thirst for autonomy was in itself a cultural constraint because they seemed to be pursuing a norm in the United States that classrooms are places of "individualism" and the "belief in one's autonomy" (Zembylas 2005). At the same time, some of the constraints against which student teachers resisted came from pressures that their mentors also experienced. One such compelling example was Amy (a fourth grade student teacher) who reported feeling angry when she had minimal instructional responsibility due to state testing during the first weeks of student teaching. She journaled that her mentor teacher was "stressed" about the forthcoming state test, which caused the students and Amy to feel stressed. Then the mentor teacher unexpectedly was absent from school for the last day and a half of testing. With a substitute teacher in the classroom, Amy wrote that she was excited to be with the students "on her own" and that the vice principal had "enough faith that I could administer an important test." However, the relationship with her mentor teacher remained a primary source of her unpleasant emotions, as she wrote at the end of the experience:

> Negative emotions were often caused by the lack of support that I felt I was getting from my mentor teacher. It was often frustrating work with her because I did not feel like I was getting the support that I needed during this student teaching process.

The emotional labor of student teaching appeared to hold a great deal of meaning for student teachers like Amy, Claire, and Marie, whose emotional practices involved trying to appease mentor teachers who they felt did not support them and trying to find a place for themselves as "teacher." Their evolving teacher identities did not seem to fit with the professional practices projected by their mentor teachers (i.e., their mentors were not the teachers they aspired to be). At the same time, the student teachers seemed very sensitive to professional expectations. Therefore, it was common for student teachers to write about how they coped with unpleasant emotions by focusing on the positive (usually related to students) and ignoring the negative (usually related to mentor teachers), as was illustrated in Marie's writing:

> While the positive emotions have made me realize this is a great career for me and I am excited to begin my teaching career, the negative emotions leave me feeling unsure of my abilities. It is hard to be around others that are so confident in their teaching every day while I am still learning – it makes me feel like I am not living up to their expectations or that I am bothering them too much by asking their advice or opinion (although the teachers are all very helpful and friendly). I have ignored the negative feelings that might make me produce lesser-quality lessons, but the thoughts are still there in the back of my head and can make their way into my lessons sometimes. I am worried that students can see when I am second-guessing myself. The positive feelings have a stronger impact on my lesson, as I feel the students can see how excited I am to teach them, and have enabled me to connect with the students.

The fulfillment that Marie attributes to students' learning and that other preservice teachers frequently described evolved into a second distinct theme. As such, student teachers often found themselves positively engaged in and fulfilled by student interactions and learning, which is discussed next.

Competence: Finding Fulfillment in Student Learning

As student teachers assumed instructional responsibilities, their contributions to student learning appeared to be intertwined with those of their cooperating teacher's instructional practices and their relationships with their mentors and students changed. Some student teaching experiences may not realize long-term individual student successes, which is one of the primary rewards reported by teachers (Hargreaves et al. 2001; Lortie 1975), but all student teachers appeared to be focused on the short-term and immediate successes of their classes. Hargreaves (2000) explained that it was common for teachers to report the emotional rewards of teaching as part of the teaching experience, which occurred with the whole class and individual students. Moreover, he explained that this sense of fulfillment was indicative of a strong emotional understanding between teachers and students. Interestingly, emotional understanding seemed to evolve with the students much sooner and more intensely than it did with mentors or other professional staff.

Student teachers typically reported being highly engaged in planning and implementing instruction, noting their interest and excitement. These emotions seemed similar to the master teachers who reported that curriculum planning that focused on student needs engaged their emotions and was sustained by their excitement about the process, revealing how student learning and teacher engagement are reciprocal (Hargreaves et al. 2001; Lortie 1975). Such reciprocity was expressed in the student teachers' journaling, surveys, and interviews, illustrating how teaching can be a very rewarding emotional practice. For example, Marie wrote at the end of student teaching:

> I am still feeling very fulfilled. At the end of all the bad days, the frustration, the failed lessons, I still feel this is a perfect match for me and what is what I will be happy doing for the rest of my life – or until I retire :). When I have a bad day, I refocus and look to how I can improve for next time rather than just give up, and I think that has a lot to do with my feeling of fulfillment.

At the same time, not every student teacher found emotional labor as easy to manage. As Flores and Day (2006) found in first year teachers' experiences, some student teachers also discovered "[t]he meanings, values, images and ideals of what it meant to be a teacher with which they entered teaching were challenged and, for many, teaching became more routine, more rule governed and less creative" (p. 230). Whitney, (a first grade student teacher), typified this experience. Whitney felt very supported by her mentor teacher and assumed instructional responsibilities early, but struggled with classroom management. Across her experiences, her first reactions appeared to be focused upon how the students were responding, but as student teaching continued, she wrote about how she had begun to manage her unpleasant feelings and the benefits that grew from this emotional labor.

For example, at the beginning of her 15-week student teaching experience, Whitney reported feeling anxious, nervous, and afraid, but still experienced more pleasant than unpleasant emotions. Like her peers, she attributed her pleasant emotions to student learning: "The way the students react to the lessons and activities – if they are enjoying themselves and learning, I feel as though the lesson/activity is successful." In addition, she explained how these feelings of success contributed to her relationships with the students as, "My reaction is happy if I see the students enjoying themselves. I think my satisfaction is evident in the way I talk to them (with a smile) and the way I allow them to interact with each other." By mid semester, Whitney reported her strongest feelings were ones of fulfillment and interest, and the most frequent were pride and confidence. When asked on the midterm survey about the strong pleasant or unpleasant emotions that she experienced most frequently, her students' successes and her feelings of competence appeared to be contributing to stronger teacher–student relationships:

> Student excitement for the activities and lessons has contributed to the positive emotions. When they enjoy the activities, time flies. Student participation is also wonderful – the students are always raising their hands and willing to participate. I smile and laugh a lot. When I know the students are enjoying themselves and understand the concepts, I sit at the tables with them and have real conversations while they work. I want to get to know them all as best as I can. I also put on music while they work, if they are quiet. It's great when they sing along to the music – it sounds like a chorus.

At the end of the 15-week experience, Whitney's strongest and most frequent emotions on the survey were amazement, pride, and sadness. She appeared to be feeling the "loss" that Goldstein and Lake (2003) found with their student teachers as well as pride in her and her students' accomplishments, even a sense of "awe":

> I can't believe how far the students have come. Many of the students have been bringing books to read to the class, books they can read with little to no help. They are all reading sentences I write on the board. They have come so far and I can't believe it.

By the end of student teaching, however, Whitney demonstrated an increasingly emotional understanding of how her emotions were influencing her teaching. At the beginning of the semester, Whitney reported that her emotional experiences were as expected and wrote: "I feel like when I am upset it shows in the way I react with the students. For example, when they misbehave I have a shorter temper and I do not let them have as much "fun" as in socialization when they are working at their tables." At midterm she wrote that emotions had been much more frequent than expected and again wrote about her frustration and how it continued to impact her decisions. She reported that she doubted herself because her classroom management frustrated her attempts to teach:

> Sometimes, when I am frustrated with their behavior, I feel like I cut them off when they need me the most. I don't mean to get short with them, but I do. I feel like they will understand what to do better if they stop the chatter and "wild" behavior.

At the conclusion of student teaching, Whitney described her emotional labor as rewarding. She appeared to understand herself better – she becomes frustrated easily and this interferes with student learning and her own teaching goals. She illustrated how her emotional understanding influenced her instructional decisions when she wrote:

> I easily become frustrated and discouraged, but I have learned that I can't reflect these feelings onto the students. I have learned to control my emotions – especially when we are having a bad day and the students misbehave. Children will be children, no matter how many times we talk about good behavior and expected first grade behavior, I know that everyone has an off-day. Moreover, I realize how important recess is for them to get out their energy – even if it is hard for me to regain control when recess is over. It's all a learning experience and it will only be positive if we work as a team!

Although Whitney's emotional management evolved over the course of 15 weeks, other student teachers described their efforts at emotional management much earlier and seemed to more quickly recognize its impact on their teaching. For example, at midterm, Claire wrote:

> In general, I think I do a good job keeping my negative emotions out of my teaching. The minute I see the children my negative feelings usually go away. My positive emotional experiences cause me to be creative, energetic, impulsive, and happy. The students can tell when I am like this and my teaching is much more effective.

The rewards of student learning were very important for all the student teachers. In addition, for many of the student teachers, relationships with their students were one of the most powerful and rewarding parts of their experience that redefined what it meant to be a teacher. As discussed in the next section, their identities as teachers appeared to change more explicitly when they experienced strong emotional relationships with their students.

Relationships with Students: Caring as Emotional Practice

A third theme that emerged in my first study of student teachers' emotions, from which the cases of Amy, Claire, Marie, and Whitney have been drawn, was centered around tensions in building relationships – relationships with students and professional relationships with mentor teachers and professional staff. Relationships with mentor teachers appear to be embedded in the tensions of autonomy/trust and competence/fulfillment. Relationships with students were important to understanding the feelings of competence and fulfillment, as student learning appeared to be a hallmark of emotional understanding. However, in that first study this theme was the least well developed because I never asked the student teachers specifically about their relationships. Therefore, I changed the final interview and inquired more directly about these relationships and included autobiographical background on student teachers' self-perceptions of how they typically displayed their emotions.

One of the most surprising initial findings from this second round of research has been the student teachers' expression of emotions during the interviews. In several of the interviews the student teachers cried when they attempted to describe their relationships with their students. For example, Beth was a student teacher in fifth grade at a highly diverse school in terms of the range of students' cultural and socio-economic backgrounds. She had completed pre-student teaching field experiences at this school, but had not been in this classroom until a month before student teaching began. Although her mentor teacher had approximately 8 years of experience, he had never supervised a student teacher and immediately let Beth begin teaching in a very supportive way, as she described, "He just pushed me right in" (smiling and laughing). I'm so happy because I learned so much more than I would otherwise." The fact that she had more in-depth teaching responsibilities for a longer period of time may have impacted her relationships with her students, but the power of those relationships appeared to change her views of teaching and her teacher identity in powerful ways.

It is important to also note that during this second study, I asked more autobiographical information related to emotions to understand how student teachers compared themselves as "emotional beings" to their "emotional practices" as teacher.

Beth described herself as "an emotional person," explaining that the students had seen her cry. She also described herself as having been a quiet student, but comfortable showing her emotions in her private life and in the classroom when she is teaching. But she was surprised at the intensity of her emotions as a teacher during student teaching and that seemed to change her views about what it means to teach. When I asked her about which emotions most surprised her about teaching, she replied, "All of them! I have never been that emotional with kids in the past, even when I was working at that school freshmen year. I have never been so attached to kids before." This recollection was so powerful she began to cry, so I inquired if she had known that teachers could form such strong attachments to their students and she replied, "Not this much." Beth seemed unaware that teachers experience such strong emotional relationships with students, although she described how her cooperating teacher had shared his "tearing up" when he was saying goodbye to last year's class. Then she added, "but he didn't feel that way about this class." Although Beth said that she did not attempt to hide her strong emotions, she did not feel like her cooperating teacher ever really acknowledged her emotions. For example, she once cried in front of her cooperating teacher because she was so happy about students' health test scores, which was a major and unexpected success, but he had focused on the positive test results – not her emotional response. This exchange of emotional understanding between student teacher and mentor is also a compelling illustration of how the norms of teaching implicitly control the expression of emotion, especially during an important developmental period such as student teaching. The exchange also suggests that such control of emotions or sharing of emotional labor is probably gendered.

Relationships with students are one of many different types of relationships that student teachers and new teachers are forming, but they were extremely important to student teachers' growing sense of what it meant to be a teacher. Hargreaves (2000) described how elementary teachers experience much stronger personal and physical emotional geographies with their students (both pleasant and unpleasant) due to their constant interpersonal contact throughout the day. Newberry and Davis (2008) reported that teachers who perceived students as needing too much support and requiring more emotional management were found to be labeled as "emotionally draining" and had more distant relationships with the teacher. Thus, the emotional labor of caring can be exhausting or may be beyond a teacher's management development. Goldstein and Lake (2003) used the lens of teacher caring to describe what student teachers are learning about teaching through their relationships with their students. They reported how many student teachers experienced a "global and immense" sense of loss at the end of their student teaching experiences, which described Beth's response to the end of her student teaching experience. Goldstein and Lake also highlighted the importance of this time of transition in learning to teach as critical for emotional understanding and reforming teacher identity:

> Our findings reveal our preservice teachers poised at a threshold of professional possibility. Working in a zone of discomfort and disequilibrium, the preservice teachers struggled with establishing their professional identity as caring teachers and coping with the tensions between caring and loss in teaching. (p. 117)

Early teaching practice offers opportunities for redefining oneself as a teacher. The student teaching experience may be a particularly powerful experience because it is the first time the new teacher truly experiences emotional practice over a sustained time and it is a highly controlled and evaluated teaching experience. During this time, student teachers actively reconstitute their identities because they struggle with their emotions, expectations, and values. In other words, they found it as a time of resistance, acceptance, and change. Marie illustrated these observations as she shared that halfway through student teaching she considered quitting, but at the end of her student teaching experience she wrote:

> Sometimes, however, I get very frustrated and think I am just done with it all. On those days, however, as soon as I see the kids, I get swept back into my happy little reality, which may be overwhelming but is very rewarding and fulfilling. If I am having a bad day and feeling overwhelmed, I try to refocus myself to make sure the important things are done and leave the rest for another day when I am better able to tackle it all. As corny as it sounds, I hope that 20 years into my career, I still have this outlook on my profession and am able to be as connected to my students as I am now. I plan to never be that jaded teacher I fear becoming, so while I hope the emotions evolve over time and experience, I don't want them to completely change.

The act of student teachers sharing their emotional practice in their journals, surveys, or interviews, or with their friends, families, and colleagues, was emotional management – which has become part of the histories they will take into their first classrooms. The purpose of these excerpts from my data was to share how readily and simply emotional practice, emotional understanding, and emotional management can be captured and are important parts of preservice teachers' lives. The challenge in researching teachers' emotions is one of parsing it in meaningful ways, for it is not difficult to find in their experiences. But then the question becomes one of what do we do with this information to improve research and practice?

Implications for Future Research and Practice

Weiss (1999) reported the relationship between school culture, including leadership practices, and teacher autonomy is paramount in first year teachers' morale, commitment, and intent to remain in the profession. Similarly Macdonald's (1999) review of the literature on teacher attrition noted that world-wide teachers' high expectations for themselves and for the profession are often not recognized by their communities. Hargreaves et al. (2001) cautioned that emotional understanding may be frustrated by curriculum and the imposition of standards. However, it may be prevented by the way we educate and structure early teaching experiences. As teacher educators we need to be more cognizant and intentional about helping teachers navigate Hargreaves' (2000) "emotional geographies." One of the important contextual features of the student teaching experiences I have examined is that they interact throughout the day with the same groups of elementary students over a 15-week period, allowing for more personal and physical closeness. At the same time the "political geography" of a student teaching experience uniquely places the student teacher in a power relationship with the students, which is not as powerful as that of the mentor teacher. Thus, student teachers have the opportunity to develop relationships with students, but these are politically juxtaposed with their mentor teachers' relationships with students. This appears to create potential for conflict between building teacher–student relationship and building a mentor–apprentice relationship.

Similarly, Goldstein and Lake (2003) passionately articulated the importance of emotional practice in teacher education in their research on teacher caring:

> Caring is often taken for granted and underdiscussed within teacher education. As the educational climate in the United States increasingly turns to talk of standards, outcomes, and accountability, there is the danger of caring being pushed even further into the shadows of our programs. However, caring teaching–learning relationships are profoundly important. We cannot allow preservice teachers to labor under mistaken impressions about what it takes and what it means to teach with care. Instead, we contend that we need to develop an orientation toward teacher education in which preservice teachers' pre-existing beliefs about caring and teaching are called into question, scrutinized critically, and then thoughtfully reintegrated into their evolving practices. (p. 129)

Moreover, Goldstein and Lake highlighted that because field experiences, like student teaching, are naturally a time of transition and instability, they offer excellent opportunities to support preservice teachers in creating "their teacherly selves."

Flores and Day (2006) also recommended that teacher education programs provide a stronger focus on opportunities to experience and reflect upon personal biography and the cultural contexts of schools to understand the tensions between them. However, with increasing teacher shortages and calls for results without attention to processes, the time required for induction into teaching has been shortened in many programs. For example, in the United States teacher education programs have been increasingly regarded by the government as unnecessary, although evidence supports the impact of student teaching and education coursework as important to teacher effectiveness and retention (Darling-Hammond and Youngs 2002).

Unfortunately, what is deemed most important is what is typically articulated in the standards-based accountability system. As O'Conner (2008) demonstrated, professional teacher standards ignore or marginalize the emotional dimensions of teaching, concluding, "The role that emotions play in teachers' work is rarely acknowledged in public policy" (p. 195). Therefore, what research and teacher education can offer is symbiotic – teacher education needs a literature base that illuminates how emotional practice is realized in a variety of school settings and over the course of teachers' careers. Teacher education also needs evidence of effective ways to discuss emotional practice and the power structures of classrooms and schools with novice teachers. Teacher education needs strong conceptual frameworks that integrate pedagogy and content knowledge with teacher identity and emotional practices and that can be clearly communicated and shared. Then teacher educators need to use these research-based sources to not only change *what* is taught, but *how* it is taught. Teacher educators need to re-examine how prospective teachers are evaluated and enculturated into the teaching profession by emphasizing critical analysis rather than assimilation (Zembylas 2005). Moreover, teacher educators need to "care for the caregivers," by incorporating mentoring and supervision approaches that not only support emotional understanding, but model it. Finally, teacher educators need to work politically to change the deficits in teaching and learning standards that are emotionally empty. The power of emotions must be valued not only at the classroom and school levels, but also in broader social and political contexts. In the preface to her book, *Feeling Power: Emotions and Education*, Boler (1999) wrote, "In order to name, imagine and materialize a better world, we need an account of how Western discourses of emotion shape our scholarly work, as well as pedagogical recognition of how emotions shape our classroom interactions" (p. xv). For those of us whose classrooms are filled with students learning to teach and for their future students, we are challenged to redefine teaching and teacher education in ways that will emphasize the love for learning and teaching our world so desperately wants and needs.

References

Boler M (1999) Feeling power: emotions and education. Routledge, New York

Cole AL, Knowles JG (1993) Shattered images: understanding expectations and realities of field experiences. Teach Teach Educ 9:457–471

Darling-Hammond L, Youngs P (2002) Defining "highly qualified teachers": what does "scientifically-based research" actually tell us? Educ Res 31:13–25

Denzin NK (1984) On understanding emotion. Jossey-Bass, San Francisco

Dove MD (Fall, 2004) Teacher attrition: a critical American and international education issue. Delta Kappa Gamma Bull 71(1):8–30

Flores MA, Day C (2006) Contexts which shape and reshape new teachers' identities: a multiperspective study. Teach Teach Educ 22:219–232

Goldstein LS, Lake VE (2003) The impact of field experience on preservice teachers' understandings of caring. Teach Educ Q 30:115–132

Hargreaves A (2000) Mixed emotions: teachers' perceptions of their interactions with students. Teach Teach Educ 16:811–826

Hargreaves A, Earl L, Moore S, Manning S (2001) Learning to change: teaching beyond subjects and standards. Jossey-Bass, San Francisco

Isenbarger L, Zembylas M (2006) The emotional labour of caring in teaching. Teach Teach Educ 22:120–134

Kardos SM, Johnson SM (2007) On their own and presumed expert: new teachers' experience with their colleagues. Teach Coll Record 109:2083–2106. http://www.tcrecord.org. Retrieved 26 Dec 2007

Knowles JG, Holt-Reynolds D (1991) Shaping pedagogies through personal histories in preservice teacher education. Teach Coll Record 93:87–113

Lortie DC (1975) Schoolteacher. The University of Chicago Press, Chicago

Macdonald D (1999) Teacher attrition: a review of the literature. Teach Teach Educ 15:835–848

Newberry M, Davis HA (2008) The role of elementary teachers' conceptions of closeness to students on their differential behaviour in the classroom. Teach Teach Educ 24:1965–1985

O'Conner KE (2008) "You choose to care": teachers, emotions and professional identify. Teach Teach Educ 24:117–126

Oplatka I (2007) Managing emotions in teaching: toward an understanding of emotional displays and caring as nonprescribed role elements. Teach Coll Record 109(6). http://www.tcrecord. org. Retrieved 22 May 2007; pp 1374–1400

Ria L, Sève C, Saury J, Theureau J, Durand M (2003) Beginning teachers' situated emotions: a study of first classroom experiences. J Educ Teach 29:219–233

Rinke CR (2008) Understanding teachers' careers: linking professional life to professional path. Educ Res Rev 3:1–3

Swanson GE (1989) On the motives and motivation of selves. In: Franks DD, McCarthy ED (eds) The sociology of emotions. JAI Press, Greenwich, CT

Tickle L (1991) New teachers and the emotions of learning teaching. Cambridge J Educ 21:319–329

Weiss EM (1999) Perceived workplace conditions and first-year teachers' morale, career choice commitment, and planned retention: a secondary analysis. Teach Teach Educ 15:861–879

Zembylas M (2003) Caring for teacher emotion: reflections on teacher self-development. Stud Philos Educ 22:103–125

Zembylas M (2005) Teaching with emotion: a postmodern enactment. Information Age Publishing, Greenwich, CT

Part III
Student and Teacher Involvement

Chapter 6
Understanding the Role of Teacher Appraisals in Shaping the Dynamics of their Relationships with Students: Deconstructing Teachers' Judgments of Disruptive Behavior/Students

Mei-Lin Chang and Heather A. Davis

Abstract In this chapter we examine the emotional by-products of developing relationships with students. We begin the chapter by reviewing the power of student–teacher relationships in promoting adaptive student outcomes including enhanced motivation and achievement. We examine the pleasant and unpleasant emotional by-products of being involved with students and the role repeatedly experiencing unpleasant emotions may play in teacher burnout. We tackle the emotional life of "challenging relationships" specifically with regard to the judgments teachers may make about student behavior that can lead to emotional exhaustion and compassion fatigue. Our central question is: When things don't "feel good," what are adaptive strategies for reframing, rethinking, and reinvesting in relationships?

Keywords Teacher appraisals · Student–teacher relationships · Adaptive strategies

> [I have] a student [who has] a difficult time staying in his seat and has had this problem the entire school year. Every time I redirected [him] and told him to get working or to return to his seat, my suggestions were met with despairing looks and frustrated sighs.... Some of his behaviors seem out of his control, as if he doesn't even realize that he's up and out of his seat or that he constantly tilts his chair backwards.... As much as I like [him], he exhausts me emotionally, mentally, and physically... and he requires more "work" and monitoring than any other student in the class (June 2008, female first-year middle school teacher).

Teaching is emotional work (Hargreaves 1998) requiring a great deal of awareness, understanding and regulation to develop and maintain supportive relationships with students. The incident above illustrates how challenging some teacher–student relationships can be; exhausting teachers emotionally, mentally, and physically.

M.-L. Chang (✉)
Department of Educational Policy and Leadership, Emory University, Columbus, OH, USA
e-mail: chang.616@osu.edu

P.A. Schutz and M. Zembylas (eds.), *Advances in Teacher Emotion Research:
The Impact on Teachers' Lives,*
DOI 10.1007/978-1-4419-0564-2_6, © Springer Science+Business Media, LLC 2009

Indeed, scholars who study teacher burnout recognize the interrelationship between conflict-ridden teacher–student interactions, teacher emotional labor, and teacher burnout (Chang in press; Maslach and Leiter 1999).

In 2006, H. Davis argued relationships between students and teachers could be characterized by patterns of interactions that happen in the dyad. In this chapter we turn our attention to the role teachers' belief about the nature of relationships and the judgments they make about student behavior can play in shaping their emotion experiences and relationship quality. In Fig. 6.1 we outline the conceptual framework for this chapter. For discussion purposes, in the model, we begin with teachers' awareness of student behavior and the judgment of that behavior as disruptive. Drawing from the literature, and our own work on teacher judgments (Chang 2009), we argue some teachers may approach disruptive behavior in less adaptive ways that can escalate conflict and contribute to leaving them feeling emotionally depleted. Specifically, we argue teachers implicit beliefs about relationships and their habitual ways of judging student behavior can leave them prone to frequently experiencing unpleasant emotions. Moreover, we argue teachers may engage in emotional labor that is unproductive and, over time, can make them prone to experiencing compassion fatigue or burnout (Chang in press).

Several assumptions underlie this chapter. The first is that emotional labor is an inherent component of maintaining long-term relationships (Hargreaves 1998, 2000; Oplatka 2007). Certainly, there are children who exhibit severe social skills or relationship problems. These children are often diagnosed and served by special

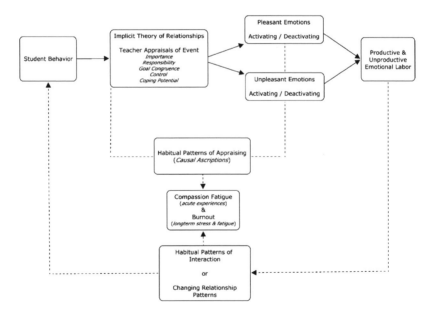

Fig. 6.1 Understanding the role of teachers' appraisals of student behavior in eliciting emotions and contributing to habitual patterns of interaction

educators who can support classroom teachers in modifying atypical behaviors. However, relationships with children diagnosed with severe behavior problems are not the focus of this chapter. We view relational conflict and student resistance/withdrawal as a natural byproduct of teachers' ongoing attempts to help children grow (Hartup 1989; Hunter 1984). Second, we assume students' also judge their teachers' behavior, experience emotions, engage in emotion labor, and select behaviors that can perpetuate conflict with teachers (see Davis, 2003; H. Davis, 2006). However, in this chapter we focus on the role teachers' judgments may play in perpetuating or changing relationship quality.

In the following sections, we begin by reviewing the power of student–teacher relationships in promoting adaptive student outcomes including enhanced motivation and achievement (Davis 2003; Corneilus-White 2008). We explore the pleasant and unpleasant emotional by-products of being involved with students (Muller et al. 1999; H. Davis, 2006). Next, we review the literature on cognitive appraisals and the role teachers' appraisals of student behavior may play in producing unpleasant affect, leading to causal ascriptions, and escalating interpersonal conflict. We then tackle the emotional life of "challenging relationships" illustrating the interplay of causal ascriptions, emotion experiences, and unproductive emotional labor. We end by exploring the nature of emotion suppression and identify ways for teachers to rejuvenate in the face of emotional exhaustion and compassion fatigue (Kees and Lashwood 1996; Olivier and Venter 2003; Radley and Figley 2007). We argue through systematic reflection, teachers can transform their own feelings, understandings, and perspectives on relationships that are not "working" for them. Our goal is to provide teachers with strategies for answering the question: When things don't "feel good," what are adaptive strategies for reframing, rethinking, and reinvesting in relationships with students?

The Power of Supportive Relationships with Teachers

A substantial body of literature has documented the importance of students' perceptions of their teacher relationships on their classroom motivation, learning, performance and school completion (Connell and Wellborn 1991; Davis 2003; Davis and Dupper 2004; Skinner and Belmont 1993). Supportive relationships with teachers serve as a form of social capital for students, providing academic and social benefits that can extend beyond the scope of a single academic year (Howes et al. 1998). In a recent meta-analysis, Corneilus-White (2008) found students' perceptions of supportive teacher relationships were correlated, on average, between 0.25 and 0.55 with academic and social outcomes including participation, satisfaction, self-efficacy, critical thinking, standardized achievement in math and language, increased attendance, reduced disruptive behavior, and higher grades. Conversely, findings suggest students' motivation and adjustment to school may be adversely affected when their relationships with teachers are distressed (Corneilus-White 2008; Finn 1993; Smyth and Hattam 2002).

While these findings highlight the importance of relationships to student learning, parallel findings suggest that even when teachers are motivated to improve relationship quality they can struggle to cultivate the kinds of relationships they desire. For example, Muller et al. (1999) found teachers made decisions about who to connect with by weighing the assets and obstacles each student brought to the relationship. These included the perception of a student's similarity, attractiveness, social skills, as well as the student's expressed desire for a relationship (Babad 1993; Baker 1999; Morganett 2001; Wang et al. 2008). These assets all contribute to getting picked from the "limited pool of eligible relationships" in the classroom (Tharpe et al. 2000, p. 56). Similarly, Newberry and Davis (2008) found some teachers may hold economic views of relationships; only investing in relationships as much as they perceive they will get out of them. These findings consistently suggest the students who need relationships with their teachers the most (i.e. those with limited interpersonal and academic skills) may be the *least* likely to be selected as relationship partners (Baker et al. 2008; Davis and Lease 2007). Moreover, with the majority of teachers in our teaching force hailing from White, middle-class backgrounds (Hoy et al. 2006), minority and economically disadvantaged students may be at risk for being systematically excluded from the social capital afforded by teacher relationships (Brown 2004; Monroe and Obidah 2004).

Within the field of education, scholars often focus on relational conflict and negativity as predictors of poor teacher–student relationships. Findings suggest students' and teachers' perceptions of emotional negativity and relationship conflict is a consistent predictor of poor academic achievement (Baker et al. 2008; Mantzicopoulos 2005). Moreover, when African-American and Hispanic students experience conflict in their relationships with teachers this conflict appears to have a more deleterious effect on their achievement and motivation compared to their White counterparts (Pianta et al. 1995). Recent studies of the interactions of white teachers with their non-White students have found these dyads may not be "in sync" with each other (Brown 2004; Irving and Fraser 1998). While conflict may be a robust predictor of relationship quality ultimately we must ask: Where does conflict come from? In a seminal study, Monroe and Obidah (2004) identified the ways in which White teachers and their non-White students became out of sync with each other by misinterpreting each other's intentions and actions as disrespectful. Their repeated judgments of disrespect resulted in increased conflict and a downward spiral for relationship quality. Interestingly, this pattern occurred despite the fact that *neither* member of the dyad intended disrespect.

In the following sections we identify several sources of relational conflict including teachers' implicit theories of relationships, the *habitual* ways in which teachers may judge problematic behavior/problem students, and the ways in which teachers may unproductively labor in their relationships with students. We align ourselves with constructivist/socio-cultural developmental scholars (Vygotsky 1978; Wertsch 1991; Devries and Zan 1996) who argue dissonance, conflict in a relationship can have meaning and purpose – particularly when relationship partners seek to understand the source of the conflict. We view conflict as a by-product of the inability to influence your relationship partner. We argue relational conflict becomes dysfunctional when it *repeatedly* results the inability to influence a relationship partner's thoughts or behaviors.

Teacher's Implicit Theories of Relationships

What does it mean to "care" about a student? Scholars such as Nel Noddings (1995) and Lisa Goldstein (1999) conceptualize "caring" as a process; that is, something teachers do rather than something they feel. They argue caring is an ethic, or a moral value, that teachers communicate to students through their selection of curriculum, their planning of a lesson, their establishment of classroom norms, and their interactions with students. From this perspective, the norms teachers establish communicate to their students the values they "care" about and their frequency and quality of interactions with individual students communicates who they "care" about.

"Caring," however, is also likely to involve more generalized beliefs about the nature of classroom relationships. Knee et al. (2003) argue people develop implicit theories about relationships that can guide them in selecting who to care about. Their work parallels the work by Carol Dweck (1996) on beliefs about intelligence as either malleable or fixed. Participants in Knee et al. (2003) study could be characterized as either holding destiny or growth beliefs about relationships. Individuals who hold destiny beliefs about relationships are likely to view potential relationship partners as either inherently compatible or incompatible. Whereas, individuals who hold growth beliefs are likely to believe that challenges in relationships, including differences, can be overcome. One's beliefs about the nature of relationships, in turn, serves as a lens for interpreting all social tasks including selecting relationship partners, perceiving the limitations of one's partner, investing effort, interpreting conflict, and persisting through differences.

These findings have important implications for teachers who are responsible for developing productive relationships with each of their students. In Fig. 6.1, teachers' implicit beliefs about relationships are hypothesized to shape their interpretation of student behavior and, in turn, their affective experience. For example, teachers who endorse destiny beliefs may interpret disruptive behavior, student resistance, or conflict as reflecting inherent incompatibility. Consistent with their findings, students judge as incompatible would be less likely to be chosen as relationship partners. Indeed, Newberry and Davis (2008) found the teachers in their study reported investing less effort and being less willing to persist through differences once students were judged incompatible.

Judging Problems, Judging Students

In the emotion literature, the judgments we make about our environment are viewed as driving the emotions we experience (Smith and Lazarus 1990; Roseman and Smith 2001). Ben-Ze'ev (2000) argues caring can be viewed as a discrete emotion state that motivates teachers to engage in different caring behaviors. From this perspective, the judgments teachers make about their curriculum and their relationships with students have important implications for whether they feel caring or indifferent. According to Ben-Ze'ev, teachers and students are more likely to care about a lesson when they judge specific elements of the curriculum to be relevant. Likewise, teachers are more likely to care about specific relationships in their class when they judge those relationships to be important or relevant to their goals/mission as a teacher. A core theme in caring then, is that it involves feeling a sense of responsibility towards someone or something. Identifying a specific relationship as important, however, may not be enough for teachers to engage in caring behaviors. In order to engage in caring behaviors, teachers must believe the caring behaviors will support them in achieving their goals (either personal or instructional), perceive they are in control of the relationship/curriculum, and perceive they are capable of managing problems that might occur. Within this framework of care, teachers' moment-to-moment judgments of importance, congruence, control, and coping potential create implicit and explicit boundaries about what they care about, such as the content and students they care about most, how much they care in the face the obstacles, and if they care enough to devote themselves to modify their approach (see Fig. 6.1).

According to Lazarus (1991), the intensity and type of emotions we experience reflect two layers of judgments: primary appraisals and secondary appraisals. In the following sections we describe the primary and secondary appraisals processes and we apply this theory to understand global relationship emotions and the more discrete emotions teachers may experience in their interactions with students. In Table 6.1, we identify five global relationship emotions: Caring/indifference (Ben-Ze'ev 2000), Hurt (Leary 2004), Affinity/disliking (Tharpe et al. 2000), Connection/alienation (Aaron et al. 1992; Wubbels, Brekelmans, den Brok, & van Tartwijk, 2006), and Compassion/sympathy (Figley 1995).

The emotion of "love" is notably absent from our list. It was a tough decision to exclude love, as the early work by Hargreaves (1994) found that warmth and love often underpin the lives and work of teachers. And yet, we hesitated because so little empirical and conceptual work has been completed on teachers' understandings and experiences of love in the classroom. One study, by Oplatka (2007, p. 1386) moved us toward exclusion as we read about the teachers' distinctions between displays of love and the emotional experience of love.

> A display of love for pupils is interpreted as caring about the pupils, an attention to their needs, an emotion that embodies verbal and nonverbal displays. But most of the respondents attach this profound and strong emotion to emotion work, suggesting, for example, that teachers might love a particular pupil and not love others. They conclude, then, that teachers are not obliged to love their pupils on the grounds that love is a very personal and internal disposition.

In many ways, these teachers' discussions of love parallel the writings of Noddings (1995) and Goldstein (1999) that portray love as process; that is, as acts teachers do in the service of caring for their students. Whereas in this chapter we

Table 6.1 Deconstructing global relationship emotions in terms of their underlying cognitive appraisals, their level of activation, and their core relational themes

Global relationship emotions	Underlying appraisals (Smith 1991; Roseman 2001)					Activation (Linnenbrink 2007)	Core relational themes for each emotion (Lazarus 2001, p. 64[a]; Tharpe et al. 2000[b]; Ben-Ze'ev 2000[c])
	Is this relevant?	Is this aligned with my goals?	Am I in control?	Can I cope with the situation?	Other		
Caring	Yes	Yes	Yes	Yes	*I am responsible*	Activating	Involves feel responsible; to have awareness of the personal, academic, and emotional situations of others (Noddings 1995)
Indifference	No					Deactivating	Involves feeling disinterested in others or events
Hurt	Yes	No	No	Maybe			Involves feeling rejected or perceiving others do not regard the relationship as sufficiently valuable or important (Leary 2004)
Affinity	Yes	Yes	Yes	Yes		Activating	Involves liking; to have an increased desire to maintain the relationship[b]
Disliking	Yes	No	No			Deactivating	Involves feeling disproval of someone's behavior or some situations
Connected	Yes	Yes	Yes	Yes		Activating	Involves a perceived proximity, and close psychological distance[b] (Aaron et al. 1992)
Alienated	Yes	No	No	No		Deactivating	Involves perceiving rejection and/or psychological distance (Leary 2004)
Compassion	Yes	Yes	Maybe	Yes		Activating	Involves being moved by another's suffering and feeling obliged and able to help[a, c]
Sympathy	Yes	Yes	Maybe	Maybe		Deactivating	Involves sorrow or concern for the distressed or needy others (Eisenberg 2000)

[a]The core relational themes were drawn from Lazarus (2001)
[b]The core relational themes were drawn from Tharpe et al. (2000)
[c]The core relational themes were drawn from Ben-Ze'ev (2000)

argue teachers need to reflect on their experiences of indifference, hurt, disliking, alienation, and sympathy we were hesitant to extend this framework to love.

In the following section, we deconstruct global and discrete emotions in terms of the primary and secondary judgments teachers may be making about the situation/relationships (Tables 6.1 and 6.2). In the far right column, we identify the core relational theme that distinguishes each emotion episode from another. We apply Linnenbrink's (2007) theory of activation to highlight how specific emotion experiences, as activating or deactivating, may lead to different types of emotion labor in the teacher–student relationships.

Primary Appraisals in the Classroom

The defining characteristic of the primary appraisal process is that one's initial judgments of events are goal-related. Thus, teachers first judge the relevance and congruence of an incident to their goals. Goal relevance is believed to be the most significant determinant in the intensity of an emotional encounter (Ben-Ze'ev 2000). The more relevant a teacher judges and an incident, the more intense the emotion experience. Within the classroom context, the intensity of nearly all global relationship emotions will reflect how relevant a teacher perceived the relationship with that child (see Table 6.1). Tharpe et al. (2000) and Aaron et al. (1992) argue teachers' judgments of relevance may, in part, be a reflection of physical proximity and the frequency and diversity of their interactions (see also Wubbels et al. 2006). Because teachers share a proximal space with students intensively, teachers are more likely to care about the students in their classes. Teachers' judgments of relevance may also be a function of their perceived psychological proximity (Muller et al. 1999; Newberry and Davis 2008); that is, a relationships may be viewed as more relevant to a teacher's goals when she perceives a students to be similar.

In addition to judging the relevance of a transaction to their goals, teachers also judge the extent to which the incident/interaction is helping them to accomplish their goals. Teachers often possess several goals in the classroom: helping students reach learning goals, following lesson plans maintaining order, and managing students' behaviors and these goals are generally tied with their personal emotions (Schutz et al. 2001). Goal congruence is defined as the extent to which teachers perceive classroom incidents as helping them to meet their goals. From our perspective, the extent to which teachers' perceive student behavior as a threat to their instructional or management goals, the more likely they are to feel hurt, or alienated from their students (Table 6.1) and to experience unpleasant emotions (Table 6.2). In summary, it is during the primary appraisal process that teachers' judgments prime them to experience an emotion, to feel that emotion intensely, and to experience a pleasant emotion vs. an unpleasant emotion.

Table 6.2 Deconstructing discrete relationship emotions in terms of their underlying cognitive appraisals, their level of activation, and their core relational themes

Discrete emotion experiences	Is this relevant?	Underlying appraisals (Smith 1991; Roseman 2001)				Activating/deactivating (Linnenbrink 2007)	Core relational themes for each emotion (Lazarus 2001, p. 64[a]; Ben-Ze'ev 2000[b])
		Is this aligned with my goals	Am I in control?	Can I cope?	Other		
Pleasant emotions							
Pride	Yes	Yes	Yes			Activating	Involves feeling self-satisfaction; taking credit for a valued object or achievement, either one's own or that of someone or group with whom we identify[a]
Excitement	Yes	Yes	Maybe			Activating	Involves feeling energized by a favorable situation or desired outcome
Hope	Yes	Yes	Maybe		*I am uncertain*	Activating	Involves the belief that the desired outcome is possible and desire to bring about the outcome[b]
Contentment	Yes	Yes	Maybe			Deactivating	Involves feeling satisfied with current states
Unpleasant emotions							
Anxiety	Yes	No	Maybe	No	*I am uncertain*	Activating	Involves facing uncertain, existential threat[a]
Fear	Yes	No	No	No	*I am uncertain*	Activating	Involves an immediate, concrete, and overwhelming physical danger[a]
Sadness/loss	Yes	No	No	No	*I am certain*	Deactivating	Involves experiencing an irrevocable loss[a]
Annoyance	Yes	No	No	Yes		Activating	Involves feeling disturbed or irritated by repeated behaviors
Frustration	Yes	No	Yes/maybe	Yes		Deactivating	Involves perceiving no control over an undesired situation caused by yourself or others
Anger	Yes	No	No	Yes		Activating	Involves perceiving someone has committed a demeaning, undeserved offense against you or yours[a, b]
Disappointment	Yes	No	No	Yes			Involves feeling defeated in your expectation or hopes

(continued)

Table 6.2 (continued)

Discrete emotion experiences	Underlying appraisals (Smith 1991; Roseman 2001)					Activating/ deactivating (Linnenbrink 2007)	Core relational themes for each emotion (Lazarus 2001, p. 64[a]; Ben-Ze'ev 2000[b])
	Is this relevant?	Is this aligned with my goals	Am I in control?	Can I cope?	Other		
Guilt	Yes	No	Yes	Yes	I am responsible	Activating	Involves feeling like you have violated certain norms[b]
Shame	Yes	No	Yes	No		Deactivating	Involves feeling like you have failed to live up to an ideal image of yourself and the desire to conceal[a, b]
Disgust/ resentment	Yes	No	No	Maybe			Involves perceiving an idea or object as indigestible[b]

[a] The core relational themes were drawn from Lazarus (2001)
[b] The core relational themes were drawn from Ben-Ze'ev (2000)

Secondary Appraisals in the Classroom

It is during the secondary appraisal process that pleasant and unpleasant emotions are further differentiated. The emotions literature is wrought with an exhaustive list of the different types of judgments individuals can make about their environment including their feelings of control, their confidence in coping with the problems/situation that arose, and their concerns about the certainty of expected outcomes (Smith and Lazarus 1990; Smith 1991; Ben-Ze'ev 2000). In this chapter, we chose to focus our attention on the role teachers' judgments of control and of their perceived ability to cope with problems. In part, this reflects our orientation toward a control-value theory of motivation (Pekrun et al. 2007; Davis et al. 2008). In some cases, we found it helpful to introduce additional judgments such as the perceived certainty of an event or one's perceived accountability. These additional appraisals were noted in column six of Tables 6.1 and 6.2.

Once teachers have judged the relevance and congruence of an incident, they must determine the extent to which the situation/problem is within their control (Roseman 2001). When the control potential is judged to be high, the intensity of emotion is likely to be high as well. For example, if the teacher perceives the student could have controlled the misbehavior, he/she may feel anger about the situation; in contrast, if the teacher perceives even the student has no control over the misbehavior, he/she may just feel annoyance or sympathy instead.

In the case of judging an event to be goal incongruent, or competing with their goals, teachers must judge the extent to which they feel confident they can cope with the problem. Coping potential is defined as the belief one holds about their ability to ameliorate or eliminate a perceived harm or threat (Lazarus 2001; Schutz and Davis 2000). It serves as "a bridge between the relational meaning of transaction and how the person feels and acts (Lazarus 2001, p. 58)." Moreover, when one judges coping potential to be high, emotional intensity is likely to be lower because coping thoughts and actions can mediate subsequent emotions. For example, in the face of aggressive behavior, if the teacher believes she can safely cope with aggressive behavior, the intensity of her anxiety or anger is likely to be reduced.

In some cases, understanding judgments of future expectancy or accountability can help teachers to identify why they experienced one emotion instead of another. Future expectancy is defined as the judgments we make about the certainty or uncertainty of an event. Keeping with Roseman (2001), feelings of uncertainty can prompt teachers to be prepared for events without reacting to commit to or avoid the event. Some of the emotions that are involved with the judgments of uncertainty are hope, anxiety, fear, and sadness. In contrast, if an event is judged as certain to occur, as in the case of fear, teachers are likely to react right away.

Accountability is defined as the extent to which we appraise ourselves, or another to be responsible for bringing about a desired outcome. For example, if a teacher judges herself to be responsible for a student's academic success, regardless of her judgment of control over a discrete failure, she is likely to feel disappointment or guilt. Weiner (2000, 2007) argues causal ascriptions, particularly the extent

to which the causes of events are deemed internal to the individual (i.e. locus) and/
or controllable by the individual are critical to understanding the experience of
moral emotions. He (p. 79) defines moral emotions as emotions that "are associated
with such concepts as *ought* and *should* and they have social norms among their
antecedents." According to Weiner (2007) moral emotions, such as compassion,
anger, guilt, and shame have served communicative functions that convey normative information to the teacher and the student. Weiner (2007) argues, it is judgments of personal accountability that are likely to compel teachers from "feeling"
care towards a student towards "enacting" caring behaviors (Kozel and Davis
2009). For example, in their study of teachers' strategies for working with "problem" students, Brophy and McCaslin (1992, p. 31) found: "Teachers … expressed
concern about the problem students sometimes directly ("My heart goes out to such
a child."), but usually indirectly. Often they were not so much personally concerned
about the individual problem student as they were accepting of their general
responsibility to do whatever they could for any of their students." In this example,
the teachers' specific judgments of non-accountability, non-responsibility for the
specific problem occurring with a student in their class, may have contributed to
perpetuating the problem (see also Brophy and Rohrkemper 1988).

Judging Conflict: Causal Ascriptions, Cultural Synchronization, and Deficit Thinking

Although emotions are elicited by the appraisals teachers make about specific situations, often, instead of appraising situations, teachers can short-circuit this process by
either drawing on a "set" of prior appraisals or by making causal ascriptions about the
child's behavior. Pekrun et al. (2007) have described the ways in which emotions may
become more "habitualized" (p. 23) as a function of repeated associations with a
given situation. As emotion experiences may be come associated with tasks, or in this
case children, the initial appraisal process may be short-circuited and the appraisal
processes become more consistent (see also affective tendencies in (Schutz et al. this
volume). In other words, when faced with a "new" conflict, teachers may not simply
evaluate the demands of the situation they may also draw on their past experiences
working with "that" child and managing similar conflicts. Over time, teachers may
begin to base their current appraisals of student conflict on their past judgments of
goal relevance, congruence, agency, and coping efficacy. Habitual judgments of student behavior can become habitual judgments of "problem students." As teachers
stop judging problems and managing situations they may begin expecting certain
emotion experiences to accompany specific students and get caught in a cycle of
unpleasant affect (see Fig. 6.1). For example, a teacher who feels anger or frustration
with the disruptive behavior of a student may come to judge the student as "defiant,"
"passive aggressive," "hostile," or "immature." In assigning these labels, teachers may
not realize that they have appraised control over the problem to an internal characteristic of the student and not to themselves.

Early studies of teacher–student conflict found teachers can misconstrue students' exuberance for hostility, or silent respect for sullen resistance (Hargreaves 1998). Thus, it is important to remember, that teachers' perceptions of what is happening in their classroom may not be calibrated with their students' perceptions. Irving and Fraser (1998) introduced the concept of cultural synchronization to describe the ways in which conflict is generated in relationships between students of minority backgrounds and their teachers when their values, patterns of interaction, and ways of being are not aligned. One misinterpretation need not define a relationship. However, when students and teachers' make repeated causal ascriptions of each others' behavior as a result of some stable, internal characteristic that lies outside of the students' control (Weiner 2000, 2007) discrete feelings of "disrespect" can become more global judgments of students as disrespectful or teachers as mean. Assuming a deficit perspective on a relationship with a student, that a student imbues an inherent deficit, can lead to teachers changing and in fact lowering their standards for student performance and the quality of their instruction (Ford and Grantham 2003).

How can teachers disrupt cycles of conflict and unpleasant affect in student–teacher relationships? In the next section we turn our eye to the literature on emotional labor and the ways in which teachers cope with unpleasant affect. We synthesize the literature on emotional labor and coping and argue teachers' deployment of event reappraisal may be an effective way for teachers to regain a task-focused perspective on disruptive behavior.

Emotional Labor/Emotion Work in Student–Teacher Relationships

To care for students requires a great deal of emotional understanding and emotional management often referred to as emotional labor (Hargreaves 1998). Initially studied among service workers, emotional labor was defined as the experience of employees when they are required to feel, or at least project the appearance of, certain emotions as they engage in job-relevant interactions (Hochschild 1979, 1983). Early findings revealed emotional labor is involved when employees are required to manage their own emotions in order to produce a desired response in their customers. When employees experienced emotional dissonance, that is when the emotions they felt and displayed were inconsistent, they were more prone to feel emotionally exhausted (Abraham 1999; Morris and Feldman 1997).

Because of the negative impact on the customer service employees, emotional labor was conceptualized as an undesired phenomenon in the customer service occupations. Conflict between customer service workers and their customers, however, embodies different characteristics than in teacher–student relationships. The duration of their relationship is briefer and bounded, in many cases, by a single interaction or a series of brief interactions around a specific problem for which the worker has limited accountability. The two people interacting are not close in physical or psychological proximity, and, if the conflict is successfully resolved, the two may never meet again. In contrast, relationships between students and teachers endure the length of an academic year during which the two members are in close physical proximity and their conflict may be public. In studying teacher emotions Hargreaves (1998) argued for a more adaptive view of emotional labor in teaching professions. Specifically, that emotional labor is an inherent phenomena of the task of teaching and therefore needs to encompass a value-free definition.

Glomb and Tews (2004) define emotional labor to include the expression and non-expression of felt emotions and can include suppression, faking, and genuine felt experiences. Emotional labor involves feeling aroused by an emotion, knowing when it is appropriate to express an emotion (i.e. display rules), and knowing how to align the emotion we display with what we genuinely feel. They argue labor is most intense when we experience a discrepancy between what we feel and what we know we are supposed to display. Emotional labor can also exist in the expression of a genuinely felt emotion. For example, it may take a great deal of labor for a teacher to appropriately express the anger she feels over an incident of disruptive behavior. From this perspective, expression and non-expression of felt emotions is a process that, to the extent that emotional labor is purposeful, may be adaptive for maintaining relationships and appropriately socializing the regulation of emotions.

Callahan and McCollum (2002, p. 282) further distinguish between emotional labor and emotion work. They define emotion work as involving the decisions individuals make to, "personally [choose] to manage their emotions for their own non-compensated benefit." In contrast, they view emotion labor as emotion management that is exchanged for some form of material or psychological compensation. This distinction reminds us that emotion management often serves an organizational function; and that teachers may manage relationships according to prescribed roles which they may or may not endorse. Indeed, Oplatka (2007) found the teachers in her study viewed engaging in emotion management as part of their own moral obligation towards students and their work and not as a function of their prescribed roles as teachers.

In this chapter, we chose to use the term emotional labor so as to emphasize our interests in the types of skills (i.e. suppression, expression, appraisal, coping) teachers use to manage their emotion experiences. Consistent with Hargreaves (1998), we view emotional labor is an inherent component of student–teacher relationships. This is because teachers serve a socializing role. They help children to acquire emotion display rules and opportunities to practice regulating their emotions (Thompson 1990, 1991). Children are in varying phases of acquiring cognitive and social skills (Davis et al. 2009) and may be less skilled in the "work" of relationships (Davis 2003). Even as they age, the task of helping children to regulate their emotion experiences and emotion displays becomes no less complex for teachers of preadolescents and adolescents. Though children in middle and high school are likely to be more adept at identifying their own emotions and are likely to have acquired knowledge of display rules, in a single day teachers may encounter more than a hundred students who are struggling with their own emotion management. Moreover, as classrooms become more diverse it is likely that teachers and students will have to work harder to develop shared interpretations of classroom events (Hoy et al. 2006). This is because when teachers and students come from culturally diverse backgrounds (Brown 2004; Monroe and Obidah 2004) they may vary with regard to what are the appropriate emotion display rules (Markus and Kitayama 1994).

Finally, it is important to remember teachers are asked to develop the relationships en mass. In addition to norms they establish, teachers' expectations for their students' behaviors and academic performance exist in a shared space (Davis and Lease 2007). Teachers' expression and non-expression of emotions in one interaction may be observed and/or discussed by the other students in the class (H. Davis, 2006). It is for this reason that teaching requires a tremendous amount of energy to know what you feel, why you feel it, and what are the underlying goals of expression and non-expression for the individual child as well as the class.

In this chapter, we argue the concept of emotional labor, in order to be useful to teachers, needs to be deconstructed into productive and unproductive labor. We believe what is lacking in current definitions is a sense of directionality; viewing labor/work as a vector moving the teachers and students toward a desired outcome. While the clarification between emotion labor and work adds to our understanding of the locus of teachers' emotion management, it fails to describe the extent to which the goals teachers are working towards are adaptive. We define productive labor as teachers' genuine attempts to get to know their students and systematically reflect on their relationships/emotions. We also define productive labor to include intermittent suppression whereby teachers may hide an emotion they genuinely feel in order to model an appropriate display rule. Consistent with Glomb and Tews (2004), we acknowledge there may also be "power in pretending" (see p. 5). That is, that productive labor may also involve intermittently pretending you feel something that you do not yet feel and creating opportunities to genuinely feel it. In contrast, we define unproductive emotional labor as teachers' attempts to routinely avoid, fake, or suppress the genuine emotions they feel. This can include "acting professional" (Newberry and Davis 2008, p. 5) and conforming with display rules even when they may not be adaptive to a child's learning.

Active and Proactive Coping with Emotions

Historically, coping has been viewed as a reaction or response to emotions. In recent decades, however, Folkman and Lazarus (1988) argued that there exists a reciprocal, dynamic relationship between emotion and coping. In other words, coping is an integral part of experiencing emotion not merely the response. Coping then, can be defined as "constantly changing cognitive and behavioral efforts to manage specific external and/or internal demands that are appraised as taxing or exceeding the resources of the person (Lazarus and Folkman 1984, p. 141)." Lazarus (2001) asserted that the evaluation of coping options is a major component in secondary appraisals, in which one appraises what can be done in the troubled person–environment relationship.

Traditionally, coping functions have been discerned as either emotion-focused coping or problem-focused coping (Lazarus 2001). Teachers who engage in problem-focused coping deploy strategies aimed at obtaining information about the disruptive behavior, or conflict and focus on changing the situation, whereas teachers who engage in emotion-focused coping deploy strategies aimed at regulating the emotions that were elicited by the events. There have been mixed findings about which coping strategy is more effective in producing adaptive outcomes (see Lazarus 2006). For this reason, Lazarus (2006) asserted these two forms of coping should not be compared to each other.

Schutz and colleagues (2004) proposed a third form of coping processes they term regaining-task-focusing processes. In regaining-task-focusing processes, one attempts to get back on task after experiencing an unpleasant emotion and regain perspective. Within the arena of test-taking regaining task focusing processes include tension reducing and importance-reappraisal strategies (see Schutz and Davis 2000). Tension reduction strategies include slowing breathing down, taking a minute to stop and stretch, or reducing off-task self-talk. Within the context of test taking, Schutz and colleagues (2004) define importance reappraisal as, "reflecting students attempts at cognitive change [that is] reconstructing the meaning of the test in their lives" (Davis et al. 2008, p. 945). Recently, Chang (2009) found novice teachers' tendency to deploy importance reappraisal strategies significantly predicted the intensity of unpleasant emotions (anger, frustration, fatigue) experienced during an incident of disruptive behavior.

The use of reappraisal, however, to cope with emotion is not limited to judgments of importance. Teachers could reappraise the alignment of an interaction with their goals, their sense of control, and their ability to cope. Lazarus (2001) notes that re-appraisal is simply an attempt to alter our emotions by "constructing a new relational meaning of the stressful encounter" and it is an effective way of coping with the stressful situations. In this chapter we argue regaining-task-focusing processes are essential to bridge the coping process from emotion-focused to problem-focused. For a teacher experiencing hostility from a student, it may be necessary for the teachers to cope with their own and the students' emotions first and then deal with the actual problem that brought on the anger. Tension reduction strategies can help reduce the arousal that accompanies emotions, while, re-appraising the situation once calm can help teachers gather more information about the situation or about the students, thus promoting the potential for teachers to face situation with a renewed sense of control. Reappraisal might involve asking: In what ways is this behavior relevant to my classroom goals? To what extent is my goals shared by the students? How can I feel in control? In what ways am I responsible for what is happening and how can I increase the student's feelings of responsibility? What do I need to cope with this situation?

Re-appraisal can also help teachers regulate the emotions they are feeling so that they re-engage with the student. According to Linnenbrink (2007), the experience of certain emotions may activate us to "do something" to modify the situations in order to approach our goals. Activated unpleasant emotions (e.g. anger, anxious) may lead to more intense engagement than deactivated unpleasant emotions (e.g. frustration, sad; see Tables 6.1 and 6.2). Just as activating emotions might lead teachers to escalate conflict with students, deactivating emotion experiences can lead teachers to withdraw from engaging with students. Learning how to monitor what you are feeling and the extent to which it provokes you to "do something" can be empowering to teachers.

More recently, proactive coping has been lauded effective in stress and emotion management. Greenglass (2002) defines proactive coping as oriented towards the future and consisting of "efforts to build up general resources that facilitate promotion of challenging goals and personal growth (p. 38)." Instead of coping reactively, proactive coping aims at goal management (i.e. making plans and building up resources for challenging goals and potential risks) rather than risk management (i.e. dealing with problems after being threatened by harm or loss). Coping in a traditional context is reactive and it reflects the compensation for loss or harm. In contrast, people who are proactive see upcoming risks and demands in the future and tend not to appraise these as threats, harm, or loss (Greenglass 2002). Therefore, proactive coping incorporates a positive approach to dealing with stressors and integrates stressors into the processes of attaining classroom goals.

Consistent with this perspective, teachers who foresee relationship challenges will be prepared for situations and will feel efficacious dealing with the problems. Oplatka (2007) argues that teachers need to be proactively attentive to students' emotional, physical, and cognitive needs, including students' verbal and nonverbal ways of communicating. Oplatka found that teachers who dedicate and invest time and energy to diagnose students' cognitive state and to be sensitive to students' welfare, stress or difficulties experience a decline in disruptive behaviors in the classroom.

In agreement with Lazarus's (2006) argument, we believe coping with unpleasant emotion needs to be examined within the context of specific situations, and judgments of productive or unproductive labor need to reflect the extent to which the teacher achieves an adaptive outcome for both the student and herself. Sole reliance on one method of coping, particularly suppression, may be problematic (see Davis et al. 2008).

Examining the Emotional Life of "Challenging" Relationships with Students

In 1995, Friedman published a report on they types of behavior problems that contribute to teacher burnout. Among the most frequently cited disruptive behaviors were talking out of turn (23%), hostility towards peers/teacher (21%), and an inattentiveness/unwillingness to learn (27%). Friedman's (1995) report corroborated work by Brophy and colleagues (1988, 1992) on the nature of "problem" students. However, few scholars have been able to identify the paths by which disruptive, problem behaviors lead to emotional stress (Bibou-Nakou et al. 1999). In the following section we examine the relationship between problematic student behavior and teacher emotion regulation using data from two datasets to illustrate.

In their seminal study, Brophy and Rohrkemper (1988) identified twelve types of students teachers judged to be problematic and carefully described the types of behaviors students were observed to engage in and how teachers managed these behaviors in the classroom. Chang (2009) recently identified nine of these typologies in an effort to understand how teachers' emotion regulation contributed to predicting burnout. She found that teachers discrete appraisals of student disruptive behavior, particularly with regard to their judgments of goal incongruence and problem efficacy, predicted the intensity of their emotion experience. Intensity, in turn, predicted their deployment of emotion and problem focused coping strategies and feelings of burnout. How can teachers remain oriented towards problem-focused coping?

In addition to making discrete ratings of their perceptions, 589 novice teachers' (19% = male, 73% = female, 8% = not reported), sampled from across the state, described an interaction with a student(s) that lead to an intense, unpleasant emotion experience. In Table 6.3, we synthesized across the Brophy and colleagues (1988, 1992) frameworks, integrating data from Chang (2009). In the first column we report relative percentages of the frequency of student behaviors reported in the Chang (2009) sample. It is important to note the higher percentages of aggression reported in the Chang sample. In the second column, we identify the common characteristics of behavior across the two data sets providing an exemplary quote from teachers in column three. In columns four through seven, we identify the ways in which appraisals of student behavior can become causal ascriptions of student deficits, identify the dominant form of suppression and corresponding display rule, and highlight they ways in which teachers may engage in unproductively emotional labor. In the final column, we offer questions that may assist teachers in reappraising these specific interactions/situations.

It is important to note that we also attempted also to group the behaviors. The challenge for teachers working with students who exhibit the behaviors in the first five columns is to manage their feelings of hurt (Leary 2004) and alienation (see Table 6.1). This is because students exhibiting withdrawn, defiant, aggressive, or underachieving behaviors are likely to be sending teachers, either directly or indirectly, cues that reject the class, the content or the relationship. Dramatic behavioral changes, too, can be experienced by teachers as rejections of relationships initially perceived as productive.

> This week, students were given an assignment that required thoughtful response, focus, and longevity. From the very beginning of the assignment … students verbalized their unwillingness to do the required task. The overwhelming rejection of my lesson plan from a majority of my students put me on the defense and made me furious.

Teachers work hard to plan lessons and create opportunities for students to learn. When students communicate to teachers their resistance to the curriculum and/or the relationship teachers must face their own feelings of rejection. In order to engage in ethical caring, and to reengage with the student, teachers may need to seek additional information and reframe the resistance they perceive. In contrast, the primary challenge teachers face when interacting with students who engage in hyperactive and immature behaviors or who experience repeated failure with academic content is to manage their feelings of frustration and sympathy. As with hurt, these feelings are deactivating and can lead teachers to withdraw from the relationship (Newberry and Davis 2008).

Table 6.3 Deconstructing relationship challenges in terms of teacher deficit thinking, typical forms of suppression and corollary display rules, forms of unproductive labor, and suggestions for reappraisal?

Relationship challenges	Student behaviors[a]	Exemplary incident (Chang 2009)	Causal ascription	Emotional suppression	Display rule	Unproductive labor[b]	Re-appraising the situation
Shyness/ withdrawl (1%)	Quiet Avoids personal interaction	When I first met [her], she was not responsive in the classroom. She interacted with her peers but communicated very little with me… Everyday I found myself asking, "Is today the day we can't find her?" It was terribly stressful and emotionally taxing	It's his/her personality He/she is not interested in relationship with me	Alienated Sadness	Affinity Indifference	Deny the problem exists Ignore student Blame student for not engaging	In what contexts does this child feel comfortable to participate? What skills does this child need to interact?
Passive-aggression (7%)	Indirectly expresses opposition and resistance Intentionally moves slowly/stubborn	A sixth grade student was making noises and shouting random words during a lesson, so he was sent out of the classroom with work to complete. He returned to the classroom after escaping the office, tore, his work in half and said "I don't have to do this stupid work," and threw the papers across the room	He/she is a complainer He/she is manipulative He/she wants attention	Annoyance Frustration	Calm Disaffected Enthusiastic	Ignore Get peers to pressure or punish Convince without listening	Why might this child *not* value the activity? What is this student interested in? How might resistance reflect low efficacy?
Defiance (18%)	Directly resists authority Frequently expresses unpleasant emotions (verbal or non-verbal) Perceived power struggle	There is a constant power struggle between myself and one of my male students. I cannot remember the details of the incident because it happens so often, but an example behavior occurs when I tell him that he can't go to the restroom at the moment, but he decides to do it anyway. He'll say things like "I'm going to go because I don't care what you say" in front of the entire class. There is a lot of "you can't control me" type of comments	He/she is disrespectful He/she is a troublemaker He I she doesn't care about school	Discomfort Anger Frustration Embarrassed Guilt shame	Indifference Confidence Enthusiasm	De-emphasize their perspectives Ignore/isolate Get peers/parents to pressure or punish	How *is* this child trying to influence you? How can I give this child more autonomy? What norms is this child critiquing? How is this child feeling marginalized?
Overt hostility/ aggression toward peer or teacher (32%)	Directly, intensely intimidates and/or threatens peers or teachers Antagonizes Easily angered Hits, pushes, damages property	I had a student tell me he "hated me and wish I would die." I came to his class as a longterm substitute teacher in October and finished the school year out. Apparently, he also challenged the previous teacher and would run through the halls trying to escape school. He became physically violent with me by hitting and punching me in front of the class. I put him on a different behavior plan than the rest of his classmates and his behavior improved about 70% within a couple months	He/she is mean/a bully He/she is dangerous	Anger fear	Calm Confidence Empathy Frustration Disappointment	Vent own anger Up the "ante" by engaging in direct conflict with student	How does this child understand authority? Why does this child feel threatened? Need to dominate? How can their dominance be transformed into leadership?

(continued)

Table 6.3 (continued)

Relationship challenges	Student behaviors[a]	Exemplary incident (Chang 2009)	Causal ascription	Emotional suppression	Display rule	Unproductive labor[b]	Re-appraising the situation
Under-achievement (2%)	Indifferent to school Does the minimum/ enough to get-by Avoids personal responsibility for academics	One of my students, who is very bright, but manages to do just enough to get by didn't turn in their homework. Then the next thing I see is them texting on their cell phone. I was so frustrated. I couldn't understand how he could care so little about the class, then disrespect me and the class, by thinking he didn't need to pay any attention	He/she does not care about school He/she is lazy	Anger Frustration Disappointment	Hope Encouragement	Trying to convince without modifying	What does this student value? Why don't they want to work towards their potential? How can I make material interesting/valuable to him/her?
Dramatic behavioral change[c] (2%)	Behavioral patterns change dramatically	I have one student who is currently not doing well in Math. She refuses to do the work, continuously disrupts class by taunting the boys in, and is very disrespectful to me. This behavior is new and is completing a 180 from her behavior in the beginning of the year. I have tried talking to this girl one on one by taking her to lunch, but she still refuses to open up to me. I honestly do not know what to do	There is nothing I can do This situation is out of my control	Frustration Disappointment Hurt Alienation	Affinity Care	Disengage Personalize without reason Press student to reconnect without understanding the underlying reasons of change	How can I support this student? Who can help me with support this student? What can I do to learn about this child as a "new" person instead of expecting him/her to be the "same"?
Hyperactivity/ distractibility (11%)	Easily excitable Often out of seat Excessive and constant movement Unable to sustain attention	A student had a difficult time staying in his seat and had had this problem the entire school year. Every time I redirected the student and told him to get working or to return to his seat, my suggestions were met with despairing looks and frustrated sighs.... The behavior to date is still not much better, but a seat change closer to my desk has helped a bit. As much as I like this student, he exhausts me emotionally, mentally, and physically and he requires more "work" and monitoring than any other student in the class	He/she can't control his/her behaviors I can't control his/her behaviors	Annoyance Frustration Sympathy	Tolerance Confidence Be in "control"	Ignore/isolate Inhibit through proximity Trying to control the student's behavior	How can I control the context? What skills does this child need to learn to control his/her behavior?

Category	Student behaviors	Example	Teacher thoughts	Negative emotions	Positive emotions	Unproductive teacher coping	Questions
Immaturity/peer-rejection (10%)	Difficulty regulating emotions Difficulty with self-control, social skills Does not assume responsibility Ignored, excluded, picked, or teased by peers	I had a fifth grade female student who has difficulty getting along with her peers She was paired with a student and they shared two clipboards. Her partner had brought them from home to use for a project. This student assumed that she would get to keep the clipboard after the project and wrote her name on it. When the student asked for the clipboard back, she completely had a temper tantrum and threw it across the room, crying hysterically because "no one likes her" and she was told that she could use it. In front of the whole class I had to control this student who has difficulty fitting in with her peers… and she was having a temper tantrum… (Female, first-year elementary teacher)	He/she is odd He/she is immature He/she can't control his/her behavior He/she can't make friends	Annoyance Helpless	Empathy Affinity	Ignore and allow peer rejection Criticize student behavior Repeatedly punishing immaturity	What social skills do the students need to get along with others? What regulating skills can the students learn to control their emotions?
Academic failure/ discouraged (4%)	Procrastinate or avoid starting Gives up easily Non-completion Avoids participation	Student who had not done homework for 2 weeks, and then comes to me with the quiz and expects me to help him with it because he doesn't know how to do it (male, third-year middle school teacher) A student broke down into tears, cried out, and was stomping his/her feet because he/she felt that he/she couldn't spell a word correctly and therefore could not participate in writer's workshop (female, first-year elementary teacher)	He/she or slow learner He/she is not smart, not talented, not college bound He/she is too far behind	Disappointment Guilt Shame	Hope Optimism	Lower academic standards and expectations Provide encouraging feedback without making modifications	What are the students' strengths? In what ways does this student need a different type instruction? What strategies do they need to learn to self-regulate and to be successful?

[a]Student behaviors were drawn from Brophy and Rohrkemper (1988, p. 8–9)

[b]Forms of unproductive teacher coping were largely drawn from Brophy and McCaslin (1992, p. 29–30)

[c]It is also important to note, dramatic behavioral change was not cited as form of problematic behavior mentioned by Brophy and colleagues nor in Freeman (1995)

Shyness/Withdraw Students

Students who tend to be quiet and avoid personal interaction present a challenge for teachers to develop relationships (Brophy and Rohrkemper 1988). Teachers may find it difficult to connect with students because of their silence and may unintentionally neglect them. "[He] was pretty much aloof and he, um, didn't have attachment to really anyone except if you loved Nintendo games and talked about them 24 h a day, then he would love you too, but we never really had that relationship"(Newberry and Davis 2008, p. 12). Because of their shyness or withdrawn behavior, teachers may waive their opportunities to engage in some classroom activities and thus marginalize them. These responses are unproductive labor because students receive no benefit to their learning when they withdraw from classroom activities and relationships. Shyness, however, does not necessary mean the student is not engaged. To engage with withdrawn students, teachers may need to re-appraise their options for interacting with students: In what context does this child feel comfortable to participate? What skills does this child need to interact? Teachers may also need to re-think the nature of engagement, as vector. For example, in the quote above the boy is interested in engaging around the topic of Nintendo. To initiate a relationship with him, his teacher may need to reappraise the relevance on Nintendo (computer games) to her curriculum. Are there ways in which his interests, or the skills associated with gaming, could be integrated in the curriculum?

Passive-Aggression and Defiance

Students who act passive-aggressive express their opposition and resistance indirectly (Brophy and Rohrkemper 1988). They do not fight with peers or attack teachers, but they may show their aggression through resistant behaviors. For instance, complaining, tearing up their own work, or dragging their feet when accomplishing tasks. Teachers may not feel anger with these behaviors but instead annoyance, even frustration. Teachers may feel hurt when interacting with students who engage in passive-aggressive behaviors if they perceive the student to be rejecting their curriculum or something that is central to their identity. Similarly, students who act defiant openly resist authority and may engage in power struggles with their teachers (Brophy and McCaslin 1992). They overtly resist authority by rejecting cooperation in the classroom activities. They may directly show they disagree with the teachers (i.e. "It doesn't matter what you say."). hey may feel angry, frustrated, and unappreciated by acts of defiance that disrupt carefully planned lessons. To cope, with passive aggressive and defiant behaviors, teachers may counter with behavior designed to regain a sense of authority/control. However, Blackburn (2005) reminds us that student defiance can have a purpose. In her study of gay and lesbian adolescents, she found students often engaged in behavioral resistance as a way of challenging teachers to re-think social and intellectual norms to which they do not ascribe.

Teachers can re-appraise acts of passive aggression and defiance by seeking understanding about why students are seeking power and what, exactly, they are critiquing? Students may not necessarily be showing resistance to the teacher, as in individual, but to learning or curriculum itself. In many cases, student incidents of passive-aggression and defiance may reflect their limited skills to appropriately articulate their positions and influence teachers to provide rationales for their activities, to rethink curricular relevance, and to question the standards they endorse. In seeking to connect with these students, teacher may need to think about the ways in which classroom the norms, they take for granted, might be marginalizing some students.

Hostile-Aggression

Perhaps the most challenging relationship problem that teachers face is overt hostility or aggression aimed at themselves or another pupil (Brophy and Rohrkemper 1988). Teachers are often intimidated or threatened by student posturing (in which students intimidate verbally or nonverbally) and aggression (Bibou-Nakou et al. 1999) and may find aggression to be among the most depleting behavior to face. Teachers may feel angry, powerless and fearful when faced with hostile behavior. Repeated experiences of hostility may result in teachers making causal ascriptions of lack of parental education or aggression in the family (García and Guerra 2004). When teachers feel threatened by the students they may feel they need to respond with an intensity that matches the aggression. This might include directly confronting students with anger and defensive language or threatening consequences. However, this form of expressive labor may be unproductive as it may damage the relationships even more.

Therefore, as an immediate response to aggression it is likely that teachers will need self-control, suppressing their own emotion experience, and displaying stern calm and confidence while facing the hostile-aggressive behaviors. Once the incident has subsided, teachers need to think about the sources of student aggression that lie within their control. Teachers can re-appraisal the situations by reflecting on the following questions: How does this child understand authority? What are their goals? Can their goals be attained another way? If a child is trying to gain power through the aggressive behaviors, how can their dominance be transformed into leadership?

Underachievement

Where as hostility and defiance represent overt rejections of a relationship, underachieving behaviors often represent subtle, covert rejections of the values teachers identify with. Underachieving behaviors often involve expressing indifference towards school (Brophy and Rohrkemper 1988). Students may act as if they just want to "get by" with their school-work despite parents' and teachers' judgments that they could "do better" (Brophy and McCaslin 1992). Over time, teachers need to monitor causal ascriptions of the underachieving students as lazy. Teachers may feel frustrated if they perceive that these students are wasting their abilities. They may try to convince them of their abilities and to work harder without considering modifying the curriculum (Graham 1994; Prawat et al. 1983). However, trying to convince students without understanding their rationales for underachievement is likely to result in unproductive labor. In reappraising the situation, teachers need to seek to understand their students' perspectives on underachievement. To what extent might the student judge the curriculum irrelevant to their goals? Given their perspective, how can we help the students to understand the values behind the tasks? Or, how can we modify the curriculum to align with what the student values?

Dramatic Behavioral Change

Students who evidence dramatic change, often leave their teachers feeling disoriented, alienated, and hurt by the change. In our sample, the teachers expressed initial hope the students would return to their "old" ways of interacting and disappointment when they did not. They may have hoped to reconnect with the students using the strategies that formerly worked. However, teachers working with students who have changed dramatically need to re-appraise the situations seeking to understand the reasons underlying the change. Is the change a function of something that happened in the classroom, or, is it a function of something students are experiencing outside of school? Usually, the dramatic behavioral changes are caused by perceived and actual crises in families, friendships, or dating relationships. Teachers seeking to reconnect with the students may also need to find different ways of interacting with them instead of expecting the students to be the "same" person.

Hyperactivity/Distractibility

Students who are excessively active and do not stay still in the class often annoy their teachers because they disrupt the flow of lessons (Brophy and Rohrkemper 1988). Over time, teachers need to be aware of causal ascriptions that excessive movement are fulfilling students' need for attention or that the student is incapable of controlling their own behaviors. These ascriptions can lead teachers to ignore behaviors which students need help learning to control or actively trying harder to control them. Teachers can re-appraise the situations and understand how contextual factors contribute to student activity and inattention as well as what skills the students need to master in order to be able to manage their own behavior. For example, teachers might ask them selves, how can I modify the classroom activities to allow them to engage their attention and energy? Can I break down the tasks into smaller chunks so that it's easier to focus on the tasks? How can I help this child develop the skills he/she needs to learn to control his/her behavior?

Immaturity/Peer-Rejection

Students who have evidence of poor self-control and limited social skills or who deny responsibility are at risk for being ignored, excluded, or teased by their peers (Brophy and Rohrkemper 1988). They may feel annoyed, challenged, or helpless in the face of student immaturity, or dealing with the relational conflicts among peers. n part, this may reflect some uncertainty about their role in promoting positive peer relationships. They may ignore situations and allow the peer-rejection, insisting students need to work it out on their own. Teachers can re-appraise the situations by thinking: In what ways is peer victimization a cultural phenomenon in our classroom? How can I change that culture? What social and emotional skills do students need to get along with others?

Academic Failure/Low Achievement

Students who experienced academic failure avoid starting or give up easily in academics (Brophy and Rohrkemper 1988). Teachers often feel it is difficult to reach low achieving students and may feel disappointed, or guilty, when they see students give up easily in academics (Prawat et al. 1983). Over time, teachers need to become aware of causal ascriptions that low achieving students are not smart, not talented, not college bound, or simply too far behind. These causal ascriptions may lead to teachers lowering their academic standards and expectations. To re-appraise the situations, teachers may need to think about the students' strengths, the contextual factors that contribute to the students' failure, and what forms of additional support might help students experience success.

Understanding Burnout and Compassion Fatigue

Up to this point, we have largely focused on the role teachers' judgments may play in their emotion experiences and emotion regulation. Our intent was to empower teachers with options for reappraising challenging behaviors they may face in their classroom. Yet, much of the literature on teacher burnout (Chang in press) and compassion fatigue notes that teachers' sense of isolation contributes to their stress.

A critical element of adaptive coping with disruptive behavior involves knowing when to seek help. In the following section we introduce the concept of compassion fatigue and outline the ways in which challenging relationships can leave teachers feeling depleted.

As teaching inherently involves emotional labor, scholars from the field of social work argue even productive emotional labor puts teachers at risk to experience burnout and compassion fatigue (Chang in press; Kees and Lashwood 1996; Olivier and Venter 2003). Compassion is an emotion we experience when we perceive that we understand the depth of another's suffering combined with the desire to alleviate it (Figley 1995). Figley (1995) and Bride and Figley (2007) argue the experience of compassion is essential in social work because effective social workers need to be able to develop rapport and empathize with their clients. With that said, empathizing with children who are experiencing crises in their lives brings with it certain risks for teachers. "The use of empathy [however] is one of the particular reasons why trauma workers are especially vulnerable to compassion fatigue" (Figley 1995). Are teachers at risk for compassion fatigue? We believe so. Consider this quote by Perry (2003):

> All too often the adults are working in difficult, resource-limited situations. The children may present with a host of problems that can confuse or overwhelm their caregivers and treaters. The pain and helplessness of these children can be passed on to those around them.... trying to work in a complicated, frustrating and often 'insensitive' system, feeling helpless when trying to heal these children – all can make the adults working with these children vulnerable to develop their own emotional or behavioral problems. (Perry 2003, p. 2)

Kees and Lashwood (1996) argue school personnel, including pre-service and practicing teachers, are frontline trauma workers for children. This is because teachers, particularly those working in higher poverty areas, work with one of the most vulnerable population in our society. In their work to serve students, they may become exposed to the traumas children face: illness, divorce, death of a loved one, victimization, and despair. Chang (2009) found that of the 500 + reports, 9% were incidents involving relationships with a severely emotionally disturbed student. An additional 3% were referenced interactions with students who were in crisis, generally as a function of something happening in their home/family.

Kees and Lashwood (1996, p. 41; see also Finke 2006) point out that bonding and connecting with clients experiencing trauma can exhaust care providers and cause them to experience compassion fatigue as teachers, "move into an exhaustion stage, where energy reserves are depleted and fatigue, apathy, and listlessness [toward the child] sets in." Moreover, teachers largely work in isolation and experience systematic fragmentation throughout their organization and may lack the necessary resources, including time, to adequately care for themselves and their students. In a study of teacher stress and compassion fatigue, Olivier and Venter (2003) found that more than 20% of the teachers from the sample were suffering from severe stress and compassion fatigue with an additional 30% of the teachers reporting moderate levels of stress compassion fatigue. While high student–teacher ratios contributed to stress, the teachers in their study appeared to experience fatigue as a function of repeated attempts to motivate and discipline their students.

Compassion fatigue has been defined as a type of secondary trauma care providers experience when they are repeatedly exposed to the emotional byproducts of their client's trauma. It has become widely adopted throughout the fields of social work (Conrad and Kellar-Guenther 2006; DePanfilis 2006; Leon et al. 1999), counseling (Sprang et al. 2007; Tehrani 2007), and medicine (Huggard 2003; Sabo 2006) to describe the factors that lead to care providers withdrawing or detaching from specific clients and/or their career. Compassion fatigue happens when care providers, like teachers, "take on their client's problems leading to mental, physical, and emotional exhaustion and feelings of hopelessness and disconnection from others (p. 207)."

When compassion fatigue happens, there is a shift in the "positivity ratio" (p. 210) whereby teachers experience more unpleasant affect in relationships with students than pleasant. Affective indicators might include pervasive anger, sadness, anxiety and even depression. Tehrani (2007) argues compassion fatigue often results in challenging providers' assumptions, beliefs and values. Thus, in addition to questioning their effectiveness as "helpers," teachers experiencing compassion fatigue may experience doubts about their purpose as teachers.

Findings in the provider literature suggest compassion fatigue often goes unrecognized, is misattributed to burnout or is easily justified by the challenge a client poses. Burnout is a phenomenon that occurs when a previously engaged teacher disengages from his/her work as a function of prolonged job related stress or strain (Chang in press). Compassion fatigue, however, "can emerge suddenly and with little warning" (Figley 1995, p. 12). Though often associated with burnout, compassion fatigue, unlike burnout cannot be reversed by a vacation or a change in the work settings (Finke 2006). It can be the result of exposure to a single traumatic event; one intensely disruptive relationship. While "detachment does not protect doctors from burnout," detachment and withdrawal from specific clients tends to be the dominant coping mechanism. Because teachers experiencing compassion fatigue are more likely to be "stuck" focusing on what is not working in the relationship, compassion fatigue also represents a potential threat for both the wellness of the teachers and students. This is because providers experiencing compassion fatigue "may lose their objectivity and their ability to be helpful" (Conrad and Kellar-Guenther 2006, p. 1073).

Four major factors have been noted as contributing to compassion fatigue: poor self-care, previous unresolved trauma, inability or refusal to control work stressors, and a lack of satisfaction at work (Radley and Figley 2007, p. 207). Research in the field of social psychology suggests fatigue may be related to high levels of emotional suppression. In a series of studies, Baumeister and colleagues (2007) documented how engaging in denial and restraint led to feeling physically depleted. And, that depletion, in turn, led to an increased likelihood of engaging in the exact behavior we sought to control. Baumesteir et al. (2007, p. 351) define self-control as "the capacity for altering one's own responses, especially to bring them in line with standards such as ideals, value, morals, and social expectations, and to support the pursuit of long-term goals." They outline responses and processes that require self-control including managing emotions, responding with kindness to a partner's bad behavior, and interacting with demanding, difficult partners. The found episodes of exerting self-control leaves individual vulnerable to engaging in the exact behavior they tried to suppress. "We observed that self-control appeared vulnerable to deterioration over time from repeated exertions, resembling a muscle that gets tired" (Baumeister et al. 2007, p. 351).

Are there alternatives to emotional suppression? At the heart of Radley and Figley's (2007) model are the judgments care providers are making about their interactions with their clients; what they call "discernment and judgment" (p. 208). They define discernment as the judgments care providers make about the relationships, highlighting again the importance of teachers appraisals of the situation. What about when intermittent suppression is necessary? In over 40% of our incidents teachers reported incidents that probably required some level of suppression either in order to de-escalate student aggression or to manage their own feelings of anxiety. It is also important to remember that Radley and Figley (2007) included self-care is critical for combating the byproducts of engaging in self-control. Self-care strategies are similar to tension reduction strategies, in that they increase positive affect and physical, intellectual, and social resources, may enable teachers to regain task-focus on solving disruptive behavior problems.

Implications for Practice and Research

In this chapter we have tried to accomplish several tasks: (1) to review the literature on the power of supportive student–teacher relationships to enhance student motivation, learning, and achievement; (2) to review the literature on the connection among teachers' discrete appraisals and their emotion experiences; and finally (3) to review the literature on emotion regulation processes with a focus on applying them to understand the ways in which teachers can productively labor in the face of student disruptive behavior.

We hope teachers reading this piece will take away several messages. First, we encourage teachers to consider their implicit beliefs about relationships, particularly with students. In general, do you tend to hold destiny or growth beliefs about relationships? How might this affect your approach toward children who are different from you? How might this affect the way you interpret student resistance, withdrawal, or conflict? Consistent with a growth view of relationships, we view student-conflict, on some level, as natural byproduct of productive student teacher relationships. We hope teachers will be more thoughtful about what and whom they *care* about in their classroom and the judgments that underlie these feelings (Ben-Ze'ev 2000). Future research may want to examine the connection between teachers' implicit theories of relationships and their approach orientations (Newberry and Davis 2008), their overall relationship quality with students, their use of suppression, and their experiences of fatigue. How might teachers with growth beliefs vary systematically in terms of their emotion experience and emotion regulation strategies?

We encourage teachers to reflect on the ways in which they labor productively. Teachers need to become aware of the emotions they are experiencing and how often they experience emotional dissonance; that is feeling one thing and expressing another. We believe teachers should be thoughtful about their rationales for displaying an emotion that is not genuinely felt and that they should ultimately seek to be *task-focused* in their emotion regulation, seeking to resolve the underlying issues in the relationship that are the source of unpleasant emotions. We caution teachers to be wary of shallow or "faux" attempts to get to know students and to be conscious of the differences between productive reflection (E. Davis, 2006) on why they feel the way they do and unproductive venting.

One of our goals when envisioning this chapter was to extend the work by Brophy and colleagues on "problem" students. Children who engage in disruptive behavior need compassion from their teachers – including displays of affection to show they care (Oplatka 2007). Without it, these students are likely to become alienated from their teachers (Finn 1989) and feel less motivated in school (Corneilus-White 2008). We believe one of the challenges teachers face is to avoid *habitually* judging student behavior in an unproductive way. We hope Table 6.3 enables teachers to be more reflective about the ways in which judgments of problem behavior can not only lead to unpleasant emotions, but also lead to judging the students themselves. We believe teachers need to be vigilant about making judgments of student behavior from a deficit perspective and we hope we offered teachers alternate ways of judging incidents that maintains their focus on *the situation* as being the problem, not the child. We encourage teachers to ask, "What is causing this situation? How can I manage this problem?" We hope teachers will think about the underlying judgments they are making, and consider re-appraising the situation: Are you really out of control? Where can you find resources for managing this situation? Is it possible to *proactively* cope with this situation?

Finally, we believe teachers need to monitor for symptoms of compassion fatigue. Ultimately, teachers are on the frontline of service for children who face challenging circumstances in their community and family. "There is an assumption that the lessons of self-care will emerge; they are embedded in all practice, ethics, and field experience courses. There is no evidence, however, that this is the case" (Radley and Figley 2007, p. 212). We hope teachers experiencing compassion fatigue will *seek* the support they need, both within the school and in their personal life, to care for themselves so that they remain compassionate and continue to serve children in need. It is important to note that in their study of 1,121 mental health providers, Sprang et al. (2007) found increased awareness and training on the symptoms and sources of compassion fatigue improved clinician self-efficacy and, in turn, reduced their levels of compassion fatigue and burnout and enhanced overall satisfaction. Huggard (2003) too argues successful interventions to reduce compassion fatigue need to address sources of fatigue in care provider's personal and professional lives as well as within the organization. We hope scholars studying emotional labor in the classroom will begin integrating the concept of compassion fatigue into their models of student teacher relationships. Moreover we encourage scholars to move away from more simplistic notions of emotional labor towards understanding the tension teachers face between "being genuine" with their students about their own emotional experience and helping students learn to regulate their own emotions by appropriately modeling display rules.

References

Aaron A, Aaron EN, Smollan D (1992) Inclusion of other in the self scale and the structure of interpersonal closeness. J Pers Soc Psychol 63:596–612

Abraham R (1999) Negative affectivity: moderator or confound in emotional dissonance–outcome relationships? J Psychol 133:61–72

Babad E (1993) Teachers' differential behaviour. Educ Psychol Rev 5:347–376

Baker JA (1999) Teacher–students interaction in urban at-risk classrooms: differential behavior, relationship quality, and student satisfaction with school. Elem Sch J 100:57–70

Baker JA, Grant S, Morlock L (2008) The teacher–student relationship as a developmental context for children with internalizing or externalizing behavior problems. Sch Psychol Q 23:3–15

Baumeister RF, Vohs KD, Tice DM (2007) The strength model of self-control. Curr Dir Psychol Sci 16:351–355

Ben-Ze'ev A (2000) The subtlety of emotions. Cambridge, MA, MIT Press

Bibou-Nakou I, Stogiannidou A, Kiosseoglou G (1999) The relation between teacher burnout and teachers' attributions and practices regarding school behaviour problems. Sch Psychol Int 20:209–217

Blackburn M (2005) Talking together for a change: examining positioning between teachers and queer youth. In: Vadeboncoeuru JA, Patel L (eds) Re/constructing "the adolescent": sign, symbol, and body. Peter Lang, New York, pp 249–270

Bride BB, Figley CR (2007) The fatigue of compassionate social workers: an introduction to the special issue on compassion fatigue. J Clin Soc Work 35:151–153

Brophy J, McCaslin M (1992) Teachers' reports of how they perceive and cope with problem students. Elem Sch J 93:3

Brophy J, Rohrkemper M (1988) The classroom strategy study: summary report of general findings. Institute for Research on Teaching, East Lansing, MI (ERIC Document Reproduction Service No. ED 295759)

Brown DF (2004) Urban teachers' professed classroom management strategies: reflections of culturally responsive teaching. Urban Educ 39:266–289

Callahan JL, McCollum EE (2002) Obscured variability: the distinction betwee emotion work and emotional labor. In: Ashkanasy NM, Zerbe EJ, Hartel CE (eds) Managing emotion in the workplace. M. E. Sharpe, Armonk, NY, pp 219–231

Chang M-L (2009) Teacher emotion management in the classroom: appraisals, regulation, and coping with emotions. Unpublished Dissertation

Chang, M-L (2009) An appraisal perspective of teacher burnout: examining the emotional work of teachers. Educ Psychol Rev

Connell J, Wellborn J (1991) Competence, autonomy, and relatedness: a motivational analysis of self-system processes. In: Gunnar M, Sroufe LA (eds) Self-processes and development. Lawrence Erlbaum Associates, Hillsdale, NJ

Conrad D, Kellar-Guenther Y (2006) Compassion fatigue, burnout, and compassion satisfaction among Colorado child protection workers. Child Abuse Negl 30:1071–1080

Corneilus-White J (2008) Learner-centered student–teacher relationships are effective: a meta-analysis. Rev Educ Res 77:113–143

Davis HA (2003) Conceptualizing the role of student–teacher relationships on children's social and cognitive development. Educ Psychol 38:207–234

Davis EA (2006) Characterizing productive reflection among pre-service elementary teachers. Teach Teach Educ 22:281–301

Davis HA (2006) Exploring the contexts of relationship quality between middle school students and teachers. Elem Sch J Special Issue Interpersonal Contexts of Motivation and Learning 106:193–223

Davis KS, Dupper DR (2004) Student–teacher relationships: an overlooked factor in school dropout. J Hum Behav Soc Environ 9:179–193

Davis HA, Lease AM (2007) Perceived organizational structure for teacher liking: the role of peers' perceptions of teacher liking in teacher–student relationship quality, motivation, and achievement. Soc Psychol Educ Int J 10:403–427

Davis HA, DiStefano C, Schutz PA (2008) Identifying patterns of appraising tests in first year college students: implications for anxiety and emotion regulation during test taking. J Educ Psychol 100(4):942–960

Davis HA, Chang, M-L, Andrzejewski CE, Poirier RR (2009) Examining smaller learning community reform (SLC) from the perspective of the learner-centered psychological principles. J Educ Change

DePanfilis D (2006) Compassion fatigue, burnout, and compassion satisfaction: implications for retention of workers. Child Abuse Negl 30:1067–1069

DeVries R, Zan B (1996) A constructivist perspective on the role of the socio-moral atmosphere in promoting children's development. In: Fosnot CT (ed) Constructivism: theory, perspectives, and practice. Teachers College Press, New York, pp 103–119

Dweck C (1996) Implicit theories as organizers of goals and behavior. In: Gollwitzer PM, Bargh JA (eds) The psychology of action: linking cognition and motivation to behavior. Guilford, New York, pp 60–90

Eisenberg N (2000) Empathy *and sympathy.* In: Lewis M, Haviland-Jones JM (eds) Handbook of emotions. Guilford, NY

Figley C (1995) Compassion fatigue as secondary traumatic stress disorder: an overview. In: Figley CR (ed) Compassion fatigue: secondary traumatic stress disorder in helpers. Brunner Mazel, New York, pp 82–101

Finke L (2006) The bond and burden of caring. J Child Adolesc Psychiatr Nurs 19:1–2

Finn JD (1989) Withdrawing from school. Rev Educ Res 59:117–142

Finn JD (1993) School engagement and student at risk. State University, US Department of Education, National Center for Educational Statistics, Buffalo, NY

Folkman S, Lazarus RS (1988) Coping as a mediator of emotion. J Pers Soc Psychol 54:466–475

Ford DY, Grantham TC (2003) Providing access for culturally diverse gifted students: from deficit to dynamic thinking. Theory Pract 42:217–225

Friedman IA (1995) Student behavior patterns contributing to teacher burnout. J Educ Res 88:281–289

García SB, Guerra PL (2004) Deconstructing deficit thinking. Educ Urban Soc 36:150–168

Glomb TM, Tews MJ (2004) Emotional labour: a conceptualization and scale development. J Vocat Behav 64:1–23

Goldstein L (1999) The relational zone: the role of caring relationships in the co-construction of the mind. Am Educ Res J 36:647–673

Graham S (1994) Motivation in African Americans. Rev Educ Res 64:55–118

Greenglass ER (2002) Proactive coping and quality of life management. In: Frydenberg E (ed) Beyond coping: meeting goals, visions, and challenges. Oxford, NY

Hargreaves A (1994) Changing teachers, changing times: teacher's work and culture in the post modern age. Cassell, London

Hargreaves A (1998) The emotional practice of teaching. Teach Teach Educ 14:835–854

Hargreaves A (2000) Mixed emotions: teachers' perceptions of their interactions with students. Teach Teach Educ 16:811–826

Hartup WW (1989) Social relationship and their developmental significance. Am Psychol 44:120–126

Hochschild AR (1979) Emotion work, feeling rules, and social structure. Am J Sociol 85:551–575

Hochschild AR (1983) The managed heart: commercialization of human feeling. University of California Press, Berkeley

Howes C, Hamilton CE, Philipsen LC (1998) Stability and continuity of child-caregiver and child-peer relationships. Child Dev 69:418–426

Hoy AW, Davis HA, Pape S (2006) Handbook of educational psychology. In: Alexander PA, Winne PH (eds) Teacher knowledge, beliefs, and thinking, 2nd edn. Simon & Schuster/Macmillan, New York

Huggard P (2003) Compassion fatigue: how much can I give? Med Educ 37:163–164

Hunter FT (1984) Socializing procedures in parent–child and friendship relations during adolescence. Dev Psychol 20:1092–1099

Irving J, Fraser J (1998) Warm demanders. Educ Week 17:56

Kees NL, Lashwood PA (1996) Compassion fatigue and school personnel: remaining open to the affective needs of students. Educ Horizons 75:41

Knee CR, Patrick H, Lonsbary C (2003) Implicit theories of relationships: orientations toward evaluation and cultivation. Pers Soc Psychol 7:41–55

Kozel S, Davis HA (2009) Teacher efficacy. In: Anderman E, Anderman L (eds) Psychology of classroom learning: an encyclopedia (PCL). Thompson, Farmington Hills, MI

Lazarus RS (1991) Progress on a cognitive-motivational-relational theory of emotion. Am Psychol 46:819–834

Lazarus RS (2001) Relational meaning and discrete emotions. In: Scherer KR, Schorr A, Johnstone T (eds) Appraisal processes in emotion. Oxford University Press, New York

Lazarus RS (2006) Emotions and interpersonal relationships: toward a person-centered conceptualization of emotions and coping. J Pers 74:9–46

Lazarus RS, Folkman S (1984) Stress, appraisal, and coping. Springer, New York

Leary MR (2004) Digging deeper: the fundamental nature of "self-conscious" emotions. Psychol Inq 15:129–131

Leon AM, Altholz JAS, Dziegielewski SF (1999) Compassion fatigue: considerations for working with the elderly. J Gerontol Soc Work 32:43–62

Linnenbrink EA (2007) The role of affect in student learning: a multi-dimensional approach to considering the interaction of affect, motivation, and engagement. In: Schutz PA, Pekrun R (eds) Emotion in education. Academic, San Diego, pp 107–124

Mantzicopoulos P (2005) Conflictual relationships between kindergarten children and their teachers: associations with child and classroom context variables. J Sch Psychol 43:425–442

Markus HR, Kitayama S (1994) The cultural construction of self and emotion: implications for social behavior. In: Kitayama S, Markus HR (eds) Emotion and culture: empirical studies of mutual influence. American Psychological Association Press, Washington, DC

Maslach C, Leiter MP (1999) Teacher burnout: a research agenda. In: Vandenberghe R, Huberman AM (eds) Understanding and preventing teacher burnout: a sourcebook of international research and practice. Cambridge University Press, Cambridge, pp 295–303

Monroe CR, Obidah JE (2004) The influence of cultural synchronization on a teacher's perceptions of disruption. J Teach Educ 55:256–268

Morganett L (2001) Good teacher–student relationships: a key element in classroom motivation and management. Education 112:260–265

Morris JA, Feldman DC (1997) Managing emotions in the work place. J Managerial Issues 9:257–274

Muller C, Katz S, Dance L (1999) Investing in teaching and learning. Dynamics of the teacher–student relationship from each perspective. Urban Educ 34:292–337

Newberry M, Davis HA (2008) The role of elementary teachers' conceptions of closeness to students on their differential behavior in the classroom. Teach Teach Educ 24:1965–1985

Noddings N (1995) Care and moral education. In: Kohli W (ed) Critical conversations in philosophy of education. Routledge, New York

Olivier MAJ, Venter DJL (2003) The extent and causes of stress in teachers in the Georgia region. S Afr J Educ 23:186–192

Oplatka I (2007) Managing emotions in teaching: toward an understanding of emotion displays and caring as nonprescribed role elements. Teach Coll Record 109:1374–1400

Pekrun R, Frenzel AC, Goetz T, Perry R (2007) The control-value theory of achievement emotions: an integrative approach to emotions in education. In: Schutz PA, Pekrun R (eds) Emotion in education. Elsevier, Amsterdam, pp 13–36

Perry BD (2003) The cost of caring: Secondary traumatic stress and the impact of working with high-risk children and families. /The Child Trauma Academy/, download at www.ChildTrauma.org.

Pianta RC, Steinberg MS, Rollins LB (1995) The first two years of school: teacher–child relationships and deflections in children's classroom adjustment. Dev Psychopathol 7:295–312

Prawat RS, Byers JL, Anderson AH (1983) An attributional analysis of teachers' affective reactions to student success and failure. Am Educ Res J 20:137–152

Radley M, Figley C (2007) The social psychology of compassion. Clin Soc Work J 35:207–214

Roseman IJ (2001) A model of appraisal in the emotion system: integrating theory, research, and applications. In: Scherer KR, Schorr A, Johnstone T (eds) Appraisal processes in emotion. Oxford University Press, New York

Roseman IJ, Smith CA (2001) Appraisal theory: overview, assumptions, varieties, controversies. In: Scherer KR, Schorr A, Johnstone T (eds) Appraisal processes in emotion. Oxford University Press, New York

Sabo BM (2006) Compassion fatigue and nursing work: can we accurately capture the consequences of caring work? Int J Nurs Pract 12:136–142

Schutz PA, Davis HA (2000) Emotions during self-regulation: the regulation of emotions during test taking. Educ Psychol 35:243–256

Schutz PA, Crowder KC, White VE (2001) The development of a goal to become a teacher. J Educ Psychol 93:299–308

Schutz PA, DiStefano C, Benson J, Davis HA (2004) The emotion regulation during test taking scale. Anxiety Stress Coping 17:253–259

Skinner EA, Belmont MJ (1993) Motivation in the classroom: reciprocal effects of teacher behavior and student engagement across the school year. J Educ Psychol 85:571–581

Smith CA (1991) The self, appraisal, and coping. In: Snyder CR, Forsythe DR (eds) Handbook of social and clinical psychology: the health perspective. Pergamon, Elmsford, NY, pp 116–137

Smith CA, Lazarus RS (1990) Emotion and adaptation. In: Pervin LA (ed) Handbook of personality: theory and research. Guilford, New York, pp 609–637

Smyth J, Hattam R (2002) Early school leaving and the cultural geography of high schools. Br Educ Res J 28:375–399

Sprang G, Clark JJ, Whitt-Woosley A (2007) Compassion fatigue, compassion satisfaction, and burnout: factors impacting a professional's quality of life. J Loss Trauma 12:259–280

Tehrani N (2007) The cost of caring-the impact of secondary trauma on assumptions, values and beliefs. Couns Psychol Q 20:325–339

Tharpe RG, Estrada P, Dalton SS, Yamauchi LA (2000) Activity theory in the classroom. In: Tharpe RG et al (eds) Teaching transformed; achieving excellence, fairness, inclusion and harmony. Westview Press, Boulder, CO

Thompson RA (1990) Emotion and self-regulation. In: Thompson RA (ed) Socioemotional development, vol 36, Nebraska Symposium on Motivation. University of Nebraska Press, Lincoln, pp 367–467

Thompson RA (1991) Emotional regulation and emotional development. Educ Psychol Rev 3:269–307

Vygotsky LS (1978) Mind in society: the development of higher psychological processes. Blackwell, Cambridge, MA

Wang SS, Treat TA, Brownell KD (2008) Cognitive processing about classroom-relevant contexts: teachers' attention to and utilization of girls' body size, attractiveness, and facial affect. J Educ Psychol 100:473–489

Weiner B (2000) Intrapersonal and interpersonal theories of motivation from an attributional perspective. Educ Psychol Rev 12:1–14

Weiner B (2007) Examining emotional diversity in the classroom: an attribution theories considers moral emotions. In: Schutz PA, Pekrun R (eds) Emotion in education. Academic, Amsterdam, pp 75–88

Wertsch JV (1991) Voices of the mind: a sociocultural approach to mediated action. Harvard University Press, Cambridge, MA

Wubbels Th, Brekelmans M, den Brok P, van Tartwijk J (2006) An interpersonal perspective on classroom management in secondary classrooms in the Netherlands. In: Evertson C, Weinstein C (eds) Handbook of classroom management: research, practice and contemporary issues. Lawrence Erlbaum Associates, New York, pp 1161–1191

Chapter 7
Antecedents and Effects of Teachers' Emotional Experiences: An Integrated Perspective and Empirical Test

Anne C. Frenzel, Thomas Goetz, Elizabeth J. Stephens, and Barbara Jacob

Abstract In this chapter we focus on teacher emotions resulting from appraisals of success or failure (i.e., teachers' achievement emotions) with respect to achieving instructional goals. We present our theoretical assumptions and empirical findings regarding the antecedents and effects of achievement emotions more generally, and specify those for the context of teaching. Assuming that teachers' emotions impact their instructional behaviour and are affected by their appraisals regarding succeeding or failing during instruction, we propose a model depicting the interplay between teachers' emotions, their instructional behavior, and student outcomes. We present results from two quantitative studies testing assumptions brought forward by the model.

Keywords Classroom goals • Appraisals • Control-value theory

Emotions matter – this is the conviction and overarching theme of all of the contributions to this volume. First of all, emotions are considered important components of overall psychological well-being (Schimmack 2008), but also of psychological suffering (Posner et al. 2005). As such, emotions have been identified as important determinants of teacher burnout, early drop-out, and retirement rates in the teaching profession (Hughes 2001; Ingersoll 2002). From this perspective, teacher emotions necessitate empirical attention for the sake of teachers' well-being and health, and for political reasons, for example, in terms of societal costs involved in early retirement and health care for overtaxed teachers. Above and beyond the importance of emotions for teachers' own lives, emotions also serve as important factors guiding teachers' instructional behaviors. Teacher emotions thus have considerable implications for student learning, school climate, and the overall quality of education. From this perspective, teacher emotions demand empirical attention for the sake of student outcomes. This latter perspective predominantly guides our approach to research investigating teacher emotions. We seek to explore teacher emotions to

A.C. Frenzel (✉)
Department of Psychology, University of Munich, Munich, Germany
e-mail: frenzel@psy.lmu.de

P.A. Schutz and M. Zembylas (eds.), *Advances in Teacher Emotion Research:*
The Impact on Teachers' Lives,
DOI 10.1007/978-1-4419-0564-2_7, © Springer Science+Business Media, LLC 2009

better understand classroom learning by linking teacher emotions, teaching behaviors, and student outcomes, which we consider to be more intricately intertwined than previously recognized in the literature on teacher emotions.

In the present contribution, we focus on the crucial teacher task of classroom instruction. In addition, we look at teacher emotions from an achievement perspective where the pursuit of success and avoidance of failure are central processes. That is, we focus on teachers' emotions resulting from their judgments of perceived success or failure with respect to their classroom goals (cf., Heckhausen 1989; Pekrun, 2000; 2006; Pekrun et al. 2007). We further focus on three important emotions, namely enjoyment, anger, and anxiety. These three emotions have been shown to be experienced most frequently in everyday life (Scherer et al. 2004) and there is preliminary empirical evidence that these three emotions play a prominent role in teaching (Sutton 2007; Sutton and Wheatley 2003).

In addressing teachers' enjoyment, anxiety, and anger related to classroom teaching, we divided the present chapter into two parts. To begin, we discuss our theoretical understanding of the antecedents and effects of emotional experiences and present corresponding empirical findings. In presenting the potential antecedents and effects of emotions, we first highlight the respective theoretical frameworks and then relate them to existing findings regarding teachers and the educational context. Integrating these perspectives on emotions in the classroom, we proffer a model of reciprocal causation between teacher emotions, teaching behaviors, and student outcomes. In the second part of the chapter, we present our own empirical data testing some of the assumptions of the proposed model and discuss related conclusions and implications for future research.

Antecedents of Teacher Emotions

An Appraisal – Theoretical Approach

Human emotions are initiated and modulated in a number of different ways. For some emotions, there likely is an evolutionarily transmitted base (e.g., Cosmides and Tooby 2000), suggesting that emotional reactions to certain situations and events have proven adaptive over time. Similarly, focusing on immediate effects between situations and emotions, neurophysiological evidence implies that emotions may be the result of early conditioning which establishes direct links between situations, perceptions, and subcortical limbic emotional reactions (LeDoux 1995). However, it has also been argued that no direct link exists between situations and events and subsequent emotional experiences, rather these situations and events first have to be cognitively appraised in order to evoke specific emotions (Clore 1994; Lazarus 1991; Roseman 2001; Roseman and Smith 2001; Scherer et al. this volume). Our assumptions on the antecedents of emotional experiences is largely grounded in such an appraisal-theoretical approach to emotions.

Within the appraisal-theoretical framework, various appraisals have been proposed as potential antecedents of emotions. Among others, the most frequently referenced appraisals include *goal congruence* (also referred to as valence), *goal conduciveness*, *coping potential* (also referred to as control), *accountability* (also referred to as agency or locus of causation), and *goal significance* (e.g., Ellsworth and Scherer 2003; Roseman 2001; Scherer 2001).

Upon examination of this list of appraisals, it is apparent that goals play an important role in the appraisal process. If a situation is appraised as *congruent with* and *conducive to the attainment of one's goals*, one will tend to experience a pleasant emotion; if a situation or event is perceived as inconsistent with or an impediment to the attainment of one's goals, an unpleasant emotion will more likely be experienced.

The dimensions of coping potential and accountability play an important role in further specifying which discrete (as opposed to general pleasant vs. unpleasant) emotions are experienced. The appraisal of *coping potential* corresponds with the judgment of whether one has the personal resources to reach a desired goal or to avoid the non-attainment of a desired goal. This appraisal is particularly relevant for the formation of anxiety which is typically felt in the case of prospective goal-incongruence paired with low coping potential (Lazarus and Folkman 1984; Scherer 1993; Smith and Lazarus 1993).

The appraisal of *accountability* corresponds with a judgment regarding the assignment of responsibility to oneself or to another person should a desired goal be blocked. This appraisal is of particular relevance for the formation of anger, which is typically experienced in the case of goal-incongruence or goal-inconduciveness paired with other-accountability (Averill 1983; Kuppens et al. 2003; Parkinson 1999; Smith and Lazarus 1993; Weiner 2007).

Finally, regarding the appraisal dimension of *goal significance*, appraisal theory holds that the intensity of any emotional experience will be enhanced if a situation is appraised as significant or relevant to oneself. Situations and events relevant to us, and our attainment of subjectively important goals, involve us emotionally. In contrast, situations and events irrelevant to us "leave us cold", that is, we do not react emotionally.

Classroom Goals and Their Appraisals as Antecedents of Teacher Emotions

As stated above, our focus is on teachers' achievement emotions. In an achievement context, standards against which success and failure can be measured and corresponding goals that can be strived for are central themes; consequently, subjective appraisals of success (goal congruent) and failure (goal incongruent) can be considered crucial for the emergence of achievement emotions (Pekrun, 2000; 2006;

Pekrun, Frenzel et al. 2007; Weiner, 1985; 1986).[1] That is, to determine which emotions a person experiences in an achievement context, one needs to identify goals and resulting standards against which that person measures his or her success and failure.

For students, such achievement standards seem to be relatively well-defined, in addition students receive frequent formal assessments that serve as feedback regarding the degree to which they have reached these standards (e.g., grades). For teachers, however, achievement standards seem to be less evident and frequent or formal assessments and feedback are mostly lacking. This is particularly true for the German school system as opposed to the US system where recent policy has set relatively clear teacher standards in terms of student achievement on standardized tests (Peterson and West 2003). Therefore, we argue that defining success and failure for teachers is not so obvious. In order to be able to posit clear hypotheses about the antecedents and outcomes of teachers' emotions, we thus need to identify teaching *ideals*, that is, teachers' overarching visions of what they desire to accomplish through instruction, and infer the resulting *goals* (implying standards) teachers use to gauge their own success or failure.

We propose that teachers strive for three overarching instructional ideals. Specifically, via their instruction, teachers aspire to influence students' (a) cognitive growth (i.e., the acquisition of declarative and procedural knowledge in academic domains), (b) motivation (i.e. topic interest, the willingness to invest academic effort, self-regulation and goal setting), and (c) social-emotional skills (i.e., empathy and thoughtfulness towards classmates and the teacher, and student compliance with classroom and school rules, i.e., discipline). Such a threefold conceptualization of higher-order instructional ideals that define successful teaching is in line with existing models of teaching effectiveness (Seidel and Shavelson 2007; Zins et al. 2004). It also corresponds with Tschannen-Moran and Hoy's (2001) threefold conceptualization of teaching efficacy (comprising efficacy for instruction, student involvement, and classroom management).

---

[1] More specifically, Pekrun suggests in his control-value theory of achievement emotions that control and value appraisals are central antecedents of emotional experiences in the context of learning and achievement (Pekrun, 2000; 2006; Pekrun, Frenzel et al., 2007). In this theory, control appraisals are defined as the amount of perceived control one has over achievement activities and outcomes (i.e., success and failure), which closely corresponds to what we call coping potential in the present contribution. Value appraisals, according to Pekrun's theory, pertain to judgments of the valence of an achievement outcome (success=positive; failure=negative), and to the personal relevance of such an outcome in a certain situation. When mapping Pekrun's appraisal terms onto the terms used in this contribution, Pekrun's term "value appraisals" imply both the aspect of goal congruence (success=goal congruent; failure=goal incongruent) and the aspect of goal significance (personal relevance of both success and failure). Despite the alternate vocabulary used in the present context, Pekrun's theory forms a central basis for our considerations regarding the formation of teachers' emotions since we focus on teachers' achievement emotions in the present contribution.

We further propose that teachers' ideals precipitate specific behavioral goals related to student achievement behavior, motivation, and social-emotional behavior. A key appraisal then involves teachers continually gauging the correspondence between these specific behavioral goals and the perceived behaviors students display within the classroom. We postulate that important appraisal dimensions for the correspondence between teachers' goals and actual student behaviors concern goal consistency, goal conduciveness, accountability, coping potential, and goal significance. For example, one specific behavioral goal based on the overarching ideal of cognitive growth may be that all students should be able to correctly set up and solve a specific set of subtraction word problems. If a student cannot set up and solve the word problems by the end of the corresponding mathematics unit, a teacher may likely appraise this behavior as goal-inconsistent. Another example, based on the overarching ideal of social-emotional skills, may be that students should remain silent while the teacher is talking. If a student is disruptive, the teacher likely appraises this behavior as both inconsistent with the goal of adequate social skills, as well as an impediment to the goal of cognitive growth (both for the disruptive student and for the class as a whole). Furthermore, the teacher will appraise who (e.g., teacher or student) was accountable for these goal-inconsistencies and goal-impediments, and will ask himself whether he has the coping potential to overcome these situations (i.e. whether he is capable of enabling the student to correctly set up and solve these types of word problems or whether he is capable of getting the students to follow classroom rules, respectively).

These appraisals of student behavior relative to classroom goals are considered to be predictive of subsequent teacher emotions. Appraisals of goal congruence and goal conduciveness should influence the pleasantness of a teacher's emotional experience. For example, a teacher should experience enjoyment if student behaviors are in line with the specific behavioral goals set for a particular lesson or unit. Furthermore, the appraisal dimensions of accountability and coping potential should be particularly important in predicting anxiety and anger. That is, teachers' emotional experiences should be dominated by *anxiety* when they doubt their ability to attain certain classroom goals through their own effort or competence, and thus feel incapable of avoiding the non-attainment of these goals (Lazarus and Folkman 1984; Scherer 1993; Smith and Lazarus 1993). Conversely, teachers should react with *anger* if a desired goal is not realized and non-attainment is appraised as other-caused (Averill 1983; Kuppens et al. 2003; Parkinson 1999; Smith and Lazarus 1993; Weiner 2007).

Finally, any teacher emotion should be affected by the appraisal of goal significance. That is, achieved or unachieved goals equated with more personal significance should result in more intense (both pleasant and unpleasant) emotional reactions. For example, a teacher should experience more intense enjoyment upon a students' success at setting up and solving a specific equation, inasmuch as he attaches personal relevance to the students' ability to solve this problem. Conversely, he should react with more anxiety and anger, inasmuch as he attaches personal relevance to a goal that is not attained.

Empirical Evidence of the Link Between Appraisals and Teacher Emotions

There are scattered empirical findings supporting our assumptions concerning the relation between teachers' attainment of behavioral goals for the classroom and teachers' emotional experiences. Interview studies support the notion that the perception of student cognitive gains causes joy in teachers. In his synopsis of interviews with a sample of 60 teachers focusing on emotions, Hargreaves (2000) quotes teachers who reported sources of pleasant emotions as, "being perceptive enough to identify a student with a learning disability and then successfully modifying their learning for them", "making a kindergarten child stick at learning to write his name", or "motivating an insecure less able child to achieve in mathematics" (all p. 818). In cases where learning gains are not made and this is appraised as caused by intentional or at least potentially changeable behavior on the part of the students, there is evidence that teachers react with anger. In this context, an important theoretical framework and rich empirical resource is Weiner's work on attribution-dependent arousal of anger and pity (Weiner 1986). Within the educational context, Graham and Weiner (1986) and Reyna and Weiner (2001) have shown that teachers' anger is caused by an attribution of students' academic failures to insufficient effort on the part of the students.

In line with our assumption that the perception of high motivational engagement among students should contribute to teachers' experience of pleasant emotions, Zembylas (2002) quotes a teacher saying, "What really makes an experience so wonderful is how fascinating it is to see kids being engaged" (p. 92). With respect to the goal of student social-emotional skills, there is also evidence that teachers' pleasant emotions are fueled by student compliance with classroom rules. For example, Winograd (2003) describes in his diary study on the emotional experiences of teaching: "When the room is quiet and I have the impression of attentiveness, I feel (...) at ease and able to use humor" (p. 1656). Typically, students are made accountable for low levels of rule compliance, which is why misbehavior constitutes one of the most frequently mentioned sources of teacher anger. Consistent with our assumptions regarding the arousal of anger, Sutton (2007) summarized in her comprehensive work on teacher frustration and anger that teachers "most commonly get angry and frustrated when their academic goals are blocked by the misbehavior, inattention, or lack of motivation of students" (p. 263).

In sum, these findings provide empirical support for our assumptions regarding appraisals related to the achievement of classroom goals and teachers' emotions. However, we lack research that has investigated the size of relationships between student behaviors as perceived by teachers on the one hand, and teacher emotions, on the other. Overall, little is known regarding the potential predictors of teacher emotions (Schutz et al., this volume).

Consequences of Teacher Emotions: Influences of Emotions on Cognition and Behavior

Influences of Emotions on Cognition and Behavior

Emotions strongly impact our behaviors and thoughts (e.g., Dagleish and Power 1999). These behavioral and cognitive consequences of emotions likely have an evolutionary basis: According to evolution theorists, emotions serve the purpose of initiating actions which over time have proven to be adaptive (i.e., they increase chances of survival, Cosmides and Tooby 2000; Dillard 1998). In that respect, emotions can be defined as reactions to perceived environmental conditions that prepare and mobilize us to manage situations in an adaptive manner (Frijda 1986; Lazarus 1991). Specifically, unpleasant emotions are typically related to avoidance behaviors, whereas pleasant emotions tend to be related to approach tendencies which allow for exploration of the unknown.

Going beyond the mere association between positive emotions and general approach tendencies, Fredrickson (2001) postulates in her broaden-and-build theory of positive emotions that the experience of joy broadens one's action repertoire. According to her theory, positive emotions not only indicate success, but they also produce or promote success by broadening thinking and easing the generation of ideas in the presence of obstacles.

Apart from the initiation of action (approach vs. avoid), emotions also influence information processing. Findings from mood research show that positive mood is closely linked to creative, holistic ways of thinking, while negative mood is accompanied by detail-oriented and rigid ways of thinking (Clore et al. 1994; Isen 2008; Mitchell and Phillips 2007; Sinclair and Mark 1992).

Finally, emotions have a deeply rooted communicative function (Anderson and Guerrero 1998; Lazarus 1991). They are related to characteristic facial features and postures that convey messages to interaction partners. For example, joyful expressions tend to serve as an invitation for interaction. While experiencing anxiety, one may express inferiority, whereas expressions associated with anger may signify a willingness to attack. Due to these expressive components of emotions, emotions can have strong effects not only on the actors, but also on their interaction partners.

Teacher Emotions and their Effects on Teaching Behavior

Drawing on the cognitive and behavioral effects of emotions, we suggest that the emotions teachers experience have effects on their teaching behavior. Due to the described emotionally induced action tendencies, *recurrent* pleasant and unpleasant emotional experiences during teaching should influence teachers' behavioral tendencies pertaining to teaching. Depending on the pleasantness of their emotions, teacher behaviors should either be characterized by general approach or avoidance tendencies. In addition, the broadening effects of pleasant emotions on thinking and information processing should provide teachers who recurrently experience pleasant emotions with a broad, easily retrievable repertoire of teaching strategies. On the one hand, this might lead to a high level of creativity and variation during lessons. On the other hand, these teachers might be able to react flexibly to concrete situations during lessons, even in the face of obstacles or difficulties. However, teachers who recurrently experience anxiety and anger in the classroom might have problems deviating from previously planned lesson scripts and might be prone to predominantly use rigid teaching strategies, including repetitive exercises.

Finally, teacher emotions may also influence the quality of teaching as a result of the expressive consequences of emotions, particularly because of their influences on enthusiasm expressed during teaching. A teaching approach characterized by enthusiasm (i.e. vivid gesture, varied tone, maintaining eye contact, humor and vivid examples) has been shown to be highly effective (Babad 2007; Gage and Berliner 1998). While it can be assumed that teachers who experience joy during teaching will exhibit increased enthusiasm, the emotions of anxiety and anger should be incompatible with an enthusiastic teaching approach.

Empirical Evidence of the Link Between Teacher Emotions and Behavior

There is a conspicuous lack of empirical findings regarding possible effects of teachers' emotional experiences on their teaching behaviors. Exceptions are Sutton (2004; 2007) who reports that teachers convey their belief that the expression of pleasant emotions makes their teaching more effective, and at the same time, that teachers are convinced that reducing their unpleasant emotions aides their effectiveness. Similarly, Witcher, Onwuegbuzie, and Minor (2001) report that American teacher candidates rated enthusiasm for and enjoyment of the profession as highly important factors influencing instructional quality. One potential shortcoming of these studies is that they only explored subjective teacher reports of the potential effects of emotions on teaching behaviors; hardly any study to date appears to have explored the relationship between teacher emotional experiences and their teaching behaviors as assessed by external observers. Exceptions are early studies from the 1950s to 1970s that documented detrimental effects of teacher anxiety on teaching effectiveness as rated by supervisors and students (Coates and Thoresen 1976). Another exception is a recent study by Kunter et al. (2008) who conducted a study examining the relationship between teachers' self-reported enthusiasm and student-reported facets of teacher behaviors. These authors confirmed that teacher-reported enthusiasm for teaching was positively related to student reports of cognitive challenge, social support, and discipline levels during instruction. Furthermore, providing support for the hypothesis that teachers' emotional experiences are related to their expressiveness and resulting enthusiasm in their teaching style, in one of our own recent studies, we could show that teachers' own ratings of enjoyment during teaching were positively related to teacher enthusiasm as rated by the students (Frenzel et al. in press).

Overall, the theoretical deliberations and empirical findings presented above point to the idea that the emotions teachers experience during teaching have important cognitive and behavioral consequences and therefore seem to be of crucial importance for teachers' instructional behavior. Consequently, they may have effects on student outcomes. At the same time, we have argued that student outcomes and the corresponding appraisals by the teachers seem to be important for the formation of teacher emotions. In that respect, we propose that teacher emotions and student outcomes are more intricately intertwined than has been recognized in the literature on teacher emotions so far. In order to depict the processes underlying the interrelations between teacher emotions and student outcomes, we propose a model, which we describe in more detail below.

A Reciprocal Model

To summarize our postulations of the antecedents and effects of teacher emotions, we propose a reciprocal model linking teacher appraisals with respect to the correspondence among perceived and desired student behaviors, teacher emotions, instructional behavior, and student outcomes. The model is displayed in Fig. 7.1.

To explain the model, we begin with given conditions in a classroom, implying certain (pre)existing levels of students' competence, motivational engagement, and social-emotional skills (i.e., student outcomes). Teachers may directly infer some of these objective conditions from formal circumstances – such as grade level or socioeconomic makeup of the classes. In many respects, though, these inferences stem from observing the students and their achievement behavior, motivation, and social behavior. We thus ascribe particular importance to teachers' subjective perceptions of these student behaviors in class. In addition, as described earlier, we propose that teachers bring with them to a classroom three overarching teaching ideals, namely student cognitive growth, motivational engagement, and the development of social-emotional skills. In each lesson, these overarching ideals, adapted to the current conditions, are translated into specific behavioral goals, implying standards for students' achievement behavior, motivation, and social-emotional behavior.

We further postulate, as described earlier, that the cognitive appraisals concerning goal congruence, conduciveness, and significance of the behavioral goals, as well as appraisals of coping potential and personal accountability represent core antecedents of teachers' emotional experiences. Finally we assume, as described above, that recurring emotional experiences should influence teaching approaches and the use of teaching strategies. Recurring pleasant emotions should be associated

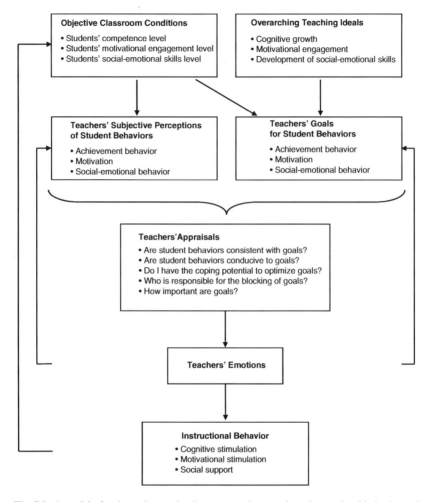

Fig. 7.1 A model of reciprocal causation between teacher emotions, instructional behavior and student outcomes

with flexible use of cognitively activating teaching strategies and a motivationally stimulating teaching approach, whereas unpleasant emotions should debilitate such flexibility and creativity during teaching. These instructional behaviors, in turn, should affect student outcomes, closing the cycle as proposed by our reciprocal model. In addition to these processes, it is conceivable that the emotions experienced in class also affect both the teachers' perceptions of the student behaviors and might lead to an adaption of their classroom goals; this is indicated by two further feedback loops in the model.

Two Empirical Studies

In the following section, we present two studies, which were designed to test certain assumptions regarding potential causes and effects of teacher emotions as depicted in our model. Specifically, these studies were aimed at exploring how teachers' enjoyment, anger, and anxiety were related to their perceptions of student behaviors and to their instructional behaviors.

Study 1: "I was anxious during this lesson" – Frequencies of Enjoyment, Anger, and Anxiety and the Link to Teacher Perceptions of Student Behavior

This study was designed to explore teacher experiences of enjoyment, anger, and anxiety in relation to teaching. In addition, we aimed to test the hypothesis that teacher perceptions of student behaviors (i.e., achievement behavior [specifically, academic performance], motivation, and social-emotional behavior [specifically, disciplined behavior]) in class should be related to their emotional experiences during teaching. The underlying assumption for this hypothesis was that the more positively teachers judge students' behaviors, the more likely teachers are appraising the situation as consistent with and conducive to their classroom behavioral goals regarding student achievement behavior, motivation, and social-emotional behavior. Consequently, teachers should report more pleasant and less unpleasant emotions. We thus expected that perceived levels of these student behaviors should be positively related to pleasant teacher emotions (including enjoyment), and negatively related to unpleasant emotions (including anxiety and anger).

We used two different methodological approaches to assess the study variables. On the one hand, we assessed teachers' general impressions of their classes' academic performance, motivation, and discipline levels. On the other hand, perceptions of student academic performance, motivation, and discipline were assessed using diaries, which the teachers filled out directly after several lessons in these classes. Likewise, teachers' emotions were assessed in a trait-like approach, asking them how they generally feel when teaching these classes, with multi-item scales assessing enjoyment, anger, and anxiety during teaching. In addition, we assessed emotions in a state-like approach, asking teachers in the diaries to indicate the degree to which they had experienced enjoyment, anger, and anxiety during the previous lesson.

This multimethod approach allowed us to explore teachers' experiences of enjoyment, anger and anxiety in detail. The trait-like approach tends to capture teachers' overall emotional experiences during teaching, and provides more reliable indicators of these emotional experiences based on multi-item scales. The state-like approach, despite its susceptibility to unreliability due to single-items, provides real-time, in vitro experiences, which are less prone to memory biases. Additionally, as a result of our multimethod approach, we could explore relationships between classroom characteristics of academic performance, motivation, and discipline on the one hand, and teacher emotions, on the other, both across and within teachers. Using the questionnaire data (trait assessments), we could explore *across teachers* whether teachers with classes they generally perceived as high performing, motivated, and disciplined report generally experiencing more enjoyment, and less anger, and anxiety than other teachers who generally perceive their classes as low performing, unmotivated and undisciplined. Using the diary data (state assessments), we can additionally explore *within teachers* how they feel during lessons in which they perceive their students as performing well, being motivated, and disciplined, compared to lessons which the teachers experience as less goal congruent in these respects.

Sample and Measures

A total of $N = 237$ teachers participated in this study. The sample was comprised of teachers from primary school ($n = 99$; 95% female[2]) and secondary school ($n = 138$; 54% female). German primary school includes grades 1 through 4. Thereafter students are streamed into three secondary school tracks based on prior achievement. The secondary school teachers from our study all taught at "Hauptschule" which is the school track with the lowest academic demands in the German three-tiered secondary school system.

The multimethod design of the study involved two assessment phases. Teachers first completed a questionnaire assessing their general judgments of the academic performance, motivation, and discipline level among the respective groups of students with a single item each ("Overall, how do you rate the level of academic performance/ motivation/discipline in this class?"). They rated these items along a three-point scale, ranging from 1 (*rather low*), to 3 (*high*). Next, teachers' enjoyment, anger, and anxiety were assessed with four items each. Items for these scales were adapted from the "Achievement Emotions Questionnaire" which was originally developed for school age and university age students (Pekrun et al. 2005; Pekrun et al. 2005). Sample items are, "I really enjoy teaching this class" for enjoyment, "Teaching this class gives me many reasons to get angry" for anger, and "When teaching this class, I am tense and nervous" for anxiety. Items were answered on a four-point Likert scale ranging from 1 (*strongly disagree*), to 4 (*strongly agree*). Each of these multi-item scales proved to be internally consistent, with Cronbach's α of .92 for enjoyment, .89 for anger, and .86 for anxiety.

The second assessment phase consisted of lesson diaries. Over the course of two weeks, teachers were asked to fill in a diary after each lesson they taught in the major subjects: German, mathematics, and science in primary school, and German, mathematics, science, and English in secondary school. In these diaries, three items assessed teachers' perceptions of students' behaviors, namely, "Students understood

---

[2] The high percentage of females is typical in primary schools in Bavaria (Bavarian State Office for Statistics and Data Processing 2008)

the material during this lesson", "Students were motivated during this lesson", and "Students were disciplined during this lesson". In addition, teachers rated the items "I enjoyed this lesson", "I was angry during this lesson", and "I was tense and nervous during this lesson". Each of these six items used a four-point Likert agreement scale.

Results

To gain a picture of the salience of the emotions of enjoyment, anger, and anxiety for teachers during teaching, we explored three indicators based on our multimethod assessment approach. First, we looked at mean values of the trait-like multi-item scales of enjoyment, anger, and anxiety. Second, we inspected mean values of all the state-level assessments of teacher emotions across the two weeks. Third, to explore the frequency of these three state-level emotions across several lessons, we calculated the proportion of lessons in which the teachers indicated a score of 3 or 4 on the four-point Likert answer scales (i.e., they agreed or strongly agreed to having experienced the corresponding emotions in that lesson). For each of these indicators, we also analyzed potential differences between primary and secondary school.

Regarding the salience of enjoyment, anger, and anxiety for teachers during teaching, each of the three indicators provided a similar picture. Table 7.1 provides mean and standard deviations separately for primary and secondary school teachers. The overall means both for trait-level and for state-level teaching enjoyment were well above the mid-point of the scale (2.5) for all teachers, but primary school teachers scored systematically higher than secondary school teachers on each of the enjoyment indicators (t-tests for the comparison of the trait scale mean/state mean and frequency scores revealed t-values of 2.76/4.22/3.24, $ps < .01$ each; effect sizes of the differences in terms of Cohen's d were .37/.59/.46, respectively).

Table 7.1 Means and standard deviations of primary and secondary teachers' reports of enjoyment, anger, and anxiety during teaching

Emotion	Assessment	Primary School Teachers		Secondary School Teachers	
		M	SD	M	SD
Enjoyment	Mean trait sum scale	3.60	0.41	3.44	0.45
	Mean of all state items	3.23	0.35	3.02	0.35
	Lesson frequency	83%		76%	
Anger	Mean trait sum scale	1.94	0.51	2.03	0.56
	Mean of all state items	1.56	0.36	1.63	0.41
	Lesson frequency	12%		15%	
Anxiety	Mean trait sum scale	1.45	0.43	1.45	0.44
	Mean of all state items	1.30	0.30	1.31	0.35
	Lesson frequency	7%		7%	

Note. Trait and state means were calculated as the sum of answers to all items divided by item number, resulting in a possible range of 1–4. Lesson frequency was calculated as the percentage of lessons in which teachers agreed or strongly agreed to have experienced the respective emotion
** $p < .01$

Anger, despite considerably lower mean levels relative to the mid-point of the scale and also lower lesson frequency as compared to enjoyment, can also be considered salient for teachers. Finally, anxiety played a comparably subordinate role in teachers' emotional experiences. However, considering the frequency of anxiety across all lessons, this emotion is not completely negligible. Both among primary and among secondary school teachers, 7% of lessons were filled with feelings of nervousness and tension.

We further proposed that teacher experiences of enjoyment, anger, and anxiety during teaching should be related to their perceptions of student performance, motivation, and discipline. To test this hypothesis, we ran a series of multiple regressions, with teacher perceptions of students' behavior as independent variables, and emotions as dependent variables. For the analyses of the trait-level scales on teaching emotions we used classical multiple regression. However, the analysis of the diary data required a multilevel approach, since diary entries were nested within teachers[3].

Table 7.2 provides the standardized weights for the regression of trait-level teacher enjoyment, anger, and anxiety on general perceived levels of student performance, motivation, and discipline in their classes. Contrary to our predictions, teachers' perceptions of students' performance level was unrelated to all three of the teacher emotion scales. However, as expected, the general perceived level of student motivation was highly predictive of teachers' trait-level emotional experiences, with positive relationships for enjoyment, and negative relationships for anger and anxiety. In addition, general perceived discipline level proved to be a strong predictor for all three trait-level emotions. The higher teachers rated the discipline levels among their students, the more enjoyment and the less anger and anxiety they reported generally experiencing when teaching these students. Overall, these models

Table 7.2 Predicting teacher enjoyment, anger, and anxiety (trait assessments): standardized regression weights from multiple regression

Teacher perception of general student behaviors [a]	Teacher self-report of emotional experience		
	Enjoyment	Anger	Anxiety
Performance	0.04	–0.10	–0.10
Motivation	0.38**	–0.28**	–0.20**
Discipline	0.42**	–0.51**	–0.46**
R^2	0.49	0.54	0.40

** $p < .01$

[a] assessed e.g. as, "Overall, how do you rate the level of performance in this class?"

---

[3]Neglecting the nested data structure would have resulted in an underestimation of standard errors since scores within teachers are dependent and similar (Raudenbush & Bryk 2002; Snijders & Bosker, 1999). We used the software package HLM 6.04 (Raudenbush, Bryk, & Congdon, 2007) to analyze the within-teacher regression weights for the regression of enjoyment, anger, and anxiety on perceived student behaviors during the lesson. In addition to taking the nested data structure into account, HLM also provides an efficient and elegant way of handling missing data by applying the full information maximum likelihood approach (Schafer and Graham, 2002).

Table 7.3 Predicting teacher enjoyment, anger, and anxiety (state assessments): Within-person standardized regression weights from multiple two-level regression

Teacher perception of student behavior in the lesson [a]	Teacher self-report of emotional experience		
	Enjoyment	Anger	Anxiety
Performance	0.30**	–0.16**	–0.09**
Motivation	0.42**	–0.15**	–0.09**
Discipline	0.25**	–0.42**	–0.22**
R^2_{within}	0.58	0.50	0.49

** $p < .01$

[a] assessed e.g. as, "Students were motivated during this lesson"

explained 49%, 54%, and 40% of the between-teacher variance of enjoyment, anger, and anxiety respectively.

Table 7.3 displays the results of the two-level regressions as performed with HLM. In contrast to the results from the multiple regressions presented above, these analyses pertain to within-teacher variations of emotions. In line with our hypotheses, each of the three facets of perceived student behaviors contributed to the prediction of enjoyment, anger, and anxiety during the lessons. Whereas teacher perceptions of student performance, motivation, and discipline during the lessons were positively related to enjoyment, perceptions of these student behaviors were negatively related to anger and anxiety during teaching. Overall, across lessons, these models could explain 58%, 50%, and 49% of the within-teacher variability of enjoyment, anger, and anxiety, respectively. School type (primary vs. secondary) did not moderate the relationship between teacher perceptions of student characteristics and teacher emotional experiences in either of the two sets of regression analyses.

Summary and Discussion

A first important finding of this study was that enjoyment was the emotion most frequently reported by both primary and secondary school teachers in our study. This supports Hargreaves' notion that classroom teaching is "charged with positive emotion" (1998, p. 835). Comparing the teachers from primary vs. secondary schools further revealed that the primary school teachers reported higher mean levels and higher frequencies of enjoyment during teaching than secondary school teachers. This might in part be explained by closer and more intense relationships among teachers and students in primary school as compared to secondary school (Hargreaves 2000; Lortie 1975). However, in contrast to Hargreaves' assertion that these closer relationships imply generally higher emotional intensity, that is both for pleasant and unpleasant emotions, in our data there were no mean or frequency differences in anger and anxiety between primary and secondary school teachers. An explanation for the similarly (low) levels of reported anger among all teachers might be internalized display rules which imply that experiencing and showing anger as a teacher is inappropriate (Sutton 2004; Winograd 2003). Similarly, teachers may not consider it socially appropriate to admit that they are anxious during teaching.

Overall, the means and frequencies of anger and anxiety were comparably low. Nevertheless, both of these unpleasant emotions do seem to play a relevant role in teacher's emotional lives, given that teachers reported experiencing anger in about 13% and anxiety in about 7% of all their lessons. Even higher frequencies might have been reported for feelings of frustration, which can be considered to be closely related, but not identical, with the emotion of anger (Schutz et al., this volume). Teachers seem to be rather open about reporting feelings of frustration (Sutton 2007).

Moreover, our data largely supported our assumption that teacher perceptions of student performance, motivation, and discipline are related to their emotional experiences. One exception was that primary and secondary school teachers' general perceptions of their classes' performance levels were unrelated to their general levels of self-reported emotional experiences. However, these teachers' perceptions of student performance within actual lessons were indeed significantly positively related to their enjoyment in these lessons, and negatively related to their experience of anger and anxiety in these lessons.

Furthermore, general judgments of the classes' motivation and discipline levels could explain between-teacher variance in the experience of teacher enjoyment, anger, and anxiety. Those teachers who rated their classes as generally highly motivated and disciplined reported less anger and anxiety than their colleagues who generally rated their classes as unmotivated and undisciplined. Likewise, within teachers, lessons in which students were judged to be motivated and attentive provoked less anger and anxiety than lessons in which students were rated less motivated and disciplined. For the emotion of enjoyment, student motivation seemed to be the most important predictor, whereas for anger and anxiety, student discipline was most relevant.

It should be noted that these effects were rather strong for the emotion of enjoyment, with almost 60% of the within-teacher variability and 50% of the between-teacher variability of enjoyment explained by these perceived student behaviors. Effects were a little smaller (about 50/40% explained within-/between-teacher variance, respectively) for the emotion of anxiety.

Study 2: "Our teacher explains things really well" – The Link Between Teacher Emotions and Instructional Behavior

The data reported here are taken from a large-scale longitudinal project analyzing students' mathematics learning and related personal and context variables across grades 5 to 9 ("Project for the Analysis of Learning and Achievement in Mathematics" PALMA, see Pekrun, vom Hofe et al., 2007).

For the present analyses, data from student and teacher questionnaires at one time point (grade 8) are reported. With these analyses, we test our hypothesis that teachers' emotional experiences during teaching are related to their teaching behaviors. The design of the study allowed us to link teachers' subjective experiences with a rather objective indicator of their teaching behavior, namely aggregated student perceptions. Several studies have documented the value of student reports, aggregated to class means, to assess instructional variables (Aleamoni 1999; De Jong and Westerhof 2001; Trautwein et al. 2006).

Sample and Scales

The student sample consisted of $N = 1,762$ grade-8 students (52% female) from 71 classes. The average class size was 24.8 students. The teacher sample consisted of these classes' $N = 71$ mathematics teachers (29% female). Within the three-tiered German tracking system in secondary school, $n = 27/19/25$ classes and teachers were from the low/medium/high track.

Teacher enjoyment, anger, and anxiety were assessed with self-report scales comparable to the ones used in Study 1. In this study, items were answered on a five-point Likert scale ranging from 1 (*strongly disagree*) to 5 (*strongly agree*). The scales were again highly internally consistent, with Cronbach's α coefficients of .87 for enjoyment, .89 for anger, and .86 for anxiety.

Students were asked to rate their mathematics teachers' instructional behavior in terms of cognitive quality, motivational quality, and social-emotional support. Cognitive quality was assessed with two sets of items, elaboration and comprehensibility. *Elaboration,* in terms of how teachers connect mathematics classroom instruction to the "real world", was assessed with five items, including "Our mathematics teacher explains many things by giving examples from everyday life". *Comprehensibility* was assessed with four items such as "Our teacher makes math so easy to understand that you can even grasp difficult concepts". Motivational quality was also assessed with two sets of items, *teacher enthusiasm* (4 items, e.g., "Our mathematics teacher tries to get students excited about the subject of mathematics") and *autonomy support* (5 items, e.g., "Our mathematics teacher allows us to try and discover our own solutions to problems"). Finally, student ratings of teacher social-emotional support, operationalized as *support after failure,* were assessed with four items (e.g., "After a bad grade, my mathematics teacher encourages me for next time"). All of these scales were highly internally consistent at the individual level, as indicated by high Cronbach α coefficients ranging between .75 and .86.

To determine whether aggregated individual-level ratings of students on these scales were reliable indicators of the respective class-level constructs, we used the intraclass correlations (ICC) Type 1 and 2 (Bliese 2000; Raudenbush 2002). Classes systematically differed in their perceptions of their mathematics teachers' behaviors, as indicated by high values of ICC(1), which ranged between .17 and .30. The corresponding high ICC(2) documented the reliability of the aggregated student ratings; they ranged between .84 and .91 (for the use of ICC(2) as a reliability indicator of class-aggregated values see e.g. Lüdtke et al. 2006).

Table 7.4 Pearson Correlations between teachers' self-reported emotions and instructional behaviors as observed by students

Aggregated student perceptions of teacher behavior	Teacher self-reported emotional experiences		
	Enjoyment	Anger	Anxiety
Elaboration	0.37*	−0.29*	−0.39**
Comprehensibility	0.30*	−0.27*	−0.41**
Autonomy support	0.28*	−0.25*	−0.34**
Teacher enthusiasm	0.34**	−0.23	−0.35**
Support after failure	0.51**	−0.29**	−0.33**

* $p < .05$; ** $p < .01$

Results

Table 7.4 shows Pearson correlations between teachers' self-reported levels of enjoyment, anger, and anxiety when teaching the respective classes, and students' aggregated ratings of their teachers' instructional behaviors. In line with our hypotheses, teacher enjoyment was positively related to student ratings of elaboration, comprehensibility, autonomy support, teacher enthusiasm, and support after failure. Interestingly, teachers' experience of enjoyment was most strongly (positively) related to students' perceptions of social-emotional support. Conversely, there were negative relationships between teachers' reported anger and students' perceptions of teacher instructional behavior. Anxiety also proved to be rather strongly negatively related to the perceived teacher behaviors.

Summary and Discussion

In this study, we could provide evidence suggesting that teachers' self-reported enjoyment, anger, and anxiety are systematically related to students' perceptions of teaching quality. Teacher enjoyment is positively related to teaching quality. Specifically, teachers who report feeling enjoyment deliver not only cognitively challenging and coherent lessons, but they are also more motivationally supportive by providing enthusiastic lectures and opportunities for autonomous student behaviors. In addition, students of "joyful" teachers reported receiving more support after failure from their teachers. Conversely, the more anger teachers experience during teaching, the lower their students rate the quality of teaching. Additionally, students rated the cognitive quality of instruction as lower and felt less socially supported by angry teachers.

Teacher anxiety, despite overall low levels, shows even stronger negative relationships with student-perceived teaching quality. Students of teachers who report being tense and nervous during teaching perceive their teachers' explanations as less elaborated and less coherent than students of less anxious teachers. Teacher anxiety is also negatively related to student ratings of teaching enthusiasm and social support. These findings underline the notion that anxiety, despite low mean levels and comparably low frequency as documented in Study 1, has important effects on teaching quality, even more so than anger.

Conclusions and Implications for Future Research

Each of the three emotions considered in the present chapter – enjoyment, anger, and anxiety – clearly are prominent, discrete emotions for teachers when they are engaged in their most important duty, namely classroom teaching. Teachers not only reported experiencing these emotions with considerable frequency, but each emotion was also systematically related to important facets of teaching quality. Specifically, the relatively low mean ratings for anxiety in no way imply that this emotion is inconsequential for teachers. Given that teachers report experiencing anxiety in approximately 7% of lessons and given its relatively strong relationship to teacher behavior as found in our study, this emotion deserves further research efforts. Future studies might also explore other emotions not considered in this study, even if their occurrences are comparably rare. For example, pride, shame, frustration, or contempt might play an important role for teachers' overall emotional well-being (e.g., Eid and Diener 2004; Grant and Higgins 2003) and might also have strong motivational impacts and thus determine teaching behaviors.

Regarding potential antecedents of teacher emotions, it is important to note that our data thus far only provide evidence regarding the relationship between teacher perceptions of student performance, motivation, and discipline on the one hand, and teacher emotions, on the other. We propose that one underlying process for these relationships is the appraisal of goal consistency and goal conduciveness provided students' achievement behavior, motivation, and social-emotional behavior is judged positively. However, these goal consistency and goal conduciveness appraisals have not directly been assessed in our study. Furthermore, in line with existing appraisal theories of emotions, we suggest that appraisals of coping potential, accountability, and goal significance may play an additional role in shaping emotional experiences, particularly in determining more precisely which discrete emotions are experienced (e.g., anger vs. anxiety). Future studies should explore the specific role of appraisals for teachers' emotional experiences. For example, the appraisal of coping potential could be explored by incorporating teacher self-efficacy beliefs. For students, the importance of self-efficacy beliefs for the experience of enjoyment and anxiety has been well documented in research (e.g., Frenzel et al. 2007; Pekrun et al. 2002; Zeidner 1998), but the relationship between self-efficacy and emotions so far does not seem to have been explored for teachers.

Regarding the appraisal of goal significance, our research thus far has implicitly assumed that each of the three overarching classroom ideals and resulting goals for student behaviors is equally important for teachers' emotional experiences. However, it is conceivable that teachers attach varying importance to these ideals. For example, some teachers may attach the highest importance to reaching high cognitive standards in their classroom, whereas others may place more importance on motivation or social-emotional growth. As a result, teachers will attach varying importance to the behavioral goals they set for their students to achieve in specific lessons. According to appraisal theory, the appraisal of goal significance should be positively related to the intensity of any emotion, both pleasant and unpleasant.

We would thus expect the attainment or nonattainment of a subjectively significant (vs. nonsignificant) goal to have stronger effects on the experienced intensity of emotions. Future studies could explore potential interaction effects between appraisals of goal significance and goal consistency with respect to classroom goals on the quality and intensity of teacher emotions.

Furthermore, it should be noted that the data presented here are correlative, thus interpretations in terms of cause-effect relationships should be made cautiously. For example, even though it is plausible, and in line with an appraisal-theoretical approach to emotions, that teachers appraisals of the attainment of their classroom goals affect their emotional experiences, it is also conceivable that the emotions teachers experiences shape their perceptions of classroom events. That is, a teacher experiencing pleasant emotions may tend to perceive his class as better performing and more motivated, and might therefore be more tolerant of minor disruptions in class than a teacher who experiences unpleasant emotions. Furthermore, just as it is plausible that teacher emotions influence the quality of their teaching, it could also be the case that certain objective classroom conditions directly influence teaching behavior. Some classes may provide a conducive environment for the implementation of certain desirable teaching strategies, e.g. high competence level among students may be conducive to the implementation of independent problem solving activities. Additionally, appraisals regarding discrepancies between desired and actual student behaviors might directly affect teachers' instructional behavior, irrespective of emotions. However, we argue that emotions are immediate and inevitable consequences of appraisals and, consequently, we propose that teacher emotions are important "catalysts" for teaching behavior.

For these reasons, we are convinced that attending to teachers' emotional experiences offers great promise for further understanding and optimizing classroom interaction processes. Emotionally positive classrooms are likely successful classrooms. Pleasant emotions enable teachers to best fulfill their teaching responsibilities and to maintain their emotional well-being and health. Additionally, enhancing *students'* pleasant emotions in the classroom should be one important goal of instruction, because these emotions are important for students' learning and achievement, and because they are an important educational goal, in and of themselves (Pekrun 2006; Pekrun et al. 2002). Classrooms, which are characterized by enjoyment of teaching *and* learning likely provide optimal grounds for overcoming obstacles and promoting positive development and achievement.

References

Aleamoni LM (1999) Student rating myths versus research facts from 1924 to 1998. *Journal of Personnel Evaluation in Education* 13:153–166

Anderson PA, Guerrero LK (1998) Handbook of communication and emotion. Academic Press, San Diego

Averill JR (1983) Studies on anger and aggression. *Am. Psychol.* 38:1145–1160

Babad E (2007) Teachers' nonverbal behaviors and its effects on students. In: Perry RP, Smart JC (eds) The scholarship of teaching and learning in Higher Education: An evidence-based perspective. Springer, New York, pp 201–261

Bavarian State Office for Statistics and Data Processing (2008) Bayerische Schulen im Schuljahr 2007/08 [Bavarian Schools in the year 2007/08]. Bavarian State Office for Statistics and Data Processing, Munich, Germany

Bliese PD (2000) Within-group agreement, non-independence, and reliability: Implications for data aggregation and analysis. In: Klein KJ, Kozlowski SW (eds) Multilevel Theory, Research, and Methods in Organizations. Jossey-Bass, San Francisco, CA, pp 349–381

Clore GL (1994) Why emotions require cognition. In: Ekman P, Davidson RJ (eds) The nature of emotion. Oxford University Press, New York, pp 181–191

Clore GL, Schwarz N, Conway M (1994) Affective causes and consequences of social information processing. In: Wyer RS, Srull TK (eds) Handbook of social cognition, 2nd edn. Lawrence Erlbaum, Hillsdale, NJ, pp 323–417

Coates TJ, Thoresen CE (1976) Teacher anxiety: A review with recommendations. *Rev. Edu. Res.* 46:159–184

Cosmides L, Tooby H (2000) Evolutionary psychology and the emotions. In: Lewis M, Haviland-Jones JM (eds) Handbook of emotions, 2nd edn. The Guilford Press, New York, pp 91–115

Dagleish T, Power M (eds) (1999) Handbook of cognition and emotion. Wiley, Chichester, England

De Jong R, Westerhof KJ (2001) The quality of student ratings of teacher behaviour. *Learning Environ. Res.* 4:51–85

Dillard, JP (1998). Foreword: The role of affect in communication, biology, and social relationships. In P. A. Anderson & L. K. Guerrero (Eds.), Handbook of communication and emotion. Academic, San Diego, pp. xvii–xxxii.

Eid M, Diener E (2004) Global judgments of subjective well-being: Situational variability and long-term stability. *Soc. Indic. Res.* 65:245–277

Ellsworth PC, Scherer KR (2003) Appraisal processes in emotion. In: Davidson RJ, Scherer KR, Goldsmith HH (eds) Handbook of affective sciences. Oxford University Press, Oxford, pp 572–595

Fredrickson BL (2001) The role of positive emotions in positive psychology: The broaden-and-build theory of positive emotions. *Am. Psychol.* 56:218–226

Frenzel, A. C, Pekrun R, Goetz T (2007) Girls and mathematics - a "hopeless" issue? A control-value approach to gender differences in emotions towards mathematics. *Eur. J. Psychol. Educ.* 22:497–514

Frenzel, A. C, Goetz, T, Lüdtke, O, Pekrun, R, & Sutton, R (in press). Emotional transmission in the classroom: Exploring the relationship between teacher and student enjoyment. *Journal of Educ Psychol.*

Frijda N (1986) The emotions. Cambridge University Press, Cambridge, UK

Gage NL, Berliner DC (1998) Educational psychology, 6th edn. Houghten Mifflin, New York

Graham S, Weiner B (1986) From an attributional theory of emotion to developmental psychology: A round-trip ticket? *Soc. Cogn.* 4(2):152–179

Grant H, Higgins ET (2003) Optimism, promotion pride, and prevention pride as predictors of quality of life. Pers. Soc. Psychol. Bull. 29:1521–1532

Hargreaves A (1998) The emotional practice of teaching. *Teaching and Teacher Educ.* 14:835–854

Hargreaves A (2000) Mixed emotions: Teachers' perceptions of their interactions with students. *Teac. Teac. Educ.* 16:811–826

Heckhausen H (1989) Motivation und Handeln [Motivation and action], 2nd edn. Springer, Berlin

Hughes E (2001) Deciding to leave, but staying: Teacher burnout, precursors and turnover. *Int. J. Hum. Resour. Manage.* 12:288–298

Ingersoll RM (2002) The teacher shortage: a case of wrong diagnosis and wrong prescription. NASSP *Bull.* 86:16–31

Isen AM (2008) Some ways in which positive affect influences decision making and problem solving. In: Lewis M, Haviland-Jones JM, Feldman Barrett L (eds) Handbook of emotions, 3rd edn. Guilford Press, New York, pp 548–573

Kunter M, Tsai Y-M, Klusmann U, Brunner M, Krauss S, Baumert J (2008) Students' and mathematics teachers' perceptions of teacher enthusiasm and instruction. *Learn. Instr.* 18:468–482

Kuppens P, Van Mechelen I, Smits DJM, De Boeck P (2003) The appraisal basis of anger: Specificity, necessity, and sufficiency of components. *Emotion* 3:254–269

Lazarus RS (1991) Emotion and adaptation. Oxford University Press, New York

Lazarus RS, Folkman S (1984) Stress, appraisal, and coping. Springer, New York

LeDoux JE (1995) Emotions: Cues from the brain. *Ann. Rev. Psychol.* 46:209–235

Lortie DC (1975) Schoolteacher. University of Chicago Press, Chicago, IL

Lüdtke O, Trautwein U, Kunter M, Baumert J (2006) Reliability and agreement of student ratings of the classroom environment – a reanalysis of TIMSS data. *Learn. Environ. Res.* 9:215–230

Mitchell RLC, Phillips LH (2007) The psychological, neurochemical and functional neuroanatomical mediators of the effects of positive and negative mood on executive functions. *Neuropsychologia* 45:617–629

Parkinson B (1999) Relations and dissociations between the appraisal and emotion ratings of reasonable and unreasonable anger and guilt. *Cogn. Emotion* 13:347–385

Pekrun R (2000) A social-cognitive, control-value theory of achievement emotions. In: Heckhausen J (ed) Motivational Psychology of Human Development. Elsevier, Oxford, UK, pp 143–163

Pekrun R (2006) The control-value theory of achievement emotions: Assumptions, corollaries, and implications for educational research and practice. *Educ. Psychol. Rev.* 18:315–341

Pekrun R, Goetz T, Titz W, Perry RP (2002) Academic emotions in students' self-regulated learning and achievement: a program of qualitative and quantitative research. *Educ. Psychol.* 37:91–105

Pekrun R, Goetz T, Frenzel AC (2005a) Achievement Emotions Questionnaire – Mathematics (AEQ-M) - User's manual. Department of Psychology, University of Munich, Germany

Pekrun R, Goetz T, Perry RP (2005b) Achievement Emotions Questionnaire (AEQ) – User's manual. Department of Psychology, University of Munich, Munich, Germany

Pekrun R, Frenzel AC, Goetz T, Perry RP (2007a) The control-value theory of achievement emotions: an integrative approach to emotions in education. In: Schutz PA, Pekrun R (eds) Emotion in education. Academic Press, San Diego, pp 13–36

Pekrun R, vom Hofe R, Blum W, Frenzel AC, Goetz T, & Wartha S. (2007b). Development of mathematical competencies in adolescence: The PALMA longitudinal study. In: M. Prenzel (ed) *Studies on the educational quality of schools. The final report on the DFG Priority Programme* Münster, Germany: Waxmann, pp. 17–37.

Peterson PE, West MR (2003) No child left behind? The politics and practice of school accountability. Brookings Institution Press, Washington, DC

Posner J, Russell JA, Peterson BS (2005) The circumplex model of affect: an integrative approach to affective neuroscience, cognitive development, and psychopathology. *Dev. Psychopathol.* 17:715–734

Raudenbush SW (2002) Alternative covariance structures for polynomial models of individual growth and change. In: Moskowitz DS, Hershberger SL (eds) Modeling intraindividual variability with repeated measures data: Methods and applications. Lawrence Erlbaum, Mahwah, NJ

Raudenbush SW, Bryk AS (2002) Hierarchical linear models. Applications and data analysis methods, 2nd edn. Sage, Thousand Oaks

Raudenbush SW, Bryk A, & Congdon R (2007). Hierarchical linear and nonlinear modeling (HLM) (Version 6.04) [Computer Software]. Scientific Software International, Lincolnwood IL.

Reyna C, Weiner B (2001) Justice and utility in the classroom: an attributional analysis of the goals of teachers' punishment and intervention strategies. *J. Educ. Psychol.* 93:309–319

Roseman IJ (2001). A model of appraisal in the emotion system: Integrating theory, research and applications. In: Scherer KR Schorr A & Johnstone T (eds) Appraisal processes in emotion Oxford, Oxford University Press, UK. pp. 68–91.

Roseman IJ, Smith CA (2001) Appraisal theory. Overview, Assumptions, Varieties, Controversies. In: Scherer KR, Schorr A, Johnstone T (eds) Appraisal processes in emotion.Oxford University Press, Oxford UK pp. 3–19.

Schafer JL, Graham JW (2002) Missing data: Our view of the state of the art. *Psychological Methods* 7(2):147–177

Scherer KR (1993) Studying the emotion-antecedent appraisal process: an expert system approach. *Cogn Emotion* 7:325–355

Scherer KR (2001) Appraisal considered as a process of multilevel sequential checking. In: Scherer KR, Schorr A, Johnstone T (eds) Appraisal processes in emotion. Oxford University Press, Oxford, UK, pp 92–120

Scherer KR, Schorr A, Johnstone T (eds) (2001) Appraisal processes in emotion. Oxford University Press, Oxford, UK

Scherer KR, Wranik T, Sangsue J, Tran V, Scherer U (2004) Emotions in everyday life: Probability of risk factors, appraisal and reaction patterns. Social Science Information 43:499–570

Schimmack U (2008) The structure of subjective well-being. In: Eid M, Larsen RJ (eds) The Science of Subjective Well-Being. Guilford, New York

Seidel T, Shavelson RJ (2007) Teaching effectiveness research in the past decade: the role of theory and research design in disentangling meta-analysis results. *Rev. Educ. Res.* 77:454–499

Sinclair RC, Mark MM (1992) The influence of mood state on judgment and action: effects on persuasion, categorization, social justice, person perception, and judgmental accuracy. In: Martin LL, Tesser A (eds) The construction of social judgments. Lawrence Erlbaum, Hillsdale, NJ, pp 165–193

Smith CA, Lazarus RS (1993) Appraisal components, core relational themes, and the emotions. *Cogn. Emotion* 7(3/4):233–269

Snijders TAB, Bosker RJ (1999) Multilevel analysis: an introduction to basic and advanced multilevel modeling. Sage, London

Sutton RE (2004) Emotional regulation goals and strategies of teachers. *Soc. Psychol. Educ.* 7:379–398

Sutton RE (2007) Teachers' anger, frustration, and self-regulation. In: Schutz PA, Pekrun R (eds) Emotion in education. Academic, San Diego, pp 251–266

Sutton RE, Wheatley KF (2003) Teachers' emotions and teaching: a review of the literature and directions for future research. *Educ. Psychol. Rev.* 15:327–358

Trautwein U, Lüdtke O, Schnyder I, Niggli A (2006) Predicting homework effort: Support for a domain-specific, multilevel homework model. *J. Educ. Psychol.* 98:438–456

Tschannen-Moran M, Hoy AW (2001) Teacher efficacy: capturing an elusive construct. *Teach. Teac. Educ.* 17:783–805

Weiner B (1985) An attributional theory of achievement motivation and emotion. *Psychol. Rev.* 92:548–573

Weiner B (1986) An attributional theory of motivation and emotion. Springer, New York

Weiner B (2007) Examining emotional diversity in the classroom: an attribution theorist considers the moral emotions. In: Schutz PA, Pekrun R (eds) Emotions in education. Academic Press, San Diego, pp 75–88

Winograd K (2003) The functions of teacher emotions: the good, the bad, and the ugly. *Teac.Coll. Record* 105:1641–1673

Witcher AE, Onwuegbuzie AJ, Minor LC (2001) Characteristics of effective teachers: Perceptions of preservice teachers. *Res. Sch.* 8:45–57

Zeidner M (1998) Test anxiety: the state of the art. Plenum, New York

Zembylas M (2002) Constructing genealogies of teacher's emotions in science teaching. *J. Res. Sci. Teach.* 39:79–103

Zins JE, Weissberg RP, Wang MC, Walberg HJ (eds) (2004) Building academic success on social and emotional learning: what does research say? Teacher College Press, New York

Chapter 8
Teacher Transactions with the Emotional Dimensions of Student Experiences with Cancer

Sue Lasky and Eileen Estes

Abstract We propose that schools have a particular place in the lives of students living with cancer, and that many teachers are largely unprepared to understand the ongoing psychosocial and physical challenges they can face. We suggest that for teachers who educate students living with cancer there may be emotional stress or satisfaction unique to their experiences that are largely uninvestigated. We also outline a phased line of research that will investigate how to develop school-based, yet community wide networks of support to provide resources than can sustain teachers through the emotionality inherent in walking with students through their cancer journeys.

Keywords Students with cancer • Teacher emotions • Ethical issues • Methodological issues

One in two men and one in three women in the US are likely to develop cancer. Among children 14 and under, the occurrence of cancer has increased by about 0.6% annually, and 5-year survival rates have also improved since 1975 (American Cancer Society 2008), with about 15 of 10,000 developing cancer (Center for Disease Control 2008). This suggests many elementary and middle school students are likely to live in close contact with the disease. Extensive research since the mid 1980s has been conducted on multiple dimensions of child and adolescent cancer, particularly possible issues students living with cancer[1] may face as they re-enter school (e.g., Kagen-Goodheart 1977; Prevatt et al. 2000; Rechis 2006).

S. Lasky (✉) and E. Estes
Department of Leadership, Foundations & Human Resource Education,
University of Louisville, Louisville, KY, USA
e-mail: sue.lasky@louisville.edu

[1] We use the term "students living with cancer" to include the student with a diagnosis, and students who have a close family member or primary care-taker living with a diagnosis of cancer (e.g., treatment, recovery, impending death).

P.A. Schutz and M. Zembylas (eds.), *Advances in Teacher Emotion Research:*   153
The Impact on Teachers' Lives,
DOI 10.1007/978-1-4419-0564-2_8, © Springer Science+Business Media, LLC 2009

While there is an extensive body of work examining student re-entry into school during or after cancer treatment, little research investigates how to support them through the unexplored topography of their cancer journey as they negotiate their ways through school (Barbarin and Chesler 1982). While many of these studies include data on teacher preparedness and knowledge pre–post a particular re-entry program, few studies foreground teacher experience or emotion during re-entry training programs, or as they teach students living with cancer during their re-entry back to school (Rechis 2006). Even fewer studies examine how to prepare teachers for the terrain they will cross as they walk with these students through their academic journeys (Barbarin and Chesler 1982; Rechis 2006)

Our collaboration (Sue Lasky and Eileen Estes) begins to address these gaps by exploring schools as networks of support for students living with cancer. Our backgrounds bridge the fields of school improvement and change (Datnow et al. 2006), teacher emotion and identity (Lasky 2005), and expressive therapies for adults and children living with cancer (Estes 2002). We come to this work as two adults living with cancer, and as professors mentoring students living with cancer. Our personal and professional experiences thus shape how we understand both our own and our students' lived experiences of cancer.

Our work extends prior theory and research in three primary ways. We have added "breadth to most conceptions of this work by including … not only the child diagnosed with cancer but the child affected by cancer in an immediate family situation" (M. Chesler, personal communication, October 9, 2008). We have developed a working definition of a person's lived experience of cancer that proposes it is a nonlinear, multifaceted, emotional and physical journey. We suggest that schools have a particular place in the lives of students living with cancer, and that many teachers are largely unprepared to teach students or understand the ongoing psychosocial and physical challenges they can face. We also suggest that for teachers who teach students living with cancer there may be emotional stress or satisfaction unique to their experiences that are largely uninvestigated.

In the narrative that follows, we first make clear our rules of evidence and methods. We then review literature related to teacher identity, notions of care related to student engagement and school culture, issues students living with cancer might face as they re-enter into their schooling, and teacher preparedness to work with students with cancer. We then propose a theoretically grounded phased line of research, and close with reflective thoughts.

Rules of Evidence and Methodology

In this section, we first set the rules of evidence for inclusion of prior work in our literature synthesis. We then describe data we used for this chapter. We also explain our data analysis.

Rules of Evidence and Database Searches

We searched Google Scholar, PsycINFO, and ERIC databases for relevant articles. One of our first decisions was to include a relatively broad array of literature; primarily, empirical investigations and literature reviews. We also included thought pieces, workshop materials, and interviews with experts that were accessible on-line. While our work takes us beyond the point of re-entry, we felt that understanding the key issues students living with cancer face re-integrating into school would lay a foundation for generating hypotheses about issues they might face over time. Between 1982 and 2006, we found only two studies that were theoretically grounded and focused analyses on teacher preparedness, and the emotions they experienced teaching students with cancer (Barbarin and Chesler 1982; Rechis 2006)

Key word searches included several permutations on the theme of "students living with cancer and their engagement in school." These included "teacher, support, cancer, students;" "cancer, re-entry, programs, teachers;" "teacher, professional development, cancer, school re-entry;" "teacher, emotion, students, cancer;" "teacher, emotion;" "students, emotion, school, cancer;" "children, cancer, re-entry, school;" "children, cancer school;" "students, cancer, support, school;" "youth, cancer, school." In these searches, one area of investigation yielded high returns: issues surrounding cancer survivor re-integration into school. One study by Barbarin and Chesler (1982) and their colleagues became a primary anchor of our work.

Data and Data Analysis

Data for this chapter are qualitative and include: prior empirical research; email communications; journal entries; methodology rule book; and field notes from conversations with people who work with students living close to cancer and who provided feedback on our working definitions and instrumentation. We synthesized the key findings from over 100 articles in the areas of programs for teachers on issues surrounding re-integration into school and issues students living with cancer can face when they return to school as well as two articles that fore-grounded teacher knowledge, concerns, and their emotional experiences working with these students.

At this stage, our work is exploratory and foundational. Generating hypotheses and working definitions, delineating stages of investigation methods of data collection for each stage, and designing instruments are a blend of intuition, knowledge gained from our lived experience, and input from experts in the field. We felt trustworthiness and fidelity (Denzin, 2008) to findings in prior work was important; as was the knowledge we gained from living closely with cancer, and the input we received from friends and colleagues. This was a foundational condition for (a) developing a working definition of the cancer experience that could capture its complex nuances and cyclical nature, (b) defining the stages of our research, and (c) developing tools for data collection. We also recognize that we are working with a population of students and teachers facing a traumatic life event, and that there are ethical and human considerations that must be kept at the forefront of our work with them.

Our data analysis was both inductive and deductive (Guba and Lincoln 1981). While we did not start with a definitive start list of possible themes (Miles and Huberman 1984), we started with ideas anchored to our fields of inquiry, our lived experiences with cancer and teaching students living with cancer, and feedback we received. We took systematic notes of findings and themes from prior work, and conversations we held with colleagues, then used these to expand and refine our original ideas.

Literature Synthesis

In this section, we present literature that is tied to the theoretical roots grounding our collaboration. In doing this, we begin to make explicit the logic that anchors our work. We first discuss research in the areas of teacher emotion, teacher sense of purpose, school climate and student engagement. We then provide a synthesis of research on issues students living with cancer face upon their school re-integration, and issues concerning preparedness and emotion that can face teachers working with these students.

Teacher Sense of Purpose, School Climate and Student Engagement

Teaching is an emotional practice (Hargreaves 2000) as well as a cognitive and technical endeavor (Beijaard et al. 2000). Feelings and emotion have a vital role in teaching, because it is through teachers' and students' subjective emotional world that they develop personal constructs, meanings, and make sense of relationships (Day and Leitch 2001). As this edited volume attests, there are a number of researchers investigating teacher emotion.

We draw primarily from prior research on teacher sense of purpose and care (e.g., Lasky 2001, 2004; Nias 1989), particularly as these relate to shaping school culture or climate and student engagement (e.g., Bryk and Schneider 2002; Teddlie and Stringfield 1993). We suggest that for students living with cancer, these dimensions of the school setting have particular importance for their long term engagement in school. We also suggest that for teachers who place primacy on developing open or caring relationships with their students, there may be distinct emotional experiences that accompany holding relationships with students living with cancer.

Teachers' primary senses of purpose are the deeper motivations behind why they teach (Lasky 2000). Through their lives as teachers, educators translate into action their sense of what is important and worthwhile (Nias 1999, p. 225).

For many teachers, their professional identity (Metz 1993), professional satisfaction (Yee 1990), and commitment to staying in the profession (Little 1996) are linked to the quality of relationships they have with their students.

Although there are clearly psychic rewards (Lortie 1975) to be gained by teachers in working with students, there is an emotional cost for teachers who develop more personal relationships with them. While some teachers receive the greatest professional satisfaction from working with their students, these relationships can also be a source of emotional pain (Lasky 2004). There can be drawbacks when teachers are too emotionally close or too emotionally distant with students (Hargreaves 2000). Yet, being "human" by developing personal rapport with them can be essential for keeping some students from giving up on themselves. This is part of the ambiguity of teaching (Siskin 1994).

Many teachers believe that to be an uncaring educator is a contradiction in terms (Best 1995). Nias (1999) made three generalizations concerning the caring purposes of teaching:

1. Most teachers regard their relationships with their pupils as a personal rather than an impersonal bureaucratic one
2. Most teachers derive, from the interpersonal nature of this relationship, a moral, as distinct from legal sense of responsibility for and accountability to pupils and often their parents
3. Most teachers feel that their moral "answerability" to pupils puts on them an obligation to "care" for them. (Nias 1999, p. 227)

Building rapport with students is, thus, a core element of some teachers' sense of purpose. For these teachers, being open and authentic with their students is essential for creating safe classroom conditions; they see building rapport as a precondition for learning. These teachers strive to facilitate student social and emotional development as much as their academic development. Being able to do this gives these teachers satisfaction that sustains them in what they describe as more constrained and less humanistic teaching conditions (Lasky 2004).

In these teachers' views, an important synergy between an emphasis on academics and a culture of caring is needed to promote optimal student learning. One without the other is incomplete. Not all teachers, however, believe this more expanded or flexible kind of student–teacher relationship is necessary for effective teaching (Beijaard et al. 2000). For those who do, many of the intrinsic rewards of teaching come from their personal and professional accomplishments with their students (McLaughlin 1993).

The relational dynamics in the school are clearly a contextual feature reflecting and creating conditions of relational safety (Little 1981). While expressions of teacher care for students is a core element of teaching, which can increase student involvement in schooling (Bryk and Schneider 2002; Shann 1999), expressions of care are expressed through the filters of one's values, gender, socioeconomic status, and culture or ethnicity (Delpit 1995; Lasky 2000; Nias 1989). In short, there is no single or monolithic understanding of care, nor is there one means of expressing it.

With that said, care in its most general sense is expressed by creating learning environments for students that increase the likelihood of their engagement in school. Before they give their full effort, students need to feel that their teachers care about them, want the best for them, and are invested in their success (Shann 1999, p. 409). When they feel unsafe, energy that can be devoted to learning is diverted to self-protection. Two core preconditions for students to learn are trust in their teachers (Tshannen-Moran and Hoy 2000, p. 550), and feeling safe in their schools (Teddlie and Stringfield 1993).

Key factors affecting student engagement include: communicating warmth and encouragement; comparing students' learning with their own past performances rather than making comparisons with other students; working together to ensure that each high-needs student has an ongoing supportive relationship with at least one school staff member; creating opportunities for students to develop supportive peer relationships and serve as peer resources to one another; and setting up firm, clear, and consistent rules and consequences (Teddlie and Stringfield 1993). While researchers have explored the various components of school culture and climate as they relate to student engagement in school, little is understood about school-level factors that can effect the long-term engagement in school of students living with cancer, or how to prepare teachers to effectively work with these students over time.

So far, we have interwoven the literature on teacher sense of purpose, care, school culture, and student engagement. In it, we make the case that these are highly integrated aspects of teachers' work lives that affect student engagement in their schooling. We also suggest that for students living with cancer, teacher orientation towards their students and school climate or culture can take on particular importance for them and their long-term engagement in school. Our review so far lays the foundation for the synthesis that follows.

Challenges Students with Cancer Face Re-entering School and Teacher Preparedness, Concerns, and Emotions

In this section, along with empirical and theoretical literature, we have included vignettes based on Estes' clinical work. These bring life to the empirical finding that more than the person diagnosed with cancer is touched with the often unanticipated news. Those close to the person and with whom the diagnosis is shared are also affected (Orbach et al. 2005; Prevatt et al. 2000).

We first discuss the array of psychosocial and physical challenges students with cancer can face when they re-enter school. We then discuss research on teacher preparedness, concerns and emotion in relation to teaching students living with cancer. We make the case that little is known about the resources teachers need to understand the long term issues surrounding students' lives with cancer. Likewise, little is understood about the contours of teachers' emotional experiences as they work with these students.

Students Living with Cancer and Their Re-integration into School

Engagement in school for students living with cancer is important for several reasons, including their future life opportunities and a sense of normalcy and routine in their lives (Vance and Eiser 2001). Students make sense of their cancer in different ways related to their cognitive development, the kinds of psychosocial support they receive, and changes in their physical functioning. They can experience changes in their self-concept, their relationships with family members and friends, and in their relationships with, or understanding of death (Hymovich 1995; Zebrack and Chesler 2002). Having a chronic illness like cancer is not linear but an "up and down process" with "good days" when a person almost "forgets" the illness and "bad days" with anxiety, treatment and its side effects (Charmaz 1991, p. 5). Maintaining a sense of normalcy in their lives is important. Inherent in this, is the array of issues teachers need information about to create safe learning conditions that can influence social integration and school engagement for these students.

Students living with cancer and returning to school face a range of issues that fall into two broad categories: Physical and psychosocial. While these can be separated – so that each can be systematically fore-grounded and back-grounded for purposes of analysis – they are inextricably interwoven. These issues can arise because the child him/herself has been diagnosed with the disease and is undergoing treatment, or they can arise when a sibling or other loved one is diagnosed

Physical issues students may face include those having to do with the effects of cancer itself, treatment or surgery, and recovery. Cancer can mean "many intrusive procedures that threaten or interfere" with students' "physical appearance and functioning" (Hymovich 1995, p. 52) and their learning in school. These include: compromised attention span and learning due to treatment or its neurocognitive late effects (Butler and Mulhern 2005; Noll et al. 1997); physical illness or discomfort because of treatment (Vance and Eiser 2001); weakened immune system (Prevatt et al. 2000); weakened bones, hair loss and baldness, exhaustion (Barbarin and Chesler 1982); slowed processing time, delayed response time, and problems with short term memory or hyperactivity (White 2003).

Psychosocial issues include the psychological and social issues a child faces as a result of living with cancer. These are in part shaped by the quality of social support and family circumstances. These issues can also be affected by a child's overall physical well-being. Thus, a child's ability and willingness to establish or maintain relational ties in school can be greatly influenced by his or her physical and psychosocial wellbeing.

Findings are quite mixed concerning the kinds of psychosocial challenges students living with cancer face when they return to school. Vance and Eiser (2001) found 18 studies that addressed school absence as an issue. A high number of school absences have social as well as academic consequences. Students may not bond with their classroom peers or they may feel alienated or isolated. They can also experience higher incidences of posttraumatic stress and related disorders than do their school-aged peers – meaning they experience high levels of distress, anxiety, and perceived life threat (Schwartz and Droter 2006). Socioeconomic status is also an issue that can affect students' engagement in school with parents from lower class backgrounds or whose children were not doing well in school before the illness reporting more negative experiences than their more middle to upper middle class counterparts (Barbarin and Chesler 1982; Chesler 2000).

Students can experience an array of emotions including increased neediness, isolation, withdrawal, anger and grief. Students can experience them during the time of a particular critical event obviously linked to their cancer experience; they can also have delayed emotional experiences (Chesler and Barbarin 1986; Vance and Eiser 2001).

The evidence we have just provided suggests that the student who is undergoing cancer treatment may be balancing fatigue, decreased physical strength or endurance while wanting to keep up with peers in the classroom and play with peers on the playground. Students may be faced with additional academic pressures if they miss several days of school due to an unexpected hospitalization or perhaps miss math class because it is scheduled when radiation treatment is scheduled. Even the youngest child may experience extreme sadness and despair if faced with the reality of having to miss school. A clinical reference for such an example is a 5-year old who had completed several months of treatment prior to starting Kindergarten. Just a few weeks after the start of school, she was told that her "cancer was back" and she would need to resume treatment, this time undergoing a bone marrow transplant. This quiet, seemingly shy child elected to tell her classmates herself that she would miss many weeks of school and why.

The student of a parent with cancer may be preoccupied on how Mom is doing while he is in school. "Is she going to the doctor's today, will she be home when I get home, is she ok at home while I am in school, does she need me?" The child who is overwhelmed with worry about the parent's wellbeing experiences great difficulty in concentrating on classroom lessons and often demonstrates decreased interest in socializing with peers. This same child is at risk of developing psychosomatic symptoms (headaches, stomach ache, etc.), which warrant leaving school early.

In the aforementioned vignettes consider the teacher's perspective. She too has to adjust to the fact that one of her students is living with cancer. Her adjustment is practical: how will I tailor classroom lessons to meet this child's needs? As the classroom teacher, she contemplates what questions are appropriate to ask her student's parents, and when the appropriate time to ask these questions might be. Her adjustment is also emotional as she deals with the questions and concerns of the other students, of their parents, and of the other teachers and school staff. In the case of the kindergartener, this teacher provided her student with the opportunity to inform her classmates of her cancer. The teacher allowed her the autonomy to relay this information in her own way and her peers were given the chance to ask their own questions.

A study conducted by Elmberger et al. (2005) brought to life the delayed emotional expression of one student whose mother had been treated for breast cancer, and the role the teachers played in informing her of the change in his behavior.

The mother of a 9-year-old son reported how her son's reaction to her cancer manifested at school – information that she received from his teacher.

> I phoned my son's teacher and she said she didn't notice anything at all but that he was a good pupil. I think my son liked school because it was a normal place, but half a year later, the teacher phoned from school and said he was misbehaving, running around telling other children he wanted to die and that he was going to kill himself. (p. 490)

Joey's teacher was initially confused by his decreased interest in his peers and classroom activities. As his psychosomatic symptoms increased in severity and frequency, he was leaving early on a daily basis sometimes less than 1 h after his mother had dropped him off. The teacher became increasingly more concerned. She was open to suggestions given by a therapist at a local cancer resource center as conveyed by his mother. She agreed to let the child call home as needed throughout the day and offered to let him each lunch in the classroom which provided them both with much needed one-on-one time. Such simple adjustments sent a strong message to the student that the teacher cared about what was going on at home and he felt supported at school. Communication between the parent and teacher increased as well. The parent realized that the teacher did not feel burdened by these alterations and also felt a great deal of comfort knowing that her child was cared for. The teacher, in turn, now felt she had the information she needed to help her student and realized that her questions about the father's health status were not viewed as "out of line" or "too personal" but deeply appreciated.

Teacher Preparedness and Emotion

Research on school re-entry of children living with cancer largely has overlooked the emotional issues teachers might face (Barbarin and Chesler 1982). Much of the previous research on professional development sessions for teachers tends to focus on evaluations of a particular program, and whether there were gains in teacher knowledge about or comfort with cancer post involvement in a program (Rechis 2006). In our search of prior work, we found two studies that were theoretically grounded and gave voice to the emotions teachers experienced when they had students in their classrooms living with cancer (Barbarin and Chesler 1982; Rechis 2006).

Barbarin and Chesler's (1982) was the first large study to explore the experiences of students with cancer from multiple perspectives. Their sample included middle-school adolescents, their parents, and their teachers. A core component of their study was an exploration of teachers' experiences who taught students re-entering school while living with cancer. Their investigation included their concerns, stressors, perceptions of preparedness, sources of support, and unexpected changes in one's orientation to life. The researchers hypothesized that the school environment, in particular, whether teachers were "able to normalize their relationships" with students and their families living with cancer, could make a significant difference in how students negotiated the stresses of re-entry. They suggested that school staff might be uncertain about how to respond to these students and could "withdraw emotionally or ignore a child, perhaps out of fear or confusion about appropriate behavior" (p. 13).

Their findings made it clear that for the teachers in their study, teaching students with cancer was an emotional experience for which they were unprepared:

> I really felt bad-like it wasn't fair. The usual reaction that someone so young is not going to grow up – he was a very responsible little boy. I guess the greatest thing was that my emotions would come in – feeling sorry for him and pity. I guess I was having a hard time dealing with the emotions. (p. 42)

Teachers in their sample spoke about the need for more informational support:

> I need more awareness training and information about what to expect during special illnesses and disabilities. How should I deal with the expected and unexpected things that happen? (p. 45)

These teachers also spoke about the difficulties in providing them professional development. In the words of one teacher:

> Every teacher is different and the training they would have to get would have to be individualized. I don't know whether you can train people to handle this, and I don't think more knowledge of cancer would have helped me one bit. (p. 46)

Barbarin and Chesler (1982) found that teaching staff working with students who had cancer consistently reported feeling personal and professional anxieties about "doing the wrong thing, managing peer relations in the classroom, and about maintaining liaison with the family" (p. 46). One of their key findings was that the difficulties school staff in their study faced with these students were "much too complex" to be solved by single professional development sessions, particularly those that offered "simple prescriptions." The authors suggested that preparing teachers to work with these students might be considered in a broader context going beyond providing information about the disease and treatment to include rich coverage of a wide range of psychosocial, emotional, practical and physical issues. They proposed developing systemic supports involving collaborations among home, school, and healthcare organizations as a way to address the multiple challenges school personnel, students living with cancer and their parents can face.

Little evidence suggests that teachers are better prepared today than they were in the early 1980s. Rechis (2006) conducted a mixed-method study that evaluated the effectiveness of a particular program to inform healthcare practitioners and school personnel about the possible challenges students living with cancer can face when they re-enter schools. She anchored her study to Hargreaves' (2001) emotional geographies framework as a way to in part explore relational closeness and distance between teachers, their students living with cancer and their families. Her mixed-method study examined both teacher pre–post knowledge and confidence gained as a result of participating in a "one-shot" 2½-h professional development session. She also explored the emotional experiences of two teachers who taught students living with cancer. An important finding was that many of her participants had some previous experience with cancer. This included their own lived experiences and those of their students; 19.2% were currently teaching a child with cancer, 23% had in the past taught a child with cancer, while 69.2% of them had family members or friends living with the disease.

The quantitative component of her study clearly indicated that teachers reported coming out of the session with greater knowledge about their students' experiences with cancer. They also felt greater confidence working with these students. She also found that coping with the possibility that a student could die from cancer changed the "typical student–teacher relationship." An emotional complexity was present, unique to working with these students and their families, including feelings of conflict, isolation, confusion, sadness, empathy, and closeness.

The teachers in her study reported that their professionalism was sometimes challenged, that they did not receive emotional support from their colleagues, nor did their colleagues appear to understand what teaching a student with cancer was like. Working relationships with students' medical teams were also largely lacking. These factors taken together created two primary obstacles for these teachers:

1. Difficulty in meeting the child's educational and emotional needs.
2. Difficulty controlling the social environment in which the child with cancer must exist. (p. 117)

When asked how they coped with their emotions, these teachers responded they handled them largely on their own. They found their commitments to the student and their parents a source of inspiration to keep going, but their senses of professional obligation sometimes kept them from sharing the depth of their emotion with the student living with cancer as the following story makes evident.

> One teacher stated that when she worked with a child with cancer, she would go into the house and deliver instruction to the best of her ability, and then drive around the corner where the child could not see her and cry. She felt that in her role as a professional it was inappropriate for her to bring anything into the house but education and hope that the child would get better. Furthermore, she seemed to have felt that her emotional outlet was to deal with her own emotions without support and in a secretive manner. (p. 34)

These two studies clearly indicate that teachers ask for informational support and experience a range of emotion when they work with students living with cancer. They also indicate the possible long-term nature of students' experiences with cancer. These combine to suggest that research going beyond student reintegration into school is needed. This includes deeper understanding of (a) students' journeys in making sense of cancer in their lives and (b) how to provide teachers with ongoing psychosocial, informational, practical, and appraisal support they need to take care of themselves and their students living with cancer.

New Directions for Investigation

In this section, we first introduce key constructs and then outline a phased line of theoretically grounded research that explores schools as a network of support for students and teachers living with cancer. Our chapter clearly makes the case that there is a need for research in this area. While there are implications for student long-term engagement in school with this line of investigation, there are also implications for teacher emotion. With the prevalence of cancer, we suggest that investigating the tools teachers might need to take care of themselves (and their students) emotionally during a period of sustained stress and uncertainty is a line of research worth considering.

We discuss cancer as an initial critical incident that often becomes a critical event in student and teacher lives. Critical incidents are highly charged moments or episodes that have considerable consequences for personal change and development (Sikes et al. 1985, p. 230). They are unplanned and unanticipated (Woods 1993a, b). Critical events are similar to critical incidents but are more enduring phenomenon that can be interpreted as both negative and positive (Sikes et al. 1985; Woods 1993a). They are more than a flashpoint and may last from a number of weeks to over a year (Fountain 1999; Tripp 1993; Woods 1993a, b).

A critical event in this context refers to the pivotal role of one's behavior in the outcome of an event (National Library of Medicine 2001). Events are designated as critical because of the way a person looks at a situation. In short, an event is identified as critical through interpretation of the significance it has for one's life (Tripp 1993). Thus, they are retrospective in nature, because it is only by reflecting back on situations that one sees them as critical. Upon diagnosis, cancer can be experienced as a critical incident in that it "hits like a sucker punch." People living with cancer often report being thrown off course or of having to regroup at this point in their lives. Likewise, cancer can be experienced as a critical event as people negotiate the rocky terrain of treatment, life options, and changing relationships.

We also use the concept of "mediated agency" (Wertsch 1991; Wertsch et al. 1993) to frame our analysis. We are particularly interested in three interactional scaffolds that shape human cognitive, psychosocial, and emotional possibilities. These are: the activities people in engage in (e.g., therapy, professional development); the tools they use such as technology or other materials for developing expertise with new language and processes (e.g., art mediums for expressive therapy; workshop materials); and norms or rules (e.g., how do we express emotion in this family, school culture) (Lasky et al. 2008; Wertsch 1991; Wertsch et al. 1993; Vygotsky 1962, 1978). We hypothesize that for people living with cancer these scaffolds may have a considerable influence on their possibilities for physical, psychosocial and emotional resilience; and how they negotiate the topography of vulnerability (Lasky 2005), survivalship, and thriving (Chesler 2000) in school settings.

A Phased Line of Research

In the section that follows, we first present a key product from the first phase of our collaboration, a working definition of a person's lived experience of cancer that makes clear the nonlinear and multifaceted nature of the journey. We then propose a line of theoretically grounded investigation that begins with gathering data on teachers' knowledge and experience working with students with cancer and then explores the possibilities of creating integrated networks of support for teachers and students living with cancer.

First Phase: The Working Definition

Our working definition reflects input from an array of people living with cancer including adult students, parents and grandparents, therapists, colleagues, and prior empirical research. It reflects our intention to portray cancer as a complex, nonlinear life experience. People can journey through predominantly despair or other unpleasant emotions to ultimately thrive (Parry and Chesler 2005); yet thriving does not mean the absence of such things as grief due to personal loss. Rather, it means one has integrated the cancer experience into his or her life, and has a tool kit and beliefs that provide structures to restore one's life and develop a deeper appreciation of uncertainty, interconnectedness, and compassion. In practical terms, what this means is that much more research attention is needed to understand the kinds of psychosocial, informational, practical, and material support teachers need to scaffold student engagement in school beyond the stage of reintegration into school.

Cancer is a critical event in one's life with life altering implications. For very young students living with a diagnosis, cancer is a "normal" part of their lives; it is what they have lived and know as far back as they have memory. A person living with cancer lives with emotional experiences including, but not limited to, enduring isolation, despair, grief, fear, and anger. The cancer journey can also be life transforming in that one finds a deeper purpose to live, and experiences greater interconnectedness, affording the opportunity to live life, rather than merely survive.

Thriving entails that one accept the reality of cancer in one's life, one's lack of control over life events and an increased confidence in one's ability to live with the uncertainty that cancer brings (Chesler 2000). This orientation to life, however, is not a linear process. It comes with living through and making sense of great losses such as death of a loved one, removal of organs or other body parts, or changes in one's identity and ability to live independently. One can reach a state of thriving and still experience powerful emotions when loved ones die, or as one experiences cancer-related triggers such as personal anniversary dates (e.g., date of diagnosis, surgeries, starting and stopping dates of treatment and monthly, quarterly, bi-annual and annual office visits, or hearing of another's diagnosis with cancer).

Going beyond survival and moving towards thriving suggests that we learn more healthy ways to process, make sense of, and live with these inevitable life events that are out of our control. Fear, anxiety, or feelings of isolation can return when one comes back around to particular life events; in these instances people learn healthier ways of making it through the emotions particular triggers elicit. For one mom, the Kentucky Derby (a long-standing local tradition, a time of great celebration, and welcoming of spring) was her trigger because it marked the anniversary of her diagnosis. She came to expect that she would have to "prepare" for the emotional setbacks she experienced, as each year she lived she revisited the calendar dates of these events. Another unexpected trigger for her was her youngest child's graduation from eighth grade – a celebration that 5 years prior she did not expect to attend.

Acknowledging these cycles as part of the cancer experience can give one the opportunity to realize and utilize his/her inner strengths and outside sources of support. As life continues, we circle back round to these cancer-related dates and unexpected life events. The initial visceral gripping of fear and negativity fades but is likely to never go away; we begin to see the cancer experience as leading to a stronger relatedness to the people we love – past and present – and feelings of compassion. The range of emotional experiences becomes a way to connect with others, and to deepen our compassion.

How one makes sense of and integrates the cancer experience into his or her life is influenced by an array of factors including type and stage of cancer, quality of healthcare, age, gender, SES, cultural or ethnic background, and psychosocial support (Chesler and Barbarin 1986). In the initial stages, persons/families are forced to rearrange their schedules to meet the demands of the medical treatment-clinic appointments, medical tests, hospitalizations, etc. These schedule intrusions may last several weeks, months, and for some, years. Once these intrusions subside, the cancer experience becomes less obvious to the outside world. Less time is spent in the doctor's office allowing for more time at home, work, and school. As seen by the outside world, the cancer becomes less visible – one's hair grows back, scars fade, appetites resume. However, the person living with it is forced to deal with the less obvious and visible repercussions of the disease.

Anger can creep up in unexpected ways and at unexpected times. In the words of one young student after she was asked, "what makes you most angry about having cancer;" she replied, "Nobody asked if I wanted it, they just gave it to me." This discussion took place several months following treatment; at a time, presumably, that her life "should have been back to normal." Likewise, deep emotional release can be triggered by hearing a particular piece of music while driving down the road, or studying for a final.

In Estes' clinical work, a pervasive contention she hears about is the idea that since the cancer is gone everyone can get back to "normal." Do I assume a cancer-free future and risk an unforeseen attack? Adult patients often discuss their need to reexamine their priorities in life asking questions such as, "what is important to me now," "how do I want to spend my time and with whom do I want to spend my time." Parents of children with cancer become vigilant regarding the possible long-term effects of treatments such as memory loss and learning difficulties-issues that may affect their child's performance at school. A secondary concern among parents is how the teacher will respond to such issues.

Inherent in our working definition of one's experience living with cancer is the emotional complexity and cyclical nature of revisiting anniversaries that can serve as triggers of emotions people living with cancer felt early in their life with cancer. In viewing the experiences of people living with cancer in this way, the need for continued support for students, their friends and families, and their teachers becomes apparent (Chesler 2000). It is the foundation of our collaboration. It provides the logic for exploring cancer beyond the point a student re-enters school during or after treatment, and for providing integrated on-going support for teachers working with these students.

Second Phase: Teacher Base-Line Data

As we were developing our working definition and conducting secondary analyses of previous literature, we were also working on study design and developing instruments for data collection. In our early conversations with several school leaders, school counseling personnel, and university colleagues, our hunch that there is no base-line data in our locale on teachers' knowledge of cancer, numbers of teachers who work with students living with cancer, or the kinds of professional development offered by local schools and districts was informally confirmed. Our collaboration at this phase addresses this gap.

Two studies Barbarin and Chesler (1982), and Murray (2000) were particularly helpful in providing theoretical grounding for developing a survey that we will use to gather base-line teacher data from schools in our locale. Murray described the development of two surveys measuring social support for children living with cancer, while Barbarin and Chesler gathered primarily interview data. Both studies highlighted specific domains of knowledge and concern to consider. We now discuss these.

In examining student experiences with cancer, Murray (2000) drew from House's (1981) notion of social support, which includes the areas of emotional, instrumental, informational, and appraisal support. Emotional support entails attending to a child's psychosocial well-being. Instrumental support entails providing materials and direct help so that people can attend to their day-to-day work. Informational support entails making sure a child has the guidance and information she or he needs to understand and adjust to living with cancer. Appraisal support entails providing a child with the tools for self-evaluation (p. 231).

Barbarin and Chesler (1982) used similar domains in the interviews they designed to understand issues and concerns parents, students, and teachers living with cancer experienced. The questions they asked teachers addressed practical, interpersonal, informational and emotional concerns. They also addressed spiritual stress or support.

At this stage, we are not looking for statistical significance, but rather for base-line data on teachers' experiences of cancer in their professional lives including their perceived preparedness, where they go for support, and the emotions they feel. In developing it, we drew from four primary areas: teacher sense of purpose and beliefs about the purposes of schooling (Lasky 2001, 2005); school culture (Hoy et al. 1991); expressive therapies (Estes 2002); and an early study on the school experiences of students with cancer (Barbarin and Chesler 1982). We also drew from the story lines experts in the field shared with us. We relied on verification and critique from teachers, principals, therapists, and oncology nurses.

We anticipate that survey results may generalize only to teachers living or working with cancer, and to schools with similar demographics and accountability rankings or status. It could be quite possible that in-school variance in teacher responses will be related to whether they themselves are living with cancer or have worked with students living with cancer. Likewise, questions pertaining to pressures teachers feel from state and federal accountability policies such as No Child Left Behind may vary by grade level, private or public status, and public Title 1 and nonTitle 1 status. Once completed, we will have base-line data on key areas in which teachers hold concerns when working with students living with cancer as identified in prior research. We will be able to determine what professional development activities teachers have engaged in, the informal and formal networks of support they rely on, and what they report as needing to work more effectively with these students.

We will also be able to examine whether there are relationships between teachers' orientations to their students and teaching, and school culture and students' engagement in their schooling. One of our hypotheses at this phase is that teachers who are more inclined to develop rapport or more open relationships with their students will be more likely to know which of their students is living with cancer. Likewise, teachers who communicate regularly with parents will be more likely to know if someone in a student's home has cancer. We also hypothesize that in schools with more open cultures (Hoy et al. 1991) teachers will have an increased likelihood of having someone they can confide in, while students living with cancer will have an increased likelihood of feeling safe. These are core elements that affect student and teacher emotional well-being and long-term engagement, and take particular importance when living with the sustained uncertainty that accompanies cancer.

We will also be able to preliminarily explore whether or how teachers' prior experiences with cancer might affect their emotional experience in school with these students. Included in this exploration are things like teachers' comfort with their students living with cancer; teachers' coping strategies, including networks of support they might be part of; and quite simply how they understand cancer. Gaining knowledge of these aspects of teachers' lived experience with the disease can help inform the next phase in our collaboration.

Third Phase: Wider Data Collection and Networking

We also plan to develop surveys for students, parents, and healthcare professionals who work with families living with cancer. Gathering data from each of these populations will involve key stakeholders who can inform a larger conversation focused on how to develop a network of support for teachers and students living with cancer. This network may include people who can provide "one-shot" professional development, but will go beyond these to create what we envision as an interconnected community-wide web of people and information that can provide resources and support appropriate to their situations. In this way, teachers, other school staff, students, and parents can have access to the things they need to act in informed ways to create school and classroom learning environments that are academically challenging, yet sensitive to the uncertain terrain teachers and students living with cancer cross. They will also have access to safe people and places for emotional support. Healthcare professionals can work in unison with schools and families to develop integrated academic and psychosocial plans. We feel this is particularly timely given the move to create more full-service schools (e.g., Calfee et al. 1998; Dryfroos 1994). The field of cancer recovery research is also expanding, and with it, the understanding that psychosocial networks of support for people living with cancer can greatly increase quality of life (J. Bull personal communication, October 10, 2007).

While our collaboration is still in its infancy, our work addresses gaps in school-based and cancer recovery research in three primary areas. First, we go beyond the student living with a diagnosis. We recognize that a student can experience psychosocial and physical stressors when close caregivers or other family members are diagnosed. We, thus, use the term "students living with cancer" to include the child or adolescent with a diagnosis and youth who live in close proximity with the disease. We propose that once cancer is diagnosed, a family and possibly a community unit are affected and begin an emotional journey of unanticipated change that can last a lifetime. Second, our working definition of a person's lived experience of cancer provides the logic for exploring students' experiences in school beyond the point of re-entry. Last, we foreground issues teachers can face when working with these students, particularly their emotional experiences and feelings of preparedness. We suggest that schools have a unique place in the extended community surrounding the student living with cancer. Understanding teacher concerns and their emotional experiences is a first step in providing them with the psychosocial and informational tools they may need to work with these students over time.

The rates of cancer diagnoses and the increased likelihood that people diagnosed with the disease will lead productive lives necessitate including this once unspoken life event in the formal ongoing professional development of teachers. How to provide integrated emotional, instrumental, informational, and appraisal support (Barbarin and Chesler 1982) is wide-open terrain for exploration. Cancer is an ongoing lived experience, yet many reintegration workshops for teachers and other school staff are short in duration, often 1–2-day workshop formats, and while some create networks of support for teachers that extend beyond the school, many do not (Prevatt et al. 2000). We propose that developing school-based, yet community-wide networks of support for teachers and students living with cancer will prove to be the route that provides the most contextually appropriate resources to go beyond the point of student re-entry into school and address their long term engagement in schooling. Key to building and sustaining these networks will be investigating the kinds of systemic linkages likely to ensure the robust endurance of them.

Closing Thoughts

There is a dimension of this collaboration we had not anticipated, and that is our own emotionality in reflecting on our personal and professional experiences with cancer. So, while we chose this work, the emotion was not necessarily comfortable.

As the earlier vignettes suggest, students do not ask to get cancer, and teachers do not necessarily anticipate their students will come to school with the myriad of challenges that are inherent in living with cancer. Yet, data on the increasing rates of cancer and the increasing likelihood of survival for those diagnosed, suggest most of us in the field of education – whether K-12 or higher education – will teach a student living with cancer. How we hold each other through the fearful, isolating, or anxious dimensions of the cancer experience while also celebrating our successes is important.

We have found that taking care of ourselves through this emotionality is an essential aspect in going the distance; of being emotionally present with our students, ourselves, our family members, and friends. We have also found that how we take care of ourselves through the lived experience of cancer includes doing this work, spending time with family and close friends, and engaging in activities that bring spiritual rejuvenation. What this means though is not formulaic, and sometimes means being open to unexpected moments of serendipity.

While writing this chapter, Lasky spent late nights working on a laptop while sitting in the chair her dad had bought for her a few months before he died; a chair she rarely used. During the last months of his life, she had sat in it for many hours listening to his stories, watching TV, or working on her laptop. While working on this chapter, her father's words of encouragement and thanks returned, "decent, Susie, decent." This was a reminder of the unexpected ways we can connect with those we love and have lost to cancer and gain inspiration or courage when they are no longer physically with us.

When Estes was approached to co-write this chapter, she did not consider rejecting such an intriguing proposal, though working in an extra project into an already full workload took some negotiating. She saw the research and writing involved as a way of broadening her clinical work with families with cancer and the possibility of expanding the mission of a local cancer resource center. The paucity of research on teacher emotions related to children living with cancer further motivated her to invest the necessary time and energy. Estes' struggle surfaced more at home both in the evenings and on the weekends. Many days she was tempted to take her work home, however, she realized her family needed her attention more so than the book chapter. In turn, she came to appreciate these imposed breaks. Estes attributes this *balance* between professional and personal life as affording her the ability to sustain the emotionality of working with families with cancer.

References

American Cancer Society (2008) Cancer facts and figures 2007. http://www.cancer.org/downloads/STT/CAFF2007PWSecured.pdf. Retrieved 20 July 2008

Barbarin O, Chesler M (1982) The school experiences of children with cancer: views of parents, educators and physicians. Research Report. University of Michigan, Ann Arbor, MI

Beijaard D, Verloop N, Vermunt J (2000) Teachers' perceptions of professional identity: an exploratory study from a personal knowledge perspective. Teach Teach Educ 16:749–764

Best R (1995) The caring teacher in the junior school. Roehampton Institute, London
Bryk A, Schneider B (2002) Trust in schools a core resource for improvement. Russell Sage Foundation, New York
Butler R, Mulhern R (2005) Neurocognitive interventions for children and adolescents surviving cancer. J Pediatr Psychol 30:65–78
Calfee C, Witter F, Meridith M (1998) Building a full-service school: a step-by-step guide. Jossey-Bass Inc., San Francisco
Center for Disease Control (2008) United States cancer statistics. http://apps.nccd.cdc.gov/uscs/Table.aspx?Group=TableICCC&Year=2004&Display=n. Retrieved 20 July 2008
Charmaz K (1991) Good days, bad days: the self in chronic illness and time. Rutgers University Press, Rutgers, NJ
Chesler M (2000) Some survivors of childhood cancer are "thriving" – Illusion or reality? A synthetic review of the literature and our empirical work. The Center for Research on Social Organization, University of Michigan. http://deepblue.lib.umich.edu/bitstream/2027.42/51,353/1/589.pdf. Retrieved 20 Aug 2008
Chesler M, Barbarin O (1986) Difficulties of providing help in crisis: relationships between parents of children with cancer and their friends. J Soc Sci 40:113–134
Datnow A, Lasky S, Stringfield S, Teddlie C (2006) Systemic integration for effective reform in racially and linguistically diverse contexts. Cambridge University Press, Cambridge
Day C, Leitch R (2001) Teachers and educators' lives: the role of emotion. Teach Teach Educ 17:403–415
Delpit L (1995) Other peoples' children: cultural conflict in the classroom. The New Press, New York
Denzin NK (2008) Emancipatory discourses and the ethics and politics of interpretation. In: Denzin NK, Lincoln Y (eds) Collecting and interpreting qualitative data. Sage, Thousand Oaks, pp 435–473
Dryfroos J (1994) Full-service schools: a revolution in social services for children, youth, and families. Jossey-Bass Inc., San Francisco
Elmberger E, Bolund C, Lutzen K (2005) Experience of dealing with moral responsibility as a mother with cancer. Nurs Ethics 12:253–262
Estes E (2002) The relationship between hopelessness and parenting stress among mothers diagnosed with breast cancer. Unpublished Dissertation, University of Louisville, Louisville, KY
Fountain J (1999, November) A note on the critical incident technique and its utility as a tool of public management research. Paper presented at the annual meeting of the Association of Public Policy and Management, Washington, DC
Guba E, Lincoln Y (1981) Effective evaluation: improving the usefulness of evaluation results through responsive and naturalistic approaches. Jossey-Bass, San Francisco, CA
Hargreaves A (2000) Mixed emotions: teachers' perceptions of their interactions with students. Teach Teach Educ 16:811–826
Hargreaves A (2001) Emotional geographies of teaching. Teach Coll Record 103:1056–1080
House JS (1981) Work stress and social support. Addison-Wesley, Reading, MA
Hoy W, Tarter CJ, Kottkamp R (1991) Open schools/healthy schools. Sage, London
Hymovich D (1995) The meaning of cancer to children. Semin Oncol Nurs 11:51–58
Kagen-Goodheart L (1977) Reentry: living with childhood cancer. Am J Orthopsychiatry 47:651–658
Lasky S (2000) The cultural and emotional politics of teacher–parent interactions. Teach Teach Educ 16:843–860
Lasky S (2001, January) School change, power, moral purpose and teachers' emotions in Ontario. Paper presented at the annual meeting of the International Congress for School Effectiveness and Improvement (ICSEI), Toronto, ON
Lasky S (2004) An exploration of teacher vulnerability in a context of large-scale government-mandated secondary school reform. Published Dissertation, Ontario Institute for Studies in Education, University of Toronto, Toronto, ON

Lasky S (2005) A Sociocultural approach to understanding teacher identity, agency and professional vulnerability in a context of secondary school reform. Teach Teach Educ 21:899–916

Lasky S, Schaffer G, Hopkins T (2008) Learning to think and talk from evidence: developing system-wide capacity for learning conversations. In: Earl L, Timperly H (eds) Professional learning conversations: challenges in using evidence for improvement. Springer, Dordrecht, The Netherlands, pp 95–109

Little JW (1981, April) The power of organizational setting: school norms and staff development. Paper presented at the annual meeting of the American Educational Research Association, Los Angeles, CA

Little JW (1996) The emotional contours and career trajectories of (disappointed) reform enthusiasts. Cambridge J Educ 26:345–359

Lortie D (1975) School teacher: a sociological study. University of Chicago Press, Chicago

McLaughlin M (1993) What matters in teachers' workplace context? In: Little JW, McLaughlin M (eds) Teachers' work: individuals, colleagues, and contexts. Teachers College Press, New York, pp 79–104

Metz M (1993) Teachers' ultimate dependence on their students. In: Little JW, McLaughlin M (eds) Teachers' work: individuals, colleagues, and contexts. Teachers College Press, New York, pp 104–137

Miles M, Huberman AM (1984) Qualitative data analysis: a sourcebook of new methods. Sage, Beverly Hills, CA

Murray J (2000) Development of two instruments measuring social support for siblings of children with cancer. J Pediatr Oncol Nurs 17:229–238

National Library of Medicine (2001) Use of the critical incident technique to evaluate the impact of MDELINE. US National Library of Medicine. Bethesda, MD. http://www.nlm.nih.gov/od/ope/cit.html. Retrieved 11 Jan 2004

Nias J (1989) Primary teachers talking: a study of teaching as work. Routledge, London

Nias J (1999) Teachers' moral purposes: stress, vulnerability, and strength. In: Vandenberghe R, Huberman AM (eds) Understanding and preventing teacher burnout: a sourcebook of international research and practice. Cambridge University Press, New York, pp 223–237

Noll R, Stehbens J, MacLean W Jr, Waskerwitz M, Whitt JK et al (1997) Behavioral adjustments and social functioning of long-term survivors of childhood leukaemia: parent and teacher reports. J Pediatr Psychol 22:827–841

Orbach T, Parry C, Chesler M, Fritz J, Repetto P (2005) Parent–child relationships and quality of life: resilience among childhood cancer survivors. Fam Relations 54:171–183

Parry C, Chesler M (2005) Thematic evidence of psychosocial thriving in childhood cancer survivors. Qual Health Res 15:1055–1073

Prevatt F, Heffer R, Lowe P (2000) Review of school reintegration programs for children with cancer. J Sch Psychol 38:447–467

Rechis R (2006) Capturing the emotional geographies of school personnel working with children with cancer. Unpublished Dissertation, The University of Texas at Austin, Austin, TX

Schwartz L, Droter D (2006) Posttraumatic stress and related impairment in survivirs of childhood cancer in early adulthood compared to healthy peers. J Pediatr Psychol 31:356–366

Shann M (1999) Academics and a culture of caring: the relationship between school achievement and prosocial and antisocial behaviors in four urban middle schools. Sch Eff Sch Improv 10:390–413

Sikes P, Measor L, Woods P (1985) Teacher careers, crises, and continuities. Falmer Press, London

Siskin L (1994) Realms of knowledge: academic departments in secondary schools. Falmer Press, London

Teddlie C, Stringfield S (1993) Schools make a difference: lessons learned from a 10-year study of school effects. Teachers College Press, New York

Tripp D (1993) Critical incidents in teaching: developing professional judgment. Routledge, London

Tshannen-Moran M, Hoy W (2000) A multidisciplinary analysis of the nature, meaning, and measurement of trust. Rev Educ Res 70:547–593

Vance YH, Eiser C (2001) The school experience of the child with cancer. CRC Child and Family Research Group, Department of Psychology, University of Sheffield, UK

Vygotsky LS (1962) Thought and language. MIT Press, Cambridge, MA

Vygotsky LS (1978) Mind in society: the development of higher psychological processes. In: Cole M, John-Steiner V, Scribner S, Souberman E (eds) A sociocultural approach to the study of mind. Harvard University Press, Cambridge

Wertsch J (1991) Voices of the mind: sociocultural approach to mediated action. Harvard University Press, Cambridge, MA

Wertsch J, Tulviste P, Hagstrom F (1993) A sociocultural approach to agency. In: Forman A, Minick N, Stone A (eds) Contexts for learning sociocultural dynamics in children's development. Oxford University Press, New York, pp 336–357

White N (2003) Educational related problems for children with cancer. J Pediatr Oncol Nurs 20:50–55

Woods P (1993a) Critical events in teaching and learning. Falmer Press, London

Woods P (1993b) Critical events in education. Br J Sociol 14:355–373

Yee S (1990) Careers in the classroom: when teaching is more than a job. Teachers College Press, New York

Zebrack B, Chesler M (2002) Quality of life in childhood cancer survivors. Psychooncology 11:132–141

Chapter 9
Emotional Scaffolding: The Emotional and Imaginative Dimensions of Teaching and Learning

Jerry Rosiek and Ronald A. Beghetto

Abstract We suggest that teachers regularly think about how to scaffold students' emotional response to the subject matter they teach. We further makes the case that when teachers think deeply about how students emotionally encounter their subject matter they are inevitably led to reflection on the social and cultural context of their students' lives. Thinking about students' emotions thus becomes one of the primary ways through which the specifics of a given subject matter and the broader sociocultural influences on student learning become intertwined in teacher thinking. This connection is illustrated with several case vignettes. In examining these cases, a second point is made: Teacher reflection on students' emotional response to the subject matter frequently elicits emotional responses from the teachers. These emotional responses, argue, are not excessive, but are necessary components of teachers' pedagogical content knowledge.

Keywords emotion · pedagogical content knowledge · scaffolding · imagination · culture

Consider a high school math teacher who developed a series of word problems organized thematically around the planning of a quinceañera (a coming of age celebration for young Mexican and Mexican-American women.) She designed the lesson to re-engage her Latino students, who had started skipping the "word problems" at the end of previous chapters in their mathematics textbook.

Similarly, consider a group of middle school boys who had been unable to tolerate the ambiguity inherent in a scientific inquiry project their teacher had assigned them. Frustrated, they had quit working, and had begun to distract other students. The teacher helped these students connect more meaningfully to the content by comparing the uncertainty they experienced in the science lesson to the uncertainty they readily accept in a basketball game (e.g., not knowing how a defender might break on the ball).

J. Rosiek (✉)
Department of Teacher Education, University of Oregon, Eugene, OR, USA
e-mail: jrosiek@uoregon.edu

P.A. Schutz and M. Zembylas (eds.), *Advances in Teacher Emotion Research:* 175
The Impact on Teachers' Lives,
DOI 10.1007/978-1-4419-0564-2_9, © Springer Science+Business Media, LLC 2009

Finally, consider a high school social studies teacher who, in an effort to make economic theories about inflation more relevant to students' lives, engaged her students in a discussion of the merits and drawbacks of a hypothetical school policy about grade inflation. Students reacted strongly to the idea that school policy might affect the value of good grades.

In the above vignettes, it is tempting to simply view the strategies used by the teachers in cold, cognitive terms. For example, it could be said that the teachers appealed to students' *prior knowledge* to engage them in the learning of new academic content or that teachers used familiar examples to cognitively support students' *understanding* of unfamiliar academic concepts. Although we agree that cognitive explanations are useful for understanding what the teachers were attempting to do, viewing these examples in purely cognitive terms obscures the emotional and imaginative dimensions that underwrite these strategies. Rather, as we will argue in this chapter, the above vignettes depict teachers who have recognized and attempted to influence their students' emotional reactions to the subject matter being taught. The particular instructional strategy illustrated in the vignettes has been called emotional scaffolding (Rosiek 2003). Emotional scaffolding engages students' imagination – using metaphor, visual representations, or narratives of content – in an effort to foster a particular emotional response to academic subject matter.

In this chapter, we consider the role of emotional scaffolding in teaching and learning specific subject matter topics. Additionally, we examine the way the process of emotional scaffolding relies on and calls forth student imaginative engagement with the content being learned. Along the way we comment on how the emotional and imaginative dimensions of teaching and learning are often neglected, and how emotional scaffolding offers a way for teachers (and researchers) to consider how to more positively incorporate emotion and imagination in the classroom. We close by returning to the opening vignettes and discussing, in more detail, how the teachers portrayed in the vignettes used emotional scaffolding to provide a more positive and enriching learning experience.

The Emotional and Imaginative Dimensions of Teaching

Unexpected Emotional Responses

Teaching and learning are processes saturated with emotion. As any practitioner of the pedagogical arts knows, inviting students to engage with academic content can result in a wide array of emotional responses. Such responses can be expected or unexpected; positive or negative; and manifest in a wide range of behaviors, including: impassioned interest, disaffected apathy, painstaking perseverance, or frustrated resistance. Predicting how students might respond to academic content is, at best, difficult. Aspects of the curriculum that seem trivial to the teacher might ignite student interest and passion, and those that seem profoundly important can be met with boredom and disaffection. Some student responses – such as disaffection, boredom, frustration, and disassociation – may impede positive and emotionally rich learning experiences thereby presenting teachers with complex instructional challenges.

Such responses are challenging because they often catch teachers off guard. Consequently, teachers – fearing the consequences of "going off track" – may choose to ignore or dismiss unexpected responses. Although teachers' reasons for dismissing unexpected student responses are somewhat understandable, doing so can result in lost learning opportunities and end up marginalizing or alienating students. Unfortunately, dismissal is a common strategy. Kennedy (2005), for instance, has reported that dismissing unexpected student responses is a habitual strategy used by teachers to avoid the derailment of their lessons. There is also evidence suggesting that prospective teachers may be inclined to develop similar dismissive strategies – based, in part, on their own beliefs, assumptions and prior schooling experiences (see Beghetto 2007a, b, 2008). Clearly, then, teachers who tend to dismiss students' responses need to be made aware of more effective alternatives.

Neglect of Emotion and Emotional Responses to Subject Matter Content

Given the emotional nature of learning, it would seem the teaching and learning literature would have much to offer regarding how teachers might better respond to unexpected, emotionally-laden student responses to subject matter content. Unfortunately, as Schutz and Lanehart (2002) have observed, "inquiry on emotions in education has been generally neglected" (p. 67). One reason for this neglect may be due to the precipitous rise of cognitive science and its profound influence on educational inquiry. Cognitive science was founded on the premise that interrelated psychological learning phenomena (cognition, emotion, culture) could be examined and understood in isolation (Anderman and Wolters 2006; Snow et al. 1996). Howard Gardner, in his account of the rise of cognitive psychology, has explained:

> [A paramount] feature of cognitive science is the deliberate decision to de-emphasize certain factors, which may be important for cognitive functioning but whose inclusion at this point would unnecessarily complicate the cognitive-scientific enterprise. These factors include the influence of affective factors or emotions, the contribution of historical and cultural factors, and the role of the background context in which particular actions or thoughts occur. (Gardner 1987, p. 6)

Although the logic of such exclusions makes a certain kind of methodological sense, in light of the intervening two decades of research on learning, such analytic compartmentalizations no longer seem tenable for the study of teaching and learning. For instance, educational psychologists have recognized the inadequacy of viewing human learning as simply the "cold" processing of information (Pintrich et al. 1993). Educational researchers in other disciplines – anthropology, philosophy, sociology – have likewise documented the importance of the affective dimension of educational processes (Boler 1999; Barbalet 2001; Reay 2000; Hargreaves 2000; Zembylas 2001, 2003; Sutton and Wheatley 2003)

This recognition seems to signal an emerging *emotional turn* in general educational research on teaching and learning. Recent years have bore witness to emotion-in-education symposia (e.g., *The Role of Emotions in Students' Learning and Achievement Symposium* at the 1998 annual conference of the American Educational Research Association; *Emotional Processes of Classroom Teacher Symposium, Teachers' Emotions, Identities, and Beliefs in the Age of School Reform*, and Inquiry *Into the Research Methods Used in the Study of Emotion in Education* at the 2008 annual conference of the American Educational Research Associations), the publication of edited volumes on the topic (e.g., Dai and Sternberg 2004; Schutz and Pekrun 2007) and special issues of academic journals (e.g., Schutz and Lanehart 2002; Linnenbrick 2006; van Veen and Lasky 2005). This research on emotion in education has underscored the role that emotion plays in teaching and learning. Still, even with this promising trend, little research has been done on how teachers might foster constructive emotional responses to specific subject matter topics.

There are a few partial exceptions to this lack of emphasis on the emotional dimension of education. For instance, there is a well developed literature on "mathematics anxiety" (Hembree 1990; Robinson and Cooper 1995; McLeod and Adams 1989); focusing primarily on mathematics anxiety as a predictor of student decisions to take mathematics courses, self-efficacy with the discipline, or general performance. There is also a significant literature on the way affect and emotion mediates the learning of reading and writing skills. A small amount of this literature addresses the emotional dimension of learning to read (DiPardo and Schnack 2004) and writers' block in adults (Rose 1985; Hjortshoj 2001). The most sustained program of research on the emotional dimensions of literacy education has been the research on *affective filters* (Krashen 1981, 1982, 2002); which pertains to the way negative emotions, such as anxiety, low interest, or low self-esteem can inhibit language learning. Little of this research, however, explores the emotional dimension of teaching specific subject matter concepts and topics. In an effort to address this limitation, we have turned to the literature on pedagogical content knowledge.

Pedagogical Content Knowledge

Over the last three decades, there has developed within the field of teacher education a robust literature on the practical dimension of teaching. Scholars in this area have undertaken an exploration of the gap between general learning theory and the particulars of teaching practice. This work has asked what is the nature and content of the insights that enable teachers to teach particular concepts, to specific students, in particular contexts in a way that is informed, but not necessarily prescribed, by a general understanding of the research on learning. This kind of insight has been conceptualized in many ways; it has been referred to as teachers' craft knowledge (Leinhardt 1990), practical knowledge (Grossman 1990), personal practical knowledge (Clandinin and Connelly 1996), and as the wisdom of practice (Shulman 1987, 2005). Those focused more on the process by which such insights can be generated and shared have advocated that teachers be prepared to engage in teacher research (Cochran-Smith and Lytle 1999), action research (Noffke 1997), narrative inquiry, and the scholarship of teaching (Huber and Morreale 2002; Shulman 2000). In a short span of time this emerging research tradition has had a considerable influence on teacher education research, policy, and practice (Darling-Hammond 1996). Teachers are increasingly seen as reflective practitioners and are expected to engage in inquiry that informs their teaching practice.

Within this growing interest in teachers' practical knowledge, we are concerned primarily with the literature that examines teachers' understanding of how to educate students about the particulars of their subject matter. This knowledge is neither identical to, nor directly derivative of, in-depth knowledge of the subject matter. Cochran et al. (1991) explain the difference:

> Teachers differ from biologists, historians, writers, or educational researchers, not necessarily in the quality or quantity of their subject matter knowledge, but in how that knowledge is organized and used. For example, experienced science teachers' knowledge of science is structured from a teaching perspective and is used as a basis for helping students to understand specific concepts. A scientist's knowledge, on the other hand, is structured from a research perspective and is used as a basis for the construction of new knowledge in the field. (p. 5)

Lee Shulman coined the phrase *pedagogical content knowledge* (PCK) to refer to this understanding of the intersection of subject matter knowledge and pedagogical practice, he described PCK as "an understanding of how particular topics, problems, or issues are organized, presented, and adapted to the diverse interests and abilities of learners, and presented for instruction" (1987, p. 8). Shulman offered that the unique knowledge that enables teaching lies at the intersection of teaching skill and the specifics of subject matter content:

> The key to distinguishing the knowledge base of teaching lies at the intersection of content and pedagogy, in the capacity of a teacher to transform the content knowledge he or she possesses into forms that are pedagogically powerful and yet adaptive to the variations in ability and background presented by the students. (Shulman 1987, p. 15)

Since the introduction of the concept of PCK into the teacher education literature, the idea has been refined and further differentiated. Smith and Neale (1989) distinguished between three aspects of PCK: knowledge of typical student errors, knowledge of particular teaching strategies, and knowledge of content elaboration. Veal and MaKinster (1999) developed a PCK taxonomy, differentiating between insights at the level of (a) the general discipline (e.g., science, mathematics, English, or history), (b) a domain within a discipline (e.g., within science: physics, chemistry, biology, or geology), and (c) topics within a domain (e.g., within physics: conservation of energy, atomic structure of matter, thermodynamics, etc.). Other scholars have distinguished between various components of pedagogical content knowledge within disciplines (Magnusson et al. 1999; Grossman 1989; Gudmundsdottir 1991; Doster et al. 1997; McCaughtry and Rovegno 2003; Mishra and Koehler 2006; Loughran et al. 2004)

Much of this literature on PCK makes reference to the importance of making curriculum relevant to student interests. One development within the PCK literature, however, focuses directly on how teachers think about and foster student emotional engagement with subject matter particulars. Rosiek, working with several teams of teachers over the period from 1992 to 2003, developed the concept of *emotional scaffolding* to describe this particular intersection.

Emotional Scaffolding

Scaffolding, as originally defined by Wood et al. (1976), focused on adults (or skilled others) "'controlling' those elements of the task that are initially beyond the learner's capacity, thus permitting him [or her] to concentrate upon and complete only those elements that are within his [or her] range of competence." Although, emotional aspects are inherent in the initial definition (e.g., the importance of student interest and minimizing frustration), the subsequent use of this metaphor often has lacked explicit recognition of the emotional dimensions of scaffolding. Recently, however, scholars (e.g., Stone 1993) have pointed out that in order to maximize success of scaffolding, additional interpersonal factors need to be considered. According to Stone, "one likely candidate in this regard is that of the affective dynamics of the [scaffolding] relationship" (p. 179).

The affective dynamics inherent in successful scaffolding are highlighted in what has been called *emotional scaffolding* (Rosiek 2004). Emotional scaffolding represents a more fine-grained differentiation of the original scaffolding metaphor and has been defined as *a teacher's use of metaphors, visual representations, and narratives of subject matter concepts to foster particular emotional responses to the content*. The definition draws on traditional conceptions of scaffolding (Wood et al. 1976) as well as recent scholarship that has highlighted the central role that emotions play in teaching, learning, and motivation (e.g., Dai and Sternberg 2004; DiPardo and Potter 2003; Schutz and Lanehart 2002; Zembylas 2007).

The concept of emotional scaffolding resulted from a series of collaborative research projects that took place over a 10-year period. The overarching goal of these projects was to refine and critique theories about teachers' pedagogical content knowledge (Shulman 1987). From 1992 to 2003, work groups of five to six teachers met regularly for a period of 1 year or more in an attempt to answer the question: "What is it that teachers uniquely need to know about teaching their subject matter – things that subject matter specialists do not need to know and that teachers of other subject matters do not need to know?" (Rosiek 2003).

The initial task undertaken by the research groups was cataloging the metaphors, analogies, and narratives they used as scaffolding for student learning of specific subject matter concepts. The first four of these projects involved 20 intern teachers at the Stanford Teacher Education Program. The Stanford Groups documented hundreds of pedagogical representations that they used to illustrate subject matter concepts in their classes. These representations were cataloged according to a variety of characteristics including, but not limited to, the subject matter to which they referred, the prior knowledge they assumed, and the effect they were intended to have (Rosiek 1995, 2003, 2005).

Several distinct kinds of scaffolding practice were identified by the Stanford groups. These included scaffolding that focused on processes of inquiry, scaffolding that drew upon insider knowledge of cultures that teachers shared with students, and scaffolding that drew on popular culture references, to name just a few. One type of pedagogical representation that emerged in the first group's work and that generated considerable conversation for all the subsequent groups was scaffolding designed to influence students' emotional response to an idea. This was called emotional scaffolding.

Subsequent research was conducted with more experienced teachers. These included: (1) the 12 teachers of the Fresno Science Education Equity Task force who met monthly for 2 years to discuss and document ways of increasing the engagement of cultural and language minority students in science education; and (2) the University of Alabama MetLife/AACTE Institute for Culturally Responsive Teaching – ten teachers gathered for six weekend long retreats for the purpose of discussing ways to increase engagement of rural, working class, African-American, Mexican Immigrant, and Native American students in the learning of a variety of subject matters; and (3) several individual teacher collaborators. These more experienced teachers critiqued and refined the concept of emotional scaffolding.

From our vantage point, these several years later, further insights continue to emerge from this data (Rosiek 2003, 2005; Rosiek and Atkinson 2005). Among the most foundational are that the participating teachers did not treat the acquisition of conceptual subject matter content as categorically separate from considerations of student motivation and affect. In fact, an appropriate understanding of the content was often thought to include emotional content – be it a calm relation to mathematics or a sense of the drama of English curriculum. Teachers in these studies rarely used cognitive/affective, concept/emotion dichotomies to initially describe their instructional planning. These were categorical distinctions imported from and at times imposed by academic discourses. At an experiential level, teachers seemed to interpret student-learning processes as an integrated fabric of emotion, content, student personal history, cultural context, and student–teacher relationship. We consider this an indicator that at some level, these dichotomies are exogenous to the reality of teaching and learning processes.

Some philosophical clarification may be helpful at this point. As we use the term, *emotional scaffolding* refers to the way participating teachers understood their pedagogical planning. It is a practical knowledge construct, and more specifically a pedagogical content knowledge construct, not a construct that originates within the post-positivist discourses of educational psychology or cognitive psychology (despite borrowing terminology from those discourses), nor in the more continental traditions of phenomenological or post-structuralist inquiry. This epistemic distinction is important, because it shifts the nature of the ontological assumptions underlying the use of the term.

Contemporary post-positivists often adopt a critical realist position (Popper 1972), maintaining that objects of inquiry maintain a great degree of ontological independence from the processes we use to describe them. In the case of cognitive psychology, claims are assumed to represent something about the actual nature of human minds and thought processes independent of the inquirer. Continental philosophers, particularly the post-structuralists, emphasize the way discursive processes play a significant roll in constructing the reality of the object of inquiry. Binary distinctions often thought to describe real differences, such as mind/body, emotion/cognition, sanity/insanity, rationality/irrationality, etc. are presented instead as arbitrary tropes that function as part of broader social and cultural discourses that encode power dynamics and protect a variety of implicit interests (Foucault 1977, 1982; Lather 1991; Petrovic and Rosiek 2007; Clandinin and Rosiek 2006; Atkinson and Rosiek 2008). Practical knowledge inquiry, at least the way we approached it, is grounded in a Deweyan transactional realism (Dewey 1934/2005). This ontology does not grant the object of inquiry a reality independent of our thought processes, nor does it allow that the reality object of inquiry is wholly the product of mental or discursive processes. Instead, it identifies the only reality we have access to as lying in the transaction between the humans and their complex social and material environment. Viewed through this lens, *emotional scaffolding* describes a reality that is located in the encounter between the intentions of the teachers and their experience of the obdurate learning processes of students.

Using this theoretical framing, our inquiries have documented the way cultural discourses and student experiences of marginality in schools become salient considerations in teachers' design of emotional scaffolding. In other instances it has identified the way teachers own emotional and educational history informs their interpretations and response to student learning needs. Of interest for our chapter is the way we now see how teachers in the studies listed above were depending on student imagination when they engaged in the process of emotional scaffolding. Teachers used emotional scaffolding to invite students out of habituated ways of thinking and feeling, and to introduce them to novel relations to subject matter content. They did so by offering students carefully tailored metaphors, visual representations, and narratives of subject matter. In order to benefit from these pedagogical gestures, students had to take an imaginative leap of sorts. When it worked students were able to experience the curriculum differently, see new possibilities, see new connections and to see themselves in the curriculum.

Scaffolding Emotion Through Imagination

Why should we be interested in the imaginative component of emotional scaffolding? Philosophers, educators, and learning theorists have long recognized the important role that engaging the imagination can play in teaching and learning. Imagination enables "possibility thinking" (Craft 2007), allowing us to consider fresh perspectives, try new things out, and move beyond *what is* to what *might or could be* (Egan 1992; Eisner 2002; Greene 1995). Imagination permits us to break from old habits, current ways of knowing, and opens gateways to new meaning and experiences (Dewey 1934/2005; Greene 1995; Vygotsky 1967/2004).

When teachers engage their students' imagination, the academic subject matter comes to life; it becomes real, present, and filled with emotion. This is because, as Egan (1992) has explained, "...when we imagine something we tend to feel as though it is real or present..." (p. 3). And yet, imagination – much like emotion – traditionally has dwelled (and often continues to dwell) in the educational shadows. For instance, Dewey (1934/2005) argued that a persistent and pernicious "false belief" is that imagination is a cognitive process limited only to aesthetic experiences. This false belief "obscures the larger fact that all conscious experience has of necessity some degree of imaginative quality" (Dewey 1934/2005, p. 283). Similarly, Vygotsky 1967/2004 observed that the imagination often is viewed as lacking "any serious practical significance" (p. 3) and thereby dismissed or discounted. The importance of engaging students' imagination rarely is given serious attention in schools and, instead, is often overshadowed by an emphasis on memorization or other standardized ways of knowing (Beghetto 2008; Egan 1992; Eisner 2002; Greene 1995).

When the imagination is overshadowed by such narrow views of knowledge, a pedagogy of "intellectual hide-and-seek" (Beghetto 2007c) may ensue. In this type of pedagogy, teachers seem to buckle under the tyranny of the lesson plan, believing that they must dismiss unexpected student reactions for fear of going off task and drifting into curricular chaos. Consequently, teachers are seen as holding all the correct answers and students aim to seek out, memorize, and parrot back those answers – leaving little room for divergent or imaginative thought, let alone imaginative exploration of new emotions. Such practices undermine the possibility that teachers can assist students who feel disaffected with the academic content.

In order for students to change their emotional relation to the subject matter – so as to better learn it – they need to let go of familiar habits of emotional response to the topic and explore new ones. This type of emotional habit breaking and exploration of new alternatives is facilitated by imaginative engagement (Egan 1992; Dewey 1934/2005; Greene 1995). By "imaginative engagement" we are not referring here to exceptional or extraordinary forms of cognition or thought. We are referring, instead, to the ordinary, frequent, even ubiquitous episodes of novel thought that are arguably essential to any learning process. In doing so we are echoing themes developed by educational philosopher John Dewey, who went so far as to claim that imagination was a central characteristic of all human experience. Specifically, he wrote "imaginative experience exemplifies more fully than any other kind of experience what experience itself is in its very movement and structure." (Dewey 1922, p. 263)

These moments of imaginative engagement that enable divergence from past habits of thought involve a degree of risk-taking, albeit of varying degrees. The anticipation of this risk, we offer, is what provides learning with some of its emotional charge and drama. And since the novelty of the thought is real, this can lead to a host of unique and unexpected subsequent reactions, which in turn may carry their own emotional charge. As such, teachers need to be able to recognize and respond to the often idiosyncratic, context dependent, and swiftly changing currents of student emotion.

Unfortunately, we live in an era that seems to emphasize convergence, rather than divergence, of thought as the goal of education. Schooling that adheres to overly prescribed standards for both the means and ends of learning may conspire against this kind of teacher responsiveness to student emotions. The resulting pedagogy – if it can even be called that – ignores myriad possibilities for engaging positive student emotion and relies instead on the fear of being wrong as the primary motivator for learning.

Such an impoverished pedagogy is not inevitable. As we will demonstrate in the next section, classroom-based research on emotional scaffolding shows that many teachers – even in the context of increasingly prescribed curriculum and pedagogy – think creatively about how to emotionally scaffold their students in order to help them better learn the specifics of their subject matter content. In fact, the very concept of emotional scaffolding was developed through inquiry conducted with teachers on their classroom practice. In order to illustrate the connection we are alleging between emotion and imagination in learning, we provide examples of how emotional scaffolding unfolds in actual classrooms.

Examples of Emotional Scaffolding

Mathematical Word Problems

Martha Salas, a high school mathematics teacher, was to teach a unit on interpreting algebraic "word problems," solving them with both graphic methods and through the elimination of variables. In planning her lesson, she anticipated that some of her Latino students, who were among the least proficient in Standard English language skills, would quickly become frustrated with these problems and give up on them. Many of these students had already been skipping the "word problems" at the end of previous chapters. In the hope of increasing the engagement of her Latino students, Salas decided to design a set of culturally tailored mathematics exercises with which these students might feel more familiar, confident, and interested. The mathematical content of the new problems were to be exactly the same as those which were presented in the text, but they were to be organized thematically around the planning of a *quinceañera* – a traditional coming out party for 15-year-old girls patterned after a wedding.

Salas wanted the first exercise to be both simple and to illustrate to her Latino students that they had some prior knowledge which would help them understand the lesson. She opened as follows:

> The young woman whose *quinceañera* this is – we'll call her Elsa – and her escort, have a combined age of 32. The escort is 2 years older than Elsa. What are their respective ages?

Her students began scribbling down the problem and applying the algorithms they had learned for solving this type of problem. Some students stalled, too intimidated or confused to even begin. However, it was not long before one of her Latino students looked up with the realization that he already knew the answer he had just arrived at mathematically. "Aaahhh…Miss Salas, this problem is eeeeasy." Salas gestured to him to keep his realization between the two of them. Other students familiar with *quinceañeras* began realizing the same thing – since a *quinceañera* is *always* held on a young woman's 15th birthday (thus the name *quinceañera*), Elsa would *have* to be 15. Simple subtraction leads to an age of 17 for the escort. Interestingly, almost all of her students at least attempted to go through the traditional algebraic calculations whether they knew this fact or not.

What is significant for the purposes of this chapter is the way Salas was thinking about the engagement of her Latino students. She created a mathematics exercise tailored to be of interest to this group of students. She intended the familiarity and positive affect associated with *quinceañera* to increase student engagement. However, she was also looking to reduce a form of negative affect. The word problems, in a language that was less familiar to students, often featuring topics and characters that were culturally unfamiliar to students, were intimidating. Salas used this first problem to lower the emotional aversion students had to the mathematics curricula she needed to teach them. The remainder of the unit involved a series of *quinceañera*-related exercises. These included calculations such as:

> Elsa will be asking friends and family members to make donations to help pay for her *quinceañera* at either the $25 contributor level or at the $100 *padrino* level. She has compiled a list of 63 people she will feel comfortable asking for donations. If Elsa's parents have agreed to spend $5,000 on this party, how many "contributors" and how many "*padrinos*" will Elsa need to have a total budget of $8,000 for her *quinceañera*?

Elsa's dress is being hand made by a local seamstress. She charges $100 plus $20 per square yard of satin and $30 per square yard of hand-made lace used on the dress, including the train. Elsa has set aside $550 for her dress. If Elsa wants no less than 25% of her dress to be lace, then how much satin and how much lace will be used in the dress?

At the *quinceañera* party there will be both a deejay and a mariachi band. The mariachis will play first and will charge $200 plus $100 per hour. The deejay charges $100 plus $50 per hour. If Elsa has set aside $800 for music and needs music for 8 h, how many hours will the Mariachis play? (Salas Case Study 1993)

Some questions involved the size of the multi-leveled cake with a fountain, the number of members of the court, and the style and text of the invitation. The culminating problem for the *quinceañera* planning lessons came on the third day, and was given as a homework assignment. In this problem, students were asked to use what they had learned about simultaneous algebraic equations, not to arrive at a definitive conclusion, but to narrow down their options and then make a personal judgment that was informed by their algebraic analysis. The problem was posed as follows:

> Elsa has $1,600 left in her budget. She can choose from two halls in which to hold her *quinceañera*. One is smaller (capacity 150 people), more elegant, and costs $800 to rent. The other is larger (capacity 500), less elegant, and costs $500 to rent. In addition, the caterer's menu includes two basic options: molé plates at a cost of $5 per guest or birría plates at a cost of $8 per guest. What is the maximum number of people Elsa can afford to invite to each hall, serving each type of food? (There will be four answers to this question.) Which arrangement would you choose and why?

Extra credit: Finally, everything is decided. Now imagine you are allowed to save money on the hall and the food and spend it on some other part of the *quinceañera*, or you are allowed to lower spending on some part of the party and increase spending on the hall and food. Would you change anything? What and why? Be specific.

By the end of the week, Salas was pleased with the lesson. Student engagement was visibly higher than it had been during past chapters focused on "word problems"[1] Salas was pleased that she had been able to culturally tailor her lesson without reducing the rigor of her subject matter.

What is salient in this example for the purposes of this chapter is the way Salas was paying detailed attention to the way students emotionally responded to specific elements of her curriculum, and the way she was engaging student imagination in efforts to transform their emotional response to the subject matter.

Salas was concerned with replacing negative emotions – an aversion to math problems presented as "word problems" among her ELL students – with positive emotions – a sense of comfort and ease with these exercises. Her effort to do so was tailored (Shulman 1988) to the cultural context of her classroom. In part, Salas sought to foster a more positive emotional relationship to her assignment simply to keep students working on them. However, she also had higher learning ambitions. She was seeking to create a sufficiently positive emotional relationship to this mathematics lesson that students would be willing to engage playfully with it.

To this end, she embedded the content of her math lesson in a topic with which the students felt familiar; one the students felt entitled to have divergent opinions about, and one that was associated with celebration and good times. Salas took advantage of the fact that there were many different possible variations on the design of a Quinceañera celebration, to scaffold students' engagement with open-ended mathematically informed inquiry and decision-making. Near the end she invited students to use the mathematics of Quinceanera planning imaginatively to make decisions about how they would design such a party. An invitation to such imaginative mathematical problem solving would not be possible without the establishment of a positive emotional relationship to the material being learned. According to Salas's interpretation of that lesson, the positive emotional relationship to the material was reinforced by the sense that it permitted imaginative play within mathematical bounds as opposed to forcing convergence to single conclusions.

---

[1]Salas assessed student engagement in a variety of ways. Based on her observations, a few brief student interviews, a short survey she had students fill out at the end of the lessons, and the percentage of work being turned in, she reported an increase in engagement by nearly all of her students. Interestingly, the increase in engagement seemed to be highest among the European-American young women in her class, followed by the Latin-American young women, the Latin-American young men, and then everyone else.

A Potentially Boring Economics Lesson

Dawnalyn Maruyama, a high school social studies teacher, taught a lesson on Keynesian economic theories and Franklin's Roosevelt's New Deal programs. Maruyama wanted to teach: (a) the ideas of inflation, deflation, and depression, (b) the question of whether the government should intervene in the economic cycle, (c) the question of where the intervention should take place, and (d) who has a stake in the answer to these questions. Maruyama's main worry was that students would find the whole notion of the monetary cycle uninteresting and would not appreciate the considerable political drama that surrounded the emergence of the New Deal programs. Anticipating student indifference, she designed emotional scaffolding for her lesson that would relate the salient features of the New Deal programs to something closer to the students' lives. She described her intentions...

> I planned to build an analogy for my students so that they could begin to understand the significance of the actions of Franklin Delano Roosevelt's New Deal administration. My purpose in telling this analogy was to give my students a story that would help them to empathize with the feelings experienced by people living through the Depression; I also thought it would help them to understand the different policy perspectives and practices implemented by governmental administrations during that era. (Maruyama Case Study 1994)

Maruyama presented students with a scenario she thought they might readily grasp and have strong opinions about: a high-achieving high school found its average grades dropping alarmingly over a few years' time. In this scenario, students who once had taken for granted they would get a job or get into some sort of postsecondary education institution were being more frequently turned down in their applications. As younger students saw this happening, their hope for the future seemed to dim. They quit trying as hard in school because it no longer seemed likely to pay off – "What's the point?" seemed to be the emerging attitude at the high school. As a result, grades at the school fell even further. A downward cycle of hopelessness and declining academic performance ensued at the school. Maruyama likened this fictional high school situation to an economic depression, where people's faith in the economy erodes, so they invest and spend very little, and as a result the economy becomes depressed.

At her fictional high school, Maruyama told her students the principal was faced with difficult choices about how to break the cycle of low morale and low grades. She described the principal's response to students as follows:

> Prevailing educational theory states that hard work and educational success create a cycle; that is, students who work hard get good grades and are, in turn, more likely to work hard... Initially, the school tried to address this problem by trying to motivate students to work harder. They started magnet programs and provided special rewards for high achieving students. This did not seem to be working, however, and the principal decided to try a new approach. Instead of focusing on increasing motivation, the school would focus on allowing their students to succeed. They would create special courses during regular school hours, in which students could enroll and get easy academic credit. Their thinking was that if students took these courses and got good grades, they would then be motivated to work harder and get better grades in the rest of their classes. (Maruyama Case Study 1994)

Setting aside the veracity of Maruyama's fictionalized claims about educational theory,[2] what is important for our purposes is the way she used this story to scaffold students' understanding of Keynsian economic theory. Notice how she did not simply try to increase students' general motivation to learn the topic. She attempted instead to provide a framework for fostering conflicted emotions about particular aspects of the historical subject matter that itself needed to be understood in terms of the conflicting interests and political passions it provoked in its own time. Maruyama was not just trying to make prosaic material exciting. She was trying to draw students into a complex emotional relationship that she considered essential to understanding this historical period. "Where history is concerned…I am convinced that if one does not empathize with the people of an era, then it is impossible to truly know history."

After the lesson was over, Maruyama reflected on what worked and didn't work. Students did get engaged – some passionately – in the discussion about school grading policy. Initially students were against the principal's plan. But as Maruyama described the consequences of the downward spiral of academic achievement to students, their opposition softened and some students changed sides – setting the stage for a more balanced debate in the class. She also reported that some, but not all, students were able to make the transfer to the Keynesian economics lesson she was teaching. Students could see why some people were angry at Roosevelt's policies, while others saw him as the nation's best hope. In the end, she concluded that her lesson had been a bit too successful at precipitating students' emotional response to the scaffolding, almost at the expense of discussing economics or the New Deal.

> My initial assessment was that, perhaps, my analogy was simply too emotionally close to my students. They simply could not separate themselves from the story enough to critically examine the issues I was presenting.

What is significant for our purposes is, first, that Maruyama developed a scaffolding strategy very precisely tailored to a particular topic within her content area and that this scaffolding strategy was focused on facilitating both a conceptual and emotional relationship to the topic. Second, we note that Maruyama's scaffolding relied upon student imagination. Students first had to be able to imaginatively visualize the grading policy scenario she presented. Then students needed to imaginatively transfer the conceptual and emotional framework developed around the fictional school to U.S. economic policy in the 1930s and 1940s.

---

[2]This analogy involves an inaccurate representation of contemporary motivational science as applied to educational processes. Ms. Maruyama recognized this later. This inaccuracy, however, is not relevant to the point being made by presenting this case. The instructor was not trying to teach motivational science, but was instead trying to teach Keynesian economics.

Whether or not her analogy was a good representation of New Deal economic policies is a more salient consideration. Ms. Maruyama came to the conclusion, recounted below, that it was not a well crafted analogy for the New Deal policies. Again, however, this does not diminish the fact that she was thinking about students emotional response to specific aspects of the subject matter in designing this lesson, and that things can be learned from her effort, whether or not it was pedagogically successful.

In this case, not all students were able to make the latter leap. This assessment, however, did not discourage Ms. Maruyama from the practice of emotional scaffolding. Instead, it inspired her to think even more carefully about how she would construct narrative analogies for this subject matter in the future.

> My school story might have been an inaccurate scaffold to build; the map did not form a precise fit....in my story I was creating a situation in which my students naturally identified with the fictional students – their own counterparts – and those students represented the impoverished population during the Depression. In teaching about Keynesian economics and federal interventions, however, I was asking my students to place themselves in the shoes of the administration – of the school and of the nation – and to critically analyze policy alternatives... I may have misdirected their emotion with my scaffolding!

Maruyama began the planning of her lesson with a concern about students not being engaged with the topic that she was teaching. However, the way she considered getting them more engaged in learning about Keynesian economics was shaped by her conception of the subject matter she was teaching – she believed students needed to be able to empathize with people in the times they were studying. Empathy is perhaps the quintessential union of emotion and imagination, as it involves placing ourselves imaginatively in another's position in order to feel what they feel.

Two Science Education Examples

There are many other examples of teachers who designed lessons to constructively influence students' emotional response to specific aspects of science content. In one case, science teacher Milo Shorris used an elaborate role playing scenario around the investigation of a fictional fish kill in a small town. Students took on the role of factory plant managers, farmers, hydroelectric dam operators, journalists, politicians, park rangers, and EPA officials, all of whom were invested in the results of the investigation. Analysis of the water samples provided by the teacher would eventually reveal one of the groups to be guilty and others innocent. As the lesson unfolded, the class would advocate for the interests of their particular characters.

Shorris reported that the role-play made exciting an otherwise boring lesson on water chemistry. Some students even falsified data in an effort to direct attention away from their character. Other students had to re-run trials to expose the falsification. This, he thought, was good scientific practice. He also observed a greater willingness to ask questions in many of his students when they were acting out their roles. The role playing, he concluded, provided some refuge from the potential embarrassment of asking ignorant questions or appearing to be personally interested in the topic.

Here, again, we see a connection between imagination and facilitating a positive emotional connection to the learning process. In this case, the teacher's emotional scaffolding was tailored to the specifics of water chemistry. It relied on students being able to imagine themselves in the roles of various professionals in the scenario he presented to them, including imaging the personal interest the various characters would have in the outcome of the science inquiry.

In another instance, Zachary Sconiers, a middle school science teacher, used a basketball metaphor to assist his students with a science inquiry lesson (Sconiers and Rosiek 2000). The inquiry lesson required students to run tests on powdered substances using liquid chemical reagents as a means to identify the contents of an unknown powdered mixture. Spanning over 3 weeks, the lesson required students to tolerate a great deal of ambiguity. When a group of boys working together became frustrated with their inability to arrive at an answer quickly, they abandoned the inquiry process and began distracting their peers.

Later, while playing basketball with these boys, Sconiers pointed out how they frequently dealt with uncertainty on the court. For example, when they drove the lane on the basketball court, he asked if they knew which direction their opponent would break while defending the basket. The students said "no," that they had to starting moving to the basket and get the opponent to commit. Once that happens, then they know what to do. Sconiers explained that a science lab was very much like that. You start the inquiry without knowing how the thing you are testing is going to react. But once you start, it will be forced to commit, and then you know what your next step is. Sconiers reported that the students mentioned the analogy the next day, when they engaged their lab. Although it did not instantly transform them into model students, he did feel the analogy was helpful and that he would use it again.

In this instance emotional scaffolding was offered improvisationally. Again it was tailored to the specifics of the subject matter content being taught – science inquiry – and it addressed the emotional response students had to that content. The analogy offered by Sconiers drew upon an experience familiar to students, and ask them to imaginatively project their positive emotional response to that familiar experience onto the less familiar experience of science inquiry. Once again, we see how the effort to foster a more positive emotional relationship to the subject matter content depended on enlisting student's imagination.

Concluding Thoughts

In this chapter we hoped to illustrate how teachers and researchers might move away from dismissing students' emotional responses to academic subject matter toward more effective ways of working with those responses. We presented emotional scaffolding as a viable means for doing so noting that the concept of emotional scaffolding resulted from naturalistic studies of teachers. This is important to note, because it underscores that teachers can (and frequently do) engage students' emotions – by providing analogies, metaphors, and narratives of those subject matter concepts – to foster positive emotional responses to academic subject matter. Building on the research literature on the emotional dimension of teaching learning, as well as research on imagination and creativity in learning, and on case examples of teachers providing emotional scaffolding to students, we have argued that imagination plays a central role in the pedagogy of emotional scaffolding.

The relationship between emotion, the teaching and learning of specific subject matter content, and what we have called imaginative engagement is multi-layered and complex. Our treatment of it in this chapter is necessarily preliminary. In this chapter we have drawn on a series of collaborative studies conducted with teachers on their practical understanding of this relationship. The assumption underlying practical knowledge research is that it provides insight into the transactional reality of teaching and learning processes. What these studies suggest is that teachers often sought to reduce or avoid negative emotional reactions to their content by presenting the content in a way that framed it with more positive emotional valence. Teachers did not assume that scaffolding process was one of passive reception. For the scaffolding to have the intended effect, students would have to be active in re-imagining their emotional relationship to the material.

The engagement of imagination, however, has its own emotional prerequisites. Imaginative engagement with a topic, as we have described it, involves some degree of risk taking for students. This risk taking carries with it its own emotional charge; students will need to feel secure enough with the topic and in the context to take these risks. This emotional need is in addition to the need for a constructive emotional response to the content and topic itself. That being said, once the imaginative engagement is established, this can be its own source of pleasure and positive affect, which can support learning.

Given these observations, we offer that efforts to address the emotional aspects of teaching and learning will inevitably require paying greater attention to the role imagination plays in teaching and learning. We believe there are many opportunities for more effectively incorporating both of these into research agendas, teacher training, and teaching practice. It is our hope that educators and researchers will continue to explore ways, such as the use of emotional scaffolding, to more effectively incorporate the emotional and imaginative dimensions of teaching and learning into the academic curriculum

References

Anderman EM, Wolters C (2006) Handbook of educational psychology. In: Alexander P, Winne P (eds) Goals, values and affects: influences on student motivation, 2nd edn. Simon & Schuster, New York

Atkinson B, Rosiek J (2008) Reading teacher knowledge research: a reader response approach. In: Lisa Mazzei (ed) Post-structural theory in education. Sage, Thousand Oaks

Barbalet J (2001) Emotions and Sociology. Blackwell, Oxford

Beghetto RA (2007a) Does creativity have a place in classroom discussions? Prospective teachers' response preferences. Thinking Skills Creativity 2:1–9

Beghetto RA (2007b) Prospective teachers' beliefs about students' goal orientations: a carry-over effect of prior schooling experiences? Soc Psychol Educ 10:171–191

Beghetto RA (2007c) Ideational code-switching: walking the talk about supporting student creativity in the classroom. Roeper Rev 29:265–270

Beghetto RA (2008) Prospective teachers' beliefs about imaginative thinking in K-12 schooling. Thinking Skills Creativity 3:134–142

Boler M (1999) Feeling power: education and the Emotions. Routledge, New York

Clandinin DJ, Connelly MF (1996) Teachers' professional knowledge landscapes: teacher stories. Educ Res 25(3):24–31

Clandinin DJ, Rosiek J (2006) Borders, tensions and borderlands in narrative inquiry. In: Clandinin DJ (ed) Handbook of narrative inquiry: mapping a methodology. Sage, Thousand Oaks

Cochran KF, King RA, DeRuiter JA (1991) Pedagogical content knowledge: a tentative model for teacher preparation. National Center for Research on Teacher Learning, East Lansing, MI

Cochran-Smith M, Lytle SL (1999) Relationships of knowledge and practice: teacher learning in communities. Review of research in education, vol 24. American Education Research Association, Washington, DC, pp 249–305

Craft A (2007) Possibility thinking in the early years and primary classrooms. In: Tan AG (ed) Creativity: a handbook for teachers. World Scientific, Singapore

Dai DY, Sternberg RJ (eds) (2004) Motivation, emotion, and cognition: integrative perspectives on intellectual functioning and development. Lawrence Erlbaum Associates, Mahwah, NJ

Darling-Hammond L (1996) The right to learn and the advancement of teaching: research, policy, and practice for democratic education. Educ Res 25(6):5–19

Dewey J (1922) Human nature and conduct: an introduction to social psychology. The Modern Library, New York

Dewey J (2005) Art as experience. Perigee Books, New York (Originally published in 1934)

DiPardo A, Potter C (2003) Beyond cognition: a Vygotskian perspective on emotionality and teachers' professional lives. In: Kozulin A, Gindis B, Ageyev V, Miller S (eds) Vygotsky and the culture of education: sociocultural theory and practice in the 21st century. Cambridge University Press, New York, NY, pp 317–345

DiPardo A, Schnack P (2004) Expanding the web of meaning: thought and emotion in an inter-generational reading and writing program. Read Res Q 39(1):14–37

Doster EC, Jackson DF, Smith DW (1997) Modeling pedagogical content knowledge in physical science for prospective middle school teachers: problems and possibilities. Teach Educ Q 24(4):51–65

Egan K (1992) Imagination in teaching and learning: the middle school years. University of Chicago Press, Chicago

Eisner EW (2002) The arts and the creation of mind. Yale University Press, New Haven, CT

Foucault M (1977) Discipline and punishment: the birth of the prison (trans: Sheridan A). Pantheon, New York

Foucault M (1982) The archaeology of knowledge. Routledge, London

Gardner H (1987) The mind's new science. Basic Books, New York

Greene M (1995) Releasing the imagination: essays on education, the arts, and social change. Jossey-Bass, San Francisco

Grossman P (1989) A study in contrast: sources of pedagogical content knowledge for secondary English. J Teach Educ 40(5):24–31

Grossman P (1990) The making of a teacher: teacher knowledge and teacher education. Teachers College Press, New York

Gudmundsdottir S (1991) Ways of seeing are ways of knowing: the pedagogical content knowledge of an expert English teacher. J Curriculum Stud 23(5):409–21

Hargreaves A (2000) Mixed emotions: teachers' perceptions of their interactions with students. Teach Teach Educ 16(8):811–826

Hembree R (1990) The nature, effects, and relief of mathematics anxiety. J Res Math Educ 21(1):33–46

Hjortshoj K (2001) Understanding writing blocks. Oxford UP, Oxford

Huber M, Morreale S (2002) Disciplinary styles in the scholarship of teaching and learning: exploring common ground. AAHE Publications, Merrifield, VA

Kennedy M (2005) Inside teaching: how classroom life undermines reform. Harvard University Press, Cambridge, MA

Krashen SD (1981) The "fundamental pedagogical principle" in second language teaching. Stud Linguistica 35(1–2):50–70

Krashen S (1982) Principles and practice in second language learning and acquisition. Pergamon, Oxford

Krashen S (2002) Explorations in language acquisition and use: The Taipei lectures. Crane Publishing Company, Taipei

Lather P (1991) Getting smart: feminist research and pedagogy with/in the postmodern. Routledge, New York

Leinhardt G (1990) Capturing craft knowledge in teaching. Educ Res 19(2):18–25

Linnenbrick EA (2006) Emotion research in education: theoretical and methodological perspectives on the integration of affect, motivation, and cognition. Educ Psychol Rev 18(4):307–316

Loughran J, Mulhall P, Berry A (2004) In search of pedagogical content knowledge in science: developing ways of articulating and documenting professional practice. J Res Sci Teach 41(4):370–391

Magnusson S, Krajcik JS, Borko H (1999) Nature, sources and development of pedagogical content knowledge for science teaching. In: Gess-Newsome J, Lederman NG (eds) Examining pedagogical content knowledge. Kluwer, The Netherlands, pp 95–132

McCaughtry N, Rovegno I (2003) Development of pedagogical content knowledge: moving from blaming students to predicting skillfulness, recognizing motor development, and understanding emotion. J Teach Phys Educ 22(4):355–368. http://www.humankinetics.com/jtpe/viewarticle.cfm?aid=1788

McLeod DB, Adams VM (eds) (1989) Affect and mathematical problem solving: a new perspective. Springer, New York

Mishra P, Koehler M (2006) Technological pedagogical content knowledge: a framework for teacher knowledge. Teach Coll Record 108(6):1017–1054

Noffke S (1997) Professional, personal, and political dimensions of action research. Rev Res Educ 22:305–343

Petrovic JE, Rosiek J (2007) From teacher knowledge to queered teacher knowledge research: escaping the epistemic straight jacket. In: Rodriguez N, Pinar B (eds) Queering straight teachers: discourse and identity in education. Peter Lang, New York

Pintrich PR, Marx RW, Boyle RA (1993) Beyond cold conceptual change: the role of motivational beliefs and classroom contextual factors in the process of conceptual change. Rev Educ Res 63:167–199

Popper K (1972) Logic of scientific discovery. Hutchinson, London

Reay D (2000) A useful extension of Bourdieu's conceptual framework: emotional capital as a way of understanding mothers involvement in their children's education. Sociol Rev 48:568–585

Robinson P, Cooper J (1995) An annotated bibliography of cooperative learning in higher education: Part III – The 1990s. New Forums Press, Stillwater, OK

Rose M (ed) (1985) When a writer can't write: studies in writer's block and other composing-process problems. The Guilford Press, New York and London

Rosiek J (1995) Affective scaffolding: studies in the pedagogical content knowledge about student motivation. Paper presented at the annual meeting of the American Educational Research Association, San Francisco, CA

Rosiek J (2003) Emotional scaffolding: an exploration of teacher knowledge at the intersection of student emotion and subject matter content. J Teach Educ 54(5):399–412

Rosiek J (2005) Toward teacher education that takes the study of culture as foundational: building bridges between teacher knowledge research and educational ethnography. In: Spindler G (ed) New horizons in the ethnography of education. Lawrence Erlbaum Associates, Mahwah, NJ

Rosiek J, Atkinson B (2005) Bridging the divides: the need for a pragmatic semiotics of teacher knowledge research. Educ Theory 55(4):231–266

Schutz PA, Lanehart SL (2002) Emotions in education: guest editors' introduction. Educ Psychol 37:67–68

Schutz PA, Pekrun R (2007) Emotion in education. Academic, San Diego, CA

Sconiers Z, Rosiek J (2000) Historical perspective as an important element of teacher knowledge: a sonata form case study of equity issues in a chemistry classroom. Harv Educ Rev 70(3):370–404

Shulman LS (1987) Knowledge and teaching: foundations of the new reform. Harv Educ Rev 57(1):1–22

Shulman L (2000) Teacher development: roles of domain expertise and pedagogical knowledge. J Appl Dev Psychol 25(1):129–135

Shulman L (2005) The wisdom of practice: essays on teaching, learning, and learning to teach. Jossey-Bass, San Francisco

Smith DC, Neale DC (1989) The construction of subject matter knowledge in primary science teaching. Teach Teach Educ 5(1):1–20

Snow RE, Corno L, Jackson D (1996) Individual differences in affective and cognitive functions. In: Berliner DC, Calfee RC (eds) Handbook of educational psychology. Macmillan, New York, pp 243–310

Stone CA (1993) What's missing in the metaphor of scaffolding? In: Forman EA, Minick N, Stone CA (eds) Context for learning: sociocultural dynamics in children's development. Oxford University Press, New York, pp 169–183

Sutton R, Wheatley K (2003) Teachers' emotions and teaching: a review of the literature and directions for future research. Educ Psychol Rev 15(4):327–358

van Veen K, Lasky S (2005) Emotions as a lens to explore teacher identity and change: different theoretical approaches. (Introduction to special issue on emotion, teacher identity and change). Teach Teach Educ 21(8):895–898

Veal WR, MaKinster JG (1999) Pedagogical content knowledge taxonomies. Electron J Sci Educ 3(4). http://wolfweb.unr.edu/homepage/crowther/ejse/vealmak.html

Vygotsky LS (2004) Imagination and creativity in childhood (trans: M. E. Sharpe, Inc.). J Russ East Eur Psychol 42:7–97 (Original work published 1967)

Wood D, Bruner J, Ross G (1976) The role of tutoring in problem solving. J Child Psychol Psychiatry 17:89–100

Zembylas M (2001) Constructing genealogies of teachers' emotions in science teaching. J Res Sci Teach 39(1):79–103

Zembylas M (2003) Caring for teacher emotion: reflections on teacher self-development. Stud Philos Educ 22(2):103–125

Zembylas M (2007) Emotional ecology: the intersection of emotional knowledge and pedagogical content knowledge in teaching. Teach Teach Educ 23:355–367

Chapter 10
Educational Psychology Perspectives on Teachers' Emotions

Paul A. Schutz, Lori P. Aultman, and Meca R. Williams-Johnson

Abstract In this chapter we focus on teacher emotion from an educational psychology lens. In doing so, we explicate some of the current theories related to the nature of emotion. In recent years, there has been renewed interest in the debates about the nature and structure of emotion in psychology and educational psychology. In other words, are there distinct categories of emotions (e.g., anger, fear) or is it more useful to conceptualize emotion with a dimensional model (e.g., pleasant vs. unpleasant, active vs. inactive)? We use those perspectives to help us understand teachers' emotions and discuss research related to how teachers negotiate relationship boundaries with their students, how teachers develop useful emotional climates in their classrooms, and how teachers attempt to deal with the emotional labor needed in negotiating their role as a teacher.

Keywords Educational psychology • Teacher emotions • Emotional labor

In essence, schooling, in whatever forms it takes, at its core involves processes of enculturalization where what is believed in and valued within and among cultures is acted and reenacted in ritualized activity settings. It is during these social histori-cal contextualized events that teachers experience, display, and/or create affective experiences. As such, affective experiences are intricately woven into the fabric of classroom experiences and it is those affective experiences and the processes involved with those experiences that are the focus of this chapter.

We approach our discussion of affective experiences from what we consider to be an educational psychology perspective. As such, we acknowledge the biological (e.g., Gray 1990), historical (e.g., Stearns and Stearns 1985), sociological (e.g., Denzin 1984), psychological (e.g., Lazarus 1991) and anthropological (e.g., Lutz and White 1986)

P.A. Schutz (✉)
Department of Educational Psychology, University of Texas at San Antonio,
San Antonio, TX, USA
e-mail: paul.schutz@utsa.edu

P.A. Schutz and M. Zembylas (eds.), *Advances in Teacher Emotion Research:*
The Impact on Teachers' Lives,
DOI 10.1007/978-1-4419-0564-2_10, © Springer Science+Business Media, LLC 2009

perspectives about affective experience, but foreground our educational psychological perspective by focusing on teaching and the study of emotions within transactions in educational contexts. To do so we begin by explaining how we make distinctions among commonly used terms for affective experiences. Next, we use data from several of our studies to explicate various affective experiences that teachers labeled emotional episodes such as frustration, anger, happiness and sadness/helplessness. Finally, we draw conclusions from these previous sections in an effort to suggest implications for research on teacher emotion, pre-and in-service teacher training and classroom activities.

Affective Experiences

There are a variety of terms used for affective experiences in the academic literature and everyday speech. Therefore, we believe it is important to begin by clarifying the distinctions we think are important to a discussion of affective experiences. Currently, based on the emotion literature to be discussed in the following sections, we believe it is useful to organize our thinking about affective experiences into three transactional processes: Affective Tendencies, Core Affect, and Emotional Episodes.

Affective Tendency

We use the term Affective Tendencies to describe somewhat stable predispositions towards certain ways of emoting (see Fig. 10.1). As such, Affective Tendencies tend to bias individuals toward particular emotional experiences that are similar to those propensities (Rosenberg 1998). Researchers interested in emotions have long made a distinction between traits (i.e., general tendency to emote in a particular way) and states (i.e., emoting during a particular event) (Davidson 1994; Ekman 1984; Lazarus 1991; Rosenberg 1998). From our perspective, affective tendencies act as lenses through which individuals view their transactions in the world. Thus, if a teacher is predisposed to view his or her school as a scary or unsafe place, he or she is more likely to interpret various situations as being potentially frightening and, as a result, experience more emotional episodes that he or she may label as anxiety or fear. These affective tendencies develop through transactions among a variety of sources that we, for discussion purposes, organize into two broad inter-related categories of influence: social-historical and individual.

Social-Historical Influences

From social-historical perspectives, researchers have accumulated evidence suggesting stronger cultural influences on affective experiences than what psychologists once

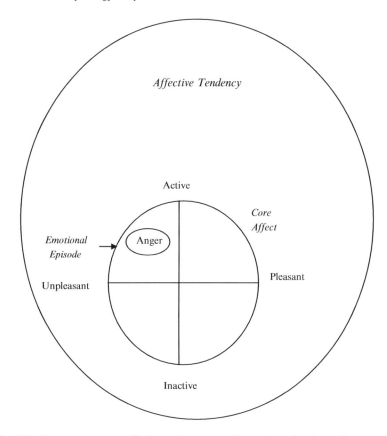

Fig. 10.1 Transactions among affective tendency, core affect and emotional episode

believed (Parkinson et al. 2005). One indication of cultural influences is a strand of research suggesting that experiences that are labeled as an emotional episode in one culture may not be labeled as such in another (Parkinson et al. 2005; Lutz and White 1986; Russell 2003). For example, Parkinson et al. (2005) indicated the English language contains around 2,000 emotion words whereas Taiwanese Chinese has a substantially reduced list of about 750 words. This suggests that affective experiences may not have similar meaning or salience across cultures.

In addition to the number of emotion terms in different cultures, researchers have also identified other potential cultural differences. For instance, there has been considerable inquiry from a cross-cultural perspective looking at the differences between individualistic and collectivist focused cultures. In a recent meta-analysis, Oyserman et al. (2002) concluded that individualistic focused cultures tend to value personal independence, uniqueness, and sometimes, personal privacy, whereas collectivist focused cultures tend to value group processes and a sense of duty or obligation to in-group harmony. These cultural differences suggest potential differences in what may be identified as an emotional episode and how that episode might be displayed.

Therefore, what is valued within a culture tends to be represented in the norms of that culture. These norms bring with them feeling or display rules (Hochschild 1983; Zembylas 2005). Display rules are basically cultural norms for how people are expected to try or try not to feel in particular situations. As such, these feeling rules help to define the nature of how and when different emotions are experienced. Individualistic cultures tend to promote open expression of the individual's emotion whereas some cultures and religious ideas value behavior or expression that promotes cooperation and harmony (Klimes-Dougan and Zeman 2007). Hence, it may be acceptable for anger to be felt and openly expressed in some cultures, but in others it is understood that anger may be felt but not communicated, even in one's facial expression (Cole et al. 2002). Thus, researchers have accumulated both cross cultural and historical evidence suggesting social-historical contextual influences related to what emotions are experienced as well as how and when we experience those emotions. However, these social-historical influences also transact with individual influences such as a person's experience, temperament and his or her behavior activation/inhibition systems.

Individual Influences

In terms of individual influences on affective tendencies, we focus on three areas that have received attention by researchers: personal experience, temperament and the behavior activation/inhibition systems. In terms of personal experience, we think it is useful to keep in mind that personal experience occurs within various social historical contexts. Elsewhere Schutz et al. (2007) used Bronfenbrenner's ecological model (1986) to represent the developmental transactions as a series of nested systems. In line with that explanation, our discussion here provides additional evidence from researchers who suggest that affective tendencies such as depression and other emotions may be passed from parents to children (or vice versa) via particular transactions in the family context (Emde et al. 1986; Larson and Almeida 1999; Larson and Richards 1994). Thus, through personal experience within their families, teachers, like anyone else, develop affective tendencies that tend to bias them towards particular core affect and emotional episodes. So if a young teacher comes from a family context where the emotional episodes such as anger or caring and love are not expressed freely, those experiences may influence affective tendencies that can be carried into and expected during classroom transactions. This suggests that, to some extent, through personal experience there is the potential for emotional episodes to become habitualized resulting in affective tendencies for particular emotional episodes (Chang and Davis this volume; Pekrun et al. 2007; Zembylas 2005).

In addition to the personal experiences that have potential to influence teachers' affective tendencies, we also discuss two other potential individual influences: temperament and the behavior activation/inhibition systems. As discussed later, both are believed to be somewhat biological in nature, but also environmentally malleable via transactions within persons' immediate (e.g., family, peers and school) and social-historical contexts (e.g., individualistic/collectivistic; historical changes).

Generally speaking the term temperament is used to describe patterns of behavioral and emotional reactivity that are thought to be relatively stable across time and situation and are thought to represent the emergence of early individual differences, in part from biological systems (Bates 2000; Goldsmith 1993). Accordingly, temperament has been characterized as a potential individual difference influence on the way emotions are expressed and experienced (Bates 2000; Goldsmith 1993).

Although there are a variety of different theories, we use the model proposed by Clark and Watson (1991) as an example of the potential individual influences of temperament on affective tendencies. Clark and Watson (1991) described two independent temperament factors: Positive and Negative Emotionality. Cross-sectional research in this area suggests that people who score high on a measure of positive emotionality are believed to show a propensity for pleasant mood states and tend to be sociable. On the other hand, people who score high on a measure of negative emotionality are believed to show a propensity for unpleasant mood states and higher levels of perceived stress (Clark and Watson 1999). In addition, there is longitudinal evidence that temperamental behaviors measured in childhood may be predictive of adult depression and mood disorders (Block et al. 1991; Caspi et al. 1996; van Os et al. 1997).

The third potential influence on affective tendencies is found in research in the area of biological or physiological psychology. There is support, via studies of brain activity, for at least two systems involved in the regulation of behavior – the behavioral activation system, which is involved in approach behavior, and the behavioral inhibition system, which is involved in avoidance behaviors (Carver and Scheier 2000; Cloniger 1987; Gray 1990). In psychology the approach/avoidance motives have been part of the emotion literature for decades, particularly in research on anxiety. In fact in 1960, Atkinson and Litwin went as far as suggesting that the "Mandler-Sarason Test Anxiety scores could indicate the strength of a motive to avoid failure" (p. 52). More recently, DeCuir-Gunby et al. (in press) reported that the approach/avoidance motives accounted for 21% of the variance in pleasant test emotions and 38% of the variance in unpleasant test emotions. Hence, the behavior activation/inhibition systems may represent basic, potentially biologically based, human processes that have the potential to influence affective tendencies.

In summary, we see Affective Tendencies as somewhat stable predispositions towards certain ways of emoting. These affective tendencies involve ways of looking at the world that have the potential to influence how individuals view their transactions in the world. In addition, affective tendencies develop through transactions among a variety of sources such as social-historical (e.g., language, individualistic/collectivism and historical) and individual influences (e.g., personal experience, temperament and behavior activation/inhibition systems). Finally, our Affective Tendencies have the potential to bias our core affect; that is, how we feel at any particular point.

Core Affect

Russell (2003) defined core affect as "A neurophysiological state that is consciously accessible as a simple, nonreflective feeling that is an integral blend of hedonic (pleasure–displeasure) and arousal (sleepy–activated) values" (p. 147) (see Fig. 10.1). So, whereas Affective Tendencies have the potential to influence how teachers feel, core affect is how they actually feel at any particular point in time. However, unlike an emotional episode (discussed later), which tends to be a response to a particular situation, core affect tends not to have an object or focus. Core affect is generally described as a continuous and fluctuating state that normally functions unconsciously (Barrett 2006a). Russell (2003) used the analogy of felt body temperature to describe core affect. In other words, people tend to be aware of extremes such as feeling hot or cold just as they may be aware of feeling "blue" or "happy", yet they may not be sure why they feel that way. However, as Russell (2003) suggests, you can talk about your core affect, just as you can talk about your felt temperature. For example, if asked, teachers would be able to describe how they feel at any particular point in time (e.g., happy, a little tired or a bit tense), yet if not asked – they may not have reflected on those current feelings.

As suggested by Russell and others, how people feel at any particular point in time can be conceptualized as a blend of two affective dimensions – valence ranging from pleasant to unpleasant and arousal ranging from high activation to low activation (Barrett 2006a, b; Linnenbrink 2007). As such, when those two dimensions are combined there is the potential for blends of at least eight potential core affective feelings (i.e., Pleasant (e.g., happy); Unpleasant (e.g., sad); High Activation (e.g., energetic); Low Activation (e.g., tired); Pleasant – High Activation (e.g., excited); Pleasant – Low Activation (e.g., serene); Unpleasant – High Activation (e.g., tense); and, Unpleasant – Low Activation (e.g., gloomy).

Therefore, we view core affect (the way one feels at any particular point in time) as a continuous range of ever-present feeling states that have the potential to become more prominent and intense based on the person's judgments (i.e., appraisal, attributions). This current way of being in the world has the potential to influence not only if an emotional episode might occur but also how that episode might be labeled. Thus, if a teacher's current core affect includes being tired and tense, a student's relatively minor classroom misbehavior may result in anger, however, if the teacher's core affect was more in line with the energetic and happy ends of the continuum – the same misbehavior may be met with joy and laughter.

In sum, core affect is basically how teachers feel at any particular point in time. How they get to that particular core affect may be influenced by any number of life events, including affective tendencies. In addition, like a felt temperature, individuals may or may not be aware of how they are feeling, and there tends not to be an object or focus to those feelings. In other words, core affect tends not to be about something in particular. Our core affect can be influenced in part by the teacher's affective tendencies and can have the potential via attributions and/or appraisals to become an emotional episode.

Emotional Episode

Although there is a great deal of discussion within the field about what constitutes an emotion, emotional experience, or emotional episode (see for example the prolonged discussions between Lazarus 1982, 1984; and Zajonc 1980, 1984 or more recently Barrett 2006a and Izard 2007), there are some common themes that have emerged. For example, a number of theorists argue that emotional episodes consist of a: physiological response, cognitive appraisal, and behavioral tendency (e.g. Frijda 2000; Izard 2007; Russell and Barrett 1999; Scherer 1984; Smith 1991). Schutz et al. (2006) further elaborated on this view by also emphasizing social and historical aspects that shape an emotional episode. They described emotional experiences as "socially constructed, personally enacted ways of being that emerge from conscious and/or unconscious judgments regarding perceived successes at attaining goals or maintaining standards or beliefs during transactions as part of social-historical contexts (p. 344)." There are two key aspects of this definition that are relevant to our discussion here (see Fig. 10.1).

Appraisals and Emotional Episodes

First, emotions involve judgments or appraisals (Boekaerts 2007; Pekrun et al. 2007; Schutz and Davis 2000; Schutz and DeCuir 2002). As suggested above, Core Affect tends to become an emotional episode via appraisal or attribution regarding what is happening during a particular event. Individuals' goals, values, and beliefs, as well as their social network are the referent points used to judge where they are in relation to where they want to be (Carver and Scheier 2000; Ford and Smith 2007; Schutz and DeCuir 2002; Schutz and Davis 2000; Solomon 1976; Powers 1971; Weiner 2007). These goals, values, and beliefs represent ways individuals, as members of social groups, position themselves during a particular life event (Boekaerts 2007; Ford 1992; Ford and Smith 2007; Markus and Nurius 1986; Schutz et al. 2001).

Thus, appraisals involve teachers' perceptions of how the pursuit of a goal progresses during an academic transaction. In most cases, these judgments tend to occur outside of the teachers' awareness, yet these judgments are seen as being key to the emotional episode (Frijda 1993; Lazarus 1991; Pekrun et al. 2007; Schutz and Davis 2000; Smith 1991). Lazarus (1991, 1999) made a distinction between primary and secondary appraisals. Primary appraisals consist of judgments related to goal relevance (i.e., is it important to the teacher's goals?), goal congruence (i.e., is it going how the teacher hoped it would?) and the type of ego-involvement (i.e., how much of the teacher's "self" or "identity" is involved?) (Lazarus 1991, 1999). These primary appraisals tend to influence the valence of an emotional episode. In other words, if the event is appraised as important and going well – a pleasant emotional episode is more likely. Whereas, if this event is appraised as being important but not going well, it is more likely that an unpleasant emotional episode will occur.

Secondary appraisals are the judgments teachers make about their potential to handle the particular situation. Key secondary appraisals are related to agency or control (Lazarus 1999; Pekrun et al. 2007; Schutz and Davis 2000) and problem-efficacy (Bandura 1997; Schutz and Davis 2000), or what Lazarus (1991) referred to as coping potential (i.e., the teacher's confidence about his/her ability to handle the situation). These secondary appraisals help differentiate among potential emotional experiences. For example, a situation that has been appraised as goal important (e.g., "It's vital for my students to do well on this standardized test") and goal incongruent (e.g., "My students did not do well on the practice test"), with secondary appraisals of self-blame (e.g., "I knew I should have done a better job of teaching") may result in shame (Turner and Waugh 2007). Alternatively, the same situation with secondary appraisals of other blame (e.g., "These standardized tests don't measure what my students know") may result in anger.

Social Construction of Emotional Episode

An important aspect of emotion episodes is that they are socially constructed and emerge from particular social-historical contexts (Denzin 1984; Lazarus 1991; Lazarus and Folkman 1984; Meyer and Turner 2007; Op 't Eynde et al. 2007; Schutz et al. 2006). In other words, emotions are "relational", such that emotional experiences do not exist as exclusive features of a person or of an environment. Particular emotional experiences involve person–environmental transactions. Consequently, in most cases there is both a social dimension of an emotional experience and the person's enactment of the particular emotional way of being.

Emotional experiences are also influenced by the particular social-historical context in which the transaction occurred (DeCuir-Gunby and Williams 2007; Lutz and White 1986; Markus and Kitayama 1994; Ratner 2007; Schutz et al. 2007; Stearns and Stearns 1985). For example, the emotional experience we label guilt is based upon developing knowledge of the ethical and legal values of a culture (Ratner 2007; Weiner 2007). As such the student or teacher must adopt the cultural value or belief of personal responsibility in order for a guilt emotional experience to occur. This suggests that the appraisals and attributions that students and teachers make are reflective of the social-historical context in which they and their social groups are embedded.

As such, when there are emotional episodes in the classroom, they reflect person–environment transactions as well as the social-historical contexts in which those transactions occur. Illustrative of this concept is an emotional school situation described in a study by DeCuir-Gunby and Williams (2007). After attending an assembly featuring a local civil rights leader, some students had intense emotional episodes including guilt, anger, and sadness. One student in particular described her classmate as being "upset, and crying". She was upset because she thought that he [the assembly speaker] was saying that she was a bad person simply because she was "white". This student was experiencing an emotion (sadness) as a result of both an environmental transaction (listening to the civil rights leader's speech) and her own social-historical context (the perceived meaning of being White). The incident is illustrative in that it describes students encountering images and discussions that were incongruent with their personal beliefs, which triggered evaluations of the self and experiencing emotions associated with that evaluation.

As indicated, from our perspective an emotional episode is a process that involves judgments about how; in this case, teachers perceive themselves to be interacting within a social-historical context (Schutz 1991; Schutz et al. 2006; Solomon 1976, 1984). In other words, as teachers attempt to attain their goals (e.g., teaching goals, life goals) or maintain their standards (e.g., social or individual norms, values, beliefs), they make judgments (e.g., appraisal, attributions) comparing what they would like to see happen (i.e., goals and standards) and what they perceive to be happening. This emoting process is the subject of the next section.

Emoting Process

Imagine a young teacher who has a belief that learning is best accomplished via problems based learning and develops classroom goals and strategies to develop problem-solving activities for her students. However, what happens if she gets a job at a school where her beliefs and goals are met with a school context where preparations for standardized tests are privileged and drill and practice is thought to be the way to best prepare students for those tests? In this situation, there is the potential for a mismatch between the goals, standards, and teacher selves of this particular teacher and the expectation expressed by other teachers, administrators, and students. In this case there may be a variety of events where this teacher has the potential to make judgments related to this mismatch. These appraisals or attributions may result in frustration, anger or even a feeling of being challenged to change how this school approached learning.

As such, the emoting process involves making judgments (i.e., appraisal and attributions) regarding where you are in relationship to where you want to be (i.e., goals and standards). Those judgments, in conjunction with teachers' affective tendencies and current core affect, have the potential to influence the type, intensity and duration of particular emotional experiences. To demonstrate this process we will share data we collected via interviews with teachers as they talk about various emotional episodes.[1]

---

[1] The data collected for these examples focused only on emotional episodes. As such, we are unable to speculate as to how affective tendencies or core affect might influence these particular emotional episodes. The theoretical framework and the authors of the research cited in previous sections would suggest that the affective tendencies teachers "bring" to an episode as well as their core affect at the time of the event have the potential to influence their experience. Future research will investigate the nature of those transactions.

Frustration: Ms. Bell

When we interviewed Ms. Bell she was in the middle of her third year of teaching. She is a fourth grade teacher of a class of 27 students. There are two other fourth grade teachers in this K-5 school that is located in a primarily rural area. Within the context of the interview, Ms. Bell made it clear that the creation of a caring, safe place where students were not afraid to ask questions was a top priority that almost consumed her. A key part of that goal was her belief that she needed to get to know her students so that she could understand and help them in times of need. In other words, this was an important teaching goal for her.

This goal was put to the test as she talked about her concern for a student who tends to be disruptive in class on some days and she was distressed by the fact that it is still occurring. She described a recent event with this student where again he was disrupting class. She expresses her frustration about this particular event and the overall situation:

> It's seven months into the school year, so I'm wondering why we haven't worked through that [her relationship with the child], but uh, it's also a child who has pretty, you know, severe problems at home. And me being aware of those, it's kind of one of those situations where I'm wondering how do we expect him to function in the classroom when he's going through that stuff at home? So it's still frustrating for me, because I feel like it's something [his classroom disruptions] we should have worked through by month seven.

For Ms. Bell, based in part on cultural expectation (i.e., teacher as caregiver) (Hargreaves 1998; Noddings 1984, 1995) and her own beliefs and goals related to the importance of creating a classroom that is a safe, caring place for students, has developed an expectation (e.g., goals and standards) which, in this case she saw as not going as planned or goal incongruent. Interestingly, she also tends not to attribute this goal incongruence to the child but instead she seems to attribute this mismatch between her expectation and what is happening to a combination of herself ("we should have worked through by month 7" – controllable) or the child's home life ("child who has pretty, you know, severe problems at home" – less controllable) resulting in her experiencing frustration during this particular episode.

Anger: Ms. Conway

Ms. Conway is in her fifth year teaching high school biology in a small city school. She has reached a point in her teaching career where she is questioning whether or not she should stay in the field. She expressed anger about her inability to motivate students, despite exerting considerable effort in her teaching.

> One kid just comes in and says, "I hate school," and another kid comes in and says, "We aren't doing anything today are we?" Another kid comes in and says, "I'm not going to be here today, I mean I'm gonna be here today, but I'm not going to be here today." Two more kids come in and say, "Do you have a pencil?" First thing in the day – it's so hard to motivate this group.

I guess you think everybody is as interested in what you are doing as you are. I think what makes me the angriest is there is no curiosity. That's where I get so jaded and feel like, "What am I here for?" There is no "I want to do this to complete my circle of learning." I mean I teach hard, and I am so exhausted when I go home from the day. I feel like the [students] learn or memorize it for a test, and after that they could just care less. I mean I hated history. I can remember how it feels to do something and have a surface understanding of it because you didn't try. I'm doing everything that [I've learned] I'm supposed to be doing to facilitate all of this love of learning. It's the best I can. I really think that it is something that would drop me out of the teaching profession at least in public school or high school or whatever.

Ms. Conway's goal is to engender intrinsic motivation in her students, but she sees her efforts are being met with apathy. She would like to see students "complete the circle of learning," indicating that she sees the learning process as a reciprocal relationship between student and teacher. However, her appraisals are frequently based on the standard of her own experience as a student. Thus, comparison of her own student identity vs. her current students' behavior becomes the standard by which she measures her success as a teacher. This comparison results in a mismatch (goal incongruence) in which her students are judged to have "no curiosity", suggesting a secondary appraisal of a lack of control leading to her anger and disillusionment.

Happiness/Enthusiasm: Ms. Stewart

In her second year of teaching sixth grade, Ms. Stewart has responsibility for covering multiple subjects with her students. When asked to describe a recent occasion when she was aware of her students' emotions, she shared the experience of a science scavenger hunt she created for her class.

They were so competitive and excited about what we were doing, and they're pushing everybody out of the way to get to me to give me their checklist. I told them that the first person to get everything checked off, I would get some little prize for them or something. So it took extrinsic motivation. But they were just, "Check mine off! Check mine off! Oh, Ms. Stewart!" They couldn't wait for somebody else to beat them to the punch. It was pretty neat. I loved it. I had a lot of fun. I reciprocated [their excitement]. I'm reflecting them or they're reflecting me. I can't quite figure out which way it goes.

Ms. Stewart admitted she enjoyed creating assignments like this to help alleviate her own tendency toward boredom with less active assignments. Her goal was to generate excitement about learning science, and she accomplished this by a hands-on activity (goal congruence). She attributed the student emotion to extrinsic motivation in the form of the prize she promised the scavenger hunt winner; however, she also shared in her interview that this was an energetic group in the classroom as well. Furthermore, she describes the "emotional contagion" that can take place in the classroom. In this case, she sees the emotional contagion as a positive teaching tool, but is not sure who is initially generating the excitement – her students, her or the activity. Ms. Stewart's episode represents a primary appraisal match between her goals and standards and what she perceived to be occurring in the classroom. In that situation, an appraisal researcher would expect pleasant emotions such joy or happiness (Frijda 1993; Lazarus 1991; Schutz and Davis 2000; Smith 1991).

Sadness/Helplessness: Ms. Walker and Ms. Collins

Teaching third and fourth graders reading for 6 years, Ms. Walker shared several stories on instructing students from working class families. There were many times she mentioned she was saddened by the student's circumstances.

> You feel like you feel helpless at that point.... I mean, they're 4th graders. You just don't expect them to have these problems that they have. And when you learn that they do, I mean, it changes your interactions with them, you know.... I just feel like I had such a privileged childhood when I look at some of the kids I have.

In this particular occurrence Ms. Walker acknowledges the difference between her background and those of her students. Ms. Walker described how she worked with her students to increase their motivation to read while maintaining a close relationship to empower them to discuss their personal concerns and issues. Working closely with the students and getting to know them as individuals is something that Ms. Walker felt aided her with her goal of motivating students to achieve. While the realization that she might not be able to protect herself from other negative forces permeates her workday with a sense of sadness, she perseveres because of her goals to increase student motivation to reading.

Unlike Ms. Walker's descriptions of having a close relationship with her students, Ms. Collins iterated she was averse to becoming too involved in the personal lives of her high school students. However, Ms. Collins teaches in an affluent high school and expressed the emotion of sadness similar to Ms. Walker's.

> I felt uncomfortable knowing all of these personal troubles and anguish, you know? I tried to just kind of keep myself focused on just the boy and just the class… These were just facts that were very sad. But, I felt like, you know, "I can get too involved here." And I don't know, what is my role here? I just felt uncomfortable with having to know so much information, but yet the kid is just in so much need…, I almost cried after leaving that day because he was just so sad. And you're thinking, "He's just 18 years old, and is so smart."… I was involved.

The complexity of the emotion of sadness is described various ways. Her goal throughout the entire incident is to emotionally protect herself from becoming involved unlike Ms. Walker, who welcomed the emotional implications of becoming entangled in the family life of her students. Ms. Collins sought to hear the facts as a way to better help her student who was struggling through a difficult time. In commiserating with the student in understanding his anger, rage and sadness her own emotional defenses declined. She was emotionally saddened because she could not protect the student, who she believed had tremendous potential and she could no longer remain emotionally distant, which is incongruent from her original goals of not becoming too involved with the student.

These recent accounts breathe new life into the idea that goal attainment and social construction influence teachers' emotional episodes. Stated more plainly, these examples highlight teachers' attempts to attain their goals, maintain standards, and make comparisons to what they would like to see happen and what is perceived to actually transpire that influence their emotional response to the events described. As indicated and illustrated in the previous examples, for teachers, emotional episodes are experienced, displayed, and/or created during classroom transactions.

Conclusions

In this chapter we suggest that emotional episodes have the potential to be influenced by teachers' affective tendencies (i.e., somewhat stable predispositions towards certain ways of emoting), core affect (.e., how teachers actually feel at any particular point in time), and the judgments (i.e., appraisal and attribution) teachers make during classroom transactions. It is important to keep in mind that the processes involved in affective experiences are bounded by and occur within social historical contexts, which have the potential to influence the type, tendency and duration of particular emotional experiences.

To date, emotion researchers have tended to investigate these three interrelated processes separately, as our examples also demonstrate. As such, researchers have typically not examined the transactions among affective tendencies, core affect, and emotional episodes. The notable exception here is the aforementioned research on affective tendencies (temperament) and emotional episodes. Therefore, from an educational psychological perspective it will be important for researchers to begin to investigate transactions and how affective tendencies, core affect and emotional episodes evolve to impact learning and teaching within the classroom. Additionally, more research is needed for educators to recognize and address these occurrences to benefit optimal positive interactions within the classroom. In other words, what do optimal classroom transactions look and feel like and how do they help teachers foster such transactions?

The research in the area of teacher emotion is important in that large numbers of teachers are leaving the profession (Dove 2004). One explanation of why teachers leave the profession so early in their career might be related to the unexpected experiences fraught with emotions within the teaching profession. For example, teaching is an occupation that involves considerable emotional labor. Emotional labor involves the effort, planning, and control teachers need to express organizationally desired emotions during interpersonal transactions. Thus, emotional labor has been associated with job dissatisfaction, health symptoms and emotional exhaustion, which are key components of teacher burnout and dropping out of the profession (Hochschild 1990; Morris and Feldman 1996). Research into emotional labor in teaching and other aspects of teachers' emotions is becoming increasingly important not only because of the growing number of teachers leaving the profession, but also because unpleasant classroom emotions have considerable implications for student learning, school climate and the quality of education in general.

Implications

The ideas and examples presented in this chapter suggest that the classroom can be an intensely emotional place. It is a socially constructed cultural context where affective tendencies and core affect are personally enacted and interacted. Teachers and students are the dominant influences – though administrators, parents, and other stakeholders may also have input into the emotional climate. Therefore, the classroom is a place where commingling of teachers' and students' emotional influences has the potential, based on individual appraisals and attributions, to create emotional episodes. As emotionally charged as schools may be, research suggests that teachers feel ill equipped to handle various types of emotional episodes they encounter in the school context (Aultman et al. in press). Teachers contend that teacher education programs either neglect or only superficially describe the emotional aspects of classroom interactions that might prepare teachers to manage emotional situations. Therefore, we suggest the emotional nature of the classroom provides several implications for the training and professional development of teachers.

Teacher educators have the opportunity to provide learning experiences in and out of the classroom. Introductory courses are typically aimed at building a foundation for field experiences that take place throughout the teacher preparation program. Teachers identify field experience as a genuine professional development opportunity. This opportunity will only be fully exploited when the complexity of the field experience, including the emotional dimension, is researched and better understood (Golby 1996; Hastings 2004). Preservice teachers do not enter into the professional arena as a blank slate (Meyer this volume). They have life experiences and personal tendencies as well as ideas and beliefs that will impact their teaching lives (Goldstein and Lake 2000). The goals preservice teachers begin to generate for their teaching practice may be built on preconceptions that have been formed from limited knowledge or misconceptions about the realities of the classroom. Hence, preservice teachers should be engaged in tasks that promote understanding of self-views a priori, so that they may build more productively and effectively on that knowledge (Bullough 1991; Cole and Knowles 1993; Hollingsworth 1989). Activities that promote teacher self-awareness can be construed as a necessary component of training. Teachers' cognizance of the individual and social historical influences on their own affective tendencies, core affect, and emotional regulation enhances their ability to anticipate classroom situations with which they may struggle. For example, reflective journaling throughout teacher preparation allows pre-service teachers to examine their views of the profession, begin to articulate their own teacher identity, reflect on their field experiences, and become more aware of their responses to emotionally-laden incidents.

Furthermore, writing teaching philosophies may aid pre-service and in-service teachers in formulating explicit teaching goals that are congruent with their own teacher identity. Teachers may also benefit from reflecting on the reciprocal nature of student–teacher relationships. Evident in the examples in this chapter is the fact that it is not just teachers' emotions in play. Students and teachers are constantly interacting, creating situations to which both react based on their own emotional influences.

Research also intimates that in-service teachers benefit from the support and advice of colleagues when dealing with emotional episodes (Aultman et al. in press; Hylen 2004; Stansbury and Zimmerman 2000; Williams et al. 2008). Establishing formal or informal relationships in schools could serve as a vehicle for this type of support. These supportive groups or relationships could be a part of the departmental structure in the school, could be the result of mentor/mentee relationships (Bullough this volume), or could be encouraged through interdepartmental contact with support personnel in the school.

The examination of emotions in this present chapter not only sheds light on the link between core affect, affective tendencies and emotional episodes, but also represents a necessary step toward future empirical investigations of teacher emotions and emotions in the classroom. The assumption that emotions influence behavior and impact the classroom climate has been valuable to educational research. However, more research is needed to further inform educators on the transactions among core affect, affective tendencies and emotional episodes to better their professional practice. In this chapter, we develop a theoretical framework that hopefully will facilitate our understandings of these transactions as well as provide a road map for future research in this area.

References

Atkinson JW, Litwin GH (1960) Achievement motive and test anxiety conceived as motive to approach success and motive to avoid failure. J Abnorm Soc Psychol 60:52–63

Aultman LP, Williams-Johnson MR, Schutz, PA (2009). Boundary dilemmas in teacher–student relationships: Struggling with "the line". Teaching and Teacher Education 25, 636–646

Bandura A (1997) Self-efficacy: the exercise of control. Freeman, New York

Barrett LF (2006a) Solving the emotion paradox: categorization and the experience of emotion. Pers Soc Psychol Rev 10:20–46

Barrett LF (2006b) Valence is a basic building block of emotional life. J Res Pers 40:35–55

Bates JE (2000) Temperament as an emotion construct: theoretical and practical issues. In: Lewis M, Haviland-Jones JM (eds) Handbook of emotions, 2nd edn. Guilford, New York, pp 382–396

Block JH, Gjerde PF, Block JH (1991) Personality antecedents of depressive tendencies in 18-year-olds: a prospective study. J Pers Soc Psychol 60:726–738

Boekaerts M (2007) Understanding students' affective processes in the classroom. In: Schutz PA, Pekrun R (eds) Emotion in education. Elsevier, San Diego, CA, pp 223–241

Bronfenbrenner U (1986) Ecology of the family as a context for human development: research perspectives. Dev Psychol 22:723–742

Bullough RV Jr (1991) Exploring personal teaching metaphors in preservice teacher education. J Teach Educ 42:43–51

Carver SC, Scheier MF (2000) On the structure of behavioral self-regulation. In: Boekaerts M, Pintrich PR, Zeidner M (eds) Handbook of self-regulation. Academic, San Diego, CA, pp 41–84

Caspi A, Moffitt TE, Newman DL, Silva PA (1996) Behavioral observations at age 3 predict adult psychiatric disorders: longitudinal evidence from a birth cohort. Arch Gen Psychiatry 53(11):1033–1039

Clark LA, Watson D (1991) Tripartite model of anxiety and depression: psychometric evidence and taxonomic implications. J Abnorm Psychol 100:316–336

Clark LA, Watson D (1999) Temperament: a new paradigm for trait psychology. In: Pervin LA, John OP (eds) Handbook of personality: theory and research, 2nd edn. Guilford, New York, pp 399–423

Cloniger CR (1987) A systematic method for clinical description and classification of personality variants. Arch Gen Psychiatry 44:573–588

Cole AL, Knowles JG (1993) Shattered images: understanding expectations and realities of field experiences. Teach Teach Educ 9(5–6):57–71

Cole PM, Bruschi CJ, Tamang BL (2002) Cultural differences in children's emotional reactions to difficult situations. Child Dev 73(3):983–996

Davidson RJ (1994) On emotion, mood, and related affective constructs. In: Ekman P, Davidson RJ (eds) The nature of emotion: fundamental questions. Oxford University Press, New York, pp 51–55

DeCuir-Gunby JT, Williams MR (2007) The impact of race and racism on students' emotions: a critical race analysis. In: Schutz PA, Pekrun R (eds) Emotions in education. Academic, San Diego, pp 205–219

DeCuir-Gunby JT, Aultman LP, Schutz PA (2009) Investigating transactions among approach/avoidance motives, emotions and emotional regulation during testing. Journal of Experimental Education, 77(4):409–436

Denzin NK (1984) On understanding emotion. Jossey-Bass, San Francisco, CA

Dove MD (Fall, 2004) Teacher attrition: a critical American and international education issue. Delta Kappa Gamma Bull 71(1):8–30

Ekman P (1984) Expression and the nature of emotion. In: Scherer K, Ekman P (eds) Approaches to emotion. Erlbaum, Hillsdale, NJ, pp 319–344

Emde RN, Harmon RJ, Good WV (1986) Depressive feelings in children: a transactional model for research. In: Rutter M, Izard C, Read P (eds) Depression in young people. Guilford, New York

Ford ME (1992) Motivating humans: goals, emotions and personal agency beliefs. Sage, Newbury Park, CA

Ford ME, Smith PR (2007) Thriving with social purpose: an integrative approach to the development of optimal human functioning. Educ Psychol 42(3):153–171

Frijda NH (1993) The place of appraisal in emotion. Cogn Emotion 7:357–387

Frijda NH (2000) The psychologists' point of view. In: Lewis M, Haviland-Jones JM (eds) Handbook of emotions, 2nd edn. Guilford, New York, pp 59–74

Golby M (1996) Teachers' emotions: an illustrated discussion. Cambridge J Educ 26(3):423–425

Goldsmith HH (1993) Temperament: variability in developing emotion systems. In: Lewis M, Haviland JM (eds) Handbook of emotions. Guilford, New York, pp 353–364

Goldstein LS, Lake VE (2000) "Love, love, and more love for children": exploring preservice teachers' understandings of caring. Teach Teach Educ 16:861–872

Gray JA (1990) Brain systems that mediate both emotion and cognition. Cogn Emotion 4:269–288

Hargreaves A (1998) The emotional practice of teaching. Teach Teach Educ 14(8):835–854

Hastings W (2004) Emotions and the practicum: cooperating teachers' perspective. Teach Teach Theory Pract 10(2):135–148

Hochschild AR (1983) The managed heart: commercialization of human feeling. University of California Press, Berkley, CA

Hochschild AR (1990) Ideology and emotion management: a perspective and path for future research. In: Kemper TD (ed) Research agendas in the sociology of emotions. State University of New York Press, Albany, NY, pp 117–142

Hollingsworth S (1989) Prior beliefs and cognitive change in learning to teach. Am Educ Res J 26:160–189

Hylen J (2004) The top ten reasons a library media specialist is a teacher's best friend. Clearing House 77(5):219–221

Izard CE (2007) Basic emotions, natural kinds, emotion schemas, and a new paradigm. Perspect Psychol Sci 2:260–280

Klimes-Dougan B, Zeman J (2007) Emotion socialization in childhood and adolescence. Soc Dev 16:203–209

Larson RW, Almeida DM (1999) Emotional transmission in the daily lives of families: a new paradigm for studying family process. J Marriage Fam 61(1):5–20

Larson R, Richards M (1994) Divergent realities: the emotional lives of mother, fathers and adolescent. Basic Books, New York

Lazarus RS (1982) Thoughts on the relation between emotion and cognition. Am Psychol 37:1019–1024

Lazarus RS (1984) On the primacy of cognition. Am Psychol 39:124–129

Lazarus RS (1991) Emotion and adaptation. Oxford University Press, New York

Lazarus RS (1999) Stress and emotions: a new synthesis. Springer, New York

Lazarus RS, Folkman S (1984) Stress, appraisal, and coping. Springer, New York

Linnenbrink EA (2007) The role of affect in student learning: a multi-dimensional approach to considering the interaction of affect, motivation, and engagement. In: Schutz PA, Pekrun R (eds) Emotions in education. Academic, San Diego, pp 107–124

Lutz C, White GM (1986) The anthropology of emotions. Annu Rev Anthropol 15:405–436

Markus HR, Kitayama S (1994) The cultural construction of self and emotion: implications for social behavior. In: Kitayama S, Markus HR (eds) Emotion and culture: empirical studies of mutual influence. APA, Washington, DC, pp 89–130

Markus H, Nurius P (1986) Possible selves. Am Psychol 41:954–969

Meyer DK, Turner JC (2007) Scaffolding emotions in classrooms. In: Schutz PA, Pekrun R (eds) Emotions in education. Academic, San Diego, pp 243–258

Morris JA, Feldman DC (1996) The dimensions, antecedents, and consequences of emotional labor. Acad Manage Rev 21(4):986–1010

Noddings N (1984) Caring: a feminine approach to ethics and moral education. University of California Press, Berkley, CA

Noddings N (1995) Teaching themes of caring. Educ Dig 61(3):24–28

Op 't Eynde P, De Corte E, Verschaffel L (2007) Students' emotions: a key-component of self-regulated learning? In: Schutz PA, Pekrun R (eds) Emotions in education. Elsevier, San Diego, pp 185–204

Oyserman D, Coon HM, Kemmelmeier M (2002) Rethinking individualism and collectivism: evaluation of theoretical assumptions and meta-analyses. Psychol Bull 128:3–72

Parkinson B, Fisher AH, Manstead ASR (2005) Emotion in social relations. Psychology Press, New York

Pekrun R, Frenzel AC, Goetz T, Perry RP (2007) The control-value theory of achievement emotions: an integrative approach to emotions in education. In: Schutz PA, Pekrun R (eds) Emotions in education. Elsevier, San Diego, pp 13–36

Powers WT (1971) Behavior: the control of perception. Aldine, Chicago, IL

Ratner C (2007) A macro cultural-psychological theory of emotions. In: Schutz PA, Pekrun R (eds) Emotions in education. Elsevier, San Diego, pp 89–104

Rosenberg EL (1998) Levels of analysis and the organization of affect. Rev Gen Psychol 2(3):247–270

Russell JA (2003) Core affect and the psychological construction of emotion. Psychol Rev 110:145–172

Russell JA, Barrett LF (1999) Core affect, prototypical emotional episodes, and other things called emotion: dissecting the elephant. J Pers Soc Psychol 76(5):805–819

Scherer KR (1984) On the nature and function of emotion: a component process approach. In: Scherer KR, Ekman PE (eds) Approaches to emotion. Erlbaum, Hillsdale, NJ, pp 293–317

Schutz PA (1991) Goals in self-directed behavior. Educ Psychol 26:55–67

Schutz PA, Davis HA (2000) Emotions and self-regulation during test taking. Educ Psychol 35:243–256

Schutz PA, DeCuir JT (2002) Inquiry on emotions in education. Educ Psychol 37:125–134

Schutz PA, Crowder KC, White VE (2001) The development of a goal to become a teacher. J Educ Psychol 93:299–308

Schutz PA, Hong JY, Cross DI, Osbon JN (2006) Reflections on investigating emotions among educational contexts. Educ Psychol Rev 18:343–360

Schutz PA, Cross DI, Hong JY, Osbon JN (2007) Teacher identities, beliefs and goals related to emotions in the classroom. In: Schutz PA, Pekrun R (eds) Emotion in education. Elsevier, San Diego, CA, pp 223–241

Smith CA (1991) The self, appraisal and coping. In: Snyder CR, Forsyth DR (eds) Handbook of social and clinical psychology: the health perspective. Pergamon, Elmsford, NY, pp 116–137

Solomon RC (1976) The passions: myth and nature of human emotion. University of Notre Dame Press, Notre Dame, IN

Solomon RC (1984) Emotions, thoughts, and feelings: emotions as engagements with the world. In: Solomon RC (ed) Thinking about feeling: contemporary philosophers on emotion. Oxford University Press, New York, pp 76–88

Stansbury K, Zimmerman J (2000) Lifelines to the classroom: designing support for beginning teachers (RJ96006901). Office of Educational Research and Improvement, Washington, DC (ERIC Document Reproduction Service No. ED447104)

Stearns PN, Stearns CZ (1985) Emotionology: clarifying the history of emotions and emotional standards. Am Hist Rev 90:813–836

Turner JE, Waugh RM (2007) A dynamical systems perspective regarding students' learning processes: shame reactions and emergent self-organizations. In: Schutz PA, Pekrun R (eds) Emotions in education. Elsevier, San Diego, pp 125–145

van Os J, Jones P, Lewis G, Wadsworth M, Murray R (1997) Developmental precursors of affective illness in a general population birth cohort. Arch Gen Psychiatry 54:625–631

Weiner B (2007) Examining emotional diversity in the classroom: an attribution theorist considers the moral emotions. In: Schutz PA, Pekrun R (eds) Emotions in education. Elsevier, San Diego, pp 75–88

Williams MW, Cross DI, Hong JY, Aultman LP, Osbon JN, Schutz PA (2008) "There is no emotion in math": how teachers approach emotions in the classroom. Teach Coll Record 110(8):1574–1612

Zajonc RB (1980) Feeling and thinking: preference need no inferences. Am Psychol 35:151–175

Zajonc RB (1984) On primacy of affect. In: Scherer KR, Ekman P (eds) Approaches to emotion. Lawrence Erlbaum, Hillsdale, NJ, pp 259–270

Zembylas M (2005) Teaching with emotion: a postmodern enactment. Information Age Publishing References, Greenwich, CT

Part IV
Teachers' Emotions in Times of Change

Chapter 11
Surviving Diversity in Times of Performativity: Understanding Teachers' Emotional Experience of Change

Geert Kelchtermans, Katrijn Ballet, and Liesbeth Piot

Abstract In this chapter we focus on the way teachers experience their job and their professional identity. Our narrative and biographical approach allows for an in-depth reconstruction of the political and moral tensions teachers experience; the pressure to reconceptualise their "selves"; and as a consequence the emotional quality of their work lives. We argue that the changes in the working conditions deeply affect teachers both in their professional actions and the emotional experience of the job. Teachers experience intense emotional conflicts as they struggle to cope with conflicting identity scenarios, the web of (conflicting) loyalties they find themselves in, etc. Our findings confirm, exemplify and deepen earlier work on vulnerability as a structural characteristic of the teaching job.

Keywords performativity · vulnerability · educational reform · diversity

In her editorial introduction to a special issue on emotions in teaching published in the *Cambridge Journal of Education*, Nias (1996) argued that affectivity is of fundamental importance in teaching and to teachers. She gave three reasons for making that claim. First, teachers do experience intense emotions in their teaching: "teachers feel – often passionately – about their pupils, about their professional skill, about their colleagues and the structures of schooling, about their dealings with other significant adults such as parents and inspectors, about the actual or likely effect of educational policies upon their pupils and themselves" (Nias 1996, p. 293). Feelings are just self evidently part of the experience of being a teacher (Hargreaves 1998, 2001). Second, "teachers' emotions are rooted in cognitions (…) one cannot separate feeling from perception, affectivity from judgment" (Nias 1996, p. 294). Teachers' thoughtful actions reflect emotional involvement and moral judgment. Finally, "neither cognition nor feeling can be separated from the

G. Kelchtermans (✉)
Center for Educational Policy and Innovation, University of Leuven, Belgium
e-mail: geert.kelchtermans@ped.kuleuven.be

P.A. Schutz and M. Zembylas (eds.), *Advances in Teacher Emotion Research:*
The Impact on Teachers' Lives,
DOI 10.1007/978-1-4419-0564-2_11, © Springer Science+Business Media, LLC 2009

social and cultural forces which help to form them and which are in turn shaped by them. The emotional reactions of individual teachers to their work are intimately connected to the view that they have of themselves and others. (…) So, the unique sense of self which every teacher has is socially grounded" (Nias 1996, p. 294). Emotion and cognition, self and context, ethical judgment and purposeful action: they are all intertwined in the complex reality of teaching. In times of educational reforms, aimed at changing teaching practices for the better, these complexities are brought to light even more prominently (Hargreaves 1998; Kelchtermans 2005; Little 1990; see also Van Veen and Lasky 2005). A careful analysis of emotions thus constitutes a powerful vehicle to understand teachers' experience of changes in their work lives. In other words, emotions reflect the way teachers make sense of the conditions they work in.

Emotions and Vulnerability

In line with Nias' analysis, we can add a fourth reason for the relevance and importance of emotions in teaching: the condition of *vulnerability* that characterizes teaching (Kelchtermans 1996, 2005, 2009). This vulnerability is not so much an emotional state or experience, but rather a structural characteristic of the teaching job. Still, the actual experience of vulnerability can trigger intense emotions. The core of that experience is "feeling that one's professional identity and moral integrity, as part of being 'a proper teacher', are questioned and that valued workplace conditions are thereby threatened or lost. Coping with this vulnerability therefore implies political actions, aimed at (re)gaining the social recognition of one's professional self and restoring the necessary workplace conditions for good job performance" (Kelchtermans 1996, p. 319).

Based on our narrative-biographical research, we have distinguished at least three elements that make up vulnerability in teaching (Kelchtermans 2005, 2009). A first element lies in the fact that teachers are not in full control of the conditions they have to work in (regulations, quality control systems, policy demands). Teachers' working conditions are to a large extent imposed on them: they work within particular legal frameworks and regulations, in a particular school, with a particular infrastructure, population of students, and composition of the staff. Essential to the experience of vulnerability, however, is not so much the fact that these working conditions are given or imposed, but rather the fact that they constitute the border or horizon within which teachers are supposed to enact their teaching. As such the conditions are not neutral, but reflect particular normative ideas about good teaching, about what it means to be a teacher and how this should be enacted. In other words, teachers find themselves in a particular context of structures, rules and norms and it is in interaction with that context that they have to work as well as develop their sense of professional identity. As others have argued, for example, the actual normative horizon of teaching and schooling is strongly dominated by the performativity discourse (Ball 2003; Jeffrey 2002; Troman 2000). Policy makers, but also the community (public opinion) tend to treat schools as institutes that have to perform a very particular task, which can be defined in terms of goals and evaluated through the measurement of outcomes. Effectiveness and efficiency become the dominant – if not exclusive – norms in the way teaching and education is thought and spoken about (Kelchtermans 2007b).

Secondly, vulnerability is reflected in the very limited degree to which teachers can prove their effectiveness by claiming that pupils' results directly follow from their actions. All teachers are aware that student outcomes are only partially determined by their teaching. Equally or even more decisive are personal factors (motivation, perseverance, etc.) or social factors, that teachers can hardly influence, change or control. It is not only difficult to prove to what extent a teacher can argue students' results are his/her own achievement, but equally difficult to know when the results of teachers' actions possibly may occur or become visible at all. Very often teachers are not allowed to witness when the seed of their efforts finds fertile ground to develop. That is why the quality control systems, based exclusively or primarily on students' test scores, are felt by so many teachers as an unfair evaluation of their work, doing injustice to their specific working conditions. This creates ambivalence among the teachers. Teachers with a high "internal locus of control" may experience high job satisfaction when student outcomes are good. On the other hand, when pupils' learning outcomes are poor, they may tend to blame themselves and feel frustrated and inefficacious. Teachers with a high "external locus of control" often ascribe student outcomes to factors outside their efforts and often beyond their control. This may have a negative impact on their personal feelings of professional competence ("I can't make a difference") and thus have a depressing effect on their motivation and eventually on their sense of self-efficacy. During their career teachers find themselves challenged to properly balance between an internal and external locus of control, between a satisfying sense of efficacy and a realistic acknowledgement of one's limited impact (Kelchtermans 1993, 1999, 2009), between exhausting personal commitment and cynical disengagement (see also Huberman 1989).

The third and most fundamental meaning of vulnerability is that teachers cannot help but make dozens of decisions about when and how to act in order to support students' development and learning, but they don't have a firm basis to ground their decisions and justify them. Even when the justification for teachers' decisions can be explicitly stated, with reference to a certain idea (argument) of good education in general and good education for this pupil here and now, that judgement and decision can always be challenged or questioned. And still, it is this capacity to judge, to act and to take responsibility for one's actions, which constitutes a key element of teachers' professionalism. There is no escape: the particular professionalism in teaching demands that one endures this vulnerability. Vulnerability is the fundamental condition a teacher "finds his or herself in". This wording is important: it reveals the inevitable element of passivity, of exposure that characterizes teaching. Although in much research, training and analysis the emphasis is on acting, planning, designing... there is also this passive dimension of undergoing, surprise, puzzlement, powerlessness.... Enduring this vulnerability, while at the same time understanding

the opportunities it creates for engaging in educationally valuable and professionally rewarding personal relationships with pupils, constitutes an ongoing challenge
and professional task for teachers throughout their careers, but also a source of
diverse, intense emotions (Kelchtermans 1996, 2005, 2009).

Vulnerability in Times of Change and Reform

It can hardly be surprising to observe that times of change and educational reform
intensify teachers' emotional experience of their job (see e.g. Hargreaves 1998;
Van Veen and Lasky 2005). A key lesson from research on educational change is
that the actual implementation of educational change greatly depends on the way
teachers make sense of that change (Fullan and Stiegelbauer 1991; Hopkins 2001).
From their sense of professionalism, but also from the particularities of their
specific professional context (that school, these colleagues and administrators, that
student population at that moment in time), teachers will interpret, question, criticize,
embrace, resist the calls for change. These sense-making processes encompass both
cognition and emotion (Nias 1996), because the implicit message in every call for
change is that the present practices are considered not to be the best possible or
even not (or no longer) appropriate to prepare future generations for their life and
participation in society. Since teaching demands a high level of investment of oneself
as a person, calls for change thus also imply a (negative) judgement about teachers'
work and thus eventually put their self-efficacies at stake. Teachers find themselves
challenged to answer the question "Am I still a good teacher?" and this has the
potential to lead to intense emotional reactions (Geijsel et al. 2001; Hargreaves
1998; Little 1990; Zembylas 2005). This further exemplifies the idea of vulnerability
as a fundamental characteristic of teaching, resulting from the fact that teaching is
an inevitably value-laden action, based on a sense of personal and moral commitment and responsibility to what is considered to be in the best interest of the students.
Since there is no consensus on what this "best interest" actually entails, teachers'
commitments and actions remain questionable.

In this chapter we want to show and analyze this interplay of vulnerability, the
confrontation with changing working conditions and teachers' (emotional) coping with them. For our argument we will draw on a study of primary schools,
which – among other changes – have seen a significant shift in the cultural and
ethnic diversity of their student population. We will start with a brief presentation
of the study and then focus on teachers' emotional experience of those changes.
Our analysis shows how these changes towards a multicultural school population,
in the context of increasing demands for accountability, constitute major challenges
to teachers we talked to and thus to their self-efficacy and the emotional quality
of their work. At the same time it will become clear that these experiences (and
thus their emotional meaning) are mediated by structural and cultural working
conditions in the school, as well as teachers' individual interpretative frameworks
(Hargreaves 2001).

The Study

The growing ethnic and cultural diversity in the Belgian society is reflected in changes in the composition of the student population in schools. These changes, however, don't affect all schools in the same way. Some schools – especially in urban areas – have witnessed a relatively fast influx of students from a variety of cultural and ethnic backgrounds – mostly of Turkish or Moroccan descent. Parallel to the growing number of these students, most of those schools at the same time have seen a significant reduction of the traditional white Belgian students. This is the so-called "white flight". It is widely taken for granted by policymakers and in the public opinion that a culturally diverse student population brings with it particular challenges and difficulties for the teachers who work there. Nevertheless, there seem to be important potential differences in the way a multicultural school population actually affects teachers' working conditions and practices. Therefore, we want to examine this phenomenon and its meaning for the school teams more systematically (also see Piot et al. in press).

The study – which is part of a larger project on the intensification of teachers' work lives (Ballet and Kelchtermans 2008; Ballet et al. 2006; Piot et al. in press) – used a multiple case design, in which one primary school was the case unit of analysis (Merriam 1998). In four primary schools, data were collected from the principal and (at least) four experienced teachers (minimal 10 years of experience). All respondents were white and had Belgian nationality, as is the case in almost the entire teaching force in the Flemish school system. Data collection was primarily done through semi-structured interviews, complemented by on-site observations and document analysis. The same interview guideline was used with all interviewees. This allowed for a certain structure in the data collection, without losing the flexibility to adjust to the particularities and idiosyncrasies of individual respondents' stories. The interview started with an open question about the three changes the teachers had experienced over the past 5 years, which had had a significant effect on their practice and on themselves as teachers. No direct questions were asked about the student population or its culturally diverse composition, since our interest was in the teachers' personal experience of the working conditions in their school. The changes mentioned by the respondents were then systematically explored in further detail during the rest of the interview.

Data were analyzed in three steps: (1) analysis per respondent, (2) analysis per school ("within-case analysis") and (3) a comparative analysis between the schools ("cross-case analysis") (Miles and Huberman 1994). First, the data of the individual teachers were analyzed. After transcription and coding of the protocol, a systematic summary report was written, presenting the relevant data of the respondent in a structured format. The fixed structure of paragraphs was the starting point for the second phase of compiling an extensive case study report in which all the data from one school were analyzed systematically. In this phase, we used the technique of "constant comparative analysis" (Glaser and Strauss 1967) to look for common patterns and recurring themes and processes. Preliminary interpretations were formulated and iteratively checked with all data. The case study reports provide a contextualized analysis of each individual school ("within-case analysis"), in which we disentangled the permanent interaction between the individual teacher, the organizational working conditions, and the external demands, as perceived by the staff. Finally, a comparative analysis of the cases ("cross-case analysis") enabled us to conceptualize the changing working conditions and their consequences for teachers' experience of their job in a more refined and analytical way and in terms of patterns and themes with a relevance beyond the cases as such.

Presentation of the Schools

The *Birch*[1] is the pseudonym for a subsidized privately run school[2], situated in a big city. The student population consists of many different nationalities. In this school, 70% of the pupils have a non-Belgian ethnic background. Until fairly recently, this school had a predominantly white, Flemish student population, with an average middle class socio-economic background. The respondents in this school are Barbara (principal); Birgit (pre-school teacher); Beatrice, Brenda and Belle (primary school teachers).

The *Elm* is the pseudonym for a subsidized privately run school with more than 50% pupils with a non-Belgian cultural background. This school has already had a culturally diverse population for many years. The respondents in this school are Eline (principal); Elsa (pre-school teacher); Emma, Erika and Edith (primary school teachers).

The *Maple Tree* is a subsidized privately run school. During the last 10 years the student population changed dramatically from predominantly white to almost 100% students with non-Belgian background. The respondents in this school are Marc (principal); Mia and Mandy (pre-school teachers); Martine and Magdalena (primary school teachers).

The *Willow* is a subsidized privately run school with a student population that is increasingly becoming diverse in terms of cultural and ethnic background. More than 50% of the pupils belong to ethnic minority groups. The respondents in this

---

[1] For reasons of anonymity the names of the respondents and schools are pseudonyms. Note that the name of the school and the names for the respondents from that school have the same first letter.

[2] In Flanders (Belgium), schools are grouped in three educational networks: (1) Community schools, being the public-authority schools provided by the Flemish government; (2) Subsidized public-authority schools, being the public-authority schools established by the provincial and city authorities; (3) Subsidized private-authorized schools, founded by private individuals, de facto associations and non-profit associations. Most of these schools are Catholic. In Flanders, subsidized private-authorized schools make up about 70% of all primary schools. They are, however, subsidized by the government in such a way that they actually operate as part of the public school system (e.g. parents don't have to pay specific or extra school fees to enroll their children). To be financed (1) or subsidized (2 and 3) by the Flemish government, schools must meet the standards for rationalization; timetabling and quality of education (cf. minimum goals).

school are the "management team" (consisting of Willy and Wilhelmina); Wivina (pre-school teachers); Wanda, Wendy and Walter (primary school teachers).

Findings

The respondents from all four schools brought up a range of different, yet often simultaneous, changes in their working conditions. More specifically, they mention changes in curriculum content, teaching methodology and new administrative duties (mostly due to systems of quality control). Teachers frequently experience these changes as authoritative calls for change, having a compelling character. They feel they have little choice but to follow up on them (Ballet and Kelchtermans 2008). At the same time, the pressure is often increased by their personal sense of obligation and commitment (Hargreaves 1994). If they feel they owe it to the pupils – because it is argued that the reform is for the students' benefit – teachers tend to just make the efforts in order to live up to these expectations and to start implementing the changes. *"It is coming to us, so I ask myself: 'how will I survive?' I think that we still want to achieve as much as we did in the past. However, we have less time to do so. We have to deal with everything much more quickly. It feels as if nothing can wait."* (Birgit). Due to the multitude as well as the simultaneous character of the changes, teachers experience a permanent lack of time (see Apple and Jungck 1996; Ballet and Kelchtermans 2008; Campbell and Neill 1994; Easthope and Easthope 2000; Hargreaves 1994). Teachers in this study also explicitly and spontaneously brought up the complex consequences the shifts in their school population – including the "white flight" – had for them. *"The first migrants arrived ten years ago in our school. At that moment, the Flemish kids started leaving. All of that happened in a short time."* (Marc). For the purpose of this chapter we focus not so much on the ethnic and cultural diversity as such, but rather on the perceived changes it brings to teachers' working conditions and to their (emotional) experience of them.

Pupils with Perceived "Language Deficiency"

The evolution towards a "concentration school" seems to have quite far-reaching consequences for teachers' working conditions. One immediate consequence is the confrontation with a high number of pupils, who have a different language back-ground and may have difficulties speaking and understanding Dutch, which is the instruction language. This language issue affects almost all aspects of school life. It not only has serious consequences for student achievement in the language courses, but also for teachers' pedagogy and communicative interactions with their students. Making these pupils acquire new subject matters requires more time, implying that – compared to the past – less curriculum content can be covered. *"Our pupils have a different starting point in their learning than those in rural schools, with an almost all white population. We can't say that children in our school end up mastering the curriculum content as those in rural schools.*" (Belle). This way, it is difficult for teachers to reach the same goals with this student population as they were used to in the past. This experience has evident emotional consequences for the teachers, since pupils' learning outcomes are an important criterion for them to judge their professional efficacy. Apart from that, student achievement is an important element in the authorities' evaluation of the educational quality. Our data show that the pupils' learning results appear to play a quite ambiguous role for teachers in an, ethnically and culturally diverse school. Firstly, teachers experience that in the current working conditions it has become impossible to maintain their previous standards on student performance. "*It becomes too much, because we feel pressure. They [the pupils] are not mastering the content although they should. So, we really want them to master that.*" (Wivina). Not being able to reach the same standards as before has a negative impact on teachers' motivation and satisfaction, according to Magdalena. "*If we conceive of satisfaction as: 'my pupils perform well' (...), then I do not have much satisfaction. Since this is simply not the case anymore.*" This way, their self-efficacy comes under pressure: "Am I still a good teacher?" (Kelchtermans 2007a). Martine argues that she – together with her colleagues in the Maple Tree – needed time to emotionally cope with the fact that pupils were performing less well. "*I had a hard time. (...) Sometimes, I am really depressed, asking myself: 'I am spending so much time and energy and I only achieve so little.' However, one should not feel swamped by these thoughts, simply because in this situation it is impossible to achieve as much as before. And there are plenty of other issues we have to take care of.*" (Martine). Trying to keep up their own "quality norms" on the one hand, while on the other hand experiencing that this is becoming very difficult to achieve brings about feelings of self-doubts and failure. When pupils do not achieve the expected results, teachers often start questioning their own competence (Kelchtermans 1996; Geijsel et al. 2001; Woods 1999). "*One starts to evaluate oneself: 'Do I have to handle things differently?' Looking at myself I couldn't help thinking that I was failing. Failing the kids, I mean. It really felt as if it was my fault, my failure and that was hard to take. After all these years in school, I really started doubting myself as a teacher.*" (Belle). As a consequence, teachers experience limits to their professional efficacy (vulnerability).

Yet, it is obvious that pupils' performances are always determined by a whole series of factors, of which the teacher's efforts (e.g. capacities, commitments) is only one. Other factors (e.g. pupils' limited mastery of the teaching language) – some over which a teacher does not have much control – also determine the outcomes. Yet, not being able to achieve one's own professional goals and norms may lead to disillusionment or powerlessness (Kelchtermans 1996). In spite of all efforts, a sense of professional failure may develop. This is reinforced by the fact that pupils' test results often are used to judge the quality of teaching and thus, indirectly, to evaluate teachers' competence and commitment (Kelchtermans 2005). Good test results are motivating to teachers, and conversely, bad results can lead towards (external) criticism and self-doubts (Kelchtermans 1996). This experience is further reinforced by the finding that in cases of formal evaluation of the pupils' results (e.g. by the Inspectorate) the same criteria seem to be applied as for schools with a different social background and with less children who have a limited mastery of the instruction language. *"All schools have to reach the same standards. But in a school like ours, everything goes much slower and more difficult than in 'rural' schools. They do not have immigrant pupils. But those new curricula are meant for all schools."* (Wanda).

Especially the respondents of the Maple Tree, Birch and Willow express their unease about the fact that the Inspectorate uses the same standards for evaluation in all schools. *"I think that policymakers are not aware of the day-to-day reality in a school like ours."* (Beatrice). As a consequence, the comparison with schools with a white and middle-class population can be quite frustrating and stressful for teachers. *"When the inspector came in my classroom, he stated: 'You are teaching a 4th Grade instead of a 5th Grade.' Yet, when I gave the pupils a test, the inspector himself said that the pupils did not understand it. So, I explained to him that we think this is just, normal and what you can expect. They try to pin it on us by saying: 'it is because you do not help them to get integrated'."* (Belle). This way, teachers feel they are being personally held responsible for the pupils' performance on the one hand, but on the other hand they feel powerless to change its actual determinants. This experience of vulnerability brought out emotions of despair, of feeling treated unfairly, yet powerless to change the conditions that actually were responsible for the outcomes.

Threats to the School's Reputation

The evolution towards a culturally diverse school does not only affect the way teachers have to conceive of their specific classroom practice (teaching; authority), but also has consequences for the perception and evaluation of the school and its teachers by "outsiders". This reputation matters a great deal to teachers, since it is considered to reflect the social recognition and appreciation of their work. Barbara, principal of the Birch, comments on this: *"Our school, the Birch, used to have a great reputation, it was known to be a really good school. We were 'the' school. Whenever I meet former students of our school, they still will talk about it as 'the' school. The colleagues, however, were confronted very quickly with this issue as the school population changed (…) And it really was a challenge, they had a hard time coping with it (…) both emotionally and mentally (…) since it demands a complete switch in our thinking."* The shift in the student population is associated in the public opinion with an increase of students with learning difficulties as well as a decrease in the overall learning outcomes. This is reflected in the "white flight". As such, teachers see the social recognition of their work threatened as the school's public reputation of having high pupil achievements, thanks to a dedicated and competent staff, is put into question. Since the teachers cannot change the school population, nor maintain the level of student achievement on which the school's reputation was based, they are facing a considerable loss in valued working conditions (social recognition). This experience of loss confronts them with the vulnerability in their job and has a deep emotional impact on their self-efficacy and motivation. It is interesting to see how in the Birch, for example, the deep emotional meaning becomes evident from the way the staff tries to cope with the developments and prove to the outside world that they – as teachers – still merit appreciation because they still work hard and take up their professional responsibility. Since their worth as teachers can no longer be proven through high student learning outcomes, the teachers intensely engage in other public activities as a symbolical way to demonstrate their continuing dedication and hard work. Social activities – like a Christmas market or school musical – that were traditionally organized by the school (a.o. for fundraising goals) and aim at involving the parents and the members of the local community, now get an extra meaning and significance in conveying the message that the reduced learning results by the students are not due to less professional skills or reduced professional commitment on behalf of staff. "*We organize all kinds of activities. We organize a Christmas market and we try to give it more appearance, so that [they – parents and local community – see] that we are still working very hard.*" (Beatrice). So, although it is both emotionally and physically adding to their workload, teachers seize all kinds of opportunities to safeguard or restore the social recognition as "proper" teachers (see also Kelchtermans and Ballet 2002). The example of the Birch illustrates the vulnerability of teachers, since their social recognition is depending on the appreciation by others. It can thus be lost at any time and therefore needs to be restored time and again. The particular meaning of social activities as in the Birch and the intense emotional value teachers attribute to it can only be understood properly against the background of this vulnerability (i.e. little control over crucial working conditions and thus over the social recognition of their professional selves).

Mediating Factors in the Organization and the Individual

The (emotional) meaning of the shifting school populations as described above, however, is not identical in all the cases of our study. The differences in the effect of the changes, reveals the mediating role of the organizational characteristics of the schools as well as of the individual frameworks teachers use to make sense of their job.

Mediating Factors in the School as an Organization

Although the cultural and ethnic diversity of the student population affected all the schools in our study, we found a striking difference between the Elm and the three other cases. The staff in the Birch, Maple Tree and Willow experiences a "*complete switchover*" (Mia), causing intense feelings of uncertainty, self-doubt, unease, diminishing self-efficacy, etc. In the Elm – in contrast – the teachers' experience of the culturally diverse student population does set a challenge, but it is far less emotionally disturbing. They rather define it in terms of frustration to bring the pupils to the envisaged learning outcomes. The neighborhoods from which the Elm recruits its pupils, have been multicultural for years and the teachers have gotten used to working with a culturally and ethnically diverse student population. *"It has always been a heterogeneous group. The people in the neighborhood are somehow used to living with a Greek next door and a Turkish neighbor on the other side. (…). It has always been like this."* (Eline). Over time, the teaching routines as well as the patterns for interactions with students and parents have been modified, developed and established in a way that allows the teachers to manage with the particularities of their school's student population. The three other schools, however, experience a pervasive rupture in the status quo. This "critical phase" (Measor 1985) is quite confronting for teachers and evokes feelings of uncertainty, uneasiness and doubts. The experience even further reinforces that meaningful others (e.g. the Inspectorate) maintain the same high standards for the pupils' learning results (see higher). The *history* of the school thus partly explains the different meaning of and emotional reaction to the changes. This further illustrates that the professional context teachers interact with, not only has a spatial meaning (place) but also a temporal one (time). The history of the Elm, as well as the personal history of the teachers in it, affects their coping with the present and the expectations about the future (see also Kelchtermans 2007a, 2009).

These historical differences in coping with change also reveal another cultural working condition that mediates teachers' experience of changes. Throughout the day-to-day practices, schools develop what Nias et al. (1989) have called a *"working consensus"* (i.e. a set of implicit and explicit understandings, norms, procedures and practices about what counts as good teaching, how this is to be achieved and what conditions are needed to do so – see also Ballet and Kelchtermans 2008; Southworth 2000). Others have referred to it as the organizational culture of the school, encompassing "the deeper level of basic assumptions and beliefs that are shared by members of an organization, that operate unconsciously, and that define in a basic 'taken-for-granted' fashion an organization's view of itself and its environment" (Schein 1985, p. 6). Although most schools do not so much reflect one monolithic common culture and levels of dissent continue to play a role (see e.g. Altrichter and Salzgeber 2000; Hargreaves 1994; Kelchtermans and Ballet 2002), there is a level of shared normative ideas, which allows that in schools certain routines develop, establishing predictable and self-evident patterns of interaction among staff members, as well as ways of coping with the job demands and calls for change. The working consensus implies that not all projects, actions or intentions need to be negotiated time and again, but can be performed on the basis of taken for granted patterns. It further allows staff members to collectively make sense of the changes and challenges they are confronted with and thus contributes to a sense of supportive collegiality and collaboration. Though the character of this collaborative support may differ (Little 1990), it is very important for teachers to feel part of a team, with some common sense of purpose and shared action routines and to be recognized as such (Kelchtermans 2006).

Furthermore *the principal* was found to play a key role in the establishment and safeguarding of the working consensus. One example of this is the importance for teachers to have the principal showing a sense of understanding of the particular conditions and difficulties they have to deal with. Walter, for example, highly appreciates the principal's supportive attitude, saying "*take it easy, there is no need to rush. Keep up the good work, but don't try to have all problems solved in one year*". A quote from his colleague Wendy further illustrates the value of explicit appreciation by the principal, especially in the difficult challenges posed by the changing school population: "(...) *she would sometimes drop by in my classroom and say things like 'you're doing great, that's cool teaching'. And it's just nice to get this appreciation, it keeps me motivated and going.*" The importance of the principal is further illustrated – though, in an negative way – in the Birch, where recurrent changes in the headship have resulted in parallel changes in school policy and priorities, but also in the fact that the working consensus is being put to question. As a result, teachers are forced to rethink and re-negotiate norms and goals. "*Right now we are also lacking a clear line to follow (...) the first principal insisted that we go this way, but the next one demands we'd go the opposite direction and the third one says we ought to move straight ahead (...) so we're like changing but not really knowing where to head (...) Well, new bosses, new rules.*" (Birgit). The lack of support and direction from the principal thus adds to teachers' sense of work pressure and uncertainty.

So, the working consensus brings about a highly valued sense of emotional comfort and reduces the experience of vulnerability in the job. As such that cultural working condition strongly mediates the emotional labor teachers have to engage in when facing changes, which force them to reconsider their work and themselves in it. It is important to stress, however, that the working consensus on changes does not necessarily work in an emotionally comforting way. It can also have unintended side-effects that add to the work pressure and to teachers' doubting of the values and norms guiding their practice, thus eventually triggering negative feelings and a questioning of their self-efficacy. A clear illustration of this was found in the Willow. One of the core ideas in this school's working consensus is the norm that every possible effort should be made as to provide every single pupil with the education he or she needs. This widely shared norm had resulted in the development of the staff's expertise on learning problems and strategies for remedial teaching as well as to organizational facilities and procedures for individualized learning trajectories for the students. Because of these efforts the school had achieved a reputation of being caring and effective for pupils with learning difficulties. As a consequence, however, the school witnessed an increased enrollment of such pupils and, eventually, a decrease in the average level of learning outcomes. "*It is a very competent teaching staff doing their best to help every single child in the classroom (...). The Student Guidance Center is also aware of these efforts. And they'll tell parents: 'In the Willow your child is looked after, teachers invest in it and work with it, even if it is low-achieving.' However, unfortunately, some schools do not share our vision or efforts (...) And this way, we end up getting all the low-achieving children from around here (...)*" (Management team). The school staff thus paradoxically becomes somehow the "victim" of its own caring role and educational commitment. "*Lately, I have been asking myself: 'Is this how we get rewarded for our efforts?' Last year, we lost several pupils. Pupils leave our school as their friends leave. As a consequence, we have a very weak class in the 6th Grade. Is this the price we have to pay for trying to provide every child with what it really needs?"* (Wendy).

Individual Sense-Making as a Mediating Factor

Teachers always interpret the changes in their working conditions (van den Berg 2002). For doing so, they rely on their personal interpretative framework: a set of cognitions by which teachers perceive their job situation, give meaning to it and act in it (Kelchtermans 1993, 2007a, 2009). This personal interpretative framework operates as a lens through which all changes, demands and expectations are perceived, interpreted and valued/evaluated. In other words, teachers' personal beliefs also mediate the (emotional) impact of changes in their job. The changes are not only filtered by the personal beliefs, but at the same time they often put these beliefs to question as those calls for change represent different normative ideas about good education. Being forced to reconsider one's deeply held beliefs on what makes a good teacher and of oneself trying to be one, does not leave teachers emotionally indifferent. In the end, their self-efficacy and self-understanding is at stake in the issue. We can illustrate this process of reflection on how to deal with the changes as well as how to maintain a positive self efficacy as teachers, by referring to the different reactions (coping strategies) of Walter and Wendy, both colleagues from the Willow, to the shifting student population and the decrease in the pupils' learning outcomes. At the same time it will be clear that changing working conditions are not just subject to collective sense-making (the working consensus as cultural working condition in schools), but also to interpretations that may differ among the members of the same school.

In Walter's personal task perception and job motivation, achieving high learning outcomes with the pupils is ranking very highly. He holds on to this personal goal, although it has become very difficult to achieve with the increased number of pupils having problems with the teaching language. This provokes deep frustration on Walter's part, especially in his teaching of language courses. Moreover, Walter finds himself having to spend more time on strictly educational tasks, which were traditionally taken care of by parents. This leaves less time for actual teaching. *"We have our task as a teacher, but nowadays, we also have to educate them permanently. I have been teaching for many years. I really achieved good results. I do not see how I could possibly achieve those now."* However, this did not seem to harm his self-efficacy, nor to result in reconsidering his task perception. Yet, for Walter's motivation the situation became unbearable and it was only solved when he gave up his role as classroom teacher and took over all the computer classes. This new task brings him a lot of satisfaction and got him out of the discouraging tensions between his aspirations as a teacher and the actual learning outcomes of his students. *"I was lucky to be asked to teach the computer lessons in all classes. If, instead, I would have had to continue teaching language and so (…). [The computer lessons] help me to find a balance [between aspirations and the changed school population] and make it more bearable."* In the end, to Walter, "benefits for pupils" remains the crucial criterion to decide on how to cope with the calls for change (also see Ballet and Kelchtermans 2008; Kelchtermans 2007a; Nias 1989). Walter thinks it is more valuable to select the essential curriculum contents instead of implementing all innovations at all costs. *"These curricula end up in my closet, I don't use them really, nor cover them entirely. I am convinced that we should not revenge ourselves on the kids because the policymakers take some particular decisions. So, we try to teach the children what we think is important (...) and that is enough of a challenge."* Walter's moral commitment towards the pupils drove him to teach the curriculum contents selectively and ultimately to give up his role as a classroom teacher.

His colleague, Wendy, on the contrary, has changed and adapted her personal task perception considerably. While in the past she tried to conscientiously work through all the curricula, she nowadays is convinced that it is more important to avoid unpleasant experiences in pupils' lives. Their emotional well-being has become the crucial issue to her. In order to achieve this – just like Walter – she treats the curriculum selectively, so that pupils will master the essential parts and experience success in their learning, and thus at the same time continue to feel good about themselves at school. Wendy explicitly justifies her decision as being most in the interest of the pupils. And she is willing to bear the consequences. For example, she does not allow her pupils to participate in the "diocesan examinations".[3] *"I take it [the curriculum] with a pinch. In the beginning, I did everything that was mentioned in the curriculum. However, if one wants to achieve everything that is written there, one gets crazy. I have resolved this by only doing what my pupils are able to take up. (...) However, we don't participate anymore in those diocesan examinations. Every class can decide whether to participate or not. I told them that I would no longer participate."* More than ever, Wendy focuses her efforts on pupils with special needs. With the pupils' well-being as the central concern in her view of teaching, she has come to think of her own role as that of an adult who students can trust and feel safe with. It makes her feel good, saves her from the frustration of the lower student outcomes and – moreover – she feels very much appreciated by the pupils. So, changing her norms and task perception added to her job satisfaction and a higher self-efficacy. *"Although I am not really trained for it, those emotional problems the pupils struggle with need to be solved. I think that in the past I would not have handled it the way I do it now. (...) If the pupils come to me and tell me confidential issues, I feel trusted and that gives me a lot of satisfaction."* In Wendy's task perception "care" increasingly gets a central place and she conceives of her job to be broader than just teaching (Campbell and Neill 1994; Kelchtermans 2007a). *"I am not just a teacher. To some kids, I am a mother figure and someone who really listens to them. So, one has to make more time for the children."* Her "caring" not only includes academic performance, but also stretches over her pupils' private lives or basic needs. *"In the past, I did not bring anything for the [poorer] children. However, nowadays, my suitcase is filled with raincoats, socks, and extra*

---

[3] "Diocesan examinations" are organized for all Catholic schools in a diocese, to allow for a comparison of their educational quality in terms of student outcomes (sixth Grades). Participation is not compulsory, nor necessary.

clothing and I hand it out to those kids who really don't have much to wear (…)" This way, she really feels like making a difference for the pupils (Isenbarger and Zembylas 2006). She gets motivation and satisfaction from aspiring these broader educational issues and not so much or not primarily from the pupils' learning outcomes.

This analysis shows that teachers do not accept changes blindly, but that they permanently negotiate, interpret and translate them, driven by the emotional need to experience a sense of meaningfulness in their job. The choices they make are grounded in their normative beliefs, their personal task perception and job motivation.

Yet, however noble these efforts, one might also argue that by lowering their expectations about students' academic achievement, teachers ironically and paradoxically may end up contributing to and reinforcing the negative social selection mechanisms of students' cultural and socio-economic background. In an effort to live up to their caring for students' needs and well-being, teachers engage in practices which possibly perpetuate the vicious circle of unequal opportunities. The data of our study not so much show a way out of this dilemma, but help to understand how processes of positive professional commitment, driven by a caring ethos and the emotional desire to make a positive difference in students' lives, can become modified and twisted through the complexities of local working conditions, eventually resulting in outcomes that no one had intended. And these outcomes not only affect the pupils, but indirectly also the teachers' motivation, job-satisfaction and self-efficacy.

Conclusion

Emotionality constitutes an inherent dimension of teachers' professionalism. Emotions are part of the work lives teachers (have to) live. In the chapter we have linked this idea to vulnerability as a fundamental and structural characteristic of teaching and being a teacher. The experience of that vulnerability encompasses a questioning of the teacher's moral personal and professional integrity and this experience can trigger intense emotions. The social recognition of being a proper teacher – a crucial condition for teachers' self-efficacy and job motivation – is never certain and can be lost any time.

By emphasizing the role of experience we also stressed the need to understand emotions in an interactionist way, reflecting teachers' particular experience of the conditions they have to work in (see also Nias 1996; Hargreaves 2001). Drawing on a study on teachers facing a shift in their student population towards more cultural and ethnic diversity (in an overall climate of increased performativity and accountability pressure), we have shown on the one hand what that vulnerability and its emotional consequences may entail, but also on the other that the emotional impact of the changes teachers are facing is mediated by both individual (personal interpretative framework) and collective (working consensus) processes of sense-making. Teachers' coping with calls for change, with experienced vulnerability and the emotions it brings differs between individuals and between contexts (both in time and space). Or as Bullough puts it: "Some teachers seek to make themselves invulnerable, immune to the possibility of failing, while others seem to enjoy risking self. Additionally, differences in the work context either heighten teachers' sense of vulnerability or diminish it, and enable or limit their ability to realize their aims and to preserve their senses of self." (Bullough 2005, p. 23).

In our approach teachers' emotions were used as representing their particular experience of their (changing) working conditions and the impact those had on their self-understanding and self-efficacy. We think that this perspective also sets an agenda for teacher education, both in the pre- and in-service phase. Teacher education programs should acknowledge that the specific "professionalism" in teaching demands more than a thorough knowledge on subject discipline and pedagogy and a mastery of the skills to effectively design, implement, and optimize learning opportunities for pupils. However important and necessary, these technical aspects of knowledge and skills (nowadays often understood and operationalized in terms of competences) capture only a part of what professional teaching entails. Taking up professional responsibility for educating pupils inevitably demands a moral commitment as well as a political astuteness in order to do justice to the pupils' needs and to find effective strategies of power and influence to establish the conditions to achieve this (Hargreaves 1995; Kelchtermans 2007a, 2009, in press). Since all of this demands teachers to commit themselves as a person, this professional stance makes emotions unavoidable. And that's why emotions are not just idiosyncratic and accidental side-effects of teaching, but are both an inherent part of as well as a condition for teacher professionalism (Nias 1996; Hargreaves 1998). Teachers' structural vulnerability further adds to this the fact that teachers don't have full control over the conditions they work in, nor over their effect on pupils' learning and that they lack an uncontested basis to ground their actions. Acknowledging, understanding and learning how to deal with this ought to be part of the curricula for teacher education.

For initial teacher education this implies the need to help future teachers coming to see the professional relevance and value of their emotional experiences and to support them in analyzing those feelings as reflecting their personal commitments as well as the (normative, political) conditions they have to work in. This may be done through reflective assignments during internship, group discussions on emotionally significant experiences in student teaching, etc. From our narrative-biographical work we have learned that different forms of guided story-telling provide powerful means to come to grips with vulnerability and emotions (Kelchtermans, in press).

Similarly activities for professional development during teachers' careers should include activities that deliberately aim at making them "read" teachers' emotional experience of changes (e.g. provoked by particular policy measures) in their working conditions and thus provide a vehicle to interpretatively disentangle the impact of those changes on their work and on themselves. This may lead to an increased awareness of the different moral and political issues that are at stake in it, and thus both encourage and equip teachers to make appropriate choices in order to critically deal with them. We realize that this stance is not evident in an international policy environment dominated by the performativity discourse and the strain that it puts on teachers (see e.g. Achinstein and Ogawa 2006; Deretchin and Craig 2007). Yet, this stance to us seems of crucial importance if we want to prevent the idea of teacher professionalism getting further reduced to a narrow technical obsession with a very specific form of effectiveness and efficiency that rules out the moral, political and emotional dimension of teaching and of being a teacher.

References

Achinstein B, Ogawa R (2006) (In)Fidelity: what the resistance of new teachers reveals about professional principles and prescriptive educational policies. Harv Educ Rev 26(1):30–63

Altrichter H, Salzgeber S (2000) Some elements of a micro-political theory of school development. In: Altrichter H, Elliott J (eds) Images of educational change. Open University Press, Buckingham, pp 99–110

Apple MW, Jungck S (1996) You don't have to be a teacher to teach this unit: teaching, technology and control in the classroom. In: Hargreaves A, Fullan MG (eds) Understanding teacher development (Teacher development series). Cassell, London, pp 20–42

Ball SJ (2003) The teacher's soul and the terrors of performativity. J Educ Policy 18(2):215–228

Ballet K, Kelchtermans G (2008) Workload and willingness to change. Disentangling the experience of intensified working conditions. J Curriculum Stud 40:47–67

Ballet K, Kelchtermans G, Loughran J (2006) Beyond intensification towards a scholarship of practice: analysing changes in teachers' work lives. Teach Teach Theory Pract 12(2):209–229

Bullough RV (2005) Teacher vulnerability and teachability: a case study of a mentor and two interns. Teach Educ Q 32(2):23–40

Campbell RJ, Neill SR (1994) Primary teachers at work. Routledge, London

Deretchin LF, Craig CJ (eds) (2007) International research on the impact of accountability systems. Teacher Education Yearbook XV. Rowman & Littlefield Education, Lanham

Easthope C, Easthope G (2000) Intensification, extension and complexity of teachers' workload. Br J Sociol Educ 21(1):43–58

Fullan M, Stiegelbauer S (1991) The new meaning of educational change. Teachers College Press, New York

Geijsel F, Sleegers P, Van den Berg D, Kelchtermans G (2001) Conditions fostering the implementation of large-scale innovation programs in schools: teachers' perspectives. Educ Adm Q 37:130–166

Glaser BG, Strauss AL (1967) The discovery of grounded theory. Aldine, Chicago

Hargreaves A (1994) Changing teachers, changing times. Teachers' work and culture in the postmodern age. Cassell, London

Hargreaves A (1995) Development and desire. A post-modern perspective. In: Guskey TR, Huberman M (eds) Professional development in education: new paradigms and perspectives. Teachers College Press, New York, pp 9–34

Hargreaves A (1998) The emotional practice of teaching. Teach Teach Educ 14:835–854

Hargreaves A (2001) Emotional geographies of teaching. Teach Coll Record 103:1056–1080

Hopkins D (2001) School improvement for real. Routledge/Falmer, London

Huberman M (1989) The professional life cycle of teachers. Teach Coll Record 91(1):31–57

Isenbarger L, Zembylas M (2006) The emotional labour of caring in teaching. Teach Teach Educ 22:120–134

Jeffrey B (2002) Performativity and primary teacher relations. J Educ Policy 17:431–546

Kelchtermans G (1993) Getting the story. Understanding the lives. From career stories to teachers' professional development. Teach Teach Educ 9(5/6):443–456

Kelchtermans G (1996) Teacher vulnerability: understanding its moral and political roots. Cambridge J Educ 26:307–323

Kelchtermans G (1999) Teacher career: between burnout and fading away? Reflections from a narrative and biographical perspective. In: Vandenberghe R, Huberman M (eds) Understanding and preventing teacher burnout. A sourcebook of international research and practice. Cambridge University Press, Cambridge, pp 176–191

Kelchtermans G (2005) Teachers' emotions in educational reforms: self-understanding, vulnerable commitment and micropolitical literacy. Teach Teach Educ 21:995–1006

Kelchtermans G (2006) Teacher collaboration and collegiality as workplace conditions. A review. Z Pädagogik 52:220–237

Kelchtermans G (2007a) Professional commitment beyond contract: teachers' self-understanding, vulnerability and reflection. In: Butcher J, McDonald L (eds) Making a difference. Challenges for teachers, teaching and teacher education. Sense, Rotterdam, pp 35–54

Kelchtermans G (2007b) Teachers' self-understanding in times of performativity. In: Deretchin LF, Craig CJ (eds) International research on the impact of accountability systems. Teacher Education Yearbook XV. Rowman & Littlefield Education, Lanham, pp 13–30

Kelchtermans G (2009) Who I am in how I teach is the message. Self-understanding, vulnerability and reflection. Teach Teach Theory Pract 15:257–272

Kelchtermans G (in press) Narratives and biography in teacher education. In: Baker E, McGaw B, Peterson P (eds.) International encyclopedia of education, 3rd edn. Elsevier, Amsterdam

Kelchtermans G, Ballet K (2002) The micropolitics of teacher induction. A narrative-biographical study on teacher socialisation. Teach Teach Educ 18(1):105–120

Little JW (1990) Teachers as colleagues. In: Lieberman A (ed) Schools as collaborative cultures: creating the future now. Falmer, New York, pp 165–193

Measor L (1985) Critical incidents in the classroom. Identities, choices and careers. In: Ball S, Goodson I (eds) Teachers' lives and careers. Falmer, London, pp 61–77

Merriam SB (1998) Qualitatitve research and case study applications in education. Jossey-Bass, San Francisco

Miles MB, Huberman AM (1994) An expanded sourcebook. Qualitative data analysis, 2nd edn. Sage, Thousand Oaks

Nias J (1989) Primary teachers talking. A study of teaching as work. Routledge, London

Nias J (1996) Thinking about feeling: the emotions in teaching. Cambridge J Educ 26(3):293–306

Nias J, Southworth G, Yeomans R (eds) (1989) Staff relationships in the primary school: a study of organizational cultures. Cassell, London

Piot L, Kelchtermans G, Ballet K (in press) Beginning teachers' job experiences in multi-ethnic schools. Teach Teach Theory Pract

Schein EH (1985) Organizational culture and leadership. Jossey-Bass, San Francisco

Southworth G (2000) How primary schools learn. Res Pap Educ 15(3):275–291

Troman G (2000) Teacher stress in the low-trust society. Br J Sociol Educ 21(3):331–353

van den Berg R (2002) Teachers' meanings regarding educational practice. Rev Educ Res 72:577–625

Van Veen K, Lasky S (2005) Emotions as a lens to explore teacher identity and change: different theoretical approaches. Teach Teach Educ 21:895–898

Woods P (1999) Intensification and stress in teaching. In: Vandenberghe R, Huberman AM (eds) Understanding and preventing teacher burnout. A sourcebook of international research and practice. Cambridge University Press, Cambridge, pp 115–138

Zembylas M (2005) Discursive practices, genealogies, and emotional rules. A poststructuralist view on emotion and identity in teaching. Teach Teach Educ 21:935–948

Chapter 12
Teachers' Emotions in a Context of Reforms: To a Deeper Understanding of Teachers and Reforms

Klaas Van Veen and Peter Sleegers

Abstract We begin our chapter by reviewing studies of teachers' emotions in relation to reforms. We examine different theoretical perspectives and methods and elaborate on the strengths and weaknesses of this relatively new field of research, adopting a social-psychological approach to emotions. We argue that this field is still in need of a coherent conceptual framework for adequately understanding teachers' emotions. Our central assumption is that reforms strongly affect teachers' emotions due to divergent reasons, varying from feeling insecure and threatened, to feeling reinforced and enthusiastic. What those studies into teachers' emotions show in general is that most reforms affect teachers' professional sense of self or identity; teachers feel their core beliefs and assumptions are at stake. At a deeper level, teachers often feel that they are not recognized as professionals, rather as employees or executors of the ideas of others. We also attempt to provide an overview of the potential issues at stake for teachers in the contexts of reforms, referring to the content, process of implementation, and teachers' agency

Keywords Teacher emotions · Educational reform · Social psychology

In the last two decades, schools have been confronted with a continuous stream of changes in their environments (e.g., demographic changes, large-scale educational innovations, socio-cultural renewal). They face, as well, different and complex restructuring demands to which they must respond. An important aim of the "restructuring" changes is to create opportunities for change at the local level and to enhance capacity building for learning in schools (Stoll et al. 2002; van den Berg and Sleegers 1996). Furthermore, schools are under considerable external pressure because of tightened "output" controls – introduced by accountability policies.

K. Van Veen (✉)
ICLON, Leiden University, Leiden, the Netherlands
e-mail: kveen@iclon.leidenuniv.nl

P.A. Schutz and M. Zembylas (eds.), *Advances in Teacher Emotion Research:*
The Impact on Teachers' Lives,
DOI 10.1007/978-1-4419-0564-2_12, © Springer Science+Business Media, LLC 2009

Research on educational change and policy implementation, however, has shown that changing teachers' practices is extremely difficult to accomplish (Fullan 2001, 2006). In our efforts to understand this, we have started to use a sense-making approach to policy implementation in order to analyze the way teachers make sense of different reforms. In this sense making approach, the way teachers interpret, adapt and transform policy initiatives is studied through the lens of teachers' cognitive processing (e.g., mental maps, beliefs and prior knowledge), the social context teachers work in and the connections teachers have towards the nature of the policy messages (Spillane et al. 2002; Coburn 2005).

Other researchers have shown that successful implementation of policy initiatives largely depends on the personal significance attached to the new situation by those involved in the reforms (Hargreaves et al. 1998; van den Berg 2002; van den Berg and Sleegers 1996). Teachers are often the individuals most involved in educational reforms and just how they perceive and react to different reforms is critical. Therefore, the key role the teacher as sense-making agent has for successful implementation is more and more recognized by scholars as a theoretical fruitful perspective for understanding the complex nature of educational change in contrast to several decades ago when a more technical, rationalistic approach towards innovation predominated (Hargreaves et al. 1998; Spillane et al. 2002).

Most of the researchers who investigate teachers' sense-making of reforms have used a rational and dispassionate cognitive perspective, neglecting the influence of motivation and affect on cognitive processing and human sense-making (cf. Hargreaves et al. 1998; Spillane et al. 2002). Reforms and their substance often affect the core behaviors that are central to one's professional self-image and, for that reason, teachers often react with strong emotion to change, both in pleasant and unpleasant ways. Although researchers stress the importance of analyzing the teachers' emotions, systematic research on the role teachers' emotions play in reform processes is still missing (Nias 1996; Hargreaves 2001; Spillane et al. 2002; van den Berg 2002), and very little research has examined teachers' emotions in relation to the current reforms or within the framework of an explicit theory of emotions (cf. Nias 1996; Sutton and Wheatley 2003). In order to better understand teachers' reaction to reforms, analyzing their emotions can provide insights ino what teachers have at stake and what is at stake in their environment.

Our aim in this chapter is to explore the role teachers' emotions have in the context of educational reforms and how analyzing teachers' emotions can help us to understand educational change and the implementation of externally mandated reforms. After briefly reviewing research on teachers' emotions, we will set out our main argument: what a policy means for teachers emotionally is constituted in the interaction among teachers' professional identity, their social context and the nature of the policy messages. We will illustrate our argument by a case of an enthusiast secondary school teacher and we will sketch a framework for understanding teachers' emotions in the context of reforms based on socio-psychological theory of emotions. This framework focuses on what teachers have at stake related to their professional self-image, the role of the context teachers work in and the problematic nature of many educational reforms. The chapter will end with a discussion of the implications of the nature and design of educational policies. This chapter builds on our previous work on teachers' emotions in the context of reforms (van Veen 2003; van Veen and Lasky 2005; van Veen et al. 2005; van Veen and Sleegers 2006), which had a strong explorative character on what teachers have at stake related to their professional identity. This chapter summarizes and elaborates those findings, especially focusing on the relationships between identity and context.

Background of Research on Teachers' Emotions

The discussion of teachers' emotions in the context of reforms is related to research on teachers' cognition and emotion, teachers' workplace, and the role of teachers in the implementation of educational innovations. Over the past 30 years, the focus of research on teachers has been primarily on their cognitions (Calderhead 1996; Richardson 1996; Richardson and Placier 2001). A central assumption within this line of research is that cognitions strongly influence behavior. In more recent research on teachers' thinking, emotions have increasingly gained attention (Hargreaves 1998, 2000, 2005; Nias 1996; Sutton and Wheatley 2003; van Veen and Lasky 2005; Zembylas 2005). Not only the importance of emotions for teaching, but also for understanding the professional lives of teachers in general is increasingly being recognized. In most of the relevant studies, it is assumed that emotions cannot be separated from cognitions and that emotions can in fact provide insight into the relations between the person and his or her surroundings. As Nias (1996) states: "neither cognition nor feeling can be separated from the social and cultural forces which help to form them and which are in turn shaped by them" (p. 294). In other words, emotions seem to be a valuable source for understanding the professional lives of teachers.

What is still missing is a systematic overview of the role of emotions in teachers' professional lives/work and the manner in which their emotions are shaped by their changing working conditions (Nias 1996; Hargreaves 1999, 2001; Spillane et al. 2002; van den Berg 2002). With regard to the relations between reforms and teacher emotions, moreover, very little research can be found to adopt an explicit theoretical framework for the understanding of emotions (cf. Hargreaves 2000; Sutton and Wheatley 2003; van Veen and Lasky 2005; Zembylas 2005).[1]

To understand teachers' emotions in a context of reforms, a theory is needed that takes both the individual and its environment into account. A starting point for such a frame can be found in social-psychological approaches to emotions (cf. Frijda

---

[1] Regarding emotions and reforms, a growing body of research can be found: Regarding reforms, a growing but relatively still small body of research can be found: Aarts et al. 2002; Dinham and Scott 1997; Gross et al. 1971; Hargreaves 1998; Huberman and Miles 1984; Jennings 1992; Kelchtermans 2005; Lampert 1990; Lasky 2005; Little 1996; Little and Bartlett 2002; Nias 1999; Schmidt and Datnow 2005; Spillane 2000; van Veen et al. 2005; van Veen and Sleegers 2006; Zembylas and Barker 2007.

1986; Lazarus 1991; Oatley 1992; Roseman et al. 1996; Schutz et al. this volume), in which emotions are perceived as the result of a dynamic interaction between the individual and its institutional and social environment. Researchers with a social-psychological approach, tend to emphasis the individual identity, exploring what one has at stake. Less attention is paid to the environment (cf. Lazarus 1991, 1999). On the other hand, sociological researchers on emotions as Kemper (1978, 2000) and educational researchers on emotions as Hargreaves (1999, 2001) focus explicitly on the environment and pay less attention to one's identity. In this chapter, we will elaborate also on the nature and role of the social context teachers' work in, in an effort to understand how teachers make sense of educational reforms. First the theoretical frame will be introduced, including a discussion of teachers' professional identity and the nature of large-scale reforms, which will be illustrated with a case study of a teacher called Lori.

Understanding Teachers' Emotions: A Socio-cognitive Framework

In the literature on emotions (Lewis and Haviland-Jones 2000; Oatley 2000), many different theoretical perspectives can be found: physiological, philosophical, historical, sociological, feminist, organizational, anthropological, and psychological. Within the various perspectives, many different questions pertaining to the nature, functions, history, context, biological aspects, cultural aspects, and social aspects of emotions are considered. In this chapter, we are not so much interested in the nature of the emotions themselves as in the significance of the various emotions for the individuals involved. We are also primarily interested in those emotions that arise from the relations between the individual and the environment. Our aim is to understand what individual teachers have at stake in a context of reforms. In other words, we are interested in what the current reforms mean for teachers, how what they think is important in their work is affected, and how they make sense of and emotionally experience different reforms. This focus leads us to a social-psychological cognitivist or appraisal theory of emotions.

Within cognitive and appraisal theories, emotions are defined as the product of the appraisal of those environmental events that are perceived as most relevant to the individual's goals and well-being (Oatley 2000). Several different appraisal theories can be found (Arnold 1960; Frijda 1986; Ortony et al. 1988; Lazarus 1991, 1999; Oatley 1992; Roseman et al. 1996; Smith 1991). Although the different theories can be seen to differ in several respects, they resemble each other in their core assumption, namely that the arousal of emotion depends on the individual's cognitive appraisal of those events considered relevant (Frijda 2000).

Emotions from a social-psychological perspective are assumed to provide insight into "what a person has at stake in the encounter with the environment or in life in general, how that person interprets self and world, and how harms, threats, and challenges are coped with" (Lazarus 1991, p 7). Emotions are assumed to occur in the interaction between the individual and the environment (Lazarus 1991).

The emphasis in our perspective is on the way the identity of the individual is affected (e.g., using theories about identity), and how individuals appraise the environment (e.g., using cognitive appraisal theories) (Scherer et al. 2001). In analyzing teachers' emotions from a social-psychological perspective, our understanding of the individual variations in the way teachers construct their personal and professional identities as well as which psychological processes underlie this construction process, may be increased. Using a social-psychological approach on emotions we hope to reveal how a person experiences the situational demand and reveals the cognitions or beliefs related to one's identity that are explicitly or often also implicitly involved. In general, pleasant emotions tend to reinforce one's identity and unpleasant ones tend to threaten one's identity. In other words, the manner in which teachers react to educational reforms is largely determined by the extent to which they feel that their professional identities are being threatened or reinforced by the reforms in question (van Veen 2003; van Veen and Sleegers 2006). In Fig. 12.1, the theoretical framework is summarized. In the following, teachers' professional identity and the nature of large-scale reforms will be discussed in more detail

Teachers' Professional Identity

Professional identity is defined generally as a constellation of teachers' perceptions with regard to how she or he views her/himself as a teacher or teachers' sense of self (Beijaard et al. 2004; Day et al. 2007; Kelchtermans 1993, 2005; Nias 1989).

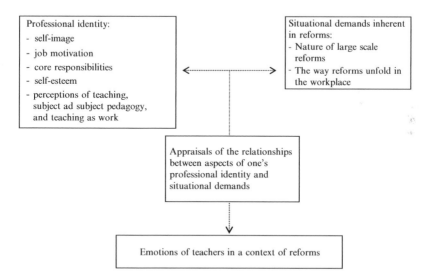

Fig. 12.1 Schematization of a social psychological approach towards emotions, derived from Lazarus (1991), applied to teachers' emotions in a context of reforms

According to Nias (1989), teachers' professional identity is a part of the "substantial self" or "a deeply protected core of self-defining beliefs, assumptions and values which, though in the first instance acquired through social conditioning, becomes so much a part of the individual's sense of personal identity that it varies very little with circumstances". She argues that most teachers have "one over-riding concern – the preservation of a stable sense of personal and professional identity (a 'substantial self,' Ball 1972) – but that this identity is realized in varying ways at different times through the developing concerns of different 'situational selves'" (p. 1258). However, recently it has been suggested that significant parts of a teacher's professional identity change continuously: In fact, teachers may be forced in this day of post-professionalism to drastically adjust their professional identity or even redefine themselves completely (Day 2002; Day et al. 2007; Hargreaves 2000).

In the literature many descriptions of professional identity can be found, often hardly defined, or referring to many divergent elements, making it an all-embracing concept that makes the concept less useful for understanding teachers' frame of reference. Therefore, we focus explicitly on certain elements of teachers' professional identity that seem to be crucial in their sense-making of the reforms. Based initially on Kelchtermans (1993) and other studies (Little and Bartlett 2002; Siskin 1994; Stodolsky and Grossman 1995; van Veen et al. 2005), we focus on a specific set of identity elements that can be distinguished to play a role, such as their perception of their self-image (the manner in which the teacher sees her/himself in general), job motivation (what motivates the person to become and remain a teacher), core responsibilities (what the teacher views as her or his essential tasks), self-esteem (the value a teacher attaches to her or his performances), and about teaching (what good teaching is and what to teach), subject and subject pedagogy (the nature and content of the subject and how to teach the subject), and teaching as work (how to work as a professional and how to work in a school organization). Distinguishing these different identity elements may allow us to gain deeper insights into teachers' frame of reference, what teachers have at stake, and the different ways of how they affect and become affected by their work context.

Situational Demands: The Context of Reforms

As stated, emotions occur in the interaction between one's identity and the situational demands. In order to understand how teachers react emotionally on different reforms, the dynamic interactions between the professional identities of the teachers and the situation or social context of teachers must be further analyzed. The important role of situation or context for understanding teachers' emotions is included in the socio-psychological framework on emotions we use, but hardly theorized or problematized.

Situation or social context is a multifaceted construct that includes both macro and micro aspects of the situation, ranging from the nature and design of nationally mandated reforms, to organizational structures, local workplace norms and rules, the daily social interactions with colleagues in school, and power and status relationships. Teachers are surrounded by other actors with their own perceptions of how teachers should work and with different policy messages which directly or indirectly affect teachers' sense making. Furthermore, emotions not only show what teachers have at stake, they also reveal the different situational demands teachers are confronted with during their work. Here, we consider how the nature and design of educational reforms (macro-level) and the way these reforms unfold in schools (micro-level) affect what teachers have at stake. This analysis of the nature of reforms refers to most of the large-scale reforms of the last 20 years. In innovation literature, most of these reforms are considered to be hardly successful (Hargreaves et al. 1998; Fullan 2006). Without stating that all reforms are failures, most of the large-scale reforms in Western countries have many of the characteristics mentioned below. The following analysis is relevant to gain deeper insights into the often complex and strong emotional context of reforms for most teachers.

The Macro Nature of Reforms

At the macro level, current educational reforms in many Western countries have affected – perhaps unintentionally – the professional identities of teachers. This seems not only to be true for those teachers whose professional orientations are incongruent with current reforms, but also for reform enthusiasts, whose enthusiasm may decline when local definitions and conditions of reform create conflicts, overwork, etc., as the case of Lori also shows (cf. Little 1996; van Veen et al. 2005). There are a variety of reasons that can explain the often-negative influence educational reforms at the macro-level can have on different aspects of a teacher's identity.

To start with, most reforms show a tendency to promote only one manner of teaching and working at school. In other words, the current "coalition" of innovations involves a more or less uniform set of expectations with regard to how teachers should work. Researchers have shown that teachers differ in their views, and do not constitute a monolithic block with the same attitudes, educational philosophy, subjective educational theory, values, or orientations towards the professional, pedagogical, and organizational aspects of their work (cf. Kelchtermans 1993; Sleegers 1999). Uniform policies therefore threaten the professional identities of numerous teachers, clearly exclude those with alternative orientations, and thereby make the profession less attractive for many. The impact of such uniform policy on the professional lives of teachers has also been questioned by those who consider plurality to be an essential part of teaching, a condition for professional vitality and growth (Klette 1997), and an important impetus for high quality education and teaching (van de Ven 1996).

The goals of educational reforms are often too broad, vague, or overly ambitious, and the proposed innovations are poorly designed. Teachers are then saddled with the immensely difficult task of translating the general aims of the innovation into concrete measures at the level of the school and classroom (Van den Berg and Sleegers 1996).

Current large-scale reforms are, in fact, bundles of innovations and, as a result, inherently complex, multidimensional, and sometimes even contradictory (Geijsel et al. 2001). Many reforms are also introduced as a consequence of organizational and/or financial changes, which suggest that the priority of the reform is not so much one of educational improvement but school reorganization or financial frugality within a national framework (Beare and Boyd 1993). Teachers can sense such a lack of clarity or misplaced focus and this will affect their cognitive and affective appraisals towards these reforms. Furthermore, teachers are often not involved in the initial design of reforms but are nevertheless expected to implement the reforms (Van den Berg 2002; Hargreaves et al. 1998), and many reforms simply do not take the individual concerns or needs of teachers seriously (Hargreaves 1996).

Most innovations are often advocated as improvements without sufficient empirical evidence of their effectiveness. Their "claim to fame" is often based on assumptions and theories formulated in a context other than the actual classroom (Fink and Stoll 1998; Popkewitz 1991). Virtually no empirical evidence can be found to assess their effectiveness in high school education, but teachers are expected to welcome empirically largely unfounded innovations and implement them as quickly and creatively as possible (cf. Hargreaves et al. 1998; van den Berg and Sleegers 1996; van Veen 2008).

Regarding teachers' agency, many teachers perceive educational reforms as providing solutions to problems that were not theirs to start with and therefore as something that simply distracts them from their daily concerns and problems (Hargreaves 1994). According to Goodson (2000), the reforms themselves represent a coalition of interests subsumed under a common rubric at a particular point in time. Teachers, however, are typically not among the people consulted with regard to the nature or scope of reforms.

While teacher involvement and commitment are currently hot issues in most reforms, teachers must still – in most cases – implement something that was created by others, developed by special committees, presented at workshops, designed by experts, and so forth. For all the talk of democratic decision-making, collaboration, and acknowledging the importance of teachers, school change is inevitably top-down (Holmes 1998), and while teacher involvement and commitment may not be the starting point for a reform but simply a strategy for implementation, teachers are often led to believe the opposite. The top-down nature of innovation or reform is not at issue here but, rather, the treatment of teachers for purposes of reform.

It also should be noted that the final implementation of a reform often occurs from a technical-managerial perspective (Fullan 2006). Reforms that initially contained very rich and promising ideas often get translated into organizational arrangements and agreements that virtually lose the original educational content. Most reforms are also poorly financed, which means that teachers have little or no time to revive the original educational content for purposes of reform and sometimes inspiration.

As a result, teachers have many legitimate reasons to resist reform. When they do, however, they are often labelled as traditional, conventional, lacking knowledge, being rigid, recalcitrant, passive, uninterested, but certainly not professional (cf. Achinstein and Ogawa 2006; Ballet et al. 2006; Gitlin and Margonis 1995; Little and Bartlett 2002; Van Veen et al. 2005).

In closing, there seems to be a growing awareness among policy makers, educational experts, and school principals to take a different approach to innovations and to take teachers more seriously. However, even if these approaches would be free of all negative aspects mentioned above, they should take into account the memory teachers have of the last decades of innovations. In other words, educational innovations have many negative connotations for many teachers. These memories have a strong emotional dimension. Emotion researchers state that especially unpleasant emotions are very persistent and it can take a long time before they fade away (cf. Fredrickson 1998; Frijda 1986). Therefore, those who are involved in educational innovations should be aware of this memory and those unpleasant emotions. It does not take much to trigger them again.

Based on the nature and design of educational reforms, as macro aspects of the situation teachers are confronted with, Blase (1991) concluded that schools "exist in a vortex of government mandates, social and economic pressures, and conflicting ideologies associated with school administrators, teachers, students, and parents" (1991, p. 1). In a situation in which the nature and the goals of most of the policy initiatives of national governments differ from the perspectives and goals teachers find relevant, one might expect strong emotional reactions and even resistance from teachers (cf. Gitlin and Margonis 1995).

Micro Nature of Large-Scale Reforms

Most of these multifaceted mandated educational reforms unfold at the micro-level called school and at that level teachers are also faced sometimes with very divergent expectations with regard to their work. For instance, the school management may adopt a more technical/management perspective on the work of teachers while subject colleagues can share the same commitment and involvement but differ with regard to their personal concerns and willingness to provide support. With regard to this micro-level of the school, different aspects can be distinguished, which affect teachers in different ways, causing different emotions.

First of all, reforms unfold in schools with their specific structures, policies, and traditions (cf. Ball and Bowe 1992; Bartlett 2001; Rosenholtz 1989). Recent research on policy implementation in schools clearly shows how teachers' sense making is shaped by the interplay between their cognitive frame of reference and the institutional routines, structures and workplace norms in schools (Coburn 2001; Spillane and Jennings 1997). As a consequence, each reform will be translated in a different way in each new context, which not only makes implementation of uniform designed innovations an almost impossible task to do, but also explains why teachers' personal experiences of the same reform sometimes differ so much. In line with this, Fineman (2000, p. 1) characterizes organizations as "emotional arenas" where "workaday frustrations and passions – boredom, envy, fear, love, anger, guilt, infatuation, embarrassment, nostalgia, anxiety – are deeply woven into the way roles are enacted and learned, power is exercised, trust is held, commitment formed and decisions made". And according to Kuzmic (1994), therefore, teachers should also be taught about "schools as bureaucratic organizations (...) and the limits and possibilities this affords those who work in such institutions" (p. 24). More specifically, as one becomes a member of a school organization they also acquire a level of "organizational literacy" (Blase 1991; Kuzmic 1994; Kelchtermans and Ballet 2002) or learning how "to handle the norms and values that prevail in an organization, to deal with a principal or with the colleagues in the staff, as well as with the parents of their pupils" (Kelchtermans and Ballet 2002, p. 1). As also Hargreaves (2001) also points out, teachers' workplace exists out of various contexts and many interactions, in which divergent issues play a role that color teachers' emotional experiences, such as political, socio-cultural, moral, professional, and physical issues.

Often the school principal plays a key role in shaping teachers' sense making and what they have at stake. School management and teachers can differ on aspects of power, different concerns, and goals (cf. Malden 1994), while often leads to emotional episodes (Kemper 1978). Recent research has shown that principals affect the way teachers interpret, adopt and appraise policy messages by buffering some policy messages and focusing attention on others (cf. Spillane et al. 2002). It also appeared that school principals influence teacher sense making through participation in social interaction that shapes the degree to which teachers engage in policy in ways that transform their practice (Coburn 2005; Spillane 1999). Moreover, school principals are sense makers themselves and use their own interpretations of new policy ideas in discussions they have with teachers in daily practice. Other research also found evidence that leadership practices such as vision, intellectual stimulation and individualized consideration affect teachers' feelings of uncertainty positively and as a consequence foster educational change indirectly (Geijsel et al. 2001).

To conclude, the way teachers appraise and experience different reforms is the result of the dynamic interplay between aspects of their professional identity and different situational demands. It is this interplay that makes most reforms complex for teachers, causing many different emotions. As described above, the situational demands teachers are faced with refer to definitions of their work, the other actors involved, and the school organizational structures, routines and local norms and rules. This interplay can explain the decline of enthusiasm of many teachers, who initially were enthusiastic about the content of the reform itself, but are faced with all other situational demands making them experience many unpleasant emotions. Lori is one of them, as her case will show. Let us now introduce the case of Lori to illustrate the value and use of this framework.

The Case of Lori

Lori is a teacher in French language and literature on a high school in the Netherlands. The case of Lori is derived from a larger research into the relationships between teachers' identity, sense-making, and emotions, the way reforms unfold in their workplaces, and the reform policies. This research is situated in Dutch secondary education, which has been subject to many large scale reforms for the last 20 years. The research has a strong qualitative approach because of the focus on teachers' subjective and situated meanings. The concept of emotions is used in the analyses as a lens to understand what those teachers have at stake and how they experience their work, workplace, and reforms.

Lori's school has been strongly innovative for the last 20 years. In 1992, when she was 25, she could be characterized as a very enthusiastic teacher regarding her students, teaching, her subject, school-wide matters, and reforms. However, during the last 15 years, she has gradually become disappointed and frustrated regarding the reforms, affecting her teaching negatively. To illustrate the theoretical framework, two strongly different snapshots are selected for this chapter: one with pleasant emotions and one with unpleasant ones. These snapshots refer to relevant moments or periods in the professional life of Lori, as Lori indicated.

It was an exciting time when Lori started working at this school in 1992 – a time of pleasant emotions. She loves her teaching, has very good relationships with her students, and is very active in developing new curriculum material. Also, she immediately becomes very active in the school organization. The school is in the middle of all kinds of changes, and most teachers are asked to be involved. Lori becomes part of a committee, which coordinates the changes towards more constructivist teaching approaches for the foreign languages. Already after 2 years, she becomes the chair of the committee. When she talks about these first years at her school, she refers to many pleasant emotions, which are related to many divergent aspects of her work and the workplace:

> You know, I felt like nothing could stop me, and that everything I did was fun. Every class I had was just exciting, full of wonderful moments with my students, who all loved being in my classes. Me and my colleagues [from her subject department] we developed so much new [curriculum] material, and, well, I didn't really care working in the evenings and in the weekends for that matter. I just felt so good… Learning new things every day… To me, it felt like a discovery. Okay, of course I had bad days, but in general, teaching was great fun…(…). And you know, I was so young then, but my colleagues and also the management saw me as one of them. I was part of the foreign language committee, and we discussed and developed so much. I felt the school was my home, and my colleagues my friends. And especially when I became the chair, I had so many plans, and we had so much space to experiment. I guess Paul [her principal back then] just had this policy of giving space and allowing almost everything. Yes, I felt so good then in so many ways

Analyzing her emotions using the social-psychological frame shows what Lori has at stake regarding her professional identity and shows the nature of the reforms. The reforms are organized strongly bottom-up, involving most teachers, strongly reinforcing Lori's sense of agency and autonomy. In this first snapshot, she feels reinforced in her professional identity in many ways. To be more specific, her task orientations, job motivation and self-esteem are all affected, which are related to her work in the classroom, the reform committee, and her colleagues and management. She likes her work and the contact with students, and she is very driven to improve her teaching. Also regarding her role in the school, she feels reinforced, taken seriously and supported. She considers her colleagues and principal as friends, and describes the school in another quote as her "second home".

The second snapshot is situated in the period of 1998–2002, and starts with a national reform being implemented, which seems to have many negative implications for Lori. The reform itself is in line with the previous one with regard to its focus on constructivist teaching. However, Lori's principal, Paul, leaves the school, and the new principal, named Barbara for this study, differs strongly in her approach of implementing the reforms. Instead of giving space to develop and experiment, the new principal, together with a small group of coordinators, design an implementation plan, referring to how the new reforms should be implemented. According to the new principal, the school has become too large, and a bottom-up strategy is not so effective. First, Lori and many of her colleagues embrace the new reforms because they strongly agree with the content. However, three things happened to Lori that caused many unpleasant emotions. First of all, due to the new implementation policy, all the work she did in the previous reform committee was slowly neglected and replaced by other ideas. Like many other committees, her committee was replaced by the reformed group of the new principal, with the promise that all the previous ideas and plans would be used and further developed. However, Lori noticed after a while that her work was not used at all, and that it was being replaced by ideas that were not as good as hers, in her view.

> It took me a while to understand that all the work we did in our committee was not used at all. You know, of course, I did understand that perhaps all those many committees were not effective and so on, but still I thought they would use our ideas and material. But no, not at all. They came with all kinds of new stuff, which was presented as new and good, but in my view it wasn't at all. Many of those ideas were actually rather stupid or silly…(…). But there seemed no space for discussion anymore. I tried, but I was told by Barbara [her new principal] that I misunderstood it all, that it was the same as my ideas, and that this was the right interpretation and so on… I still can get so mad about this. I felt so angry and upset… You know, first, I was really willing to listen and to work along… and I worked along actually… (…). But maybe the thing that upset me most was that their ideas were so superficial…(…) or maybe it is that all my previous work was simply neglected

A second thing that happened as a consequence of the reforms, referred to her subject, French language and literature. Due to the national reforms, the curriculum of seven courses was increased to 14 courses. One consequence of this, which affected her course and some other courses, was that the contact hours for her subject in the case of some classes were reduced to only 1 h per week. Moreover, the content was reduced to reading only, which is one of the four skills taught in a foreign language class (the others are talking, listening, and writing). A very negative consequence for Lori was that in the cases of having only one contact hour per week, she felt unable to really establish good positive relationships with her students, which resulted for the first time in her professional life in having classroom management problems.

> I still can hardly talk about this. I felt so uneasy and insecure. I just could not get contact with those kids, and how can you when you hardly have the time to learn their names? They didn't like French anymore, they made silly jokes… I even one time walked out crying… You know, I had no idea what was happening to me. I always had great classes and so much fun and good contact with my students, but in those classes, no… (…). Even in those classes that I still had for more than one hour, I started to feel insecure… okay, I still had good times there, but they couldn't compensate for the other classes… I really felt so bad

Besides, being forced to only focus on reading skills in those contact hours was strongly incongruent with her subject pedagogical views, in which all four sub skills should be integrated[2]. However, in her school, hardly any of her colleagues or the school management supported her in her resistance against this situation:

> they said, it's just part of the reforms, and there is rationale for it, and there were language teachers involved in the group [at a national level] who designed this, and so on and so on, just very frustrating. And that was against all good sense, and against the basic principles of subject pedagogy, well, like I was a fool or something, somebody traditional, or whatever, just very insulting it was, especially, now [a few years later], they changed that policy again, saying it was a mistake, but that was not what they said back then, no not all, oh, I still can get so mad

Due to the changes in her local environment, Lori's practice became more and more individualized and the quality of the interactions with her colleagues eroded. As a consequence, she began to feel more and more unhappy and her school did not feel like her "second home" anymore as she once had described it.

Analyzing this second snapshot, which is full of unpleasant emotions, it again shows that Lori has many aspects of her professional identity as a teacher at stake. The nature of the reforms differs strongly from the first snapshot especially her sense of agency and autonomy. The new reform committee neglected her task orientations, or how she thought the work should be done. Furthermore, it affected her self-image as an involved and professional teacher; others replace her ideas, her subject pedagogical views are neglected, and she is even accused of being traditional. What seems to affect her professional identity most is that she is having classroom management problems in the 1-h classes. It all affects her job motivation and her involvement in her work. From being taken seriously and having a lot of autonomy, the new implementation policy reduces her to an executor of ideas of others. The lack of open discussion and the dominance of the new reforms classify her in the category of traditional teachers, which is quite a shock to her. Lori finds herself disagreeing with many issues regarding the new implementation policy and implications of the reforms. Furthermore, her sense of agency is being eroded: she is not taken seriously anymore as a professional.

Concluding Remarks

In order to understand the problem of educational change, we used a cognitive approach on policy implementation and argued that one plausible explanation for these problems is the process of framing and sense making by teachers. Our emerging line of research has contributed to our understanding of policy implementation by providing a sense-making approach that helps to analyze and unpack how teachers

---

[2] In this view, she was not alone. Many of her subject colleagues all over the country protested. After a few years, the ministry of education decided to replace these part-subjects, as they were called, by the previous situation, in which each class has more contact hours per week and all sub skills are integrated again.

and school principals construct ideas from policy messages and use them to transform their practices (Spillane et al. 2002). Since the last decade, increasing attention is paid to the role of "hot cognition" or emotions in the context of reforms. We believe that teachers' emotions provide a valuable lens to gain a deeper understanding of teachers' professional live in times of reforms.

In this chapter we sketched our socio-psychological framework to analyze teachers' emotions. Based on this framework, we use teachers' emotions as a frame to analyze the process of identity construction by teachers and how this process is shaped by the macro and micro situation teachers work in. Our framework includes different elements of the professional identity of teachers (such as their perception of their self-image, job motivation, core responsibilities, self-esteem, teaching and subject pedagogy, and teaching as work) and aspects of the situation (such as the nature and complexity of reforms, the institutional structures, the nature and quality of interaction, leadership). We also pay attention to the dynamic interplay between the professional identity and the situation, because it is through these interactions that emotions come to the fore. In line with the sense making approach to policy implementation, in our framework emotions are considered to be a function of; (a) the nature and message of policy signal, (b) elements of teachers' professional identity and (c) the local and social context in which teachers attempt to make sense of their lives.

We believe that this framework can help scholars to generate more and new insights in the role of teachers' cognition for policy implementation and increase the quality of research in this field. The framework makes it possible to identify relevant categories of variables to be selected and can also be used to generate hypotheses that can be tested. Furthermore, researchers can use the framework to analyze differences between the way teachers appraise educational reforms and identify patterns of sense making by teachers and school principals in schools and in the system.

The current educational reforms and the expectations that the reforms bring with them have been found to generally intensify the work of teachers (Ballet et al. 2006; van Veen 2008). As Hargreaves (1994) has observed, teachers are expected to do more and more with frequently less support. In addition, many teachers have been found to experience considerable ambiguity due to the often contradictory expectations and vaguely formulated goals contained in the reforms. Teachers can also experience a marked loss of self-esteem due to reduced levels of autonomy and professional responsibility in conjunction with increased levels of accountability. Furthermore, the unfolding of reforms in school can affect the nature and quality of the staff relationships and social interactions, leading to a shift from high-trust relationships to low-trust relationships (Calderhead 2001). Because of this, policy makers should pay attention to the possible effects of this in the long term.

According to Fredrickson (1998), the primary function of positive emotional experiences is to promote the availability of personal resources and thereby provide for innovation and creativity in thought and action. Frijda (1986) argues that unpleasant emotional states orient people towards proximal, immediate events. In the long term, both types of emotions can have strong consequences for people's somatic health (illness), morale (general well-being), and social functioning (Lazarus 1991). With regard to teachers, unpleasant emotions can lead to illness, burnout, and early departure from the profession in the long run (Calderhead 2001; Vandenberghe and Huberman 1999).

Such unpleasant affects should obviously be avoided, for, as Leithwood et al. (2000, p. 27) have observed:

> Historically, the profession of teaching has attracted a disproportionate number of people extraordinarily dedicated to the mission of children's welfare; most other types of organizations can only dream of approaching such levels of dedication to their corporate missions. Reform-minded governments would do well to consider what is lost by squandering such a resource, and what the costs would be of finding an equally effective replacement.

We therefore hope that the framework can also help policy makers to become more aware of the key role teachers play during the implementation of policy initiatives and the unintentional effects of large-scale reforms on the emotional well-being of teachers. Similarly, teachers' perceptions of their own task should be clearly and seriously taken into consideration for the successful implementation of reforms as the congruence or incongruence between their perceptions and the expectations imposed by the reforms appear to be a strong determinant of their emotional well-being. As also found and argued by Day et al. (2007), not only do teachers matter for the quality of education, but more crucial for teachers' motivation to work and to improve education is that they should experience and feel that they matter. What often seems to be forgotten is that improving education and teaching is a goal that most teachers value and feel deeply about. The main challenge for all those involved in innovations is to understand these emotions and organize teachers' work and reforms in a way that will make positive use of those emotions, dedication, and motivation.

References

Aarts M, van den Berg R, Sleegers P (2002) Teachers' personal interpretations of intensified working conditions in Dutch secondary schools. Paper presented at the annual conference of the American Educational Research Association, New Orleans

Achinstein B, Ogawa RT (2006) (In)Fidelity: what the resistance of new teachers reveals about professional principles and prescriptive educational policies. Harv Educ Rev 76(1):30–63

Arnold MB (1960) Emotion and personality: Vol 1 Psychological aspects. Columbia University Press, New York

Ball S (1972) Self and identity in the context of deviance: the case of criminal abortion. In: Scott R, Douglas J (eds) Theoretical perspectives in deviance. Basic Books, New York

Ball SJ, Bowe R (1992) Subject departments and the implementation of National Curriculum policy: an overview of the issues. J Curriculum Stud 24(2):97–115

Ballet K, Kelchtermans G, Loughran J (2006) Beyond intensification towards a scholarship of practice: analysing changes in teachers' work lives. Teach Teach Theory Pract 12:209–229

Bartlett L (2001) A question of fit: conceptions of teacher role and conditions of teacher commitment. Unpublished Ph.D. Dissertation, University of California, Berkeley, CA

Beare H, Boyd WL (eds) (1993) Restructuring schools. An international perspective on the movement to transform the control and performance of schools. Falmer, London

Beijaard D, Meijer P, Verloop N (2004) Reconsidering research on teachers' identity. Teach Teach Educ 20:107–128

Blase JJ (ed) (1991) The politics of life in schools. Power, conflict, and cooperation. Sage, Newbury Park

Calderhead J (1996) Teachers: beliefs and knowledge. In: Berliner DC, Calfee RC (eds) Handbook of educational psychology. Macmillan, New York, pp 709–725

Calderhead J (2001) International experiences of teaching reform. In: Richardson V (ed) Handbook of research on teaching, 4th edn. American Educational Research Association, Washington, DC

Coburn CE (2001) Collective sensemaking about reading: how teachers mediate reading policy in their professional communities. Educ Eval Policy Anal 23(2):145–170

Coburn CE (2005) The role of nonsystem actors in the relationship between policy and practice: the case of reading instruction in California. Educ Eval Policy Anal 27(1):23–52

Day C (2002) School reform and transitions in teacher professionalism and identity. Int J Educ Res 37:677–692

Day C, Sammons P, Stobart G, Kington A, Gu Q (2007) Teachers matter: connecting work, lives and effectiveness. Open University Press, McGraw Hill, Berkshire

Dinham S, Scott C (1997) The teacher 2000 project: a study of teacher motivation and health. University of Western Sydney, Nepean, Perth

Fineman S (ed) (2000) Emotion in organizations, 3rd edn. Sage, London/Thousand Oaks

Fink D, Stoll L (1998) Educational change: easier said than done. In: Hargreaves A, Lieberman A, Fullan M, Hopkins D (eds) International handbook of educational change. Kluwer, Dordrecht/Boston/London, pp 297–321

Fredrickson BL (1998) What good are positive emotions? Rev Gen Psychol 2:300–319

Frijda NH (1986) The emotions. Cambridge University Press, Cambridge

Frijda NH (2000) The psyhologists' point of view. In: Lewis M, Haviland-Jones JM (eds) Handbook of emotions, 2nd edn. Guilford, New York/London, pp 59–74

Fullan M (2001) The new meaning of educational change. Teachers College Press/RoutledgeFalmer, New York/London

Fullan M (2006) The future of educational change: system thinkers in action. J Educ Change 7(3):113–122

Geijsel F, Sleegers P, van den Berg R, Kelchtermans G (2001) Conditions fostering the implementation of large-scale innovation programs in schools: teachers' perspectives. Educ Adm Q 37(1):130–166

Gitlin A, Margonis F (1995) The political aspect of reform: teacher resistance as good sense. Am J Educ 103:377–405

Goodson IF (2000) Social histories of educational change. J Educ Change 2(1):1–26

Gross N, Giacquinta J, Bernstein M (1971) Implementing organizational innovations: a sociological analysis of planned educational change. Basic Books, New York

Hargreaves A (1994) Changing teachers, changing times. Teachers' work and culture in the postmodern age. Cassell, London

Hargreaves A (1996) Revisiting voice. Educ Res Jan/Feb:1–8

Hargreaves A (1998) The emotions of teaching and educational change. In: Hargreaves A, Lieberman A, Fullan M, Hopkins D (eds) International handbook of educational change. Kluwer, Dordrecht/Boston/London, pp 558–575

Hargreaves A (1999) Teaching in a box: emotional geographies of teaching. Keynote at the 9th Biennial Conference of the International Study Association on Teachers and Teaching conference, Dublin

Hargreaves A (2000) Mixed emotions: teachers' perceptions of their interactions with students. Teach Teach Educ 16(8):811–826

Hargreaves A (2001) The emotional geographies of teaching. Teach Coll Record 103(6): 1056–1080

Hargreaves A (2005) Educational change takes ages: life, career and generational factors in teachers' emotional responses to educational change. Teach Teach Educ 21(8):967–983

Hargreaves A, Lieberman A, Fullan M, Hopkins D (eds) (1998) International handbook of educational change. Kluwer, Dordrecht/Boston/London

Holmes M (1998) Change and tradition in education: the loss of community. In: Hargreaves A, Lieberman A, Fullan M, Hopkins D (eds) International handbook of educational change. Kluwer, Dordrecht/Boston/London, pp 242–260

Huberman AM, Miles MB (1984) Innovation upclose: how school improvement works. Plenum, New York

Jennings N (1992) Teachers learning from policy: cases from the Michigan reading reform. Unpublished Doctoral Dissertation, Michigan State University, East Lansing, MI

Kelchtermans G (1993) Getting the story, understanding the lives – from career stories to teachers' professional-development. Teach Teach Educ 9(5–6):443–456

Kelchtermans G (2005) Teachers' emotion in educational reforms: self-understanding, vulnerable commitment and micropolitical literacy. Teach Teach Educ 21(8):995–1006

Kelchtermans G, Ballet K (2002) The micropolitics of teacher induction. A narrative-biographical study on teacher socialisation. Teach Teach Educ 18(1):105–120

Kemper TD (1978) A social interactional theory of emotions. Wiley, New York

Kemper TD (2000) Social models in the explanation of emotions. In: Lewis M, Haviland-Jones JM (eds) Handbook of emotions, 2nd edn. Guilford, New York, pp 45–58

Klette K (1997) Teacher individuality, teacher collaboration and repertoire-building: some principal dilemmas. Teach Teach Theory Pract 3(2):243–256

Kuzmic J (1994) A beginning teacher's search for meaning: teacher socialisation, organisational literacy, and empowerment. Teach Teach Educ 10(1):15–27

Lampert M (1990) When the problem is not the question and the solution is not the answer: mathematical knowing and teaching. Am Educ Res J 27(1):29–64

Lasky S (2005) A sociocultural approach to understanding teacher identity, agency and professional vulnerability in a context of secondary school reform. Teach Teach Educ 21(8):899–916

Lazarus RS (1999) Stress and emotion, a new synthesis. Free Association Books, London

Lazarus RS (1991) Emotion and adaptation. Oxford University Press, New York/Oxford

Leithwood K, Steinbach R, Jantzi D (2000) Identifying and explaining the consequences for schools of external accountability initiatives. Or what in the world did you think I was doing before you came along? Paper presented at the annual meeting of the American Educational Research Association, New Orleans, April 2000

Lewis M, Haviland-Jones JM (eds) (2000) Handbook of emotions, 2nd edn. Guilford, New York/London

Little JW (1996) The emotional contours and career trajectories of (disappointed) reform enthusiasts. Cambridge J Educ 26(3):345–359

Little JW, Bartlett L (2002) Career and commitment in the context of comprehensive school reform. Teach Teach Theory Pract 8(3/4):345–354

Malden B (1994) The micropolitics of education: mapping the multiple dimensions of power relations in school polities. J Educ Policy 9(5&6):147–167

Nias J (1989) Primary teachers talking. A study of teaching as work. Routledge, London

Nias J (1996) Thinking about feeling: the emotions in teaching. Cambridge J Educ 26(3):293–306

Nias J (1999) Teachers' moral purposes: stress, vulnerability, and strength. In: Vandenberghe R, Huberman AM (eds) Understanding and preventing teacher burnout, a sourcebook of international research and practice. Cambridge University Press, New York, pp 223–237

Oatley K (1992) Best laid schemes: the psychology of emotions. Cambridge University Press, Cambridge, UK

Oatley K (2000) Emotion: theories. In: Kazdin AE (ed) Encyclopedia of psychology, vol 3. American Psychological Association/Oxford University Press, New York/Oxford, pp 167–171

Ortony A, Clore GL, Collins A (1988) The cognitive structure of emotions. Cambrdige University Press, Cambridge, UK

Popkewitz TS (1991) A political sociology of educational reform: power/knowledge in teaching, teacher education, and research. Teachers College Press, New York

Richardson V (1996) The role of attitudes and beliefs in learning to teach. In: Sikula J (ed) Handbook of research in teacher education. Macmillan, New York, pp 102–119

Richardson V, Placier P (2001) Teacher change. In: Richardson V (ed) Handbook of research on teaching, 4th edn. American Educational Research Association, Washington, DC, pp 905–947

Roseman IJ, Antoniou AA, Jose PE (1996) Appraisal determinants of emotions: constructing a more accurate and comprehensive theory. Cogn Emotion 10:241–277

Rosenholtz S (1989) Teachers' workplace: the social organization of schools. Longman, New York

Scherer KR, Schorr A, Johnstone T (eds) (2001) Appraisal processes in emotion. Theory, methods, research. Oxford University Press, New York

Schmidt M, Datnow A (2005) Teachers' sense-making about comprehensive school reform: the influence of emotions. Teach Teach Educ 21(8):949–965

Siskin LS (1994) Realms of knowledge: academic departments in secondary schools. Falmer, London

Sleegers PJC (1999) Professional identity, school reform, and burnout: Some reflections on teacher burnout. In M. Huberman & R. Vandenberghe (Eds.), Understanding and preventing teacher burnout: A sourcebook of international research and practice (pp. 247–255). Cambridege: Cambridge University Press

Smith CA (1991) The self, appraisal and coping. In: Snyder CR, Forsyth DR (eds) Handbook of social and clinical psychology: the health perspective. Pergamon, Elmsford, NY, pp 116–137

Spillane J (1999) State and local government relations in the era of standards-based reform: standards, state policy instruments and local instructional policy-making. Educ Policy 13(4):546–572

Spillane J (2000) Cognition and policy implementation: district policy-makers and the reform of mathematics education. Cogn Instruct 18(2):141–179

Spillane J, Jennings N (1997) Aligned instructional policy and ambitious pedagogy: exploring instructional reform from the classroom perspective. Teach Coll Record 98(3):449–479

Spillane JP, Reiser BJ, Reimer T (2002) Policy implementation and cognition: reframing and refocusing implementation research. Rev Educ Res 72(3):387–431

Stodolsky SS, Grossman PL (1995) The impact of subject matter on curricular activity: an analysis of five academic subjects. Am Educ Res J 32(2):227–249

Stoll L, Bolam R, Collarbone P (2002) Leading for change: building capacity for learning. In: Leithwood K, Hallinger P (eds) Second international handbook of educational leadership and administration . Kluwer, Dordrecht

Sutton RE, Wheatley KF (2003) Teachers' emotions and teaching: a review of the literature and directions for future research. Educ Psychol Rev 15(4):327–358

van de Ven P (1996) Moedertaalonderwijs. Interpretaties in retoriek en praktijk, heden en verleden, binnen- en buitenland [Mother tongue education. Interpretations in rhetoric and practice, present and past, at home and abroad]. Dissertation, Wolters-Noordhoff, Groningen

van den Berg R (2002) Teachers' meanings regarding educational practice. Rev Educ Res 72(4):577–625

van den Berg R, Sleegers P (1996) Building innovative capacity and leadership. In: Leithwood K, Chapman J, Corson D, Hallinger Ph, Hart A (eds) International handbook of educational leadership and administration. Kluwer, Dordrecht/Boston/London, pp 653–699

van Veen K (2003) Teachers' emotions in a context of reforms. Unpublished Thesis, University of Nijmegen, Nijmegen, the Netherlands

van Veen K (2008) Analyzing teachers' working conditions from the perspective of teachers as professionals. In: Ax J, Ponte P (eds) The profession of teacher in Dutch educational praxis. Sense Publishers, Rotterdam

van Veen K, Lasky S (2005) Emotions as a lens to explore teacher identity and change: different theoretical approaches. (Introduction to special issue on emotion, teacher identity and change). Teach Teach Educ 21(8):895–898

van Veen K, Sleegers P (2006) How does it feel? Teachers' emotions in a context of change. J Curriculum Stud 38(1):85–111 van Veen K, Sleegers P, Van de Ven P (2005) One teacher's identity, emotions and commitment to change: a case study into the cognitive-affective processes of a secondary school teacher in the context of reforms. Teach Teach Educ 21(8):917–934

VandenBerghe R, Huberman AM (1999) Understanding and preventing teacher burnout, a sourcebook of international research and practice. Cambridge University Press, New York

Zembylas M (2005) Teaching with emotion: a postmodern enactment. Information Age Publishing, Greenwich, CT

Zembylas M, Barker H (2007) Teachers' spaces for coping with change in the context of a reform effort. J Educ Change 8:235–256

Chapter 13
Implementing High-Quality Educational Reform Efforts: An Interpersonal Circumplex Model Bridging Social and Personal Aspects of Teachers' Motivation

Jeannine E. Turner, Ralph M. Waugh, Jessica J. Summers, and Crissie M. Grove

Abstract Professional-development is often a catalyst for transforming research-based theories and findings into best-teaching-practices and increased student-achievement within whole-school reform efforts. In the following chapter, we present a theoretical model that integrates social aspects of personal motivation (i.e., Self-Determination Theory), personal aspects of motivation (i.e., Control-Value Theory), and circumplex models of interpersonal relationships to understand factors that affect teachers' implementation of promising ideas presented in professional development. From a Self-Determination Theory perspective, individuals' intrinsic motivation is facilitated through environmental supports of three elements: autonomy, competence, and relatedness. From a Control-Value Theory perspective individuals' motivations and emotional correspondents are due to personal judgments regarding issues of personal control (e.g., agency/self-efficacy) and personal values (e.g., goals). We integrate these theories, and present a circumplex model to describe two primary dimensions of principals' interactional behaviors that provide overt and covert messages about their support (or lack of support) for teachers' autonomy and competence. We propose that principals' supportive or unsupportive behaviors merge with teachers' personal values and perceptions of control to shape teachers' motivations for implementing high-quality professional development for whole-school reform.

Keywords teacher emotions • teacher motivation • interpersonal • interactions

With the goal of boosting students' engagement, learning, and achievement; high-quality professional development is often sought as a catalyst for transforming research-based theories and findings into best-teaching educational reform efforts. If the educational reform and professional development are high-quality and

J.E. Turner (✉)
Department of Educational Psychology and Learning Systems, Florida State University, Tallahassee, FL, USA
e-mail: turner@mail.coe.fsu.edu

P.A. Schutz and M. Zembylas (eds.), *Advances in Teacher Emotion Research:*
The Impact on Teachers' Lives,
DOI 10.1007/978-1-4419-0564-2_13, © Springer Science+Business Media, LLC 2009

research-based, how do social aspects (e.g., teachers' interactions with their principals) interact with teachers' personal characteristics (e.g., their perceptions of personal values and efficacy) in ways that facilitate or hinder their motivation to apply newly-learned skills and content knowledge? Understanding factors that affect teachers' implementation of promising ideas presented in high-quality professional development activities as part of educational reform efforts is important because their implementation can ultimately impact students' achievement (Turner et al. 2006).

In the following chapter, we present a theoretical model that integrates social aspects on personal motivation (i.e., Self-Determination Theory) and personal aspects of motivation (i.e., Control-Value Theory). Furthermore, we propose that emotional foundations, developed through teachers' interpersonal interactions with individual contextual authorities (e.g., individual principals and/or district authorities), merge with teachers' personal values and personal perceptions of control to shape their motivations. These interactions take place in ways that influence dynamically teachers' motivations for implementing high-quality professional development to obtain or maintain high-quality teaching.

Specifically, we integrate three theoretical perspectives, Self-Determination Theory (Deci and Ryan 2000), circumplex models of interpersonal interactions (Benjamin 1974; Freedman et al. 1951; Leary 1957), and Control-Value Theory (Pekrun 2000). From the perspective of Self-Determination Theory (SDT), principals' supports for personal autonomy, personal competence, and interpersonal relatedness facilitate teachers' intrinsic motivation (i.e., energized behaviours that are rewarded by doing an activity, without regard to receipt of external rewards). A circumplex model is then used to describe two primary dimensions of principals' interactional behaviors that provide overt and covert messages about their support (or lack of support) for teachers' autonomy and competence. Finally, from the perspective of Control-Value Theory (CVT), teachers' subjective judgments regarding perceptions of personal control (e.g., agency/self-efficacy) and personal values (e.g., goals) merge into their emotions and motivations. Hence, teachers' on-going evaluations of social aspects and personal aspects act as a catalyst for their emotional reactions and motivations, which strengthen or weaken their implementation efforts of professional development and reform efforts.

Implementing Professional Development and Reform Efforts: The Role of Teachers' Emotions

Researchers have revealed that teachers' continued professional growth, in ways that support students' learning, is an important element of successful schools (Billig et al. 2005). These post-graduate educational experiences are expected to augment teachers' instructional repertoire, thereby helping teachers keep their instructional practices current. With respect to high-quality, educational reform efforts, scholars have suggested that teachers will not teach differently unless their instructional models or pedagogical understandings have been elaborated or altered (Hashweh 2003; Leinhardt 2001). Indeed, some scholars contend that professional development should focus on shifting teachers' models of instruction to more complex, effective models of teaching and learning (Kent 2004). In support of this claim, Haim et al. (2004) found that, compared to levels of content knowledge, the most important factor influencing changes with regard to teachers' instructional choices was a shift in teachers' cognitive instructional models. High-quality, educational reform efforts often require substantial modifications to teachers' instructional models. Consequently, teachers may be required to make changes in ways that challenge their beliefs about teaching and learning. These changes, in turn, may challenge teachers' personal identities and values as teachers.

Within this context, professional development for educational reform can initiate strong emotional reactions in teachers (Darby 2008; Lasky 2005; Reio 2005). Indeed, Reio (2005) discussed "the influence of reform on teacher identity, emotion, risk taking, and learning" (p. 992). He suggested that, within the context of educational reform, aspects of teachers' personal identities influence the emotions that teachers experience and the levels of risk-taking (e.g., making substantial changes; feeling embarrassed) they are willing to accept. Consequently, the emotions that teachers experience and the risks they are willing to take may impact their learning and development, which, consequently, may impact their personal identities. Reio (2005) maintained that educational reform efforts "must take into account that teachers have natural emotional reactions to change that have both positive and negative influences on the construction of their professional and personal identity. All too often, unfortunately, change evokes negative emotions due to insufficient information and vague perceptions of unnecessary loss" (p. 992).

We propose that teacher-principal[1] interpersonal interactions may be critical to teachers' perceptions of reform, their emotions, and their motivations to implement high-quality professional development for educational reform. In particular we propose that, under positive conditions of support from school principals, the dynamic interplay of teachers' and principals' motivations and emotions may facilitate teachers' motivation to apply newly-learned skills and content knowledge gained through high-quality professional development.

To begin, we describe our overarching model for bridging social and personal aspects of teachers' motivation for reform. Then we review literature that further describes and supports components of the model from the perspectives of (1) social influences on individual motivation, (2) authority-behaviors and interpersonal interactions, and (3) personal aspects of teachers' motivation. We conclude with suggestions for future research.

---

[1]We use the term "principals" to signify persons of authority. Respectfully, we acknowledge that, in addition to principals, other persons of authority have central importance in role-hierarchy relationships and interpersonal interactions with teachers. Such persons may include district leaders, school principals, school leadership teams and other persons of authority who interact with teachers.

An Interpersonal Circumplex Model Bridging Social and Personal Aspects of Teachers' Motivation

Similar to findings with regard to students' learning-related perceptions, teachers' perceptions of environmental supports (SDT, Deci and Ryan 2000) and their perceptions of personal control and personal values (CVT, Pekrun 2000) may facilitate or hinder their motivation to (1) *learn* from professional development and (2) *implement* professional development (Grove 2007, 2008; Turner and Grove 2008). The construct connecting teachers' perceptions of principals' supportive behaviors and their individual motivations is that of principals' interpersonal behaviors, which create an emotional climate.

As Fig. 13.1 illustrates, teachers' motivation for implementing professional development and educational reform efforts is influenced by (1) environmental supports for teachers' personal autonomy, values, and competence, (2) the emotional climate established through their interpersonal interactions with the principal (or contextual authorities), and (3) their own personal values, perceptions of control, competencies, and emotional experiences. Aspects of interpersonal interactions drive teachers' appraisals of environmental supports that interact with their personal appraisals of control and values, thereby impacting their ongoing emotions and motivations for implementing their newly-learned skills and content knowledge, which has the potential to influence students' learning and achievement. Student-outcomes subsequently can influence principals' supports for teachers' motivations, principals' interpersonal behaviors, teachers' personal motivations, and teachers' implementation of professional development, thus creating dynamic processes.

Consistent with dynamical systems theories (e.g., Op 't Eynde and Turner 2006; Waugh 2002, 2003a, b) each component is connected dynamically through interactive reciprocal feedback loops. This means that each component influences, and is reciprocally influenced by, each of the other components. Although fairly stable patterns may develop (e.g., principals' leadership styles, teachers' values, teachers' perceptions of efficacy), reciprocal feedback loops allow for the possibility of flexibility, adaptations, adjustments, and other changes that can occur within each component (e.g., principals may come to value teachers' input because of the relationships they develop with them, teachers' values or perceptions of efficacy may change because of their interactions with principals).

Across the model four related categories of social aspects and personal aspects of motivations are aligned: (1) Autonomy/Control (i.e., perceptions of the principal's autonomy support and teachers' individual perceptions of control), (2) Values (e.g., the principal's valuing the promotion of students' mastery goals over performance goals and teachers' valuing/promoting students' mastery goals over performance goals), (3) Knowledge and Skills (e.g., the principal's acknowledgement and promotion of teachers' knowledge and teachers' maintenance and development of domain knowledge and pedagogical knowledge), and (4) emotions (i.e., the principal's emotions; the emotional climate that develops through interpersonal interactions; teachers' personal emotions associated with appraisals of personal control, values, skill, and emotional climate) (see Fig. 13.2).

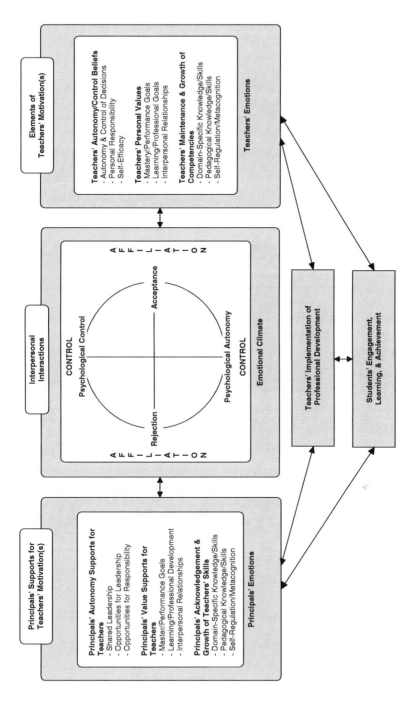

Fig. 13.1 An interpersonal circumplex model bridging self-determination theory and control-value theory

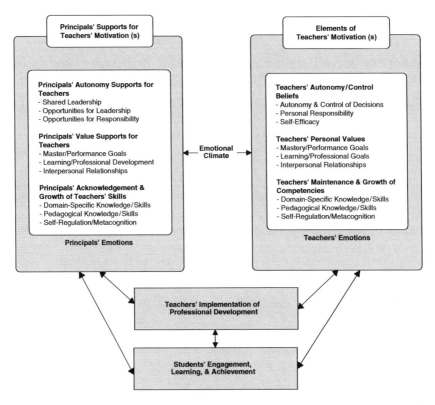

Fig. 13.2 Alignment of components: principals' supports for teachers motivation and elements of teachers' motivation

From the teachers' perspective, their motivations will be impacted by the extent to which they believe their principals' supports their control-related perceptions, their values, and their competencies. Additionally, teachers' own control beliefs, personal values, competencies, and emotions will influence their motivations for implementing newly-learned skills and content knowledge. Which component will create the greatest influence on teachers' in-the-moment motivation will depend on the strength on the individual components as well as teachers' own perceptions and interpretations of the various components within the current time-frame.

Social Support for Intrinsic Motivation: Self-Determination Theory

The notion that environmental factors can impact an individual's motivations is consistent with Deci and Ryan's Self-Determination Theory (Deci and Ryan 1985, 2000; Ryan and Deci 2000). A foundational tenet of SDT is that, while humans may have natural tendencies to pursue their own interests, that pursuit most often requires external support. Hence, SDT provides a foundation for understanding ways in which principals may influence teachers' personal control-related and value-related appraisals for implementing newly-learned skills and content knowledge for educational reform.

Deci and Ryan's (2000) theory is based on the assumptions that humans are active, growth-oriented organisms who are naturally inclined toward integration of psychological elements into a unified sense of self and integration of themselves into larger social structures. Proponents of SDT tend to suggest that it is part of the adaptive design of the human organism to engage in interesting activities, to exercise personal capacities, to pursue connectedness in social groups, and to integrate intrapsychic and interpersonal experiences into a relative unity (ibid., p. 229).

Furthermore, proponents of SDT proposes that humans have three foundational, psychological needs that must be met for healthy functioning and for the promotion of intrinsic motivation: the needs to experience *competence, autonomy*, and positive interpersonal *relatedness*. When social aspects facilitate individuals' basic needs for competence, autonomy, and interpersonal relatedness, they are more likely to perceive that their actions are "self-determined," and they are more likely to experience intrinsic motivation (involvement in an activity is personally rewarding). When individuals perceive their actions are not autonomous (i.e., the environment uses coercive, external controls for promoting motivation), personal intrinsic motivation is thwarted. For our purposes, SDT helps to explain the impact of principals' support (or lack thereof) on teachers' intrinsic motivation for implementing newly-learned skills and content knowledge for educational reform.

Researchers have shown that principal–teacher relationships may influence teachers' implementation of professional development (Grove 2007, 2008) and can affect teachers' classroom practices (Beachum et al. 2008). These researchers have focused on the relationships between principals and teachers and the effects of these relationships on teachers' cognitions, motivations, behaviors, and feelings. For example, Scribner's (1998) research demonstrated that teachers who saw their principals as "supportive" of professional development – compared to those who saw principals as controlling "gatekeepers" of information – also had intrinsic motivation for learning professional development content and held beliefs of high personal efficacy (i.e., perceptions of competence). Similarly, Ellett et al. (1997) found a strong relationship between teachers' ratings of positive teacher–administrator relationships and their perceptions of increased opportunities for professional development. Furthermore, Ellett et al. (1997) found that teachers' reports of having a positive professional learning environment predicted their sense of efficacy and human caring. They suggested that opportunities for teachers' learning are more likely to occur when administrators and teachers have positive relationships (i.e., principals fostered teachers' autonomy, competence, and positive relatedness) and that having an environment that fosters teachers' learning specifically impacts teachers' positive perceptions efficacy (i.e., competence). Finally, Ciani et al. (2008) found that feelings of teacher community – encouraged by trust, collaboration, and support from administration – predicted teachers' perceptions of collective efficacy, which in turn predicted their perceptions of individual teacher efficacy (i.e., competence) and mastery classroom goal structures.

With respect to research on school reform efforts, Lasky's research (2005) showed that when teachers felt safe (i.e., emotionally supported through positive relationships) to take risks of becoming visibly stressed and embarrassed in front of others, they were more willing to be vulnerable professionally during the uncertainty of changes. Additionally, Darby's (2008) investigation of teachers' emotions and professional self-understandings during reform efforts demonstrated that when teachers experienced positive professional development relationships with coaches and university faculty who provided competency-supports, they felt less fear and intimidation and they were able to make requested changes that resulted in positive student outcomes.

Power of Role Hierarchies

One reason that principals' support has an important influence on teachers' personal work-related motivation and emotions is that a relationship between principals and teachers is enacted within a role hierarchy and across a relational history (Darley 2001; Grove 2007). The role hierarchy incorporates levels of authority and power that are associated with individual participants' role structure (e.g., principal's and teacher's). Principals impact the environmental resources and autonomy provided to teachers. Consequently, consideration of teachers' personal cognitions, emotions, and motivations in relation to their principals' decisions and behaviors (i.e., the extent to which teachers believe principals support their autonomy and competence) may be crucial to understanding teachers' implementing newly-learned skills and content knowledge.

We propose that principals' support for teachers can be facilitated through the emotional climate and environmental supports in which principals initiate and enact supportive (or unsupportive) interpersonal interactions. Hence, these interpersonal interactions may create constructive or unconstructive emotional climates for subordinate teachers' implementation of newly-learned skills and content knowledge within the contexts of local efforts (school and/or district) and statewide efforts to achieve educational reforms.

In a negatively-valenced climate, teachers may struggle for personal autonomy, experience unpleasant emotions (e.g., anger, despair), and/or have appraisals of low efficacy for their abilities to implement the educational reform efforts (e.g., Sandholtz and Scribner 2006). Additionally, they may have low expectations and low valuation for professional development tasks and the potential outcomes of educational reforms. In a positively-valenced climate, teachers' may have perceptions of autonomy support, experiences of pleasant emotions (e.g., enjoyment, hope), and high expectancies and valuation for professional development tasks and the potential outcomes of educational reforms. Using the circumplex model as a theoretical framework for understanding the emotional climate that is generated via the principal–teacher relationship, in the following section we outline the processes through which interpersonal interactions may bridge principals' behaviors and teachers' appraisals.

A Circumplex Model of Principal–Teacher Interpersonal Interactions

Drawing upon theory and empirical evidence with respect to systems communications (Watzlawick et al. 1967; Creton et al. 1993) and interpersonal interactions (Benjamin 1974; Freedman et al. 1951; Leary 1957), we suggest that every education-related communication carries both an informational message and a relational message (i.e., an underlying emotional/relational communication). The relational aspect is often communicated through nonverbal behaviors, such as voice tone and facial expressions. When individuals interact over time, interactional patterns are established.

Leary and his colleagues (Freedman et al. 1951; Leary 1957), as well as Wubbels and colleagues (e.g., Wubbels et al. 1993; Wubbels and Brekelmans 2005; Wubbels and Levy 1993) have advocated using an interpersonal circumplex model to describe educational interpersonal interactions. Leary (a clinical psychologist) and his colleagues developed an interpersonal behavioral classification system known as a *circumplex model* (for a history of circumplex models, see Wiggins 1996). Through analysis of clinical interactions (e.g., patient–therapist interactions, group discussions), Leary and his colleagues categorized interpersonal behaviors along two dimensions: *Affiliation* (i.e., Hostility – Love) and *Control* (i.e., Dominance – Submission). Using a circumplex structure, they arranged interpersonal behaviors around a two-dimensional circular space. The two dimensions of the circle-space are divided further into eight octants, with each octant describing a position relative to the two coordinates (e.g., Benjamin 1974, 1996; Lorr 1996; Wiggins 1996; for example, see Fig. 13.3).

A circumplex model implies circular order, such that opposite octants are most dissimilar and negatively related to one another, and adjacent octants are more similar and more positively related to one another. Wiggins (1996) explained that, "the circle design involves dimensional classification in which category membership ... is continuous rather than discrete and in which elements are distributed continuously around the perimeter of a circle, with each fuzzy category emerging into its neighboring categories" (Wiggins 1996, p. 226). Circumplex models have been developed and validated (e.g., Wiggins et al. 1989) to explore an array of psychological phenomena such as levels of interpersonal interactions (Benjamin 1996), clinical interactions (Kiesler 1996), parental behavior (Schaefer 1965), and emotions (Barrett and Russell 1999).

For more than 25 years, Wubbels and his colleagues (e.g., Wubbels and Levy 1993; den Brok et al. 2006; den Brok and Levy 2005; Levy et al. 2003) have used a circumplex model to investigate the importance of teachers' and students' interactions and relationships (for a review, see Wubbels and Brekelmans 2005).

Within the role-hierarchy milieu in which teachers and students interact, Wubbels and colleagues' research began with the assumption that these interactions are driven by teachers' behaviors that subsequently impact students' behaviors. Wubbels and Levy's (1993) circumplex model used the dimensions of Opposition – Cooperation (*Proximity*) and Dominance – Submission (*Influence*) to classify teachers' Control-related and Affiliation-related behaviors in relation to students. Their studies regarding teacher–student classroom environments have shown strong associations among students' perceptions of teachers' controlling behaviors, teachers' affiliation behaviors, and measures of students' outcomes. For example, emotionally hostile teacher-behaviors (i.e., oppositional) were found to be associated with lower levels of students' achievement, while emotionally supportive teacher-behaviors (i.e., cooperative) were associated with higher levels of students' achievement (den Brok et al. 2006; Goh and Fraser 2000).

A few scholars have adapted Wubbels' circumplex model to investigate principal–teacher interactions (Creswell 1997; Fisher and Creswell 1998; Fisher et al. 1995). These researchers modified Wubbels, Creton, Levy, and Hooymayers' (1993) teacher–student interpersonal circumplex model to accommodate principal–teacher interactions. Investigating associations between teachers' ideal preferences for their principals' behaviors and their perceptions of principals' actual interpersonal behaviors, Cresswell (1997, Cresswell and Fisher, 1999, Fisher and Creswell, 1998) found differences between teachers' "ideal" and "actual" ratings. For example, compared to their ratings indicating the behaviors that principals were currently displaying, teachers wanted their principals to engage in more cooperative interpersonal behaviors, and use fewer opposing behaviors. More importantly for our purposes, Creswell (1997) found strong associations between teachers' perceptions of the independence their principals gave them (i.e., autonomy-support) and the extent to which teachers felt empowered (i.e., personal control). Additionally, teachers' higher ratings of principals' tendencies to interact with disapproving interpersonal behaviors (i.e., not supporting interpersonal relationships) was associated with negative perceptions of the school environment (i.e., school climate).

A Circumplex Model of Principal–Teacher Interpersonal Interactions

In Fig. 13.3, we present a circumplex model that integrates Fisher and Creswell's (1998) circumplex model (Creswell and Fisher 1998; Fisher and Creswell 1998; Fisher et al. 1995) of principals behaviors towards teachers and Schaefer's (1965) circumplex model of parental behaviors. Although Fisher and Creswell's (1998) model targets our population of interest (principals and teachers), Schaefer's model uses descriptive labels that more closely align Self-Determination Theory in relation to Control-Value Theory. Both circumplex models allow for the conceptualization of the emotional climate that is created by various affiliative qualities and differentials in power, authority, and personal

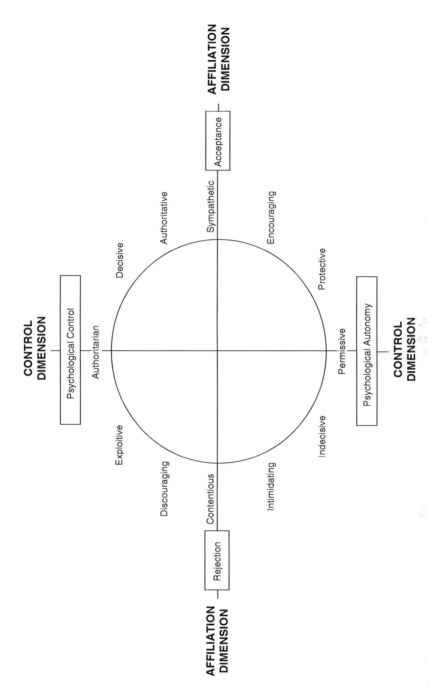

Fig. 13.3 A circumplex model of principal–teacher interactions

resources found within the role-hierarchy milieu that exists between individual principals and individual teachers.

Our model includes the fundamental facets of previous theories and we apply them to specific theoretical considerations of teacher–principal interpersonal interactions: (1) the Affiliation and the Control dimensions, (2) conceptual alignment of social aspects (i.e., SDT) and personal aspects (i.e., CVT), and (3) from teachers' perspectives, identification and use of pertinent theoretical labels that address specifically the interpersonal dynamics between teachers and principals. In our model the *Control* dimension encompasses the continuum, Psychological Control – Psychological Autonomy, and the *Affiliation* dimension includes the continuum, Rejection – Acceptance. The unique labels of the circumplex model are consistent with historical interpersonal models of interpersonal behaviors, from clinical and personality psychology (Freedman et al. 1951; Leary 1957; Benjamin 1974, 1996), social and lifespan developmental psychology (Waugh 2002), child development and parenting behavior (i.e., Schaefer 1965), and educational leadership (Creswell and Fisher 1998; Fisher and Creswell 1998; Kremer-Hayon and Wubbels 1993).

Each of the labels around the circumplex model denote individual principals' behaviors toward teachers, with each octant describing a position relative to the control and affiliation dimensions. The octants around the circumplex describe the interpersonal behaviors that individual principals present to individual teachers. These octants are labelled as follows: *decisive, authoritative, encouraging, protective, indecisive, intimidating, discouraging, and exploitive.* Each octant, opposite in the circle, is proposed to be most dissimilar and most negatively related to the octant on the other side of the circle, and each adjacent octant is proposed to be more similar and more positively related to the two adjacent octants.

We believe that the interactional process dimensions of *Control* and *Affiliation*, provide a lens through which we can understand better principals' enactment of principal–teacher interpersonal transactions. Additionally, we believe that, over time, the enactment of these interpersonal transactions can lead to the development of principals' individual communication patterns or styles with respect to teachers. Furthermore, over time and in relation to their respective principals, teachers develop appraisals, expectations, and emotional interlinkages regarding their principals' interpersonal styles. The dynamical and reciprocal (i.e., bidirectional influences and effects) interplay between (1) principal–teacher transactions, (2) individual principals' and individual teachers' communication/interactional patterns or styles, and (3) individual principals' and individual teachers' appraisals, expectations, and emotional interlinkages contribute to the creation of an emotional climate within which a teacher functions within a specific school and within a given school system. Hence, the emotional climates established by principals may strongly influence teachers' motivations for implementing professional development. However, teachers' motivations may also be strongly influence by internally-generated perceptions and goals. We discuss this perspective in the following section.

Teachers' Motivations and Emotions: Control-Value Theory

Focusing on factors that shape individuals' emotions and respective motivations, Control-Value Theory (CVT), Pekrun (2000, 2006) suggests that, if individual teachers do not hold a modicum of perceived *value* and perceived *control* with respect to the enactment of newly-learned skills and content knowledge, they will not experience positive emotions and energized motivation concerning their efforts. Pekrun and colleagues posit that two classes of appraisals – "subjective control over achievement activities and their outcomes ... and the subjective values of these activities and outcomes" (Pekrun 2006, p. 317) – are of primary importance for understanding reciprocal and dynamical processes among individuals' emotions (e.g., enjoyment, fear), cognitions (e.g., perceptions, appraisals), and motivations (e.g., approach, avoidance; intrinsic or extrinsic goals). For example, just as teachers' perceptions of control and values may influence the extent to which they experience pleasantly-valenced or unpleasantly-valenced emotions about implementing newly-learned skills and knowledge, the emotions they experience may influence subsequent appraisals of control and values related to their motivations.

Previous research regarding teachers' motivations has examined relationships among variables with respect to teachers' perceptions of personal control (most often defined as expectancy perceptions regarding personal control and self-efficacy), values (most often defined as perceptions concerning valued personal goals), and to a lesser extent, their emotions. For example, with respect to teachers' motivation for implementing professional development, van Eekelen et al. (2006) analyzed teachers' interviews for their perceptions and experiences about mastering new skills and found three groups of teachers regarding their *will to learn* ("a psychological state in which the learner has a desire to learn" p. 410). These groups were identified as (1) those who do not see the need to learn (i.e., have low value) (2), those who wonder how to learn (i.e., concerns about control), and (3) those who are eager to learn (i.e., experience pleasant emotions).

CVT (Pekrun 2000, 2006) posits that teachers' appraisals about their abilities to control aspects of their activities include personal identity-related beliefs (e.g., Wenger 1998), attributions about the causes of their successes and failures (e.g., self-generated or other-generated; Weiner 1985), and their appraisals about their abilities to regulate actions to attain desired outcomes (e.g., self-efficacy beliefs; Bandura 1986, 1989). Depending upon individuals' appraised levels of control, they experience different emotions. For example, low levels of control can be associated with feelings of anxiety, while high levels of control can be associated with feelings of confidence.

In a comprehensive model of teacher-motivation, low levels of teachers' expectancies for personal control and expectancies for success in their classrooms were related to low levels of teachers' professional engagement, especially when teachers had high valuing for goals that were difficult to attain (de Jesus and Lens 2005). Additionally, findings from a study conducted by Roth et al. (2007) showed strong, positive relationships among teachers' ratings of personal autonomy, teachers' self-efficacy for teaching, and their perceptions of personal accomplishments (Roth et al. 2007). These findings are consistent with CVT in that appraisals of personal control interact with appraisals of personal values to influence motivations and emotions.

With respect to personal values, the primary foci of the value component within academic motivation have been individuals' goals (e.g., social goals, mastery goals) and their reasons for engaging in academic tasks (e.g., intrinsic incentives such as personal interest, extrinsic incentives such as monetary rewards). Value-/goal-related research has linked teachers' job satisfaction (an emotional element) with a focus on mastery goals for their students (a value element, Papaioannou and Christoduoulidis 2007). With respect to educational reform efforts, Lasky's research (2005) demonstrated that teachers' identity, which included their perceptions of agency, influenced their willingness to be professionally vulnerable (an emotional element) during the uncertainty of reform efforts. Furthermore, changes in teachers' control perceptions throughout the reform effort impacted their emotional reactions, their willingness to take risks, and their ultimate implementation of teaching practices. Consistent with CVT, teachers' were more willing to take the risks involved with implementing change when they valued the potential outcomes that change could provide.

Finally, CVT posits that ongoing appraisals of control and value, with subsequent emotions and motivations, in turn, lead to further shifts in cognitive appraisals, emotions, and motivations. Supporting this claim, Darby's (2008) study regarding teachers' specific emotions and their self-understanding during comprehensive reform revealed that teachers' feelings of fear were initiated when their professional self-understandings (i.e., aspects of their identity) were threatened. However, supportive interactions from coaches and university faculty facilitated teachers' conceptual changes. In particular, when teachers were involved with collaboration (i.e., given opportunities for control) they were willing to take on challenges associated with instructional changes. Furthermore, Darby's results showed that, as teachers made changes to their instructional practices, they saw increases in students' learning, which prompted boosts in self-efficacy, self-esteem, and instigated emotions of pride and excitement. Consistent with CVT, these cognitive appraisals and pleasant emotions seemed to further enhance teachers' motivation to continue the reform program.

Influence of Social Interactions on Individual Motivation

As suggested by Darby's (2008) research, CVT recognizes that individuals' appraisals of environmental factors (e.g., messages from authorities) will affect their motivations and emotions (Pekrun 2006). This occurs because environmental authorities deliver information directly related to individuals' perceived levels of control and perceived levels of valuation. Messages received through important social interactions include "induction of values, autonomy support, goal structures and achievement-related expectancies of significant others, as well as feedback and consequences of achievement" (Pekrun 2006, p. 325). According to CVT, individuals' appraisals of these socially-delivered messages mediate the motivational and emotional impact of situational factors.

One factor that may influence a principal's willingness to act in autonomy-supportive ways is the degree to which principals and their subordinate teachers share professional values. Analyzing interview data, Grove (2007) found that, when teachers shared similar values with their respective principals, a positive relational affiliation was established. For example, if (1) individual principals held mastery orientations toward students' learning (i.e., promoted a focus on students' mastery of skills vs. students' high performance on standardized assessments), and (2) individual teachers also held mastery orientations (i.e., provided students with mastery-focused messages and activities), then individual principals were more likely to promote positive relationship affiliations by supporting individual teachers' autonomy and competence (Grove 2007).

The same phenomena occurred when principals and teachers shared performance-focused goals. Having shared-values seemed to foster principals' confidence in teachers' capabilities as well as principals' willingness to provide the teachers with self-autonomy. These teachers implemented successfully those high-quality, professional development strategies and reform efforts that principals and teachers both supported. Thus, when principal's perceived that teachers' behaviors confirmed the principals' beliefs, the principals were more likely to establish a positive emotional climate through interpersonal interactions that were low in principals' control and high in principals' affiliation behaviors.

Interestingly, Grove's results also suggested that when principals held performance-focused goals and teachers held mastery-focused goals, the teachers often chose to pursue their goals and not the principals, even if the actions could foster a lowering of principals' autonomy support. This result suggests that personal motivational factors (e.g., individual values) may take precedence in influencing teachers' behaviors when the factor has higher strength than those coming from social influences.

Implications and Future Research

CVT researchers highlight the importance of individuals' values for promoting personal motivation, a variable that SDT researchers do not directly emphasize. In contrast, SDT researchers focus upon the extent to which individuals perceive that contextual authorities' support their development of personal competence and the extent to which contextual authorities promote interpersonal relatedness, variables that CVT researchers tend not to directly address. Given that these two theories are frequently used to investigate students' academic motivations, we believe these two theories may work in tandem to reveal social and personal aspects that affect teachers' motivations for implementing high-quality professional development for educational reform.

Our synthesis and new theoretical framework can open avenues for research and theory for advancing our understandings of dynamical and reciprocal processes in teachers' learning endeavors. These processes underlie the rich full range of interpersonal characteristics that underpin hierarchical interactions in education. Further research is needed to articulate, elaborate, extend, validate, and revise the theoretical framework presented in this chapter. Here, we have focused on the interpersonal interactions of teachers with their principals (and other authorities) within the context of professional development for whole school reform; however, we recognize that the model could be used to investigate hierarchies of other learning situations as well.

In our current research, we are using the model to investigate ways that teachers' perceptions of their principals' autonomy-, competence-, and value-supports influence the school climate and teachers' personal motivations and emotions for implementing whole school reform. Initial results from investigating a whole-school reading initiative (Roehrig et al. 2008) have suggested that teachers, who were given autonomy through collaborative school leadership, also held more positive reasons (i.e., "because it was good for them" or because of intrinsic motivation), for participating in the reform program. On the other hand, teachers who indicated they did not participate in collaborative leadership were more likely to hold extrinsic reasons (i.e., they were required to participate by administration) or felt amotivated (i.e., a lack of motivation) for participating in the reform program. Additionally, teachers' who indicated they had been given more control over their classroom decisions (i.e., provided with autonomy-supports) felt higher levels of teaching efficacy, positive motivations for the reform program, and job satisfaction.

Further research is needed to understand how interactional behaviors impact teachers' motivations. Along with investigating elements of principals' support and school climate, understanding the dynamic interconnections among these variables and teachers' specific emotions, cognitions, and motivations can help identify specific environmental supports (or lack of supports) that lead to different trajectories of teachers' willingness or resistance for educational reform. We are particularly interested in ways that the interpersonal circumplex model of principal–teachers interactions can help define and describe teachers' perceptions of their principals' on-going behaviors that influence their motivations and emotions. Along this line of inquiry, the circumplex model may be used to investigate similarities and discrepancies between principals' perceptions of their own interpersonal behaviors and teachers' perceptions of their principals' interpersonal behaviors. For example, using Wubbels' interpersonal circumplex model (Wubbels et al. 1991, 1993), Fisher et al. (1995) compared teachers' perceptions of their interpersonal behaviors with students' ratings of their teachers' interpersonal behaviors. They provided professional development that targeted discrepancies between the two perceptions to help teachers improve their interpersonal interactions with students. A similar procedure could be used to help principals' improve their interpersonal interactions with teachers. By showing principals the discrepancies between their own perceptions of their behaviors and teachers' perceptions of their behaviors, principals may learn more effective and efficient interpersonal leadership behaviors.

We believe that affiliative, positive dynamics of human interaction lie at the heart of great and successful high-quality education and educational reform, and merits continued empirical inquiries. In the educational process, when authorities provide autonomy-, competence-, and value-supports – thus creating positive interactional climates – both supervisors and subordinates may transcend individual differences in the interest of working together and learning together – ascertaining and enlivening the education and educational opportunities of all who participate in learning endeavors.

References

Bandura A (1986) Social foundations of thought and action: a social cognitive theory. Prentice-Hall, Englewood Cliffs, NJ

Bandura A (1989) Self-regulation of motivation and action through internal standards and goal systems. In: Pervin LA (ed) Goal concepts in personality and social psychology. Erlbaum, Hillsdale, NJ, pp 19–86

Barrett LF, Russell JA (1999) The structure of current affect: controversies and emerging consensus. Curr Dir Psychol Sci 8(1):10–14

Beachum FD, Dentith AM, McCray CR, Boyle TM (2008) Havens of hope or the killing fields: the paradox of leadership, pedagogy, and relationships in an urban middle school. Urban Educ 43(2):189–215

Benjamin LS (1974) Structural analysis of social behavior. Psychol Rev 81:392–425

Benjamin LS (1996) A clinician-friendly version of the interpersonal circumplex: structural analysis of social behavior (SASB). J Pers Assess 66(2):248–266

Billig SH, Jaime II, Abrams A, Fitzpatrick M, Kendrick E (2005) Closing the achievement gap: lessons from successful schools. U. S. Department of Education, Office of Vocational and Adult Education, Washington, DC (ERIC Document Reproduction Service No. ED491863)

Ciani KD, Summers JJ, Easter MA (2008) The influence of academic context on the motivational beliefs and classroom practices of high school teachers. Contemp Educ Psychol 33:533–560

Creswell J (1997) A study of principals' interpersonal behaviour and school environment. Unpublished Doctoral Dissertation, Curtin University of Technology, Australia

Creswell J, Fisher D (April, 1998) A qualitative description of teachers' and principals' perceptions of interpersonal behavior and school environment. Paper presented at the meeting of the American Educational Research Association, San Diego, CA

Creswell J, Fisher D (April, 1999) A school level environment study in Australia. Paper presented at the annual meeting of the American Educational Research Association, Montreal, QC, Canada

Creton H, Wubbels T, Hooymayers H (1993) A systems perspective on classroom communication. In: Wubbels T, Levy J (eds) Do you know what you look like? Interpersonal relationships in education. London, England: RouledgeFalmer Press, pp 1–12

Darby A (2008) Teachers' emotions in the reconstruction of professional self-understanding. Teach Teach Educ 24:1160–1172

Darley JM (2001) The dynamics of authority influence in organizations and unintended action consequences. In: Darley JM, Messic DM, Tyler TR (eds) Social influences on ethical behavior in organizations. Lawrence Erlbaum Associates, Mahwah, NJ, pp 37–52

de Jesus SN, Lens W (2005) An integrated model for the study of teacher motivation. Appl Psychol Int Rev 54:119–134

Deci EL, Ryan RM (1985) Intrinsic motivation and self-determination in human behavior. Plenum, New York, NY

Deci EL, Ryan RM (2000) The "what" and "why" of goal pursuits: human needs and the self-determination of behavior. Psychol Inq 11:227–268

den Brok P, Levy J (2005) Teacher–student relationships in multicultural classes: reviewing the past, preparing the future. Int J Educ Res 43:72–88

den Brok P, Brekelmans M, Wubbels T (2006) Multilevel issues in research using students' perceptions of learning environments: the case of the questionnaire on teacher interaction. Learn Environ Res 9(3):199–213

Ellett CD, Hill FH, Liu X, Loup KS, Lakshmanan A (1997, March) Professional learning environment and human caring correlates of teacher efficacy. Paper presented at the annual meeting of the American Educational Research Association, Chicago, IL

Fisher D, Creswell J (1998) Actual and ideal principal interpersonal behavior. Learn Environ Res 1(2):231–247

Fisher DL, Fraser BJ, Cresswell JC (1995) Using the questionnaire on teacher interaction in the professional development of teachers. Aust J Teach Educ 20:8–18

Freedman MB, Leary TF, Ossorio AG, Coffey HS (1951) The interpresonal dimension of personality. J Pers 20:143–161

Goh SC, Fraser BH (2000) Teacher interpersonal behavior and elementary students' outcomes. J Res Child Educ 14(2):216–231

Grove CM (2007) The importance of values-alignment within a role-hierarchy to foster teachers' motivation for implementing professional development. Unpublished Doctoral Dissertation, Florida State University, Tallahassee, FL

Grove CM (2008, March) Self-determination theory and control-value theory in a professional development for teachers: from motivation to implementation. Paper presented at the annual meeting of the American Educational Research Association, New York, NY

Haim O, Strauss S, Ravid D (2004) Relations between EFL teachers' formal knowledge of grammar and their in-action models of children's minds and learning. Teach Teach Educ 20(8):861–880

Hashweh MZ (2003) Teacher accommodative change. Teach Teach Educ 19:421–434

Kent AM (2004) Improving teacher quality through professional development. Education 124(3):427–435

Kiesler DJ (1996) From communications to interpersonal theory: A personal odyssey. J Pers Assess, 66(2):267–282

Kremer-Hayon L, Wubbels T (1993) Supervisors' interpersonal behavior and teachers' satisfaction. In: Wubbels T, Levy J (eds) Do you know what you look like? Interpersonal relationships in education. RoutledgeFalmer, London, England, pp 113–122

Lasky S (2005) A sociocultural to understanding teacher identity, agency, and professional vulnerability in a context of secondary school reform. Teach Teach Educ 21:899–916

Leary T (1957) Interpersonal diagnosis of personality: a functional theory and methodology for personality evaluation. Ronald Press, New York, NY

Leinhardt G (2001) Instructional explanations: a commonplace for teaching and location for contrast. In: Richardson V (ed) Handbook of research on teaching. American Educational Research Association, Washington, DC, pp 333–357

Levy J, den Brok P, Wubbels T, Brekelmans M (2003) Students' perceptions of interpersonal aspects of the learning environment. Learn Environ Res 6(1):5–36

Lorr M (1996) The interpersonal circle as a heuristic model for interpersonal research. J Pers Assess, 66(2):234–239

Op 't Eynde P, Turner JE (2006) Focusing on the complexity of emotion-motivation issues in academic learning: a dynamical component systems approach. Educ Psychol Rev 18:361–376

Papaioannou A, Christoduoulidis T (2007) A measure of teachers' achievement goals. Educ Psychol 27(3):349–361

Pekrun R (2000) A social cognitive, control-value theory of achievement emotions. In: Heckhausen J (ed) Motivational psychology of human development. Elsevier, Oxford, England, pp 143–163

Pekrun R (2006) The control-value theory of achievement emotions: assumptions, corollaries, and implications for education research and practice. Educ Psychol Rev 18(4):315–341

Reio TG (2005) Emotions as a lens to explore teacher identity and change: a commentary. Teach
    Teach Educ 21(8):985–993
Roehrig A, Turner JE, Petscher Y (2008) Evaluation of the Florida Reading Initiative for the
    NorthEast Florida Education Consortium. Unpublished Manuscript
Roth G, Assor A, Kanat-Maymon Y, Kaplan H (2007) Autonomous motivation for teaching: how
    self-determined teaching may lead to self-determined learning. J Educ Psychol 99:761–774
Ryan RM, Deci EL (2000) Self-determination theory and the facilitation of intrinsic motivation,
    social development, and well-being. Am Psychol 55:68–78
Sandholtz JH, Scribner SP (2006) The paradox of administrative control in fostering teacher
    professional development. Teach Teach Educ 22:1104–1117
Schaefer ES (1965) Configurational analysis of children's reports of parent behavior. J Consult
    Psychol 29:552–557
Scribner JP (1998, October) Teacher efficacy and teacher professional learning: what school leaders
    should know. Paper presented at the meeting of the University Council for Educational
    Administration, St. Louis, MO
Turner JE, Grove CM (2008, March) Investigating situational aspects and personal aspects of
    teachers' motivation and emotions for implementing whole school reform. Paper presented at
    the annual meeting of the American Educational Research Association, New York, NY
Turner JE, Biscoe B, Harris B (2006, April) Great expectations of Oklahoma's whole school
    reform model: evidence of student achievement gains. Paper presented at the annual meeting
    of American Educational Research Association, San Francisco, CA
van Eekelen IM, Vermunt JD, Boshuizen HPA (2006) Exploring teachers' will to learn. Teach
    Teach Educ 22:408–423
Watzlawick P, Beavin JH, Jackson D (1967) The pragmatics of human communication. W. W.
    Norton & Co., New York, NY
Waugh RM (2002) A grounded theory investigation of dyadic interactional harmony and discord:
    development of a nonlinear dynamical systems theory and process-model. Unpublished
    Doctoral Dissertation, The University of Texas at Austin, Austin, TX
Waugh RM (2003, May) A nonlinear dynamical systems process-model of dyadic interactional
    harmony and discord. Paper presented at the meeting of the Fifteenth Annual Convention of
    the American Psychological Society, Atlanta, GA
Waugh RM (2003, July) A self-reflexive, holographic nonlinear dynamical systems process-theory
    of dyadic interactional harmony and discord. Paper presented at the meeting of the Thirteenth
    Annual International Conference of the Society for Chaos Theory in Psychology & the Life
    Sciences, Boston, MA
Weiner B (1985) An attributional theory of achievement and motivation and emotion. Psychol Rev
    92(4):548–573
Wenger E (1998) Communities of practice: learning, meaning, and identity. Cambridge University
    Press, Cambridge, UK
Wiggins JS, Phillips N, Trapnell P (1989) Circular reasoning about interpersonal behavior:
    Evidence concerning some untested assumptions underlying diagnostic classification. J Pers
    and Soc Psychol, 56(2):296–305
Wiggins JS (1996) An informal history of the interpersonal circumplex tradition. J Pers Assess
    66(2):217–233
Wubbels T, Brekelmans M (2005) Two decades of research on teacher–student relationships in
    class. Int J Educ Res 43:6–24
Wubbels T, Levy J (1993) Do you know what you look like? Interpersonal relationships in education.
    RoutledgeFalmer, London, England
Wubbels T, Brekelmans M, Hooymayers H (1991) Interpersonal teacher behavior in the classroom.
    In: Fraswer BJ, Walberg HJ (eds) Educational environments: evaluation antecedents and
    consequences. Pergamon, Oxford, England, pp 141–160
Wubbels T, Creton H, Levy J, Hooymayers H (1993) The model for interpersonal teacher behavior.
    In: Wubbels T, Levy J (eds) Do you know what you look like? Interpersonal relationships in
    education. RoutledgeFalmer, London, England, pp 13–28

Chapter 14
Beliefs and Professional Identity: Critical Constructs in Examining the Impact of Reform on the Emotional Experiences of Teachers

Dionne I. Cross and Ji Y. Hong

Abstract In this chapter we examine the effects of both nationwide and local efforts to improve the state of our educational system in the areas of mathematics and science. Although these mandates are designed at the federal level, the grueling task of implementation is often bestowed on the local school districts and, ultimately, on teachers who are most closely connected to learning. Reform in these domains often involves teachers transitioning from a traditional, didactic teaching approach to one that is student-centered and inquiry-based. Changing teaching practice is an emotionally laborious and challenging process, as it often involves modifying teachers' existing beliefs about the domain, teaching and learning, and also reshaping their professional identity as a teacher. We will discuss the influence of teachers' domain-specific beliefs and professional identity on their emotional experiences as teachers attempt to incorporate reform-oriented practices in their mathematics and science classrooms. Our discussion will also include findings from empirical studies related to these issues with descriptions of teachers' experiences from emic perspectives.

Keywords Professional identity · Reform · Teacher emotions

Developing and maintaining productive interpersonal relationships with students and colleagues is a central part of the teaching profession. As with most professions that involve caring for others, emotions tend to lie at the core of teachers' daily experiences. Emotions tend to become more salient to teaching during this current age of educational reform, a period in education that is replete with change. Reform at the national and state level is often more abstract and dispassionate as it is enacted through policy, curriculum and administration. However, within schools these changes are experienced at a more individual and personal level as they

D.I. Cross (✉)
Mathematics Education, Indiana University, Bloomington, IN, USA
e-mail: dicross@indiana.edu

P.A. Schutz and M. Zembylas (eds.), *Advances in Teacher Emotion Research:*
The Impact on Teachers' Lives,
DOI 10.1007/978-1-4419-0564-2_14, © Springer Science+Business Media, LLC 2009

involve making adjustments and modifications to how teachers have traditionally enacted their roles in the classroom and how students have come to view schooling. They also involve changes in teaching practices where teachers are required to modify the ways they instruct, interact with their students and often to the curriculum they are teaching.

In the areas of mathematics and science, orchestrating instruction in new ways often involves teachers transitioning from a traditional, teacher-centered instructional approach to one that is student-centered and inquiry-based. Changing teaching practices is an emotionally laborious and challenging process, as it involves modifying teachers' existing beliefs about their respective disciplines, teaching and learning, and also reshaping their professional identity as a teacher (Schutz et al. 2007). This interplay of psychological constructs results in both pleasant and unpleasant emotions that have the potential to influence the level of success with which the reform objectives are implemented. We will begin our discussion by defining and providing an overview of education reform within mathematics and science education. We use reform as the context within which we examine the relationship between teachers' beliefs, professional identity, and emotions, how beliefs and identity influence the formation of a goal, and how they all work in concert to shape emotional experiences. This discussion will be situated within the context of teachers' attempts to incorporate reform-oriented practices into their mathematics and science classrooms and so will include findings from empirical studies related to these issues, with descriptions of teachers' experiences from emic perspectives. We will conclude with implications for pre-service teacher education and in-service teacher professional development.

Reform in Mathematics and Science Education

Reform within the fields of mathematics and science education focuses not only on students developing a broad knowledge base in these disciplines, but more generally on students developing dispositions[1] towards mathematics and science as disciplines of inquiry (NCATE 2002; NCTM 2000; NRC 1996). This also involves students developing competence in their ability to generate ideas that are considered reasonable within the epistemology of the discipline, and being able to critically assess the validity of these ideas. Specifically, within science education the focus is on students engaged in the practices of science to become more knowledgeable about scientific inquiry and the nature of science (Aikenhead and Ryan 1992; Ineke et al. 2007); and within mathematics education, for students to have personal knowledge of mathematical concepts and be able to think and reason powerfully about mathematical ideas.

---

[1] Dispositions refer to an individual's attitudes and beliefs towards a specific discipline coupled with his/her self-concept with regard to the discipline.

In the most recent reform efforts focusing on pedagogy, attempts have been made to translate these notions of expertise in the disciplines into classroom practices. For example, to help students develop into scientifically literate citizens, the National Science Education Standards (NSES) (National Research Council 1996) and Benchmarks for Science Literacy (American Association for the Advancement of Science 1993) have suggested "inquiry-based instruction". The NSES recommendations describe the inquiry-based classroom as an environment where students are encouraged to construct their own knowledge and understanding of science through asking probing questions and investigating these questions to find answers. This is a move away from top-down teaching approaches in which teachers present decontextualized scientific knowledge to students, and instead focuses on encouraging students to not rely on an external rational authority as to what constitutes scientific 'truth' and to become active participants in the development of scientific ideas.

The field of mathematics education has similar goals, primarily focused on producing students who are powerful mathematical thinkers. In line with NCTM's *Principles and Standards for School Mathematics* (2000) and *Professional Standards for Teaching Mathematics* (1991), reform teaching describes an instructional approach geared towards students communicating their mathematical ideas, and thinking and reasoning in powerful ways. As such, engaging in mathematical practices such as conjecturing, problem solving, exploring and investigating mathematical ideas, affords opportunities for students to deepen their understanding of mathematics (Franco et al. 2007).

Incorporating these goals into one's teaching practices requires making significant changes for most mathematics and science teachers. Because teachers' pedagogical decisions and behaviors in the classroom are connected to beliefs about their discipline, who they conceive of themselves as teachers and how they should act in the classroom, forced changes of any kind will cause internal cognitive and affective struggles. Examining teachers' emotional experiences as they engage in educational reform is a rich context for exploring the complex nature of these constructs because of the strong emotional connections teachers have to their work and the interconnectedness of emotions with cognitions (Kelchtermans 2005).

The Role of Beliefs, Identity, Goals and Emotions in Reform-Based Classroom Practice

In order to explicate the relationship between beliefs, identity and goals, and their influence on teachers' emotional experiences in the context of reform, we organized these constructs in a hypothetical model. This hypothetical model (Fig. 14.1) emerged from the analyses of data accumulated from several research projects investigating teachers' emotions, emotional awareness and regulation in relation to general schooling, classroom transactions and pedagogical and curricula reform (Cross in press); Hong (under review) provide detailed descriptions of this research).

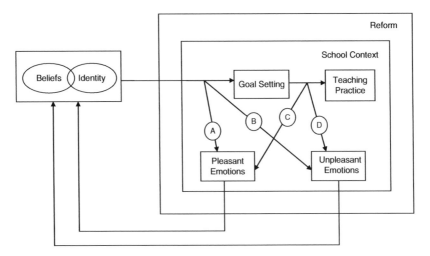

Fig. 14.1 Hypothetical model of the relationship between BIGE

Beliefs

Psychologists often define beliefs quite broadly to include epistemological beliefs
– beliefs about the nature of knowledge and how knowledge is obtained (e.g., Hofer
and Pintrich 2002; Schraw and Olafson 2002); interpersonal beliefs including self-
efficacy beliefs, teacher efficacy beliefs etc. (e.g., Ashton 1984; Bandura 1997)
and domain-specific beliefs to include views about specific academic disciplines
(e.g., Raymond 1997; Tobin and McRobbie 1996). In this chapter we will focus
primarily on the latter and secondarily on interpersonal beliefs as they relate to
teachers engaging in their profession (namely, teacher efficacy beliefs). Domain-
specific beliefs describe a teacher's belief about the nature of knowledge within a
particular discipline and how concepts within the discipline are best taught and
learned. These beliefs are interconnected and so teachers' ideas about the most
effective pedagogical approaches tend to be derived from how they conceptualize
the discipline. For example, mathematics teachers who design lessons where students
are taught isolated mathematical facts and procedures to be memorized by rote often
hold the belief that mathematics comprises a set of disconnected bits of knowledge
that mathematicians long ago discovered. These beliefs about the discipline and
how students come to know and understand mathematical and scientific concepts
shape the role teachers enact in the classroom by prescribing how they interact with
their students, the instruction and learning goals they set and how they design
instruction to meet these goals.

The relationship between emotions and beliefs can be described as interconnected
and interdependent as both constructs influence each other and influence peoples'
actions (Frijda and Mesquita 2000; Schutz et al. 2007). Beliefs comprise the organization and content of a person's thinking that are presumed to drive that person's
actions (Bryan and Atwater 2002). Beliefs are personal, stable and are considered to

be very influential in determining how individuals frame problems and organize tasks (Nespor 1987; Rimm-Kaufman and Sawyer 2004). As such, we regard beliefs as an individual's personal thoughts and ideas about him/herself, the world and their perceived role in it, developed over time through interaction and membership in various social groups, that are considered by the individual to be "true" (Cross in press). Researchers in this area have also suggested that beliefs are often precursors to action, specifically with regard to teachers' pedagogical decisions (Pajares 1992; Torff and Warburton 2005), and are very influential on teachers' emotions and subsequent classroom behavior (Schutz et al. 2007).

Simultaneously, emotions are considered to be powerful determinants of what people think is true and are thereby very influential in the formation of new beliefs, and modifying and altering the strength of existing beliefs (Frijda and Mesquita 2000). We do not see these views as contradictory but powerful perspectives that provide a framework for understanding the antecedents, causes and impact of teachers' emotional experiences. Although there is not strong empirical evidence in support of this theory, Frijda et al. (2000) along with Frijda and Mesquita (2000) make a compelling argument for emotions being the driving force behind the actualization of beliefs. They state that, "although beliefs may guide our actions, they are not sufficient to initiate action" (p. 3). Frijda and Mesquita (2000) describe this process of emotion-induced action and further articulate the ways in which emotions influence beliefs.

They propose four key features of emotions that explain their influence on beliefs. These include instrumentality, motivational force, control of scope of thought and, motivational bias. Emotions tend to focus our thinking on particular aspects of the event that will help us achieve our goals. In this regard, they provide the necessary motivation we often need to persevere towards goal attainment and to help us focus and avoid distractions that may interfere with us achieving our goals. In this respect, the 'emotion-steered thinking' that results from the emotional experience may influence our decisions to persist or cease particular behaviors, selectively distribute attention towards pre-existing beliefs that appear to support our goals, or generate new functional beliefs that would better enable us to meet our objectives. By exploring the interdependent, cyclical relationship between beliefs and emotions and how they impact teachers' pedagogical decision-making, we provide empirical data to support the theoretical relationship between emotions and beliefs and contribute to the growing body of research on emotions in educational contexts.

Identity

The beliefs teachers hold, are not only situated in the context or content, but also within the person's unique beliefs system (Kagan 1992). The beliefs system that an individual has developed over time becomes connected with their sense of self or identity. The 'self' is crucial in constructing the way we interact with the environment and make judgments in a given context (Day et al. 2005, 2006; Lasky 2005; Van den Berg 2002). Thus, the way teachers perceive themselves influences their choice of action and judgment, thereby making identity a critical factor in understanding teachers' classroom behaviors. We agree with Beijaard et al. (2000) idea that teachers' professional identity is a framework established and maintained through the interaction in social situations, and negotiation of roles within the particular context. Mead explained that, "The self is something which progressively develops; it is not initially there, at birth, but arises in the process of social experience and activity" (Mead 1934, p. 135). In other words, humans act and interact on the basis of meaning, and so the emerging identity is the product of a social and interactive process involving continuous interpretation and negotiation of interactions, transactions and objects. Accordingly, professional identity is a dynamic, continually changing, and active process that develops over time through the interaction with others in a given context, specifically the working environment (Cooper and Olson 1996; Kelchtermans 1993; Watson 2006). Thus, identity is continually being formed and reformed through the way we internalize the environment, negotiate interactions, and externalize ourselves to others.

For any individual, emotions play an important role in the process of forming an identity. This connection between identity and emotion has been discussed among various researchers (Fogel 2001; Frijda 2001; Hermans and Hermans-Jansen 2001; Harter 1998; Kunnen et al. 2001) who point out that self-evaluation is an essential process in forming an individual's sense of self, and the act that connects these two constructs. For example, a negative self-evaluation arises only if the individual deems the particular transaction important or relevant. If she evaluates that the nature and meaning of a particular transaction is significant to her, then emotions are elicited depending on how well aligned the outcome of the transaction is with her expectations. Thus, opinions about oneself cannot be separated from the emotions and the context where the emotions arise.

For teachers, their professional identities embody how teachers view themselves in their instructional role and how they portray themselves to their students and colleagues. These mental representations of themselves are intimately intertwined with emotions. What teachers believe constitute knowledge in mathematics or science, and the process through which students obtain this knowledge informs the ways they orchestrate learning in the classroom and their responsibilities in the learning process. Through this relational process between students and the teacher in the classroom transaction, the teacher experiences diverse emotions. As Kunnen and her colleagues mentioned, these emotions provide formative conditions from which the sense of self and identity emerge (Kunnen et al. 2001). Accordingly, teachers' professional sense of self is shaped by their beliefs about the discipline and the emotions induced during classroom transactions and other relationships and dynamics in the school. Therefore, the teacher's professional identity is a critical dimension in understanding teachers' behavior, judgment, and subsequent emotional experiences in the classroom. Implementing reform policies and practices ultimately ask teachers to reshape their professional identities by adopting different roles and perspectives. Several researchers have noted this mechanism, and emphasized teachers' professional identity as one of the most important factors for successful implementation of a reform agenda (e.g., Lasky 2005; van Veen et al. 2005).

Educational researchers have focused on the threat reform posed to teachers' professional identity, and they have explored the lens of teacher emotions, individual agency, and vulnerability. As an extension of these discussions, we include the "goal" to fully understand how teachers' beliefs, identity, and emotions are related, and function in the context of reform as both beliefs and identity shape the long-term (broad teacher goals) and immediate (instructional) goals teachers develop.

Goal

When reform mandates are conveyed to individual teachers, they are not simply decoding the message; rather they understand and interpret the new information based on their preexisting beliefs and schemas (Schmidt and Datnow 2005), and then set classroom goals in accordance with the degree of acceptance of the reform agenda. Goal setting is a key dimension in executing the reform plan, because teachers' behaviors, strategies and decisions are guided by their goals (Schutz et al. 2001). As motivation researchers have studied, people initiate and persist at behaviors to the extent that they believe the behaviors will lead to desired outcomes or goals (Deci and Ryan 2000; Ford 1992; Schutz 1991). That is, the classroom goal determines what behaviors will be elicited, what decisions will be made, how much effort and energy will be invested, and what the quality of the performance will be. Thus, we need to further examine how teachers set goals, and how the goal setting is related to other critical psychological constructs such as beliefs, identity, and emotions.

By definition, goal is a future oriented concept, and it is not impersonal or abstract motivation; rather it is deeply intertwined with the individual's desire, aspiration, or intention (Markus and Nurius 1986). For example, goals like "using constructivist curriculum" should be understood "my using constructivist curriculum". In other words, the self cannot exist in isolation, but it is connected with future goals. Markus and Nurius (1986) further explained the relationship between a goal and one's self-perception using the concept of "possible self". When one's self represents the individual's ideas of what one would like to become, and what one is afraid of becoming, we call these "possible selves". In particular, the former is called the "hoped-for self", and the latter is called the "feared self". Possible selves are cognitive manifestations of future goals, aspirations, and fears, and also possible selves are shaped by both the individual's past experiences and current interactions within particular social context (Markus 1983; Markus and Nurius 1986; Markus and Sentis 1982; Markus and Wurf 1987). The possible self is another way to understand teachers' professional identity with the emphasis of time dimensions, especially the future.

When teachers set the classroom goals based on the information about the reform, it cannot be separated from the individual teacher's possible selves, which are based on the teacher's past experience and present interactions in a given context – experiences and interactions shaped by the teacher's domain-specific beliefs and diverse emotions. If the way the individual teacher envisions herself in the classroom is the same as the roles and expectations required by the reform, then she is more likely to set a classroom goal aligned with the reform agenda. However, if the way she thinks about herself as a teacher does not line up with those required by the reform agenda, then she either attempts to change her self-perception as a teacher, ignore the reform altogether, or may make peripheral changes to the instruction while still not accepting the core vision of the reform.

As we discussed earlier, teacher identities are "the result of an interaction between the personal experiences of teachers and the social, cultural, and institutional environment in which they function on a daily basis" (van den Berg 2002, p. 579). As active agents, individual teachers have the ability to make choices and carry forth action within a given context, and thus can influence their school lives and environment while at the same time they are shaped by what is required by the context and social structure (Giddens 1979). So while teachers are able to independently define and portray their roles in the classroom, the roles are influenced by and shaped within the boundaries of the social context.

Emotions

When teachers assimilate the new ideas mandated by the reform agenda into their existing beliefs and identities, it is inevitably accompanied by various emotions (Schmidt and Datnow 2005). There are a variety of ways that emotions are described in the literature, however to acknowledge both the social and cognitive dimensions of the construct, we will use Schutz et al.'s (2006) definition of emotions as "socially constructed, personally enacted ways of being that emerge from conscious and/or unconscious judgments regarding perceived successes at attaining goals or maintaining standards or beliefs during transactions as part of social-historical contexts" (p. 344). First of all, emotions are relational and socially constructed. That is, emotions involve relationships of the subject with a particular object such as one is angry at something, happy about something, and so on (Denzin 1984; Lazarus 1991). Thus, person–environmental transactions are essential for emotional experiences. For teachers, the person–environmental transactions usually occur during attempts to reach their classroom goals. The goal functions as a reference point where teachers compare and judge consciously or unconsciously their position in relation to the goal. Individual teachers constantly evaluate and interpret classroom transactions and encounters to judge whether they are beneficial or harmful to the goal attainment. These judgments they make about the ability of classroom transactions to facilitate their goals are referred to as appraisals (Lazarus 1991, 1999). Appraisals cannot be separated from the social-historical context in which the individual is embedded. In the context of reform, teachers are exposed to new objectives and standards, and the process of coping with the reform mandates entails teachers' instructional goal setting, appraisals about perceived success at attaining the goals, and emotions emerging during the transactions and as a result of the appraisals. For example, if an individual teacher appraises that the classroom transaction does not facilitate her attaining the classroom goal, then unpleasant emotions may be elicited. In the next section we present teachers' descriptions of their emotional experiences as they underwent educational reform.

We examine their experiences as both products and factors in the complex interplay of beliefs, identity, goals and emotions (BIGE).

Explicating the Paths

From the teachers' descriptions of their experiences with reform we observed that there were generally four paths that lead to pleasant or unpleasant emotions. We acknowledge that there are other paths, but for illustration purposes, we focus on these four. We observed that these emotional responses tended to determine the fidelity with which teachers would implement the reform. Below we explain the relationships between the constructs and include teachers' descriptions of their experiences with reform that explicate the trajectory of these paths.

Path A

Path A illustrates how pleasant emotions are elicited through the process of adopting and interpreting the reform mandate based on teachers' beliefs and identity, and the process of setting instructional goals for their classroom teaching derived from the interpretation and adaptation. Implementation of reform often takes a top-down approach, where the reform policies and objectives are conceived at the state or federal level and then passed down the line to school districts where teachers are presented with the objectives. When presented with the particular reform, teachers determine whether the mandates are aligned with their own existing beliefs about how they should instruct in general, what types of instruction work best for particular types of students and the role they want to play in the classroom. Teachers' assessments of how well the reform mandates and their goals are aligned tend to elicit particular emotions that guide subsequent decisions, their willingness to implement, and the fidelity with which they do implement the reform practices. This is exemplified in the case of Ms. Oakley, a science teacher who opted to come and teach in the U.S. to help meet the demand for qualified science teachers at the middle and high school levels. When asked why she decided to come to the United States to teach, she responded with excitement, explaining that this was an opportunity for her to teach more effectively by incorporating the necessary technological resources – resources she expected would be readily available in U.S. schools,

> I was looking for challenge, I had gotten a bit bored with what I was doing at home and so I fancied something new and different and advanced... The curriculum looked the same but... I was thinking that this, being a western country that the schools would be better resourced than they actually are [at home in the United Kingdom]... I understood from people I know who are Americans that parents take education quite seriously so I was expecting much more resources than I actually found.

Prior to making her decision, she had examined the U.S. curriculum and the teaching philosophy underlying science education in the U.S., and thought it fit with her own ideas about how science is best taught. Ms. Oakley firmly believed that students are to be actively engaged in the scientific processes of exploration and investigation, thereby making laboratory work a crucial aspect of science instruction. She described her expectations of the U.S. classroom and why she was initially attracted to the idea of teaching in the U.S.

> As a science teacher, I firmly believe that science is a practical subject and so I was expecting…I guess ahm…something…I was expecting things to be a lot more technological because I regarded America as a much more technologically advanced country. I used to work as an engineer and I have worked with American engineers and I was expecting that kind of thing to be much more here [in the U.S. classroom]. And also generally…just equipment so that students can do some really hands on investigations so they can really learn it [science concepts].

In the case of Ms. Oakley, her beliefs about science and how science should be taught aligned well with the reform objectives. As a result, she experienced pleasant emotions of excitement at the prospect of teaching in the U.S. Although this excitement was later thwarted because the U.S. classroom did not meet her expectations, Ms. Oakley's experience provides a good example of how the interplay of beliefs, identity and goals within the context of reform can elicit pleasant emotions. Ms. Oakley believed that science embodied a process of inquiry and so students should be engaged in the practices of science involving conjecturing, exploring and investigating. To facilitate this way of learning she believed that her role was to establish an environment where students could have opportunities to construct their own knowledge through engagement in authentic scientific experiences. Her perception of the alignment between these beliefs, her identity, and the reform objectives, led to feelings of excitement and pleasure.

The emotional experience itself tends to influence teachers' existing beliefs or identities. A number of researchers have noted the influence of emotions on the beliefs (Frijda et al. 2000; Lazarus and Smith 1988; Schutz et al. 2007). In particular, when there is satisfaction and pleasant emotions like Ms. Oakley experienced, the emotions take the role of maintaining or confirming her existing beliefs. So for Ms. Oakley, the feelings of affirmation generated from the alignment between her pre-existing beliefs, and the reform objectives served to strengthen those beliefs and shape her instructional goals. The way a teacher sees herself and a teacher's perception about her role as a teacher are not separated from the emotions she experiences (Hong under review). Pleasant emotions tend to support her views and sense of self as a teacher. Thus, when the reform agenda is introduced, the emotional responses generated from the perceived alignment between the reform objectives and teacher's sense of self may reinforce the teacher's existing identity, which may in turn affect their teaching practices.

Path B

Path B represents how teachers' unpleasant emotions are elicited in the process of setting instructional goals for their classroom teaching based on the negotiation between their existing beliefs and identity, and the changing of teaching practices suggested in the reform agenda. The movement towards educational change is based on the premise that incorporating a different approach, strategies or materials will yield better results. However, this change is often not well received by teachers for several reasons. From our research we noted two cases that followed Path B. In the first case, teachers responded negatively to reform because they believed that the very nature of the reform suggested that they are ineffective in their jobs. They interpreted reform to mean that their current performance is unsatisfactory and thus needs to be modified in order to increase achievement levels. This often has a debilitating impact on their teacher efficacy and identity, especially for those teachers who are inexperienced or have low teacher efficacy. For other teachers who consider themselves successful, evidenced by their ability to meet school-based accountability standards, reform is often viewed as a 'passing fancy' or the latest trend in education, soon to be forgotten. In these cases, the reform may threaten their teacher self as it is interpreted as a rejection of them as teachers. This interpretation often leaves teachers disgruntled, eliciting feelings of anger and resentment.

For example, Mr. Andrews, a tenth grade biology teacher with 3 years of experience at a suburban high school in the southeastern U.S., considered himself to be a successful teacher and the teaching profession quite rewarding. Mr. Andrews was enthusiastic and positive about teaching in general, but responded quite unfavorably when asked about inquiry-based learning. He considered reform practices such as implementing inquiry-based learning as "one of those recirculating ideas that people are pushing", but not really effective in his classroom.

> If you're a classroom teacher, you're either good at it or you're not good at it. I don't care what fancy way they tell you to teach, or whether you're doing inquiry-based labs, or you're doing teacher-focused or student-focused, or whatever. If you know how to teach, you know how to teach. Everybody tries to come in and tell you, you have to do this, that and the other to be successful and that's not really true, but that's the type of stress that they're putting on teachers.

In this case, Mr. Andrews associated student success with having good pedagogical skills. These skills, from his point of view did not necessarily include any of the reform-based practices associated with science teaching, such as inquiry-oriented activities or engagement in laboratory activities. Rather, successful teaching can occur in spite of all these 'fancy' techniques. Mr. Andrews already considered himself a successful teacher and these new practices were not aligned with his own. He perceived the reform message to mean that he was not an effective teacher. This assessment posed a threat to both his teacher identity and efficacy and so elicited unpleasant emotions in the form of stress. Experiencing these unpleasant emotions resulted in Mr. Andrews rejecting the new learning approach and continuing with his old way of teaching. They also made him more resolute in his current way of thinking.

Teachers, from their personal and professional experiences form beliefs about types of students, how they learn and instructional methods that work well for them. Specifically, some teachers hold that low-achieving students do not have the skills or the ability to learn mathematics and science through inquiry methods. Rather, they believe that students who have not performed at high academic levels learn best when they are taught concepts through direct instruction and are provided with opportunities to practice. In this second case, the objectives of the reform that generally promote inquiry-oriented activities and student-centered teaching approaches are in opposition to the teachers' beliefs about pedagogy and students' learning.

This case is illustrated in a study investigating the impact of mathematical argumentation and writing on ninth-grade students' understanding and achievement of algebra concepts. Teachers experienced a range of emotions when initially approached to be participants in the study (Cross 2008). Mr. James, an experienced ninth grade mathematics teacher, was initially interested in being a participant in the study. There were two phases to the study and he had consented to be a participant in phase one, which focused on examining teachers' domain-specific beliefs about mathematics. The second phase involved teachers engaging their students in discourse-oriented and writing activities centered on the concepts they had covered in class. For these activities to be successful it required the teacher to prioritize student thinking and discourse, thereby relinquishing their role or position as the epicenter of classroom activity. A few days after discussing the objectives of the research Mr. James responded by email,

> Although I agree with the premise of your work as applied to students who are on grade-level, the majority of my students are way below grade level and are wrestling with basic concepts. Yes, I would like to have them engaged in conversations about Algebra, but I find myself delighted if they simply perform basic operations. Additionally, I'm afraid that even the time involved…would be both a distraction and take away from instructional time.

Mr. James thought about the objectives of the research and the practices that it would require him to incorporate into his classes. He considered them in light of the type of students he thought he had and how he believed they learned best. His beliefs about his students and their learning needs were not in concert with the reform-oriented classroom practices and so he anticipated frustration in trying to engage them accordingly, thus leading him to decline participation in the study.

When there is a mismatch between the teacher's existing beliefs and what is required by the reform, teachers may experience unpleasant emotions such as stress or frustration. In other words, the teacher's existing beliefs and the appraisal of the alignment between the beliefs and the situation worked as a determinant of certain emotions. As stated earlier, emotions may also influence the content and strength of an individual's beliefs (Frijda et al. 2000; Schutz and DeCuir 2002; Schutz et al. 2007). In particular, Gross's (1998) discussion of emotional regulation, specifically the response-focused approach, suggested that after certain emotions are induced, there is response modulation which directly influences physiological, experiential, or behavioral responses. For example, when teachers experience unpleasant emotions in adopting the reform practices, it may hinder them from further exploring the situation or opening themselves to different teaching practices and strategies. Additionally, according to Leiter (1992) who talked about the relationship between efficacy beliefs and emotions, unpleasant emotions such as burnout and stress often lead to a crisis in the individual's efficacy beliefs. As a number of self-efficacy researchers have noted (e.g., Bandura 1997; Pajares 1996; Pajares et al. 1999) the weakened efficacy beliefs are often associated with the avoidance tendency for the activities. Thus, teachers who experienced unpleasant emotions in the process of setting their classroom goals may choose not to invest effort and to simply avoid the reform mandate and the unpleasant emotions associated with enacting that mandate.

Path C

Once teachers set goals for their classroom, they will strive to achieve those goals, whether it is fully aligned with the reform agenda or not. Path C shows how teachers experience pleasant emotions in the process of implementing classroom goals into their daily teaching practices within particular classroom and school contexts. As we discussed previously, these goals are the result of negotiation between the individual's beliefs, identity, and social context, and thus, it determines teachers' behaviors, decisions, and efforts to attain those goals. Teachers, as active agents, try to achieve their goals, and also make judgments consciously or unconsciously regarding how well their goals are being attained in their classroom. Lazarus (1991) explained that these cognitive appraisal processes are a key part of emotional experiences. For example, if an individual teacher perceives that a transaction or encounter is relevant to her classroom goal, and if the transaction facilitates the goal attainment, then pleasant emotions are more likely to be elicited. This appraisal process foregrounds the importance of context or the environmental realities affecting the outcome.

In Hong et al.'s study (under review), Ms. Bailey, a tenth grade biology teacher at a rural school, mentioned that her own view of teaching science was perfectly aligned with inquiry teaching and learning suggested by NSES. She readily embraced the reform practices without significant psychological conflict, although there were time, resource, and curriculum restraints in her school. She explained that the inquiry-oriented instruction increased students' learning, and thus she appraised that it helped her to achieve her classroom goals resulting in a satisfactory academic year. She described her experience using inquiry-teaching methods as an "awesome" one,

> I think many students are lazy thinkers. Inquiry learning makes a student become an active thinker and learner. It is awesome when you watch light bulbs go off in their heads because they arrived at a thought on their own.

In the same study, a ninth grade physical science teacher, Mr. Benjamin, described himself as "an inquiry-based teacher". He had a group of academically diverse students and so tried to focus every aspect of his lesson around inquiry-based learning. He believed that self-derived knowledge is remembered for a lifetime, and thus students who discover things on their own or with the assistance or guidance of a science teacher will be life-long learners. Inquiry-based teaching approaches afforded opportunities for students to gain meaningful knowledge and skills, thereby allowing Mr. Benjamin to meet his classroom goals. The congruence between his classroom goals and the products of inquiry learning resulted in joy and excitement.

> I feel great bursts of enjoyment when students learn on their own and begin to 'love science' and school. Inquiry-based learning is greatly enjoyed by teachers and students. They love it!

For both Ms. Bailey and Mr. Benjamin, their classroom goals of helping students to gain the natural desire to learn and to become well-rounded citizens were attained through inquiry-based instruction, and thus pleasant emotions were elicited.

For these teachers their beliefs about science and pedagogy aligned well with the reform, and so they were open to incorporating new practices into their classrooms. In trying this new instructional approach the teachers were satisfied that the students were engaged and truly learning to be scientists, thus pleasant emotions were elicited. These feelings of satisfaction served to both strengthen the teachers' existing beliefs about the nature of science and science teaching and also sustain the effort to truly transform their classrooms into inquiry-focused spaces. Both Paths A and C elicit pleasant emotions, but we see these two paths as distinct with regard to how the teacher perceives the alignment of his/her instructional goals with the reform objectives (Path A) and adaptation and translation of these goals into teaching practices (Path C). We contend that a teacher's experience with reform can follow Path A but not ultimately lead to Path C. Two cases in particular describe this phenomenon. The first is when pleasant emotions are elicited because the teacher considers the reform practices to be aligned with her own vision of teaching but anticipates the difficulty in implementing these practices and chooses not to. Second, the case where the teacher *perceives* that his/her own beliefs about the discipline and teaching are compatible with the reform objectives, however, in actuality they are not. So the reform objectives are filtered through the teacher's existing beliefs about the discipline resulting in the reform practices being implemented with minimal fidelity (Yerrick et al. 1997).

Path D

Path D illustrates how teachers experience unpleasant emotions in the process of implementing reform-oriented classroom goals into their teaching practices. If an individual teacher perceives that a transaction is related to her valued classroom goal, but it thwarts attaining the goal, then these appraisal processes lead to unpleasant emotions (Lazarus 1991). For example, Ms. Bona, a biology teacher with two years of teaching experience, became extremely frustrated when attempting to incorporate inquiry-teaching methods. Although she acknowledged the value of using inquiry-based methods and its theoretical underpinnings aligned well with her own teaching philosophy, she considered it only partially effective in meeting her instructional goals. Considering her students and the concepts she was expected to cover in the curriculum, she concluded that not all material is best-taught and learned through inquiry methods. In her classroom, she assessed that only about 10% of the time involved inquiry learning, because the inquiry method hindered her from attaining her classroom goal. She wanted her students to grasp scientific concepts correctly, but inquiry-based teaching practices did not facilitate her achieving the goal.

> It can be very frustrating for the students and the teachers when the students do not arrive at an answer that is correct. Process skills are very important, but the right answer can also be very important so the students do not support misconceptions they may have.

Ms. Oakley, who we discussed earlier, a teacher from another country, who had left her job as an engineer to enter the teaching profession, also experienced such unpleasant emotions. Ms. Oakley moved to the U.S., because she expected to teach physics and physical science using better resources and technology. She believed that lab-based activities were important for students' learning, but the school did not provide enough support for purchasing equipment and planning and organizing curriculum. Ms. Oakley was initially excited about the opportunity to work in an environment that supported her teaching philosophy and that would allow her to engage her students in inquiry science. However, as the academic year progressed she recognized that the resources were not available for her to teach in the desired manner and so had to default to more traditional teaching methods. This incongruence between her expectations or goals, the school context and her classroom teaching practices did not facilitate her moving towards the goal attainment and thus resulted in her experiencing frustration, annoyance, and stress. She described her feelings when asked about her teaching experiences during her first year in the U.S.,

> I'm starting to feel very, very frustrated and just annoyed with the whole process really. Um, in terms of specifics, uh, I guess one of my continual…continuing problems really is the uh, the resources that have come from the State as far as the curriculum is concerned. The textbook and the resources that go with it um, it's, it's just annoying that it's inconsistent… It is just shocking to me the lack of understanding on the part of administration about the importance of lab work and the importance of equipment and a basic understanding of the cost involved and also the logistics and planning of lab-based learning, and the importance that it has on learning a science. I was amazed at the lack of equipment available for use.

Both Ms. Bona and Ms. Oakley had beliefs about their discipline that aligned well with the theoretical base and objectives of science reform. However, there were school, curriculum and student-related factors that served as impediments to them meeting their classroom goals. These factors were inconsistent with what the teachers wanted in the classroom and so served as a deterrent to the teachers attaining their instructional goals. Evaluations of their teaching situations led to negative appraisals resulting in unpleasant emotions. When teachers experience unpleasant emotions in the process of implementing their classroom goals, the result may be emotion-induced action or inaction. On one hand, feelings of frustration may lead teachers to be less creative and innovative in seeking solutions and developing alternative teaching strategies to meet the goal. For example, feelings of helplessness and powerlessness hindered Ms. Oakley from using her power as an active agent to confront the unsupportive school administration and implore them to provide the necessary resources and equipment. On the other hand, feelings of anger may motivate teachers to address the issues that were impeding progress towards their goals. Unfortunately, the unpleasant emotions experienced by the teachers across the research projects discussed here discouraged them from trying to make any further changes to their practices.

Based on previous research (Ashton and Gregoire 2003; Gregoire 2003; Hargreaves 2005) we hypothesize that there may be a path where the emotional experiences lead to belief change. For example, Mr. James's beliefs about student learning (previously discussed) may have been amenable of change if he had been willing to implement the discourse and writing practices in his classroom *and* they had lead to increased student engagement and mathematical understanding. However, there was no evidence of belief change for the teachers in our studies.

Summary

Emotions are vital and integral parts of teaching and learning, therefore if we intend for educational changes and reform efforts to be successful we must come to a better understanding of emotions and acknowledge the emotional dimensions of teaching and teacher development (Hargreaves 2005; Lasky 2005; Schmidt and Datnow 2005; Schutz et al. 2006; van Veen et al. 2005). As we have discussed above, the intensity and quality of the emotional responses of teachers in the context of reform are results of how individual teachers view the reform policies and objectives in relation to their beliefs, goals, and identities. These induced emotions in turn also serve as powerful influences for confirming or challenging their existing beliefs, identities, or teaching practices. As we illustrated in the model, the psychological constructs of emotions, beliefs, identities and goal setting are not separate responses, but interconnected and interdependent and tend to operate as a unit. Thus, in the chapter, we attempted to understand how they are related and function within the context of reform. When teachers are introduced to the reform initiatives, they adopt it and translate it into their classroom goals based on their existing beliefs, standards, and experiences. Teachers' beliefs about the nature of knowledge and the most effective pedagogical approaches influence the extent to which they accept and translate reform objectives into instructional goals (Czerniak and Lumpe 1996; Handal and Herrington 2003). These processes also cannot be separated from teachers' professional identities. The way teachers view themselves, the way they portray themselves to others, and the roles and perspectives they take are reflective of the beliefs teachers hold (Kagan 1992). Teachers' sense of self are portrayed and actualized through the effort to achieve the goal, and also teacher identities are defined by the goals, desires, or aspirations, because these future-oriented perceptions provide the evaluative and interpretive context for their view of self (Markus and Nurius 1986; Markus and Wurf 1987). Thus, the complex interplay of both these constructs, beliefs and identities, affect teachers' classroom goal setting.

Depending on whether the goal is aligned with teachers' existing beliefs or identities, it elicits different emotions. These emotions subsequently impact the teaching practices and pre-existing beliefs. For example, Ms. Oakley, whose beliefs about teaching science were aligned with the reform objectives, experienced pleasant emotions such as excitement in the process of setting the goal for her classroom. Although these feelings did not persist throughout the year, her initial feelings of satisfaction served to affirm her pre-existing beliefs about science and science teaching. However, another teacher, Mr. Andrews, thought that teachers' successful pedagogical skills did not necessarily require having reform-based practices, and so his beliefs or experiences of teaching science were somewhat contradictory with the reform mandate. Thus, he perceived the reform message negatively, which threatened his identity as a teacher, thereby eliciting unpleasant emotions and resulting in a rejection of the reform-based practices.

Once teachers develop goals based on their beliefs, identities, and diverse interactions, the goals tend to guide and direct decisions and efforts about teachers' instructional practices (Deci and Ryan 2000; Ford 1992; Schutz 1991; Schutz et al. 2001). In their attempts to achieve the goal, individual teachers evaluate the personal significance of the classroom transactions in relation to the goal, and also assess how well they can handle or manage the transactions. The meaning and personal stake an individual teacher ascribes to a classroom transaction, and the results of the appraisals provoke emotional reactions. For instance, for Mrs. Bailey, a tenth grade biology teacher, her classroom goal was to help students think actively and independently using inquiry-based methods. When she evaluated that her instructional practices worked well in attaining the goal, she felt excitement and fulfillment. However, all teachers do not always experience these pleasant emotions. Ms. Bona talked about her unpleasant emotions when the classroom transactions and inquiry practices did not help her to improve student knowledge of science concepts. She wanted her students to develop accurate understandings and to grasp correct scientific concepts. However, she concluded that the inquiry-based instructional practices lead students to arrive at incorrect answers, and to develop misconceptions. The inquiry-based instructional practices did not serve as an effective mechanism through which she could attain her goals and so her appraisal of the classroom events led to her experiencing unpleasant emotions, such as frustration and disappointment, and subsequent default to initial teaching practices.

Teaching is an emotional practice; emotions permeate the overall educational context. We attempted to understand teachers' emotional experiences in relation to their beliefs, identities, and goals in the context of teachers' efforts in coping with the reform mandates. Given this understanding, we provide implications for teacher educators, policy makers, and school administrators.

Implications for Teacher Education and Professional Development

The strength of an emotional response influences teachers' decisions to persist or change a particular behavior, specifically in relation to instructional practices. Understanding the antecedents of these emotional responses can allow professional developers and teacher educators to approach reform differently, resulting in greater positive effects. As we have discussed, teachers have varied responses to change in general, and specifically in relation to adopting reform-based practices. A crucial factor that determines how teachers respond to reform is their domain-specific beliefs. Therefore, the first step in accomplishing successful reform implementation is addressing teachers' beliefs about the epistemology of their discipline and teaching and learning within that discipline. This change will not occur in a single session but requires a continuous process of awareness, confrontation and reflection coupled with opportunities for teachers to develop authentic mathematical and scientific points of view. Specifically, engaging teachers in experiences that will engender dispositions towards science and mathematics as socially constructed disciplines of inquiry, will help to support efforts to implement reform.

The experiences of these teachers suggested that in addition to awareness and understanding of the psychological factors that influence teachers' decision-making, those involved in working with teachers to successfully implement reform-based practices or curricula must also be cognizant of the physical, social and contextual factors that support or impede teachers efforts to change. We would suggest that when pleasant emotions are elicited, the likelihood that teachers will accept, adopt and implement reform mandates increases. Given that there are at least two ways that teachers experience these emotions (see Paths A and C), it is important that access to these paths be facilitated and not hindered. However, we must also note that teachers are embedded in particular school and social contexts. Thus, we must consider the other contextual factors such as curriculum development, interpersonal and power relationships within the school, and school culture, in order to fully capture how emotions are related to teachers' reform-based teaching practices.

To better facilitate access to these pathways, it is important that teachers be provided with the necessary resources to perform these practices. Examples of the resources that would help teachers better enact reform-based practices are: (a) intellectual resources, such as exposure to new pedagogical teaching practices that are aligned with the objectives and (b) materials, including technology, software, lab resources, manipulatives and reform-based activities, tasks and text books. In cases where reform objectives align with teachers' beliefs and support their existing professional identities, having the required instructional supports will allow teachers to achieve their projected goals. Teachers like Ms. Oakley who embraced educational change and reform may become discouraged and frustrated when the lack of the proper resources prevents them from engaging students in inquiry-based scientific and mathematical activities. Inability to teach in these ways interferes with the teachers' intended roles in the classroom and their ability to actualize their instructional goals leading to feelings of disappointment, irritation and frustration. The unpleasant emotions coupled with the pressures of meeting school-based accountability standards may lead to teachers resorting to more traditional teaching approaches that tend to require less time and resources. Further, persistent feelings of frustration and stress may ultimately lead to teachers deciding to leave the profession (Carlyle and Woods 2002; Hong under review; Hughes 2001).

Teachers' initial responses to reform are also often negative. In situations where teachers interpret reform objectives to be in opposition to their beliefs about how students come to acquire knowledge in their respective disciplines and their roles in the learning process, may lead to anger, anxiety, and frustration. Awareness of the varying beliefs and experiences that teachers bring to teaching and the ways that they inform instructional practices is imperative in appropriately initiating teachers to reform and in designing professional development. Teachers who consider their current practices and ways of teaching as successful may interpret the reform as a message that their efforts are no longer valued. It is therefore important that when presenting the reform objectives that they are presented as evidence-based approaches, grounded in empirical research, that support the development of students' understanding and achievement in mathematics and science. This will alleviate concerns of teachers like Mr. Andrews, that the current reform is merely another 'passing fancy' or that the proposed changes are merely superfluous trimmings on established practices.

Additionally, teachers are often skeptical of whether inquiry approaches will be successful for all types of students. Specifically, these concerns tend to be related to low-achieving and bilingual students and whether or not they will learn through these more self-directed and independent approaches. To diminish this skepticism and increase these teachers willingness to be innovative, it is important that teachers be provided with specific examples of successful efforts with students they can identify as similar to their own. In so doing teachers can feel more efficacious about adopting reform-based practices through these vicarious experiences. These examples should be accompanied with strategies that have proven successful in addressing the diverse needs of their students.

Researchers (Yerrick et al. 1997) have reported that teachers tend to filter reform goals through their existing beliefs and perspectives, often resulting in staggered or unsuccessful implementations. It is therefore important that professional developers and educational researchers be specific about the ways that reform objectives are different from current teaching approaches. Understanding that current practices are connected to teachers' orientations towards their discipline is the first step in designing successful professional development (Park Rogers et al. 2008). Teachers who have had years of success using traditional methods will have difficulty in embracing change and so presenting a convincing argument about why reform-based practices better support the kind of independent and critical thinking necessary for developing expertise in the disciplines is crucial.

Unsuccessful reform implementation occurs not only when teachers reject the reform goals but also when institutional and contextual factors hinder the teachers' efforts to implement the reform as intended. Student-directed learning and inquiry-based approaches in general often require more classroom time than more traditional forms of instruction. Reform does not exist in isolation but in conjunction with other schooling concerns such as covering the curriculum, addressing the academic standards, time, and dealing with students with diverse needs. Often, teachers whose beliefs and teacher selves align with reform objectives default to more traditional methods because they find it difficult to adopt inquiry approaches when restricted by the old infrastructure and accountability measures. In this regard, teachers' concerns must be addressed and measures put in place to allow teachers the opportunity to transition with ease and success.

Similar to difficulties teachers experience in transitioning, students also experience challenges in changing to this new way of learning. In this regard, it is necessary to continuously scaffold the learning process for the students so they remain encouraged and motivated to engage with these new learning approaches. Undoubtedly, there will be failures for both teachers and students in the initial stages of change and so it is important for school officials to acknowledge this and allow teachers and students the time to transition without penalty for these initial failures. For example, understanding that in the transition year the positive effects of these approaches will often not be visible and so suspend teacher and student accountability for standardized tests and grade point averages in the initial year of transition.

In considering institutional or contextual factors, we also need to note the importance of acknowledging teachers' autonomy and authority. Several researchers have found that when schools mediate the reform mandates under the assumption that teachers can be mechanically remodeled to fit the demands of reform mandates, then it often results in threatening their teacher identities (Day 2002; Lasky 2005; Lofty 2006; Sloan 2000; van Lier 2007). As Kelchtermans (1996) also claimed, teachers' sense of vulnerability and their emotions are shaped by experiences of power and powerlessness. Thus, it is important to acknowledge teachers' agency and empower them, so that they can have the opportunity to be actively involved in decision making and problem solving in school activities, which may in turn lead them to feel less vulnerable and perceive the change as less threatening to their professional identities. If teachers' professional identities are threatened, it inevitably influences their beliefs and emotions in a negative way (O'Connor 2008). When this happens, we cannot really expect meaningful changes at the classroom level, which is the most important and necessary point of change.

Designing instruction and orchestrating learning in ways that allow students to meaningfully engage with scientific and mathematical concepts, to develop students' critical thinking and reasoning skills and to become more autonomous in their approach to learning are the main objectives of reform in science and mathematics pedagogy. Teachers are at the forefront of these efforts as they are the ones who are ultimately responsible for student learning because they interact with the students directly. In addition to dealing with the already emotionally charged schooling environment, to incorporate instructional changes, teachers must also resolve the inter-psychological tensions that arise between BIGE (beliefs, identity, goals, and emotions). Understanding the relationship between BIGE, the role the constructs play in teachers' classroom behaviors and instructional decisions, and how to help teachers modify their domain-specific beliefs and identities to better align with the reform philosophy, are the necessary steps in easing the transition for teachers and also improving the success rate of reform implementation.

References

Aikenhead G, Ryan A (1992) The development of a new instrument: views on science-technology-society. Sci Educ 76(5):477–491

American Association for the Advancement of Science (1993) Benchmarks for science literacy. Oxford University Press, New York

Ashton P (1984) Teacher efficacy: a motivational paradigm for effective teacher education. J Teach Educ 35(5):28–32

Ashton P, Gregoire M (2003) At the heart of teaching: the role of emotion in changing teachers' beliefs. In: Raths J, McAninch A (eds) Teacher beliefs and classroom performance: the impact of teacher education. Information Age Publishing, Greenwich, CT, pp 99–122

Bandura A (1997) Self-efficacy: the exercise of control. WH Freeman, New York

Beijaard D, Verloop N, Vermunt JD (2000) Teachers' perceptions of professional identity: an exploratory study from a personal knowledge perspective. Teach Teach Educ 16(7):749–764

Bryan L, Atwater M (2002) Teacher beliefs and cultural models: a challenge for science teacher preparation programs. Sci Educ 86(6):821–839

Carlyle D, Woods P (2002) The emotions of teacher stress. Trentham, Stoke-on-Trent

Cooper K, Olson M (1996) The multiple 'I' s of teacher identity. In: Kompf M, Dworet D, Boak R (eds) Changing research and practice. Falmer, London, pp 78–89

Cross D (2008) Creating optimal mathematics learning environments: combining argumentation and writing to enhance achievement. Int J Sci Math Educ. http://dx.doi.org/10.1007/s10763-008-9144-9. Retrieved Oct 2008

Cross D (in press) Alignment, cohesion and change: examining mathematics teachers' belief structures and their influence on instructional practice. J Teach Educ

Czerniak C, Lumpe A (1996) Relationship between teacher beliefs and science education reform. J Sci Teach Educ 7(4):247–266

Day C (2002) School reform and transitions in teacher professionalism and identity. Int J Educ Res 37:677–692

Day C, Elliot B, Kington A (2005) Reform, standards and teacher identity: challenges of sustaining commitment. Teach Teach Educ 21(5):563–577

Day C, Kington A, Stobart G, Sammons P (2006) The personal and professional selves of teachers: stable and unstable identities. Br Educ Res J 32(4):601

Deci EL, Ryan RM (2000) The 'what' and 'why' of goal pursuits: human needs and the self-determination of behavior. Psychol Inq 11(4):227–268

Denzin NK (1984) On understanding emotion. Jossey-Bass, San Francisco, CA

Fogel A (2001) A relational perspective on the self and emotions. In: Bosma HA, Kunnen ES (eds) Identity and emotion: development through self-organization. Cambridge University Press, Cambridge, pp 93–114

Ford ME (1992) Motivating humans: goals, emotions, and personal agency beliefs. Sage, Newbury Park, CA

Franco C, Sztajn P, Ortigão MIR (2007) Does reform teaching raise all students' math scores? An analysis of the role that the socioeconomic status of students plays in closing the achievement gap. J Res Math Educ 38(4):393–419

Frijda NH (2001) The self and emotions. In: Bosma HA, Kunnen ES (eds) Identity and emotion: development through self-organization. Cambridge University Press, Paris, pp 39–57

Frijda N, Mesquita B (2000) Beliefs through emotions. In: Frijda N, Manstead A, Bem S (eds) Emotions and beliefs: how feelings influence thoughts. University Press, Cambridge, pp 45–77

Frijda NH, Manstead A, Bem S (2000) The influence of emotions on beliefs. In: Frijda N, Manstead A, Bem S (eds) Emotions and beliefs: how feelings influence thoughts. The University Press, Cambridge, pp 1–9

Giddens A (1979) Central problems in social theory: action, structure and contradiction in social analysis. University of California Press, Berkeley, CA

Gregoire M (2003) Is it a challenge of a threat? A dual-process model of teachers' cognition and appraisal processes during conceptual change. Educ Psychol Rev 15(2):147–179

Gross JJ (1998) The emerging field of emotion regulation: an integrative review. Rev Gen Psychol 2(3):271–299

Handal B, Herrington A (2003) Mathematics teachers' beliefs and curriculum reform. Math Educ Res J 15(1):59–69

Hargreaves A (2005) The emotions of teaching and educational change. In: Hargreaves A (ed) Extending educational change. Springer, New York, pp 278–295

Harter S (1998) The development of self-representations. In: Eisenberg N (ed) Handbook of child psychology, vol 3, 5th edn, Social, emotional, and personality development. Wiley, New York, pp 553–617

Hermans H, Hermans-Jansen E (2001) Affective processes in a multivoiced self. In: Bosma HA, Kunnen ES (eds) Identity and emotion: development through self-organization. Cambridge University Press, Paris, pp 120–150

Hofer B, Pintrich P (2002) Personal epistemology: the psychology of beliefs about knowledge and knowing. Erlbaum, Mahwah, NJ

Hong J (under review) Pre-service and beginning teachers' professional identity and its relation to dropping out of the profession

Hong J, Oliver S, Vargas P (under review) Science teachers' professional identity and beliefs in the context of reform

Hughes RE (2001) Deciding to leave but staying: teacher burnout, precursors and turnover. Int J Hum Resour Manage 12(2):288–298

Ineke H, van Driel J, Verloop N (2007) Science teachers' knowledge about teaching models and modeling in the context of a new syllabus on public understanding of science. Res Sci Educ 37(2):99–122

Kagan D (1992) Implications of research on teacher belief. Educ Psychol 27(1):65–90

Kelchtermans G (1993) Getting the story, understanding the lives: from career stories to teachers' professional development. Teach Teach Educ 9(5–6):443

Kelchtermans G (1996) Teacher vulnerability: understanding its moral and political roots. Cambridge J Educ 26(3):307–323

Kelchtermans G (2005) Teachers' emotions in educational reforms: self-understanding, vulnerable commitment and micropolitical literacy. Teach Teach Educ 21(8):995–1006

Kunnen ES, Bosma HA, Van Halen CPM, Van der Meulen M (2001) A selforganizational approach to identity and emotions: an overview and implications. In: Bosma HA, Kunnen ES (eds) Identity and development: development through selforganization. Cambridge University Press, Cambridge, pp 202–230

Lasky S (2005) A sociocultural approach to understanding teacher identity, agency and professional vulnerability in a context of secondary school reform. Teach Teach Educ Int J Res Stud 21(8):899–916

Lazarus RS (1991) Emotion and adaptation. Oxford University Press, New York

Lazarus RS (1999) Stress and emotions: a new synthesis. Springer, New York

Lazarus R, Smith C (1988) Knowledge and appraisal in the cognition–emotion relationship. Cogn Emotion 2:281–300

Leiter MP (1992) Burn-out as a crisis in self-efficacy: conceptual and practical implications. Work Stress 6(2):107–115

Lofty J (2006) Quiet wisdom: teachers in the United States and England talk about standards, practice and professionalism. Lang Publishing, Inc., New York

Markus H (1983) Self-knowledge: an expanded view. J Pers 51(3):543–565

Markus H, Nurius P (1986) Possible selves. Am Psychol 41(9):954–969

Markus H (1982) The self in social information processing. In: Sentis K, Suls J (eds) Psychological perspectives on the self. Erlbaum, Hillsdale, NJ, pp 41–70

Markus H, Wurf E (1987) The dynamic self-concept: a social psychological perspective. Annu Rev Psychol 38:299–337

Mead GH (1934) Mind, self & society from the standpoint of a social behaviorist. The University of Chicago Press, Chicago, IL

National Council for the Accreditation of Teacher Education (NCATE) (2002) Professional standards for the accreditation of schools, colleges, and departments of education. NCATE, Washington, DC

National Council of Teachers of Mathematics (1991) Professional Standards for Teaching Mathematics. Reston, VA

National Council of Teachers of Mathematics (2000) Principles and standards for school mathematics. Reston, VA

National Research Council (1996) National science education standards. National Academy Press, Washington, DC

Nespor J (1987) The role of beliefs in the practice of teaching. J Curriculum Stud 19:317–328

O'Connor K (2008) 'You choose to care': teachers, emotions and professional identity. Teach Teach Educ 24(10):117–126

Pajares MF (1992) Teachers' beliefs and educational research: cleaning up a messy construct. Rev Educ Res 62(3):307–332

Pajares F (1996) Self-efficacy beliefs in academic settings. Rev Educ Res 66(4):543–578

Pajares F, Miller MD, Johnson MJ (1999) Gender differences in writing self-beliefs of elementary school students. J Educ Psychol 91(1):50–61

Park Rogers M, Cross D, Trauth-Nare A, Buck G, Gresalfi M (2008) First year implementation of a project-based learning approach: the need for addressing teachers' orientations and professional experience in the era of reform. Paper presented at the Annual Meeting of the American Educational Research Association, San Diego, CA

Raymond A (1997) Inconsistencies between a beginning elementary teacher's mathematics beliefs and teaching practice. J Res Math Educ 28(5):550–576

Rimm-Kaufman S, Sawyer B (2004) Primary-grade teachers' self efficacy beliefs, attitudes toward teaching, and discipline and teaching practice priorities in relation to the responsive classroom approach. Elem Sch J 104(2):321–341

Schmidt M, Datnow A (2005) Teachers' sense-making about comprehensive school reform: the influence of emotions. Teach Teach Educ 21:949–965

Schraw G, Olafson L (2002) Teachers' epistemological world views and educational practices. Issues Educ Contrib Educ Psychol 8(2):99–148

Schutz PA (1991) Goals in self-directed behavior. Educ Psychol 26(1):55–67

Schutz PA, DeCuir JT (2002) Inquiry on emotions in education. Educ Psychol 37:125–134

Schutz PA, Crowder KC, White VE (2001) The development of a goal to become a teacher. J Educ Psychol 93(2):299–308

Schutz PA, Hong JY, Cross DI, Osbon JN (2006) Reflections on investigating emotions among educational contexts. Educ Psychol Rev 18(4):343–360

Schutz PA, Cross DI, Hong JY, Osbon JN (2007) Teacher understandings, thoughts and beliefs about emotions in the classroom. In: Schutz PA, Pekrun R (eds) Emotions in education. Elsevier, San Diego, CA, pp 215–233

Sloan K (2000) Teacher agency and the TAAS: maintaining the ability to "act otherwise". Paper presented at the Annual Meeting of the American Educational Research Association, New Orleans, LA, April

Tobin K, McRobbie C (1996) Cultural myths as constraints to the enacted science curriculum. Sci Educ 20:223–241

Torff B, Warburton EC (2005) Assessment of teachers' beliefs about classroom use for critical thinking activities. Educ Psychol Meas 65:155–179

Van den Berg R (2002) Teachers' meanings regarding educational practice. Rev Educ Res 72(4):577–625

Van Lier L (2007) Action-based teaching, autonomy and identity. Innov Lang Learn Teach 1(1):46–65

Van Veen K, Sleegers P, Van de Ven P-H (2005) One teacher's identity, emotions, and commitment to change: a case study into the cognitive–affective processes of a secondary school teacher in the context of reforms. Teach Teach Educ 21:917–934

Watson C (2006) Narratives of practice and the construction of identity in teaching. Teach Teach Theory Pract 12(5):509–526

Yerrick R, Parke H, Nugent F (1997) Struggling to promote deeply rooted change: the 'filtering effect' of teachers' beliefs on understanding tranformational views of teaching science. Sci Educ 81(2):137–160

Part V
Race, Gender and Power Relationships

Chapter 15
An Exploratory Study of Race and Religion in the Emotional Experience of African-American Female Teachers

Ken Winograd

Abstract The study examines the emotional experience of five African-American female teachers in the Pacific northwest. The existing literature on emotion rules and teachers' emotions is referenced and critiqued for its possible misrepresentation or marginalization of teachers of color. Using interview data, the study found that race and religion shape the emotional response of teachers. The teachers tended to reference race and racism as well as their religious or spiritual beliefs to contextualize teaching experience and accompanying emotions, including the use of emotions to manage and reconceptualize their professional identities. In the end, it appears that for these African-American teachers, in particular, the intersection of race, religion and emotion serves both personal and political interests.

Keywords Professional identity · Reform · Teacher emotions

In 1998-99, I took a sabbatical from my position as an education professor and returned to the classroom, as an elementary teacher of first-third graders. Among the self-studies I conducted that year was an examination of my emotions as a teacher (Winograd 2003, 2005). This chapter is a response to the *colorblindness* (Delgado 1995) of these earlier studies. When I did the 2003 study, I was oblivious to the limitations of my findings as they related especially to race. I was oblivious to the implications and dangers of colorblindness in educational research as well as colorblind representations in media and texts generally. This chapter is also a response to the literature on teacher emotions. While teachers of color may have been participants in the extant research on teacher emotions, few empirical studies, if any, have explicitly sought understandings of the emotional experiences of teachers of color.

K. Winograd (✉)
Teacher and Counselor Education, Oregon State University, USA
e-mail: winograk@oregonstate.edu

P.A. Schutz and M. Zembylas (eds.), *Advances in Teacher Emotion Research:*
The Impact on Teachers' Lives,
DOI 10.1007/978-1-4419-0564-2_15, © Springer Science+Business Media, LLC 2009

As such, this is an exploratory study of the emotions of African-American female public school teachers living in the Pacific northwest of the United States. The goal of this chapter and research is to do some problem posing around this question and to advocate for more research on the emotions of teachers of color.

Rationale for Study

It was projected in 2003 that students of color in the US would comprise approximately 40% of the total population (US Department of Education, 2003) and by the year 2050 the total population of people of color in the US would surpass 50% (El Nasser 2008). Already, more than half of *students* attending public schools in our nation's largest cities are students of color. However, the number of teachers of color does not nearly approximate the number of students of color.

> The prospective teacher population is . . . predominantly white. The enrollment of schools, colleges, and departments of education (SCDEs) in the late 1990s was 495,000. Of these students, 86 percent were white; about 7 percent were African American; about 3 percent were Latino. The number of Asian–Pacific Islander and American Indian–Alaskan Native students enrolled in SCDEs is negligible (Ladson-Billings 2001, p. 4).

Many leading African-American education researchers argue that students of color benefit from teachers of the same racial or cultural group because these teachers bring greater empathy and interest than white teachers (Delpit 1995; Foster 1995, 1997; Ladson-Billings, 1994, 2005). I am not suggesting that African-American teachers can be effective only with African-American students, or that white teachers can not be effective with students of color. Still, the need for African-American teachers for African-American students is especially acute; these students need teachers who understand their experience, who can inspire and cajole them in culturally congruent ways, and who can provide powerful role models for what these students might envision for themselves (e.g., Wilder 2000).

An important new body of scholarship has emerged since the 1990s in the area of teacher emotions (e.g., Schutz and Pekrun 2007; Sutton and Wheatley 2003; Zembylas 2005a, b). There has been significant theoretical work that has contextualized emotions, including teacher emotions, in broad socio-cultural frameworks (e.g., Boler 1999; Zembylas 2005a, b). However, most of the empirical work on the emotional experience of teachers has centered on lives of Euro-Americans, and empirical work on the lives of teachers of color has been largely unexamined. This tendency towards colorblindness in the empirical literature on teacher emotions also reflects larger problems in teacher education, generally, regarding its sensitivity to culture in the preparation of teachers. There continues to be uneasiness among African-Americans educators that teacher education in the United States has much work to do regarding culture and teacher preparation. Although there has been progress, there still is a tendency for teacher education to normalize whiteness and, thereby, marginalize the experience and world view of teachers from historically oppressed groups (e.g., Delpit 1995; Ladson-Billings 1991).

The study in this chapter aims to address this missing link in the teacher emotions literature with the larger goal of developing more culturally sensitive cultures in teacher education programs for preservice teachers of color. By understanding this aspect of African-American teachers' experience, and by extension the idea that teachers from non-dominant cultures experience and display culture-specific emotions, only then can teacher education more effectively continue to diversify the educational work force.

Conceptual Frameworks

I use three theories to support my interpretation of the data: the research and theory of emotions and teaching; Afrocentric epistemology of Patricia Collins and W.E.B. DuBois; and Critical Race Theory.

Emotion and Teaching

Lazarus (1991), whose work reflects a more individualistic, cognitive approach to emotions, attributes agency to individuals who are constantly making appraisals based on their goals for the activity, including decisions on how to cope with and behave emotionally in different situations. Although social structure and culture play a part in Lazarus' theory, these factors are more prominent in other theories in social psychology and sociology on emotions (e.g., Goffman 1959; Hochschild 1983; Kemper 1978). In large part, emotional experience reflects the needs of institutions and the roles that people serve in those institutions (Gerth and Mills 1953). "Social factors enter not simply before and after but interactively during the expression of emotion" (Hochschild 1983, p. 211).

From a social-interactionist perspective, expressions of emotion serve to defend social norms and beliefs and have a socio-functional purpose (Armon-Jones 1986). Emotions are "functional in that they are constituted and prescribed in such a way as to sustain and endorse systems of belief and value" (Armon-Jones 1986, p. 57). Reflecting the idea that emotion and personality reflect social structure and role, Sarbin (1986) maintains that emotions and how we respond emotionally are "tied to values, to conditions that involve one's identity" (p. 91). Similarly, in their work on teachers' emotions, Hargreaves (1998) and others (Nias 1996; Schutz and Pekrun 2007; Zembylas 2005a, b) embed their analyses in social, political and moral contexts in order to explain how teachers feel and display emotions. While there are differences in the conceptual frameworks of these researchers, they all conceptualize (teacher) emotions as social construction, reflecting the imperatives and values of institutions and cultures but also the interests and personalities of individuals.

Feminists and other criticalists examine questions of how the experience and display of emotion may be a site of *or* a site for political transformation; and how emotions may serve to maintain the status quo social control of dominant patriarchal, hierarchical capitalist systems *or* how emotions may be used to disrupt these systems (e.g., Boler 1999). Harrison (1985), for example, argued that the emotion, anger, can be a vehicle for social change. Jaggar (1989) termed *outlaw emotions* to be unconventionally unacceptable emotions. Like Boler (1999) and Campbell (1994), she found a strong relationship between emotions and power. "Only when we reflect on our initial puzzling, irritability, revulsion, anger, or fear may we bring to consciousness our 'gut level' awareness that we are in a situation of coercion, cruelty, injustice or danger" (p. 161). Jaggar maintained that outlaw emotions can lead to change only when feminists (women and men) share their experience, by naming their experience as particularly cruel, unjust, and so on and then by forming alternative subcultures within the dominant (male) stream. When outlaw emotions are the expression of a collective, then these emotions may be "politically and epistemologically subversive" (p. 160).

Feeling Rules and Emotion Management

There are certain *feeling rules* – historically determined and locally redefined, that influence how people (and teachers) experience and display emotion. The education profession does have generalized, somewhat loose, notions about how teachers are *supposed* to emote. These rules are not necessarily taught formally to teachers, but they are collaboratively constructed in the everyday work of teachers, students, principals, parents, and teacher educators among the intersecting dynamics of race, class, geography, age, gender and personality. Rules about emotional behavior are constructed in particular schools as well as the general culture of teaching, represented in sources such as NCATE's guidelines for professional dispositions, findings reported in education psychology textbooks regarding the affect of "effective teachers", an amorphous mass of images and messages from the culture of teacher education, expressions about teaching in media and the arts in the larger society, and the culture's collective memory of teachers working in schools. For example, teachers generally are supposed to enjoy children, enjoy their work, maintain a patient and kind front, become angry with children infrequently, not show extreme emotions, show emotional self-control, and so on.

When teachers do not display or feel emotions that they are *supposed* to have, they may do what is known as emotional labor or emotion management. Thoits (1990) defined emotion management as "deliberate attempts by the individual to change one or more components of his or her subjective experience in order to bring that feeling in line with normative requirements" (p. 192). Emotion management work is typically required in "every political regime, of every cultural hegemony" (Reddy 2001, p. 121).

Hochschild (1983) distinguishes two somewhat dramaturgical strategies for emotion management: deep acting and surface acting. In deep acting, the person gets into the role, almost like method actors, and there is no disconnect between their outward appearance and generally how she feels. For example, a teacher who is grumpy just before school may purposefully remember wonderful past images of her students, her reasons for going into teaching, and her love of her students. Through this purposeful "exhorting (of) feeling" or making use of his imagination, the teacher is able to both appear and feel happy when the students come through the door. However, if the teacher is unable to draw on imagery or experience to exhort feeling that is appropriate to the situation, then she may simply look the part without the accompanying feeling. The surface effects associated with emotions, such as smiling, frowning, sighing, and laughing, are a put-on and do not reflect how the individual is really feeling. Hochschild 1983) warns of the dangers of surface acting: It can lead to an alienation of our working lives and our more natural selves. We become alienated from the part of our self that does the work.

Instead of being simply an alienating experience, emotion management can be a satisfying or even liberating experience, since it can lead the worker to enhance his involvement in activity that is fundamentally meaningful. The more the norms or values inherent in the work role have been internalized by the worker, the more likely emotional labor will lead to a sense of personal well-being (Ashforth 1993). For example, Yanay & Shahar (1998) found that the emotional labor in a therapeutic setting led to increased empathy and caring by the therapist. In a study of food market clerks, Tolich (1993) distinguished emotional labor regulated by another person, such as an employer or supervisor, from emotional labor that is regulated by the worker. Tolich (1993) maintained that emotional labor led to deeper feelings of satisfaction regarding work when the employee controlled the emotion work.

Emotion management entails the reshaping of one's emotions in relation to goals of the organization or culture, goals that are more or less fixed. Zembylas (2005b) suggests that the metaphor of emotion management is too limiting for the teacher, a concept that makes little room for the use of emotions to engage in liberatory or transformational identity work. Zembylas uses a concept from the work of Reddy (2001), emotion *navigation*, which entails a more fluid and dynamic emotional response to experience, a process that allows more space for the person to use emotions to explore or alter identity, perhaps even redefine the situation or modify goals in order meet larger higher level aims or ideals. The process of navigation can lead to transformation of identity, implying "purposive action, whereas changes of goals…are carried out in the name of higher priority goals" (Reddy 2001, p. 122).

Zembylas (2005b) studied a kindergarten teacher who engaged in this type of emotion work: by initiating and directing her own emotional freedom, transforming earlier feelings of suffering, low esteem and shame, by resisting the dominant emotional culture of the school and "…creating spaces for emotional freedom in her classroom–through empathetic understanding and affective alliances" (p. 479). According to Reddy and Zembylas, emotional control is where political power is played out, determining who gets to express certain emotions and when and where, those quintessentially important emotions that shape, guide and redirect high level priorities and related actions. Teachers have what Zembylas calls "spaces for emotional freedom" and they have the ability to resist external normalized rules for emotion, although he is clear that some constraints are virtually inevitable. "…emotions are not the anti-cognitive domain of life but rather the very site of the capacity to effect change" (Zembylas 2005b, p. 470).

Critical Race Theory

Critical Race Theory, in the 1990s, was a response to Critical Legal Studies, which apparently did not fully consider racism in its critique of meritocracy in the United States (Crenshaw et al. 1995). Critical Race Theory addresses how the legal system privileges white people and how these systems structure racial progress only incrementally and never enough to truly challenge the hegemony of white interests. Furthermore, critical race theorists argue that the existing legal system tends to reproduce and legitimate the existing system, even when legal reforms *appear* to be making progress. A huge goal of CRT is the taking of action to "eliminate racial oppression as part of a larger project to eradicate all forms of oppression" (Ladson-Billings 1999, p. 257). Barnes (1990) eloquently and unequivocally articulated the goal of CRT, "…to transform a world deteriorating under the albatross of racial hegemony" (p. 1864–1865).

Most research done in education using the CRT perspective has critiqued curriculum, instruction, assessment, school funding and desegregation (Ladson-Billings 1999). This study uses CRT to understand the emotional experience of African-American teachers, using four ideas or features of CRT (Delgado 1995).

First, racism is a normal feature of life in the United States. While this may seem obvious to people of color and their allies, the notion of racism as a "permanent fixture of American life" and as normal and natural provides an important counter-narrative to a prevailing liberal idea that racism is no longer pervasive in US society and, instead, is an historical artifact in what some liberals mistakenly promote as the current post-racial period.

Second, scholars with a CRT perspective believe that people of color and other oppressed peoples ought to tell their own stories, where the "writers analyze myths, presuppositions, and received wisdoms that make up the common culture about race and that invariably render blacks and other minorities one-down" (Delgado 1995, p. xiv). There are three reasons for inviting oppressed peoples to tell their own story (Delgado 1989; Ladson-Billings 1999). First, the stories people tell reflect their positions as they relate to the class, race, nation, gender, sexual orientation, etc. Second, stories serve a validation function for out-group members, providing them with a vehicle to assert their personal/collective identities and engage in cultural self preservation. And third, stories told by the out-group have the potential to help the in-group to de-center and become conscious of their unconscious racism.

A third feature of CRT is that whites have been the primary beneficiaries of social reform, like civil rights legislation, although the manifest intention of this reform is the improvement of the lives of the out-group. For example, there is some scholarship that suggests affirmative action was driven by the need to establish women in leadership positions in the military (Guy-Sheftall 1993); or that the Brown v. Board of Education ruling was shaped, in large part, by the Cold War imperative that the United States be viewed internationally as a beacon of social justice and freedom (Bell 1980).

The fourth idea of CRT is its critique of liberalism and its claims that social systems in the United States (i.e., the legal system, the educational system) are neutral, colorblind and merit-based. In education, for example, proponents of colorblindness argue that research-based practices work for all students when, in fact, the relative effectiveness of various approaches to teaching may be culture-dependent (e.g., Delpit 1995). White teachers may claim not to "see" color in their students, but this is problematic when racial stereotyping of students may marginalize some students and privilege others. CRT can help question dominant assumptions as they relate to neutrality and colorblindness in research on teacher emotions.

Finally, I am aware of my status as white (male) person with unearned privilege that comes along with being white and male. I am also aware of the debate around the question of white researchers using Critical Race Theory in their own scholarship. One aspect of CRT is making central the voices of the people who are the focus of the research, but in the present research my voice is still central to the narrative. I try to include more direct quotations that capture the experiences of my participants. I also realize the difficulty in trying to re-present the experience of others whose experience is radically different than mine, especially when the participants' lives have been shaped by oppressions that I can only experience vicariously. As a white person, I do not pretend that I can "understand" the experience of people of color. I also realize that white people, in all facets of life including educational research, often and easily co-opt and re-invent African-American initiatives and innovations (Sleeter 1994). However, I believe that CRT can critique the taken-for-granted hegemony of whiteness in education practice and research and also re-position the gaze of those in the majority away from a deficit view of people of color. Bergerson (2003), a white scholar grappling with her use of this perspective, said, "I do not intend to say that white voices are necessary to legitimize critical race scholarship, but (instead) to emphasize the importance of incorporating CRT's tenets into our work to show that norms and assumptions about racism are changing" (60). My use of CRT also reflects my belief that social justice happens effectively in the context of alliances between white people and people of color.

An Afrocentric Epistemology

In order for me to make sense of the emotional experience of my five participants from, specifically, an African-American feminist perspective, I draw upon several core ideas of two African-American scholars, W. E. B. DuBois and Patricia Collins. DuBois developed the idea of *double consciousness*, the notion that African-Americans have learned to see the world through multiple perspectives because of their subordinated status as slaves, as second-class citizens during Jim Crow and even through the post civil-rights period of a racism that is largely unconscious and imbued in social structures and white identity. Living outside the dominant discourse, African-Americans have had to learn the ways of the white majority, in order to survive, in addition to learning their own racial culture. Lewis (1993) argues that these "two souls, two thoughts, two unreconciled strivings" (Franklin 1965, p. 215) have led African-Americans to perceive more deeply into everyday experience, with an "intuitive faculty enabling him/her to see and say things about American society that possessed heightened moral validity" (Lewis 1993, p. 281). Double consciousness is viewed here as a strength, an asset, a virtue, giving African-Americans a "transcendent position allowing one to see and understand positions of inclusion and exclusion—margins and mainstreams" (Ladson-Billings 2000, p. 260).

A second concept germane to the present study is Afrocentric Feminist Epistemology, developed by Patricia Collins (1990) and others (but I will focus on the work of Collins exclusively here). One central idea from this epistemology is the ethic of caring, the "appropriateness of emotion in dialogues", personal expressiveness and deeply empathetic relations. Collins explains that these three dimensions of caring permeate African-American culture, especially that of African-American women. Collins also notes the similarity of this Afrocentric value on caring with similar ways of knowing and caring by white women (e.g., Belenky, et al. 1986) and the inextricable linkage of personality, intellect and emotions. While the Afrocentric and feminist ideas about the reason/emotion relation are similar, Collins notes that the only institution that has supported white women's expression of emotion has been the family. African-American women, however, have long had the support of the Black church along with the family, institutions that have both invited and nurtured the expression of deep caring (rejecting the reason/emotion dichotomy).

Method

I interviewed five African American teachers who work in urban schools in the Pacific northwest area. The interviews occurred in early fall 2008. I interviewed the teachers at their schools, except Lisa, with whom I interviewed at her home.

Participants

Here is a brief description of the five participants, all African-American and female.

1. Yolanda is 28 years old and married. She has been a classroom teacher for four years, all in high schools as a science and mathematics teacher. She currently

teaches in a suburban school district near Vancouver, WA where approximately 90% of the students are Euro-American. Yolanda was born in Arkansas and moved to the Pacific northwest when she was two years old. She occasionally travels back to Arkansas to visit family.

2. Carol taught as an elementary teacher for 11 years in public schools in a city in the Pacific northwest. The schools had predominantly African-American student populations and integrated teaching staffs. Carol was born and raised in the same city. She just completed a doctorate in education at an area university and has begun her first job as an assistant principal.

3. Lisa is 30 years old, is married to a minister and they have two children. She teaches first grade at an elementary school with an African-American population of approximately 65%. She has taught for five years, all in this same school. The teaching staff at her school is predominantly Euro-American. Her mother is from eastern Oregon, and her father is from Arkansas. Lisa and her mother came to an urban part of the state when she was eight years old. Her mother still works as an accountant for the country government.

4. Pat is approximately 45 years old and she has taught for 15 years, mostly in public schools as a special education teacher. Before working in an urban area in the Pacific northwest, she worked in Los Angeles city schools. She has taught mostly in integrated schools. The middle school where she now works is 67% Euro-American, 30% Latino, and 3% African American. The school has no African-American teachers and around half of the staff is Latino.

5. Leticia is in her mid 30s, and she has been a social worker for the last 12 years. Her work has always been in non-profit education programs. She currently works as a teacher of teenagers, mostly African-American, who do not attend the public school system, such as teenage mothers. Her colleagues are white, African-American, and Latin-American. Leticia was born and raised in a large city in the Pacific northwest.

Data Collection and Analysis

I collected data exclusively through five interviews. Each audio-taped interview lasted approximately 90 min. I transcribed the audio-tapes verbatim, and each interview yielded roughly seven pages of text (typed, 12 in. font, one inch margins). The interviews were semi-structured, and I used set interview questions (see Appendix) which led to open-ended discussion. My research focus was an examination of the intersection of culture and emotions, so the interview questions explicitly addressed aspects of culture (in this case, African-American culture) of interest to me.

I used an analytic inductive approach (Lincoln and Guba 1985) to organize the data and then generate categories and assertions as they related to my research questions. After each interview, I slightly revised the interview questions, based on the teacher's responses, and emerging patterns and categories that I imposed on the data. Clearly, I was interested in how African-American woman teachers experienced the emotions of teaching. I was already versed in the research literature on African-Americans and stress. With some background knowledge in the experience of professional African-American women, I used sensitizing concepts to shape and direct my coding of the data.

I initially read the data and engaged in coding of words, phrases, sentences or paragraphs that I used in the analytic categories from my own self-study of teacher emotions (Winograd 2003), particularly emotion rules and emotion management strategies. These three categories framed the interview questions and also served to initiate and guide the analysis process. I organized the initial codes into look-alike groupings, and gave each grouping a categorical name (e.g., use of prayer, treatment of students based on race, etc). I searched the data for discrepant cases or aberrant data and was careful to note exceptions to the central findings.

The central explanatory concept of this research is that emotion and culture are inter-related, so the theoretical schemes presented in the next section are all organized around this idea. The schemes, or categories, are preliminary and more work needs be done to understand variation within and between the categories. There were dimensions of emotion work done by these teachers that seem relevant to most teachers, across cultures. For example, many of their strategies for managing emotions are no different than what studies of white teachers have found, like deep breathing, going for walks, problem solving, etc. I did not report or expand on some of these "non-cultural" responses, since my purpose was to understand the cultural dimensions of emotion. In the end, the teachers' narratives were structured by my questions, and I wonder how much more or what else I could have learned if I had constructed more open-ended questions and then had the time to return for a second round of interviews. The focus of the participants' stories related to their experience of living and teaching in the Pacific northwest. I imagine that African-American teachers in different parts of the country would show some differences with this group.

The credibility of my assertions, or validity to use a traditional term in social science research, is addressed in two ways. First, I did some cross-case analysis of the interviews; common patterns among the five participants provide some confidence that the findings are not overly idiosyncratic or an artifact of the researcher's imagination. Second, I searched the literature on African-American culture, teachers, stress and history, again, in search of similarities with patterns I constructed from the data. (I did my study of the literature before data and during data collection.) The goal of qualitative research often is to build theory, so the aim here is do just that: to develop "explanatory power" and not generalizability (Strauss and Corbin 1998). As substantive theory, the outcome of this research will be to speak to the specific case of five African-American public school teachers in the Pacific northwest. Because the sample size is so small, especially, I make no claim that the precision and power of my assertions are anything but partial.

Findings

Emotion Rules

There were three emotion rules that dominated the interviews: honesty, caring, and differential treatment of students based on race.

Honesty

Most frequently, the five participants indicated that effective teachers are honest, mostly with their students but also with parents and colleagues. Although teachers acknowledged that some faking is necessary when teaching, being direct and honest with students tended to dominate teachers' relations with students. According to Carol, when she began teaching…

> …I never really tried to hide my emotions per se. And I try to have honest conversations with students about my feelings and to use them as learning opportunities for the students.…There was laughter and many different emotional levels on a given day. I think I am very open to all kinds of emotions.

Pat has worked to balance honest emotional display and the more distanced detachment typical in the dominant discourse for being a professional. Still, she says, "It goes both ways…the kids know that I am human. I get mad like they do, I'm happy like they are, and I'm sad like they are. I am tired some days…. I think the kids…appreciate honesty."

Like the others, Leticia believes strongly in this honesty rule, emphatically stating:

> These kids come here already wounded after being told, you can't. You can't make it here, so go over there. It is important for us to be more open and more honest about our emotions and where I am with you so you know that I am not hiding my self from you. 'You are irritating me right now. I'm not really happy with you right now.'

There was a racial dimension in Carol's honesty with parents about their children's progress, specifically the importance of not "sugar coating" information given the challenging racist world in which these students have to live.

> I have to be very real with parents. I don't sugar coat anything with them because we don't have the luxury to do that. We are fortunate in this country, we can fail and come again. For African American students you can't fail too many times and come again. I mean, it's just another ball game. And I am very blunt with the families. (African Americans) don't have a lot of room, we have to work twice as hard.

All of the teachers indicated that they are honest with students even if the teachers are having an "off day." Carol said, "I would be having kind of a bad day, and remarkably the students would rally around me and that picks me right up…to get out of whatever mood I'm in that's not so happy and we end up laughing together." Yolanda also indicated the value of being honest with students if the teacher is not feeling "up":

> I think I am pretty direct with students because it's so easy for you and anybody else to recognize when I'm not in my normal mode….so when I'm not feeling (good) on a certain day

then I have to be honest with my students and communicate with them, 'today is not a good day, I'm not happy, let's get through this stuff....I think students feel...want to help me....

Related to the honest expression of emotions, there appears to be a sense from the teachers that they do feel comfortable in expressing positive emotion in a more or less unrestrained manner, emotions such as joy, love, and even sadness. (As a white male teacher, I have felt restrained to show these extreme emotions, generally). Pat cried openly in front of her students when she heard her mother was very ill. Carol in her early years would cry with her students, almost routinely. Lisa is frank about the range of emotions she displays with her students. "I display emotion from enthusiasm to anger...and I am very playful and I like to sing a lot and I joke around with my kids. I'm honest with them...they know when I'm mad."

Caring

A second emotion rule indicated by teachers is caring for the whole child. Caring simply about the academic progress of students is inadequate from the perspective of these teachers. Caring means that teachers establish relationships with parents, spend time with students outside the school, and engage in physical displays of caring such as hugging. According to Lisa, her sternness is tempered by her love for students,

> ...and they know I love them too because we have fun....They don't think that I don't like them because I am so involved in their lives; The first week (of school), I call their homes, let them know how they are doing....I give hugs everyday, before they leave they have to give me a hug and we play around a lot....If they think you don't like them, they won't care and they won't listen to you.

Pat echoed this idea, saying, "Kids need to know you care. They respond better to positive and negative reinforcement if it comes from someone who cares. Almost like you love them...I think for the minority kids, they need to feel like you love them."

Physical expressions of caring, like hugging, appeared to be consistent parts of emotion rules for teachers among these women. Pat and Leticia both worked with middle school and high school aged students, but they both insisted on the need to hug students, in spite of the risks of intimate physical contact with students. Leticia, who works with teens in an alternative school, said,

> I hug them. I don't think I could get away with this in the public schools....The hug that I give them, the hug I shouldn't be giving them, is the only one they're going to get that day. And I would be willing to risk someone writing me up for that. I don't care because that's what they need and that's why I am here....They're going to fire me for hugging a kid or they're going to let me do my job and watch this kid blossom.

Differential Treatment of Students Based on Race

I asked the teachers if they show emotions differently with white and African American students. There was consensus among the five teachers that the emotional display of teachers reflects, *in part*, the race of the students. With the exception of Lisa, the teachers agreed that African-American teachers, when compared to white teachers, will tend to be more honest with African-American students, more directive and "in your face," and more expressive when displaying emotions. Pat, Carol and Leticia said that with white students, they would be more reserved and more distanced in routine situations that entailed some kind of emotion display. Carol said that she will tend to be firmer and more "in your face" with African-American students, but she acknowledges that how she redirects white and black students also depends on the relationship she has with the parents.

> I'm known to be animated and so if I am upset with a student, I would be animated so they would not only see it in my words but see it in my movement. I use a lot of hand gestures and I might have closer eye contact and I might draw in closer and have a conversation in that way...and I might be a little more firm....but with a white student I might be a little softer, but firm...and it depends because I also base it on the relationship I have with the parents....

Leticia is afraid of offending white students who might be unfamiliar with certain African-American ways of talking. She said, "I am there...emotionally open and truer to them, my black kids, because I have a filter in my brain saying...not to offend or violate some cultural difference."

Pat also considers race along with other factors in shaping her emotional response to students. "But I can see where I am over the top for some of the kids and I have had to level it for my white kids because they don't fully pick up on the emotional cues...."

There appears to be some agreement, among the five teachers, that overt and loud displays of anger are inappropriate or ineffective, and students are more effectively redirected through calm and restrained emotion displays. The teachers all observed that African-American teachers will tend to engage in firm and "in your face" emotions with their African-American students (e.g., moving face closer to student's face; speaking with more tense and directive manner). These African-American teachers will tend to tone down or avoid overt anger displays with African-American students because of shared tacit knowledge about language, history, and norms for behavior. Instead of raising the voice in some anger display, African-American teachers use perhaps a combination of guilt and cajoling aimed at "racial uplift," to manage students' behavior or emotions.

Leticia described this idea of the "guilt trip." "Without saying word for word what is going on...with a black kid, I can say, 'you know better' and I can then walk away because they do know and I know they know." Both Leticia and Carol said they use the word, disappointed, when talking to African-American students, when redirecting some aberrant behavior. Carol said, "I will let them know if I am disappointed in them, my expectations are much higher...I will not tolerate."

Navigating Emotional Landscape

I asked teachers to discuss stressful experiences -- times they had experienced despair, depression, or anxiety. As we discussed this question, I followed up with a leading question that targets the intersection of oppression and emotions: "Do you

ever experience racism or sexism on the job? How does this effect you emotionally?" The five teachers all responded to this question without much hesitation,
and they all had much to say. Racism tended to dominate the responses, and comments about sexism were mentioned but not nearly as much as racism. When
responding to racist episodes, the three most common emotions they experienced
are irritation, anger and anxiety.

As the teachers related stories that contained negative emotions (irritation, anger
and anxiety), I asked them what they do to "deal with" or cope with these emotions.
They all mentioned strategies that were familiar to me as a white teacher and
researcher of white teacher emotions (e.g., deep breathing, exercise, talking to
friends, direct and honest talk, smoking cigarettes, pedagogic problem solving, crying,
eating, nothing, drinking tea, humor, hugging, reframing and prayer). I focus on
two strategies that appear to be unique to African-American women, at least this
group of African-American women: first, the use of race and their racial identity
and, second, prayer. The teachers tended to use these two strategies to reframe, or
redefine stressful situations, so their use of emotion enabled the construction of new
goals: that of freedom (their own) and that of racial progress (for society).

Use of racial identity

All five teachers indicated a sense of almost *chronic* anxiety that white colleagues
or white parents will describe them as ineffective, disorganized, or lackadaisical in
their work. Leticia said, "I've always had to work harder, so I don't think it goes
away. I am always aware of…what I'm wearing." Leticia mentioned the anxiety
when she hears from whites that African-American teachers work better with
African-American students, "that we will be considered only with black kids…like
we're not good teachers of students of other cultures. But I have the same
relationship with white students as I do with black students."

Carol mentioned the ongoing anxiety of the prospect of being perceived as incom-
petent, especially by white people: "Oh my goodness, absolutely and maybe more so
than most people…that is one thing that bothers me more than anything and I am
more cognizant of that than anything I could ever think of. And I'm the only person
of color on the faculty here…" Yolanda talked passionately of the ongoing anxiety
about having to prove one's self as an African American *and* a woman.

> I think you have to prove yourself being African American because you are coming to the
> classroom or coming to a setting prejudged and that's from the larger society…with the
> stereotypes….This is a professional setting with predominantly white people so you have
> to make sure that being a minority you live up to the best of your ability so you can get rid
> of those stereotypes because you know this is what people already think about my race or
> my culture or my people. I have to show the people I am working (effectively) so they can
> trust me in my position. I'm not like you think I am. I am not like the stereotypes….When
> you come into the classroom, students are not used to seeing African-American teachers
> and I know being a woman is different than being a man because even men have a cer-
> tain…dominance or authority in the classroom, whether black or white. So being a woman
> and being African American…you still have the majority race in the classroom who are

looking at you with these same stereotypes. Now, you have to prove to them, I know what I'm talking about. I know my subject and I am the right person for this job.

The teachers all indicated explicitly that they deal with on-going anxiety by simply working harder, being more organized, spending more time in the classroom than, perhaps they would have if they were white. Pat attributed her work ethic to her mother.

Lisa, who alluded to race much less frequently than the other four participants, has always worked in schools with predominantly African-American student populations and also with African-American colleagues. She indicated she gets angry when she thinks about the world that her African-American first graders must traverse.

Just not knowing what's going to happen to them after they leave my classroom as they grow up…is all they've learned going to dismissed, are they going to make it, are they going to be another statistic, in jail? Can they stay out of trouble or will they have a baby early…just thinking about the political system…?

Yolanda used the word, *irritated,* to describe her reaction to racial slights from her white high school students, particularly when they use racial stereotypes when talking to her.

I think what bothers me most are the racist comments of sarcasm where…because I am African-American, students think they could just say, "What's up, homey?" or "Yeah, right on, my brother or my sister?" These white students will just start talking to me in dialect.

Carol and Leticia both experienced similar racist slights from their colleagues, and, like Yolanda, they claimed to be more irritated than angry.

I've had staff say…oh…Carol, I need to ask you some questions, because you're street-wise…Well, I've never lived on the street! And everyone who knows me would laugh at that. And then they may have the nerve to say the topic they want to discuss is drugs because they need someone with expertise in drugs…which I would be the last person!

Leticia worries that her ability to use both African-American dialect and standard English may alienate her colleagues, who she has already observed to hold racist stereotypical views of language and what is expected of African-American speakers of English.

It is so irritating…associates from school, say, 'you speak so white.' How do you speak white? I speak proper English when I need to and I joke about being bilingual since there's a definite dialect I slip into when I go home. African-American teachers can slip into that dialect…and also be having a conversation that (white teachers) do not understand, and so then I worry that my co-workers might feel alienated like I'm trying to say something about them that I'm not…because I am trying to connect with the students.

Leticia becomes angry with her African-American students who do not take full advantage of their educational opportunities, and this anger derives from her understanding of African-American history and racism.

That's when my emotions get flared up because…what has always been a privilege for some kids was fought for by others groups of people and…they don't know the history, that's the frustration I feel. The anger comes from the history of being disrespected, all the effort that has come into even my being able to go to college. ...I'm trying to get these kids to understand, it used to be illegal to teach a black person to read in this country. You know, if you were caught writing, you got your hand chopped off....

Two ways that the teachers deflected racist slights or the pain of racism was to use these situations as teaching events or, in some cases, to ignore the racist incident and, in turn, attribute the incident to *ignorant* white people. Carol, for example, describes how she responded positively to a racist slight from a white elementary student.

I had students come up to me, and they say, I don't like people that look like you. At first, I didn't understand what they were saying, so they would point to my skin and I would say, ok, that's ok. You don't have to like me, but we're all going to respect each other while we are in our classroom and I said that we are going to absolutely like you and care for you while you are here.

Carol said she feels more pity for the racist than anger because "they are in some kind of inner turmoil...they're not at peace with themselves and that's why they're lashing out at other people...." Carol does confront racism in the workplace but not in a way that is going to "kill someone's spirit."

One of Lisa's African-American students, a first grader, looked at a high-quality of display of student work and surmised that it was probably done by white students. Lisa responded to this stereotype by confronting the boy directly (in a developmentally appropriate way). "I keep telling them (the African-American students) that they can do things that they think they can't. The can go to college, they can get good jobs, they can get good grades...they can do well in life."

Yolanda felt strongly about confronting racism as teaching opportunities.

I know there's stereotypes about African-American people that we talk a certain way, well that's not true. When that happens, I confront that person and everyone in the classroom and educate them that not every African-American talks that way....It's important that you take time out to educate students about culture because they don't know.

Pat described getting ignored at a workshop for teachers, which she believed was racially motivated. While she does get angry at times, it seems that she quickly reframes the anger by putting the onus for the event on the white antagonist. "I think... my first response is to be angry. It bugs me. But again, I say a little prayer, and that's their problem, not my problem....I have sort of brushed it off and keep going."

Prayer

Initially, I didn't ask the teachers directly if they used prayer, religion, or spirituality in their work. When I asked, how did they manage or cope with stress on the job, prayer was mentioned as a central strategy by four of the five individuals. One teacher, Pat, did refer to her relationship with god, praying for students and spirituality in general, but it was not as central to her professional identity as it was to the other four teachers.

The teachers believed teaching is a "gift" or calling from god (even Pat, although not to the extent of the others). All the teachers appeared to use aspects of their religious or spiritual faith in their everyday work: to deal with stress and also to inform or shape their work with students. Carol characterizes teaching as a gift, an outcome of her relationship with god. She believes this is typical of African-American teachers, saying,

> The calling…is one of the spiritual gifts. Everyone who becomes a believer, everyone is given a spiritual gift and they're supposed to use that gift. And there are all kinds of gifts and teaching is one of them. And you use this gift to impact people's lives…There hasn't been one African-American teacher who I've met who hasn't felt that way (about teaching as a calling). I don't always agree with how they perceive their calling, but there hasn't been anyone I have met who hasn't attached some spiritual piece to it.

Letitia also senses that her work with youth is a calling. When stressed out, she reminds herself, "…I feel god has directed me to do this. So there's not enough hours in the day to do my job here. And I pray about aspects of the job that I will never have the time to do…." Yolanda, in characterizing teaching as a god-given gift, referenced Romans 8.28 which says,

> 'All things work together for the good, for those who love the lord and are called to do things in his purpose,' what he wants you to do, if you're willing to do that, then he's going to take care of it. So he already lets you know, 'I'm going to work it out if you believe in me and if you are doing what I've gifted you to do.' I know that in being gifted to teach…I know whatever I need to get through the day, he's going to work it out for me.

All the teachers said they pray at school, for their students and for themselves. Lisa said, "I pray for my kids, here at the school. I ask for patience. I've asked god for wisdom, for what to do with this particular girl….I pray for staff and how I deal with gossip….As a Christian, I care for my students, what happens to them out of school, at home, their moms and dads." Letitia has a bible in her desk and also a book of daily meditations called prayers for the workplace. She also prays to help make sense of problems. "(When) one of my kids is struggling, I pray about it… what's the best way to help them…I don't have children so these are my children and I tell them, I will pray for you and also for myself so I don't say the wrong thing to you today."

Pat was raised as a Catholic but is currently non-practicing. When she prays, "I just say, help me through this situation, basically….Please help me do well with the kids. It's basically a conversation. I feel like I'm on a first name basis with god (she laughs) and we talk or I talk and he listens and responds accordingly." Pat believes that African-American teachers are more spiritual or religious than white teachers. Yolanda prays, regularly, to support her teaching. "Before each class, even if it's just wisdom to explain the lesson the best way I can, even it it's the night before for me to retain everything….If I have a difficult class or a difficult student, lord help me…deal with this student or help me deal with this class…so I use my faith all the time…to deal with all types of adversity."

When asked about coping strategies for stress, both Yolanda and Carol referred to a verse from Peter 5:7 that conceptualizes god as a force that can actually assume the stress or anxiety held by a believer. "Casting the whole of your care [*all your anxieties, all your worries, all your concerns, once and for all*] on Him, for He cares for you affectionately and cares about you watchfully."

God, here, is a divine presence in the lives of these teachers, a divine presence that may assume or "take on" the stress and anxiety off of these teachers' shoulders. I imagine these teachers using this verse to consciously and deliberately transfer their negative emotions onto god. My last interview was with Lisa, and I asked her about this verse. She knew it well and also used it in her prayers.

Discussion

While I am tentative about making generalizations about the emotions of African-American female teachers from just five interviews, it does appear that culture and race matter in how these five women do the work of emotions. It appears that the beliefs and stated actions of these women reflect aspects of Africanist epistemology of both Collins (1990) and DuBois (Franklin 1965). One dimension of Collins' African-American feminist epistemology is caring, and the deeply caring, almost loving, relationship with students, colleagues and parents was apparent in the interviews. A fictive-kin or matriarchal relationship between African-American female teachers and students has been researched by others (Foster 1995, 1997; Jeffries 1997). In this study and elsewhere, this caring is reflected in a discourse style that embraces the open display of emotions including much expressiveness and an animated style of interaction, physical touching, and teachers taking on a "mother" role for students during the school day.

DuBois' (Franklin 1965) notion of the "double consciousness" of African-Americans may enable African-Americans to perceive and understand issues of difference and in/exclusion differently than people in the dominant (white) racial group. Viewed as an asset or strength, the ability of people of color to more readily see multiple perspectives includes the "intuitive faculty enabling him/her to see and say things about American society that possessed heightened moral validity" (Lewis 1993, p. 281). In the present study, this heightened consciousness about race and differences may have influenced teachers to understand the importance of varying their emotional display based on the race of their students. One of the participants, Pat, was explicit when she articulated that effective African-American teachers are able or need to be able to code-switch *emotionally*. They are able to *read* situations and conversational partners and adjust their emotion response accordingly.

African-Americans have lived in the United States in a subordinated position in relation to white people, and in order to survive, it has been an imperative for them to study the thinking and behavior of the dominant racial group. African-Americans have a heightened understanding of difference, power and discrimination. This broader perspective, in part, has helped these African American women teachers problematize emotional experience beyond the psychological, which is the modal response of white teachers to emotional stress in the workplace. By being able to problematize emotional experience in a moral context of racism, inclusion/exclusion, and social justice, this understanding may help African-American teachers to use emotions as a site of political resistance on behalf of social justice (Reddy 2001; Zembylas 2005b).

The emotion management, or navigation, in which the teachers engaged tended to lead to emotional freedom (Reddy 2001; Yanay & Shahar, 1998; Zembylas 2005b), a situation where the teachers constructed their own goals in order guide their emotion work and the emotion rules that shaped this work. Much of the emotional stress in the lives of these professional women results from racism: from the angst of observing the self-destructive behavior of their African-American students, to the everyday racist slights and stereotypes directed at them from students and colleagues, and the anxiety felt from some amorphous expectation, usually coming from white people, that they are not "doing the job." When these teachers feel irritation, anxiety or anger stemming from perceived racism, they described situations in which they would instantiate goals for teaching that are aimed at racial progress and social justice. When Yolanda feels anger at students who direct racial stereotypes at her, she finds the motivation to respond to these racist slights as teaching events, to help her students understand the meaning and implications of racist language. Leticia's contextualizes her irritation with the poor work ethic of her African-American students by renewing her aim to help her students know African-American history and the potential of education in their lives. There is arguably a "rule" in the culture of teaching in the United States that discourages the explicit examination of racism and race history. Given their position as African-American teachers, these women are perhaps more prone to violate this rule.

The emotional suffering of the experience of African-American teachers, from the Jim Crow period to the current period, is indisputable, and it makes sense that *racial uplift* has been central in the vision of African-American teachers (e.g., Ladson-Billings 1994; Ross 2003). The teachers in the present study tend to respond to their own emotional stress of racism by working harder, by aiming to be exemplary role models for both white and African-American students, by helping students understand and change their racist behavior and by inspiring African-American students to use the system to their advantage. This racializing of emotional experience has, I believe, liberatory outcomes for these teachers. Still, the psychic burden on these teachers is enormous, to stay vigorated and motivated to do this kind of political work, since the *race work* of being African-American teachers is obviously total, everyday, all day, especially in typical public schools which will have some number of white students and teachers. Of course, I imagine there are many African-American teachers who eschew this political work, so I imagine they navigate the emotional landscape of racism differently than the teachers in this study.

Prayer also appears to be second core strategy utilized by these teachers to help navigate their way around and through emotional rules. The grounding of experience in spirituality or religion is part of west African and African-American tradition (Bacchus and Holley 2004; Mbiti 1970; Shorter-Gooden 2004; Weinberg 1970). African-American educator Lisa Delpit (Ladson-Billings 2005) suggests that the harsh conditions of racial oppression have given rise to the desire for spirituality, moving its practitioners outside rational thinking, as a heuristic to make sense of oppression but also to use religion as a vehicle to engage in liberatory practice.

> The ability to overcome when it seems impossible is regularly and readily attributable to
> some force beyond individual effort—for many Black people that force is God, for others
> it may be referred to as a 'spirit' or ancestors. Whatever they perceive to be the source of
> this higher power or strength, Black people throughout history have merged the sacred and
> the profane as the only ways to live mentally, emotionally, and psychically healthy lives.
> (Delpit, in Ladson-Billings 2005, p. 137).

When mired in the emotional turmoil of teaching, the five teachers all referenced instances where they used their own religious aspirations, or goals, which in turn shaped the emotional experience of teaching. In fact, most of the teachers indicated a belief that they were "gifted" by god to do the work of teaching, and this high level goal of doing god's work tended to help teachers reframe, reduce or circumvent debilitating emotions often felt in challenging teaching situations, like despair, depression and anger.

The teachers in this study feel that racism is an indisputable and on-going condition for all people in the United States (Delgado 1995), so the use of race to organize and shape their emotion work makes sense. In turn, prayer and religion in African-American traditions has its origins in the terrible suffering of slavery and Jim Crow Prayer, so the spiritual or religious practice of our five teachers, similarly, operates as a higher level goal that shapes their emotion work. In the tradition of their forebears among African-American teachers for whom racial uplift was central to the teaching mission, these five teachers work to merge the sacred and the material reality of teaching in an imperfect world. Whitfield and Klug (2008), drawing on American Indian tradition, call for teachers to be "healers" who "bring wholeness to the individual and shared insights to the community...." (16). Certainly, the African-American teachers in this study exemplified care for the whole child, care for themselves and their race whose emotions are shaped by the imperative to survive and heal their worlds.

Implications for Research and Teacher Education

The findings suggest that culture matters in understanding the emotions of teachers of color. Obviously, more research needs to be done with teachers who represent a wide range of cultures and races and across grade levels. Certainly, there is a need for teachers to tell their stories, in their own words. In the present study, my use of their words is truncated and disjointed, especially due to space limitations in this book. Ethnographies that make room for more sustained narratives by teachers would fulfill the goals of "storytelling" from a CRT perspective. I encourage white researchers to develop relationships with teachers of color and, taking care not to co-opt or *own* the stories of the teachers, support teachers of color in the writing of oral and written narratives about the emotional experience of teaching. For teacher educators now, engaging preservice teachers of color in conversations about race and emotion are recommended, including discussions of the use of race and religion to structure teachers' uses of emotion to achieve their goals for education. Teacher educators should work with their students to include the question of the intersection of religion and emotion work in teaching, at the same time taking care that this examination of students' religious orientations do not become overbearing or a micro-political threat to these or other students.

Appendix

Interview Questions

What are your rules for how you emote in the classroom?

Do you ever feel tension between how you are supposed to emote and how you actually feel? What do you do about this?

Do you ever feel angry or depressed or down in the dumps when teaching? What do you do to change this?

How do you see your role as teacher? What is your goal as teacher?

Do you ever experience racism or sexism on the job? How does this effect you emotionally? What do you about this emotion?

What role is there for religion or spirituality in your life, if any?

Do white teachers relate differently to black students and white students? Do you relate differently to white and black students?

Do you feel that you need to always be proving your competence, to your supervisors, colleagues and parents? If yes, what emotion do you have in response to this feeling?

What brings you satisfaction on the job? What motivates you?

Are you honest with your students about your emotions? Do you hide your emotions?

References

Armon-Jones C (1986) The social functions of emotions. In: Harre R (ed) The social construction of emotions. Blackwell, Oxford, pp 57–82

Ashforth RE (1993) Emotional labor in service roles: the influence of identity. Acad Manage Rev 18:88–115

Bacchus DN, Holley LC (2004) Spirituality as a coping resource: the experiences of Black professional women. J Ethnic Cultur Divers Soc Work 13:65–84

Barnes RD (1990) Race consciousness: the thematic content of racial distinctiveness in Critical Race scholarship. Harv Law Rev 103:1864–1871

Belenky MF, Clinchy BM, Goldberger NR, Mattuck J (1986) Women's ways of knowing. Basic Books, New York

Bell D (1980) *Brown v. Board of Education* and the interest convergence dilemma. Harv Law Rev 93:518–533

Bergerson AA (2003) Critical race theory and white racism: is there room for white scholars in fighting racism in education. Int J Qual Stud Educ 16:51–63

Boler M (1999) Feeling power: emotions and education. Routledge, New York

Campbell S (1994) Being dismissed: the politics of emotional experience. Hypatia 9:46–66

Collins P (1990) Black feminist thought. Unwin Hyman, Boston

Crenshaw K, Gotanda N, Peller G, Thomas K (eds) (1995) Critical race theory: the key writings. The New Press, New York

Delgado R (1989) Symposium: legal storytelling. Mich Law Rev 87:2073

Delgado R (1995) Legal storytelling: storytelling for oppositionists and others: a plea for narrative. In: Delgado R (ed) Critical Race Theory. Temple University Press, Philadelphia, pp 64–74

Delpit L (1995) Other people's children: cultural conflict in the classroom. The New Press, New York

El Nasser H (Feb 12, 2008) U.S. growth spurt seen by 2050. USA Today

Foster M (1995) African-American teachers and culturally relevant pedagogy. In: Banks JA, Banks CM (eds) Handbook of research on multicultural education. MacMillan Publishing USA, New York, pp 570–581

Foster M (1997) Black teachers on teaching. The New Press, New York

Franklin JH (1965) Three Negro classics. Avon Books, New York

Gerth HH, Mills CW (1953) Character and social structure: the psychology of social institutions. Harcourt, Brace, New York

Goffman E (1959) The presentation of self in everyday life. Doubleday, New York

Guy-Sheftall B (1993, April) Black feminist perspectives on the academy. Paper presented at the annual meeting of the American Educational Research Association, Atlanta, GA

Hargreaves A (1998) The emotional practice of teaching. Teach Teach Educ 14:835–854

Harrison BW (1985) Making the connections: essays in feminist social ethics. Beacon, Boston

Hochschild A (1983) The managed heart: commercialization of human feeling. University of California Press, Berkeley, CA

Jaggar A (1989) Love and knowledge: emotions and feminist epistemology. In: Jaggar A, Bordo S (eds) Gender/body/knowledge: feminist reconstructions of being and knowing. Rutgers University Press, New Brunswick, NJ, pp 145–171

Jeffries R (1997) Performance traditions among African-American teachers. Austin & Winfield, San Francisco

Kemper TD (1978) A social interactional theory of emotions. Wiley, New York

Ladson-Billings G (1991) Returning to the source: implications for educating teachers of Black students. In: Foster M (ed) Readings on equal education: qualitative investigations into schools and schooling, vol 11. AMS Press, New York, pp 227–244

Ladson-Billings G (1994) The dreamkeepers: successful teachers of African American children. Jossey-Bass, San Francisco

Ladson-Billings G (1999) Just what is Critical Race Theory, and what's it doing in a nice field like education. In: Parker L, Deyhle D, Villenas S (eds) Race is – race isn't: Critical Race Theory and qualitative studies in education. Westview Press, Boulder, CO, pp 7–30

Ladson-Billings G (2000) Racialized discourses and ethnic epistemologies. In: Denzin NK, Lincoln YS (eds) Handbook of qualitative research, 2nd edn. Sage, Thousand Oaks, CA, pp 257–278

Ladson-Billings G (2001) Crossing over to Canaan: the journey of new teachers in diverse classrooms. Josey-Bass, San Francisco

Ladson-Billings G (2005) Beyond the big house: African American educators on teacher education. Teachers College, New York

Lazarus RS (1991) Emotion and adaptation. Oxford University Press, New York

Lewis DL (1993) W. E. B. DuBois: biography of a race 1868–1919. Henry Holt, New York

Lincoln YS, Guba EG (1985) Naturalistic inquiry. Sage, Beverly Hills, CA

Mbiti JS (1970) African religions and philosophy. Praeger, New York

Nias J (1996) Thinking about feeling: the emotions in teaching. Cambridge J Educ 26(3):293–306

Reddy WM (2001) The navigation of feeling: a framework for the history of emotions. Cambridge University Press, Cambridge, UK

Ross R (2003) Witnessing and testifying: black women, religion and civil rights. Fortress Press, Minneapolis

Sarbin TR (1986) Emotion acts: roles and rhetoric. In: Harre R (ed) The social construction of emotions. Basil Blackwell, Oxford, pp 83–97

Schutz PA, Pekrun R (2007) Emotion in education. Elsevier, Amsterdam

Shorter-Gooden K (2004) Multiple resistance strategies: how African-American women cope with racism and sexism. J Black Psychol 30:406–425

Sleeter C (1994) White racism. Multicultural Educ 1(4):5–8

Strauss A, Corbin J (1998) Basics of qualitative research. Sage, Thousand Oaks, CA

Sutton RE, Wheatley KF (2003) Teachers' emotions and teaching: a review of the literature and directions for future research. Educ Psychol Rev 15:327–358

Thoits PA (1990) Emotional development: research agendas. In: Kemper T (ed) Research agendas in the sociology of emotions. SUNY Press, Albany, NY, pp 180–203

Tolich MB (1993) Alienating and liberating emotions at work: supermarket clerks' performance of customer service. J Contemp Ethnogr 22:361–381

U.S. Department of Education (2003) Overview of public elementary and secondary schools and districts: school year 2001–02: statistical analysis report. NCES 2003-411.

Weinberg M (1970) W. E. B. DuBois: a reader. Harper & Row, New York

Whitfield PT, Klug BJ (2008) Teachers as 'healers'? Multicultural Perspect 6(1):43–50

Wilder M (2000) Increasing African-American teachers' presence in American schools: voices of students who care. Urban Educ 35:205–221

Winograd K (2003) The functions of teacher emotions: the good, the bad and the ugly. Teach Coll Record 105:1641–1673

Winograd K (2005) Good day, bad day: teaching as a high wire act. Scarecrow Education, Landham, MD

Yanay N, Shahar G (1998a) Professional feelings as emotional labor. J Contemp Ethnogr 27:346–374

Yanay N, Shahar G (1998b) Professional feelings as emotional labor. J Contemp Ethnogr 27:346–374

Zembylas M (2005a) Teaching with emotion: a postmodern enactment. Information Age Publishing, Greenwich, CT

Zembylas M (2005b) Beyond teacher cognition and teacher beliefs: the value of ethnography of emotions in teaching. Int J Qual Stud Educ 18:465–487

Chapter 16
The Emotionality of Women Professors of Color in Engineering: A Critical Race Theory and Critical Race Feminism Perspective[*]

Jessica T. DeCuir-Gunby, Linda A. Long-Mitchell, and Christine Grant

Abstract In this chapter we suggest that although the number of African American and Latina professors of engineering has increased in the last decade, engineering faculty and engineering student populations remain grossly overrepresented by White men. Because of this, African American and Latina women professors often experience unique difficulties that stem from their race, gender, and the intersection of their race and gender. The purpose of this chapter is to use a Critical Race Theory (CRT) and Critical Race Feminism (CRF) framework to explore the emotions associated with being underrepresented women professors of color in engineering. In doing so, the authors focus on CRT's tenet of Whiteness as Property, particularly the elements of the right of use and enjoyment and the right to exclude. Also, we utilize intersectionality theory from CRF to examine the interaction of race and gender in the experiences of the participants (Crenshaw, 1989). Our analysis concentrates on the emotions involved in interacting with faculty and students. Finally, we discuss strategies for coping with race and gender-related stress in academia.

Keywords Critical race theory · Women in science · Emotionality

Women of color[1] are cognizant of both their racial and gender identities. There are experiences that are unique to being people of color; likewise there are experiences unique to being women. However, there are many experiences that combine race

J.T. DeCuir-Gunby (✉)
Department of Curriculum & Instruction, North Carolina State University, Raleigh, NC, USA
e-mail: jessica_decuir@ncsu.edu

[*]This material is based upon work supported by the National Science Foundation under Grant No. 0545269. Any opinions, findings, and conclusions or recommendations expressed in this paper are those of the authors and do not necessarily reflect the views of the National Science Foundation.

[1]The terms "women of color" and "people of color" refer to underrepresented minority groups including African Americans, Latinos, and Native Americans. Asians are not included because they are overrepresented in engineering.

P.A. Schutz and M. Zembylas (eds.), *Advances in Teacher Emotion Research:*
The Impact on Teachers' Lives,
DOI 10.1007/978-1-4419-0564-2_16, © Springer Science+Business Media, LLC 2009

and gender. Thus, women of color must view their experiences from the perspective of being both people of color and women. This is particularly true in academia. It is not uncommon to be the only African American or Latina[2] and/or the only woman in an academic program and/or department. Since women of color are often the "only ones", they are in the precarious positions of negotiating both race and gender.

The purpose of this chapter is three fold: (1) to explore the racist experiences of women professors of color in engineering; (2) to examine how these experiences impact their identities; and (3) to discuss the emotions and coping strategies associated with these experiences. The discipline of engineering is a particularly relevant context in that women of color are more grossly underrepresented in this area than most other technological and scientific fields (Nelson 2007). We begin the chapter by discussing relevant literature regarding race and gender demographics in engineering, identity and engineering, and emotions, emotional labor and coping. Next, we describe the foundations of our analytical lens including critical race theory, focusing specifically on whiteness as property as well as critical race feminism's intersectionality theory. We then present findings through the telling of the women professors' counterstories. Lastly, we provide a general discussion of the study and offer implications to help women professors of color cope with the unpleasant emotions they experience in the engineering profession.

Race and Gender Demographics in Engineering

Professors of color are grossly underrepresented in engineering. Studies show that people of color, regardless of their gender, are less likely to be represented as faculty members as well as instructors in engineering with people of color making up only 5.6% of chemical engineering, 6.6% of civil engineering, 3.6% of electrical engineering, and 4.3% of mechanical engineering faculty, while White men make up 67.5% of chemical engineering, 66.2% of civil engineering, 62.2% of electrical engineering, and 63.7% of mechanical engineering faculty in "top 50"[3] schools in the United States (Nelson 2007). In addition, faculty of color are less likely than White faculty to be tenured in engineering. For instance, only 4.7% of chemical engineering, 4.4% of civil engineering, 3.0% of electrical engineering, and 2.8% of mechanical engineering faculty of color are tenured, full professors (Nelson 2007).

Although people of color are underrepresented in engineering, there are increasing numbers of women faculty members in engineering. For instance, from 2001 to 2006, the number of women science and engineering faculty increased 33 % at the University of Michigan (University of Michigan Advance Program 2007). Although the numbers are increasing in many institutions such as the University of Michigan,

---

[2] African American and Black are used interchangeably as well as Latina(o) and Hispanic.

[3] A "top 50" ranking is based upon research expenditures as determined by the National Science Foundation.

there are still too few women teaching in engineering as compared to the number of men faculty members, regardless of rank. Also, women represent only one-fifth of undergraduate and graduate students in engineering and earn only 15% of doctorates awarded in engineering (National Academy of Sciences, National Academy of Engineering, and Institute of Medicine, 2007). In addition, once women obtain faculty positions in engineering, they are less likely to be tenured full professors than men (National Research Council 2006). Women on average only hold between 3 to 15% of full tenured professorships in science and engineering in "top 50" schools (Young 2004).

Just as people of color and women in general are underrepresented in engineering, studies show that women of color are even more underrepresented in science and engineering schools. According to a report by Mannix (2002), only 2.1 % of African American and 2.9 % of Hispanic women are tenure track or tenured professors in engineering schools. Nelson (2007) found that in the "top 50" universities, women of color are extremely underrepresented. They found only 22 African American, 24 Hispanic, and 1 Native American women faculty members in "top 50" engineering departments (chemical, civil, electrical, and mechanical) in the United States. In addition, studies show that women professors of color in engineering are less frequently awarded tenure and are full professors than other groups. More specifically, White women and men of all racial groups are much more likely to be full professors and to be awarded tenure than Black and Hispanic women professors (Nelson 2003). In fact, Mannix (2002) found that only 1.3% of Black women have been awarded the rank of full professor while only 2.2% of Hispanic women are ranked at full professor in engineering.

Racist and Sexist Experiences of Women Faculty of Color

The under-representation of women of color who teach in engineering schools has an impact on their experiences as faculty members. Nelson and Rogers (2004) reported that the low representation of women professors of color in engineering disciplines exacerbates a learning and work environment that feels alienating and unfair to women faculty of color. It is well-know that women encounter prejudiced attitudes and sexist treatment across a wide variety of contexts (Kaiser and Miller 2004; Swim, Cohen & Hyers, 1998). Sexism is a victimizing experience that severely limits the options of women and can serve as an obstacle to their career success (Jegelian, 1976). Gender harassment is a commonplace workplace stressor that warrants serious attention (Piotrkowski 1998). This may particularly be applicable to women who work in the male-dominated profession of engineering. Ranson (2005) who studied women in engineering in the work environment reported that many of them encountered overt sexism at work. In addition, in a study that explored the climate factors in the academic work environment of science and engineering faculty, findings indicated that women faculty of color reported overhearing disparaging comments about women and people of color. Members of the faculty also reported observing gender, racial-ethnic discrimination, and uninvited sexual attention. In addition, women faculty of color reported experiencing relatively high rates of racial and ethnic discrimination (UM Advance, 2007). Similarly, Jackson (2004) found that women and faculty of color described themselves as discouraged, less supported, and think that the tenure process is less fair compared to their White male colleagues' social experiences.

The research literature does explore several reasons for women of color's under-representation as engineering faculty (Vargas 2002). Women of color are less likely to go into and remain in engineering when they lack mentors and role models (Aquirre 2000). When women professors of color are not hired, treated fairly and retained, women students of color perceive that they will be treated similarly (National Research Council 2006). For example, it is well documented that women faculty receive lower salaries than their male counterparts; even when you speak to women of color in departments that are relatively diverse, many of them are not happy, report a lack of promotion and recognition, as well as complain of lower pay than men (National Research Council 2006). Women students who might aspire to pursue their studies in engineering and even become faculty who teach in the discipline may feel discouraged about making this their career choice due to the lack of women faculty available to them as role models/mentors and based on their observations of how their role models/mentors are treated (National Academy of Sciences, et al., 2007). The shortage of recruitment efforts that students and other faculty observe in engineering departments may send a clear message that having an ethnically and sexually diverse faculty is not a priority. The lack of presence of women of color and their recruitment at universities has contributed to a poor work atmosphere and experience for those that are faculty members (Young 2004). The perception that women professors of color are not treated fairly and equally influences women students of color's decision to leave engineering (Nelson and Rogers 2004). Women engineering professors of color may arrive at the difficult decision to leave the field based on how these challenging experiences impact how they view themselves. Ultimately, all of the issues associated with the underrepresentation of women of color in engineering impacts their identities as people of color, women, and as engineering professors.

Identity as Engineers

Because of the underrepresentation of women of color in engineering, the racial and gender identities of women faculty of color in engineering are salient. Within the workplace, their gender and racial identity intersects with career (Chinn 1999). This intersection of identities impacts their experiences, particularly since the culture of the engineering profession is associated with a White, masculine identity. Robinson and McIlwee (1991) asserted that the work environment of engineers and engineering professors dictates patterns of thought and behavior that make it difficult for women to be integrated professionally. From the perspective of gender and work, women engineers are a small and unique group of women who are attracted to and selected into engineering (Ronen and Ronen 2008). Therefore, women in engineering are required to possess some resilience to sustain themselves and achieve success in the profession. Chinn (1999) reported that the resilient professional identities of the women engineers in her study were formed early on in their socialization processes. The identities of these women were found to be constructed primarily from their families. This early protective agent appeared to reinforce their resilient behaviors in the male-dominated, competitive profession of engineering. Chinn (1999) also reported that women engineers of color in her study were willing to adapt to more aggressive behaviors to succeed in a male-dominated, competitive environment. It has also been found that women engineers of color often avoid showing weakness by maintaining physical activity and fitness as signs of competence, wearing loose-fitting clothes, simple hairstyles, minimal makeup to show signs of competence, seriousness, and male solidarity (Arthur 1993). These practices help them to send clear messages that they are serious engineers. In addition, having to engage in these practices often create occupational stress for women faculty of color (Smith and Witt 1993). As such, women faculty of color have to effectively cope with the unpleasant emotions associated with race-related stress in the workplace.

Emotions, Emotional Labor, and Coping

Because of the difficulties they face within the workplace, women faculty of color in engineering often experience unpleasant emotions, which often result in increased emotional labor. Emotional labor is the effort used in trying to change emotions or feelings (Hochschild 1983). According to Hochschild (1979), emotional labor involves addressing three types of emotions: cognitive emotions (changing ideas, feelings, and associated ideas), bodily emotions (changing physical symptoms of emotions such as sweating), and expressive emotions (changing facial gestures). For all professors, there is emotional labor in research, teaching and committee work. However, being a woman of color in engineering involves employing more emotional labor in that they are expected to hide emotions that are a result of issues with both race and gender (Bellas 1999). This places women of color in an emotional double bind, forcing them to learn how to cope with the unpleasant emotions they experience (Erickson and Ritter 2001).

One way of coping with unpleasant emotions is that women of color tend to engage in escapist coping strategies as solutions to their stressful experiences (Folkman and Moskowitz 2004). For instance, many women of color avoid careers in which they anticipate experiences of racism and sexism (Evans and Herr 1991). This may explain why most Black and Hispanic women gravitate to careers traditionally dominated by women and those that give them minimum exposure to racial and gender discrimination. According to Kaiser and Miller (2004), when individuals are insufficiently prepared to cope with events appraised as harmful or unable to secure potential gains, they frequently avoid or disengage from the situation. Women of color often cope with unpleasant emotions associated with discrimination they experience by withdrawing emotionally and avoiding specific situations. This contributes gravely to the underrepresentation of African American and Hispanic female faculty in engineering.

Another way of coping with unpleasant emotions is that women of color often engage in problem-focused coping strategies (Folkman and Moskowitz 2004). The use of problem-focused coping strategies is a more positive way of dealing with unpleasant emotions. Specifically, women of color often utilize three coping resources: psychological resources (e.g., optimism, resilience, etc), sociofamilial resources (e.g. family, friends, etc), and cultural resources (e.g. racial pride, religion, etc) (Utsey, Giesbrecht, Hook, & Stanard, 2008). Utilizing natural support systems in coping with challenging life experiences is a strength of people of color. In particular, African American and Hispanic professional women are more likely to utilize cultural resources such as praying and meditating (Bacchus and Holley 2004) and sociofamilial resources including support from families and friends (González-Morales, 2006). Psychological, cultural, and sociological resources appear to provide these professional women safe options for dealing with the difficulties they face professionally daily. These important resources provide women professors of color an essential outlet for coping with the very real emotions they experience associated with being discriminated against in their work environments.

As discussed, women of color are underrepresented in the various disciplines of engineering. In addition, they often experience racism and sexism within the academic workplace, causing an increase in unpleasant emotions (Bellas 1999). Because of the prevalence of racism and sexism particularly in engineering, it is imperative to take race and gender into consideration when discussing the experiences of women faculty of color in engineering. Critical Race Theory (CRT) and Critical Race Feminism (CRF) provide useful lenses for such a discussion.

A Critical Race Theory and Feminism Perspective

Critical Race Theory (CRT) emerged in the 1970's as a response to the US legal system's slow and sometimes nonexistent approach to addressing legal issues concerning race and racism (see Delgado and Stefancic 2001). CRT examines the interrelationship of race, racism and power. The goal of CRT is to help challenge and eventually help eradicate the legal manifestations of racism and White privilege. As described by DeCuir and Dixson (2004), CRT involves 5 tenets: (a) Permanence of Racism (Bell 1992); Whiteness as Property (Harris 1993); (c) Interest Convergence (Bell 1980); (d) Critique of Liberalism (Gotanda 1991); and (e) Counterstorytelling (Delgado 1989). The *permanence of racism* examines how racism remains an enduring component of all aspects of society; *whiteness as property* explicates the power and privilege associated with Whiteness; *interest convergence* explores how the advancement of people of color is accommodated only when Whites can benefit; the *critique of liberalism* discusses race consciousness (e.g. the notion of colorblindness) and the systematically slow progress in reaching racial equality; and counterstorytelling is a means of allowing the voices of marginalized to be heard rather than silenced. (For a more in-depth discussion of the tenets of CRT, see DeCuir and Dixson 2004). Because of the unique experiences of women of color in engineering as well as the Whiteness of the field of engineering, this chapter uses counterstorytelling to explore the tenet of Whiteness as property in the stories of women faculty of color in engineering. Counterstorytelling is used because it allows for the challenging of the normal discourse in engineering, that of White men. Likewise, Whiteness as property is a useful perspective in that highlights the power inherent in Whiteness and the homogeneity of engineering.

Counterstorytelling

Counterstorytelling is an essential component of CRT. Counterstories can be defined as "stories of those individuals and groups whose knowledges and histories have been marginalized, excluded, subjugated or forgotten in the telling of official narratives" (Peters & Lankshear, 1996, p. 2). It is a method in that it involves allowing participants to tell their own stories. Specifically, counterstorytelling challenges the majority discourse and reality by allowing the unheard voices of the marginalized to be heard and for others to relate to those stories (Delgado 1989; Solórzano, and Yosso 2002).

Counterstorytelling allows marginalized groups to provide an alternate vision and helps the majority to question their social reality. In addition, counterstorytelling provides the majority a means of learning how to see and understand the perspectives of others and thereby challenges the majority's ethnocentric view (Delgado 1989). For example, since the election of Barack Obama to the United States presidency, there has been much commentary on the state of racism in the US. The majority story explains that by electing the son of White mother and African, Muslim father, during a time of great economic troubles, demonstrates that race is not an issue in US politics. However, the counterstory explains how electing one African American as US president does not erase the fact that Obama was the first African American to be a major party nominee. Nor does it eradicate the extreme underrepresentation of African Americans in the US Senate, House of Representatives, gubernatorial offices, mayoral offices, and countless other political positions. This chapter uses counterstorytelling in a similar way to allow the voices of women of color in engineering to be heard and simultaneously challenge the dominant discourse in engineering.

Whiteness as Property

Whiteness as property describes how White racial identity or Whiteness has value and can be discussed in the same manner as property (see Harris 1993). Whiteness shares the same rights of property including possession, use, and disposition. These rights include transferability rights, the right to use and enjoyment, reputation rights, and the right to exclude others. *Transferability* suggests that Whiteness is passed on from one generation to another; the *right to use and enjoyment* refers to the maintenance of White identity and the associated privilege; *reputation* rights highlights the salience of White identity and its need of protection; and *the right to exclude* describes how White identity is accompanied by a sense of entitlement, including the right to include and exclude others (For a more detailed description of Whiteness as Property in terms of racial identity development, see DeCuir-Gunby 2006).

Although CRT is a useful tool in exploring the experiences of people of color, CRT focuses almost exclusively on issues involving race. CRT does not make other issues such as gender central to understanding the experiences of people of color. Critical Race Feminism (CRF) (Wing 2003) emphasizes the importance of understanding that both race and gender are essential to the identities of women of color. Intersectionality theory, an aspect of CRF, is a particularly useful theoretical lens to help analyze the experiences of women of color.

Critical Race Feminism

Critical Race Feminism is a perspective that grew out of Critical Legal Studies (CLS), CRT, and feminist theory during the 1990's (Wing 2003). CLS challenges the objectivity of the law and its use to oppress the powerless; CRT specifically questions racism and power in the law; and feminist theory examines the unfair treatment of women. CRF combines these approaches, creating a movement to challenge unfair legal practices in terms of the combination of race and gender. A basic component of CRF is intersectionality theory. Intersectionality theory, also referred to as multiplicative identity, suggests that women of color are often not included in discussions of racial or gender legal issues (Crenshaw 1989). Instead, issues of racism are most often seen as issues impacting African American men while issues of sexism are seen as issues impacting White women. Women of color are not fully represented in that they are both people of color and women. They are often forced to choose between race and gender in that most legal problems are addressed using race-based or gender-based approaches. Thus, intersectionality theory examines how racial identity intersects with gender identity (Carbado and Gulati 2001). Specifically, intersectionality theory challenges the idea that women of color are "white women plus color" and suggests that their "identities must be multiplied together to create a holistic One when analyzing the nature of the discrimination against them" (Wing 2003, p. 7).

As Crenshaw (1989) explains when discussing women of color, "single issue analyses" of only race or gender are problematic. The experiences of women of color must include the intersection of race and gender as well as the multiplicative nature of their identity. Intersectionality is useful to help analyze the manner in which race and gender intertwine. This aspect of CRF is used in this chapter to analyze the participants' unique experiences as being both people of color and women, how their multiple identities are shaped within engineering, and the impact of these issues on their experiencing of unpleasant emotions and coping.

A CRT and CRF Analysis

Context/Participants

Sampling for the study was purposive in that study participants[4] included women faculty members of color that attended the first of a series of summits in July 2007 on mentoring women of color in engineering. The goal of the summit was to obtain women faculty members' perspectives on the best practices for the recruitment, retention and promotion for women of color in engineering as well as provide information on the mentoring of women of color in engineering. The participants in this study included 11 women engineering professors of color (7 African American and 4 Hispanic/Latina/Latin) from various universities across the country (see Table 16.1). They were from a range of disciplines (five electrical, three mechanical, and three civil/environmental engineering) and held a variety of academic ranks (six assistant, two associate, and three full professors).

Table 16.1 Participants

Name	Race/ethnicity	Faculty rank	Discipline
Dr. Keisha Benson	African American	Full Professor	Electrical engineering
Dr. Rochelle Collins	African American	Full Professor	Mechanical engineering
Dr. Jennifer Plummer	African American	Full Professor	Mechanical engineering
Dr. Alexandra Chappelle	African American	Associate Professor	Civil/Environmental engineering
Dr. Maria Valenzuela	Hispanic/Latina	Associate Professor	Mechanical Engineering
Dr. Cheryl Brown	African American	Assistant Professor	Electrical engineering
Dr. Consuela Ward	Latin	Assistant Professor	Civil engineering
Dr. Jasmine Davenport	African American	Assistant Professor	Electrical engineering
Dr. Catalina Núñez	Hispanic/Latina	Assistant Professor	Civil engineering
Dr. Ramona Fernandez	Hispanic/Latina	Assistant Professor	Electrical engineering
Dr. Valerie Jenkins	African American	Assistant Professor	Electrical engineering

Note. Race/ethnicity is listed as described by each participant.

---

[4] All of the names used in this chapter are pseudonyms.

Data Collection Procedures

The participants in this study were solicited from the aforementioned summit. During the summit, the researchers asked for volunteers to share their experiences as women professors of color in engineering. The 11 participants agreed to be interviewed. One-to-two hour personal interviews (Rubin and Rubin 2005) were conducted with each participant via telephone during fall 2007. Semi-structured interview schedules were used for the personal interviews in order to capture the experiences of the participants (Rubin and Babbie 2007). All interviews were audio-taped and later transcribed for analyses. Follow-up interviews are to be collected after the final summit, which is to be held during summer 2009. These future interviews will address successes that the participants have had as professors as well as the pleasant emotions that are associated with such experiences.

Data Analysis Procedures

After the interviews were transcribed, they were imported into ATLAS.ti 5.0 software program. ATLAS.ti 5.0 allows for the organizing and coding of text data. After coding, we then used thematic content analysis to analyze the interviews (Coffey and Atkinson 1996). Thematic content analysis is the process of determining the "categories, relationships, and assumptions that inform the study participants' view of the world" (McCracken 1988, p. 42). These categories, relationships, and assumptions are determined through the process of inductive coding. In coding the data, we used a three-step process: identifying, organizing, and interrelating themes. First, we identified patterned regularities or significant themes that appeared across all participants' stories (Wolcott 1994). Next, we organized themes according to frequency. Last, the various themes were connected and contexualized to the broader research literature. This three-step process allowed for the emergence of three major themes: (1) *Racist and sexist interactions with engineering colleagues*; (2) *Racial and gender prejudice in teaching in the engineering classroom; and* (3) *Coping with racism and sexism.* We used the query tool of ATLAS.ti 5.0 to provide quotations for each of the themes. Multiple coders were used to code the data in order to establish consistency in the interpretation of data (Golafshani 2003).

Exploring the Counterstories of Women Professors of Color in Engineering

The first theme that emerged from the data concerns relationships and interactions with engineering colleagues. Many of the participants described the difficulties they experienced with their colleagues that were based upon race and gender.

These difficulties often negatively impacted their academic experiences and career development. These experiences included devaluing their ability as well as unfairly distributing resources.

Being the only one or one of the few women of color faculty members often means being asked to serve on working committees. Although women of color agree to participate in order to share their perspectives, they often find that their presence is cosmetic and they are not seen as being able to contribute or add substantive value. They are victims of tokenism in that they are forced to engage in activities that reinforce their minority status and are seen as minority-oriented practices (Aguirre, 2000). For instance, when serving on committees such as faculty hiring committees, white men asserting their power and right to exclude based upon race and gender, often silenced their voices. Serving in such functions requires expending additional emotional labor. Dr. Consuela Ward, a Latin assistant professor of civil engineering and the only woman in her department, described her experience on a faculty search committee and how such experiences are "emotionally draining":

> [It] was an awful experience, too. I was the chair of the committee only in name. The other members, especially the department chair, had really control over the whole situation. And…a lot of the time – and this is also another example of the part that I had to fight. Some of the things that he wanted me to do, I really didn't agree. I really didn't think that was the right thing to do as far as that committee, and how – you know…everything was conducted…And the one comment that he made during that whole hiring process that was terrible – he asked me, he's like, 'Well, do we need to worry about Affirmative Action?' And I said, 'Yes. Yes, I'm taking all of this into account.' And he said, 'Well, we really don't need to worry too much about hiring a woman. Because we're already above our quota.'…. It was really, really hard. At the time I was very – I was speechless. I did not expect that…And I'm the one with experience in the field, and all of that. And emotionally it's just…it's draining.

Although they were often asked to be on search committees, their opinions were not always appreciated. Despite having vast experiences that added great depth to search committees, they were often ignored. This was frustrating for the women in that they knew that their perspectives were not valued. They were only seen in terms of race and gender, particularly in being able to satisfy requirements set by their respective schools' policies on diverse search committees. Dr. Maria Valenzuela, a Latina associate professor of mechanical engineering explained,

> you always have to have a minority [on a]…hiring committee. And I'm a two-fer. So many of my colleagues are like, 'Please, Maria. Please. Just be in the short hiring committee for us. Because there's three white guys, and we need you.' It's like, okay, because then they can check two boxes. They have a minority and a woman.

In addition to their perspectives not being valued, the women were not always provided with the tools they needed to be successful as an engineering professor. When first joining the faculty at her university, Dr. Valerie Jenkins, an African American assistant professor of electrical engineering was promised lab space but did not receive it until a year later. Lab space is essential to the academic success of engineering faculty. The more lab space an engineering professor has, the more equipment can be stored, the more graduate students she can support, and the more research she can potentially produce. Not having adequate lab space can greatly hinder a professor's progress, especially a beginning professor. Also, not having lab space presented additional emotional labor. Valerie felt that she was differentially treated because she was African American and a woman. Although she knew that she had the right to have lab space, she felt "afraid" to speak up and felt voiceless. She explicated:

> I was promised lab space, but was not given it until a year later...I felt like that would not have happened to a white male faculty. I mean, well, with all the people that came in my same year, not – no one else had the same issues with having a lab space – of lab space that I had...Your first year of coming in, you're trying to really – you know, establish good rapport with people. And I felt like I didn't press the issue because I was afraid of appearing to be argumentative....I mean, it really did. It also – you know, it creates – it created an environment where I really felt always behind my other colleagues....they didn't make a big rush about getting me lab space, because probably they didn't have expectation that I would do that much here anyway. You know, that's the way I interpret it...I think that's where the subtle hints of discrimination come in, when people have low expectations of you. So they don't try to hinder your progress. But you know, you're ignored... I always have that in the back of my mind. I always feel a year behind my other colleagues because of that.

The second major theme that emerged from the data was the interactions with students. All of the women described negative confrontations with engineering students in the classroom. Because the majority of engineering students are white men, the women perceived that the difficulties were based upon differences in race and gender. The women felt that their students were overly antagonistic. Many of these students questioned the authority and knowledge of the women as engineering professors. These difficult interactions often elicited unpleasant emotions from the women.

Many students questioned the women's authenticity as "real engineers" and their identity as teachers of engineering. Dr. Alexandra Chappelle, an African American associate professor in civil/environmental engineering described how many of the White men in her classes negatively viewed her background as an environmental engineer. She explained how she was often insulted by such students' prejudicial attitudes:

> Civil engineering, I like to refer to as the last bastion of white maleness...So the fact that I was teaching environmental engineering, which they [the students] saw as...soft, which in engineering is just the ultimate insult... And so a lot of times – you know, when they realized I wasn't a civil engineer, in their mind that translated to – she's not an engineer. And so I think that, coupled with the fact that I was black and I was female – you know, wasn't – they weren't really interested in that.

In addition to questioning their credentials as engineers, all of the participants discussed how their students, mostly White men, would question their teaching, both privately (e.g. in their offices) and publicly (e.g. in front of the class while teaching). Dr. Cheryl Brown, an African American assistant professor in electrical engineering, stated that she was often "irritated" and "bristled" by the comments that her white men students often made regarding her teaching strategies and knowledge of engineering. She described a common exchange she has had with white male students:

> But it was the way they came at me with – the arrogance. That's what kind of – it bristled a little bit. You know. That the way they come at you with… 'Well, I know you're only here for this quota. But must you teach like that? I don't think its right.' You know, it was kind of condescending. That kind of – that kind of irritated me just a wee bit. I actually had students who would… I had one young man. And he would walk up to me after class. And he would say, 'Well, Dr. Brown, I think your lecture went okay today. I would tell you that you need to work a little bit more on the way you pose questions. Maybe do a few min – more in-class activities. But the topic you taught on today was okay. But maybe we need more power. You need to do a little bit more work on your lecture.' He would do this almost every day. He would come up and critique my lecture. Really sarcastic, I was like 'Well, you know what? Thanks for the feedback. You have a great day, okay?'

While all of the women experienced negative exchanges with White men in the classroom, it was often difficult to separate negative feelings regarding a particular student and an entire class/course. Difficulty with particular students would often poison the women's feelings towards a particular class and/or course. Dr. Catalina Núñez, a Latina assistant professor in civil engineering explained how this happened to her. She stated:

> I think there is a prejudice around women. And around – about…Hispanic people…. So this is sometimes difficult because at the beginning, when they start going to a class, maybe they are unsure if you are capable….to teach the subject that you are assigned…There was a particular student who was in the mood of always, like, questioning and…and…like, disrespectful questions…It was very difficult for me to – to stay in class…The relationship with the class, I think it was very difficult to me. The rest of the semester I was…like, not very well motivated with this class.

Although the women all experienced racist and sexist interactions with students in the classroom, these negative interactions did not stop once the course ended. Through end of course evaluations, many students would still find ways to challenge the women's identities as engineering professors, by questioning their knowledge, credentials, and authority. Through the use of course evaluations, their criticisms were immortalized on paper. Dr. Rochelle Collins, an African American full professor in mechanical engineering discussed how she was angered regarding the racial comments that students made but also angered at the fact that her White colleagues, particularly White men, did not have to deal with such issues. She explained:

> I remember at least two racially motivated…student comments on evaluations over the years. Two or three. So – okay. And it's fractionalized, that's not bad. But let's face it. My [White] colleagues don't have to deal with that. So – so it angers you…Well, you're… you're angry mostly because…why do you need to be dealing with this?...But you know, what ignorance. And to even have to deal with this, and then not be able to…not really able to deal with it, right?...All you can do is read it. But you're not actually able to address it. Because you're – you're not sure who that came from…And so there's nothing you can do to correct it.

A third theme that emerged from the data was coping with racism and sexism. The women in the study discussed the use of both negative and positive coping strategies when attempting to address their experiencing of unpleasant emotions. Specifically, the women discussed escapist coping practices (Folkman and Moskowitz 2004) including not using their time wisely and questioning their identities as professors.

All of the participants explained that they often wasted a lot of time attending to the wrong things such as the prejudiced comments they often heard instead of focusing on things that mattered. This escapist coping strategy helped to yield unpleasant emotions such as anger and frustration. Dr. Jennifer Plummer, an African American full professor in mechanical engineering explained:

> I know that I have spent…a lot more energy…on…just being frustrated than just doing my work… But, I spent a lot of time and energy on the wrong thing… I spent a lot of time being frustrated and angry… I knew who I was before I came here. But I – you know, you end up questioning it sometimes. And I am here why? But I spent a lot of time and energy that I could've spent…doing other things, like writing papers. I spent a lot of time and energy being just frustrated and annoyed and angry.

Similarly, many of the women questioned their career choices and subsequently their identities as both engineers and professors. They wondered if they should continue careers as engineering professors. Several even contemplated changing to drastically different careers. Dr. Alexandra Chappelle explicated:

> I went through – you know…a phase where I felt like – you know, that I had chosen the wrong profession. That I wasn't any good at whatever I was doing. That I really needed to consider different options altogether. That I wasn't cut out to be an engineer. That I wasn't cut out to be in academia. You know. That maybe I should go open a travel agency, or do something totally different with my life.

Such escapist coping strategies of dwelling on the problems and contemplating career changes are common amongst women professors of color in engineering (Kaiser and Miller 2004). However, such strategies are not productive or effective. In order to help combat the differential treatment that women of color in engineering often receive, it is necessary to develop effective means of addressing the problems. As described by the women, it is necessary to develop resilience by effectively coping with the unpleasant emotions experienced from interacting with colleagues and students. Specifically, the women mentioned how they take care of self, have support networks, engage in mentoring relationships, and develop professionalism and professional identities.

Several of the women discussed that in order to positively cope with the unpleasant emotions that they feel in the workplace, they often had to make sure that they were taking care of themselves. They utilized cultural coping resources (Utsey, et al. 2008) and engaged in activities that helped them to maintain their mental, physical and spiritual well-being. For example, they exercised in order to reduce stress, ate healthily to stay physically strong, and meditated and prayed to keep their minds clear. As explained by Dr. Alexandra Chappelle, it is important to make "time and space" for you and your well-being.

Another important strategy to counter unpleasant emotions is to utilize sociofamilial coping resources by developing a support network (Banyard and Graham-Bermann 1993; Utsey, et al. 2008). All of the participants mentioned that they had elaborate support systems consisting of family, friends and colleagues. As explained by the women, having a support network is crucial to their well-being. It is important to have people you can share your feelings with, particularly those that offer unconditional support. As described by Dr. Consuela Ward, "After I complain and whine and cry,

I have a really, really supportive family. My husband is extremely supportive. So are my parents; I usually call them. I usually call them and ask for advice." A support network is important because as Dr. Alexandra Chappelle explained, "[you can] pick up the phone bawling and crying and screaming about anything and everything. And they'll be there, and vice-versa."

A third problem-focused coping strategy, utilizing sociofamilial coping resources (Utsey, et al. 2008), is obtaining a mentor (Grant 2006). It is important to "use your resources," as mentioned by Dr. Keisha Benson, an African American full professor in engineering, by having someone help you navigate the tenure process. It is particularly helpful to have someone that has been successful in dealing with racism and/or sexism in the workplace, particularly in dealing with colleagues and students. Dr. Jasmine Davenport, an assistant professor of electrical engineering explained, "mentoring just helps you just – you know, bypass a lot of mistakes. And you don't have to do all those lessons learned. You can learn from other people's lessons, and things like that...It does help you immensely."

A last coping strategy, using psychological coping resources (Utsey, 2008), is the necessity of developing a sense of professional identity as an engineer including working hard, being knowledgeable of your field, and always being academically prepared. Because racism and sexism exists in the field of engineering, women of color will often be subjected to double standards. They will not receive the same opportunities and benefits that White men receive. Also, women of color will often be judged more harshly when they make mistakes. Thus, it is important for women of color to be informed and confident regarding their knowledge and abilities as engineers. This will give colleagues and students less opportunity to criticize. As described by Dr. Ramona Fernandez, a Latina assistant professor of electrical engineering:

> I have to prepare myself ... I have to show people that I really have the knowledge, the skills...I have to show my peers and the students and the other faculty that I'm as good as any other faculty, or better. Better. Because I – because being a minority and you have to show that you are not just the same. That the – your peers, you are better than your peers. But...the other thing is, just keeping updating, reading, improving myself. You have to learn something new every day. Because why? Because you have to show that you are as good or better than the other people [White men].

CRP and CRF: Challenging the White and Male Identity of Engineering

In this chapter, we examined the experiences of women faculty of color in engineering by telling their counterstories, stories that challenge the normative discourse. Specifically, we utilized both critical race theory (whiteness as property) and critical race feminism (intersectionality theory), to focus on the interconnectedness of race and gender on women of color's experiences, the emotions associated with those experiences, and the coping resources used to address those emotions. The women faculty members' counterstories demonstrated that the very presence of women of color in engineering challenged racial and gender norms. However, in doing so, women professors of color in engineering often experienced unpleasant emotions such as anger and frustration regarding their interactions with White men faculty members and students.

CRT's tenet of *whiteness as property*, specifically the right to exclude suggests that being White and having a White identity means being entitled to power and privilege and having the right to exert these racial benefits by discriminating against those that are not White. The tenet of whiteness as property is useful in helping examine the counterstories of the participants in that the field of engineering exemplifies notions of power and privilege based upon race. Since engineering is seen as a white discipline, this perspective assumes that people of color do not belong in engineering. This attitude is embraced by many White faculty members and students, creating racially-charged environments for women of color and challenging the non-White identity of engineering. In particular, these negative attitudes contribute to not valuing people of color's perspectives, as in the search committee experiences of both Dr. Consuela Ward and Dr. Maria Valenzuela, the hindering of professional development as in the experience of Dr. Valerie Jenkins, and the discrediting of the credentials and knowledge as described by Dr. Alexandra Chappelle, Dr. Cheryl Brown, Dr. Catalina Núñez, and Dr. Rochelle Collins.

Although engineering is viewed as a white discipline, it is also seen as primarily being a discipline for men. While White women are seen as outsiders because of their gender, they are included because of their White identity. Women of color, on the other hand, are seen as not belonging and are viewed as outsiders because of both their racial and gender identities. It cannot be assumed that the experiences of White women are the same for women of color. As such, the intersection of race and gender has to be taken into consideration. However, it is often difficult to determine if what women faculty of color experience stems from race, gender, or both. Because women of color are both women and people of color, one cannot discount the multiplicativeness of race and gender identities or their intersection.

As demonstrated by the previously described experiences of all of the participants in this study, it can be argued that their negative racial and gender experiences impacted their identities as engineers. When normative expectations differ from one's identity (e.g. racial and gender), there is an increase in the experiencing of unpleasant emotions. The resulting emotional labor leads to a negative impact on one's well-being or identity (Ashforth and Humphrey 1993). Further, when identity with a social group differs from one's organizational role, one can experience emotive dissonance and self-alienation (Ashforth and Humphrey 1993). Because women of color are neither men nor White, their presence challenges the homogeneity of engineering and the traditional engineer identity. Women faculty of color constantly have to negotiate both their racial and gender identities, and in turn, their identities as engineers. Women faculty of color must constantly attempt to redefine what it means to be an engineering professor by challenging the traditional view of engineering as White and male. However, the process of negotiating an identity that is not considered normative is stressful. They must learn to effectively manage their racial and gender identities and cope with the unpleasant emotions that they experience.

However, it must be added that having to develop strategies to effectively cope with the negative emotions caused by racial- and gender-related stressors in itself can be an extra layer of stress and emotional labor (Vargas 2002).

Implications

Most college faculty members experience unpleasant emotions in the workplace. However, for women faculty of color, particularly in the male-dominated field of engineering, it is even more problematic. The best way to help women faculty of color to effectively address and cope with unpleasant emotions in the workplace is to provide them with additional sociofamilial coping resources, particularly more women faculty of color. Institutions need to be committed to changing the environments of engineering departments by increasing the number of women faculty of color in engineering (National Research Council 2006). In order to do so, predominately White institutions should develop relationships with HBCUs and other minority-serving institutions. Developing a pipeline is necessary to increase the number of women of color in engineering graduate programs and eventually increase the number of women of color who are interested in careers in academia. Second, there should be more funding for women of color in engineering. People of color often do not attend graduate school because of inadequate funding. Targeted funding sources will help enable women of color to attend graduate school. Last, while in graduate school, women of color should be encouraged to go into academia rather than industry. In doing so, while in graduate school, they should receive adequate training on conducting research, obtaining grants, and teaching.

In addition, in order to help women faculty of color develop effective coping strategies, it is imperative that researchers better understand the emotions experienced and the coping strategies used by women faculty of color in the workplace. Researchers need to examine pleasant emotions regarding coping. Although this paper focused only on unpleasant emotions, women of color do often experience many pleasant emotions in the workplace. In particular, stress-related growth often involves experiencing pleasant emotions or coping strategies as a result of successfully enduring a stressful situation (Folkman and Moskowitz 2004). By attempting to better understand the role of pleasant emotions in the workplace, researchers will provide women of color with more positive options in coping as well as offer tools for developing resilience.

Conclusion

Although this study was conducted utilizing the counterstories of women professors of color, it is important to realize that these women are representative of numerous women faculty members in various disciplines across the country. Many women professors of color experience challenges stemming from the combination of racism and sexism. By engaging in effective coping strategies, women faculty of color will be able to cope with the unpleasant emotions that they experience. They will be able to succeed in the workplace while maintaining a positive identity as women professors of color.

References

Aquirre A Jr (2000) Women and minority faculty in the academic workplace: Recruitment, retention, and academic culture. Jossey-Bass, New York

Arthur LB (1993) Clothing, control, and women's agency: The mitigation of patriarchal power. In: Fisher S, Davis K (eds) Negotiating at the margins: The gendered discourses of power and resistance. Rutgers University Press, New Brunswick, pp 66–84

Ashforth BE, Humphrey RH (1993) Emotional labor in service roles: The influence of identity. Acad Manage Rev 18(1):88–115

Bacchus DN, Holley LC (2004) Spirituality as a coping resource: The experiences of professional Black women. J Ethnic Cultur Divers Soci Work 13(4):65–84

Banyard V, Graham-Bermann S (1993) A gender analysis of theories of coping with stress. Psychol Women Q 17(3):303–318

Bell, D A (1980). *Brown v. Board of Education* and the interest convergence dilemma.

Bell D (1992) Faces at the bottom of the well: The permanence of racism. Basic Books, New York *Harv Law Rev, 93*, 518–533.

Bellas ML (1999) Emotional labor in academia: The case of professors. Ann Am Acad Polit Soc Sci 561:96–110

Carbado DW, Gulati M (2001) The fifth Black woman. Contemporary Legal Issues 11:701–729

Chinn P (1999) Multiple worlds/mismatched meanings: Barriers to minority women engineers. J Res Sci Teach 36(6):621–636

Coffey A, Atkinson P (1996) Making sense of qualitative data: Complementary research designs. Sage, Thousand Oaks, CA

Crenshaw, K. (1989). Demarginalizing the intersection of race and sex: A Black feminist critique of antidiscrimination doctrine, feminist theory and antiracist politics. University of Chicago Legal Foru 139–167

DeCuir JT, Dixson A (2004) "So when it comes out, they aren't that surprised that it is there": Using critical race theory as a tool of analysis of race and racism in education. Educ Res 33(5):26–31

DeCuir-Gunby JT (2006) "Proving your skin is white, you can have everything:" Race, racial identity and the property rights in Whiteness in the Supreme Court Case of Josephine DeCuir. In: Rousseau C, Dixson A (eds) Critical Race Theory and Education: All God's children got a song". Routledge, New York, pp 89–111

Delgado R (1989) Storytelling for oppositionists and others: A plea for narrative. Mich Law Rev 87(8):2411–2441

Delgado R, Stefancic J (2001) Critical race theory: An introduction. New York University Press, New York

Erickson RJ, Ritter C (2001) Emotional labor, burnout, and inauthenticity: Does gender matter? Soc Psychol Q 64(2):146–163

Evans KM, Herr EL (1991) The influence of racism and sexism in the career development of African American women. Journal of Multicultural Counseling and Development 19(3):130–135

Folkman S, Moskowitz JT (2004) Coping: Pitfalls and promise. Ann Rev of Psychol 55:745–774

Golafshani N (2003) Understanding reliability and validity in qualitative research. Qual Rep 8(4):597–607

González-Morales MG, Peiró JM, Rodríguez I, Greenglass ER (2006) Coping and distress in organizations: The role of gender in work stress. Int J Stress Manage 13(2):228–248

Gotanda N (1991) A critique of "Our constitution is color-blind". Stanford Law Rev 44:1–68

Grant C (2006) Mentoring. In: Pritchard PA (ed) Success strategies for women in science: A portable mentor. Elsevier Academic Press, Burlington, MA, pp 83–106

Harris C (1993) Whiteness as property. Harv Law Rev 106(8):1707–1791

Hochschild AR (1979) Emotion work, feeling rules, and social structure. Am J Sociol 85(3):551–575

Hochschild AR (1983) The managed heart: Commercialization of human feeling. University of California Press, Berkeley, CA

Jackson J (2004) The story is not in the numbers: Academic socialization and diversifying the faculty. Nat Womens Stud Assoc J 16(1):172–185

Jeghelian A (1976) Surviving sexism: Strategies and consequences. Personnel Guidance J 2:307–311

Kaiser C, Miller C (2004) A stress and coping perspective on confronting sexism. Psych Women Q 28(2):168–178

Mannix, M. (2002). Facing the problem. *Prism, 12(2) 18-24* .

McCracken, G. (1988). *The long interview*. (Vol. 13). Sage, Thousand Oaks: Sage.

National Academy of Sciences, National Academy of Engineering, and Institute of Medicine. (2007). *Beyond bias and barriers: Fulfilling the potential of women in academic science and engineering*. National Academies Press, Washington, DC

National Research Council (2006) To recruit and advance: Women students and faculty in science and engineering. National Academies Press, Washington, DC

Nelson D (2003) The standing of women in academia. Chem Eng Prog 99(8):38–41

Nelson D (2007) A national analysis of minorities in science and engineering faculties at research universities. file: ///C:/Documents%20and%20Setting/schitraporselvi/Local%20Setting/Temp/SPiCE.html#http://cheminfo.ou.edu/~djn/diversity/Faculty_Table_FY07/07Report.pdf. Retrieved 8 Dec 2008

Nelson D Rogers D (2004) A national analysis of diversity in science and engineering faculties at research universities. file:///C:Documents%20Settings/schitraporselvi/Local%20Setting/Temp/SPiCE.html#http://cheminfo.ou.edu/~djn/deversity/Faculty_Tables_FY07/07Report.pdf. Retrieved 6 Nov 2008

Peters M, Lankshear C (1996) Postmodern counternarratives. In: Giroux H, Lankshear C, McLaren P, Peters M (eds) Counternarratives: Cultural studies and critical pedagogies in postmodern spaces. Routledge, New York, pp 1–39

Piotrkowski CS (1998) Gender harassment, job satisfaction, and distress among employed White and Minority women. J Occup Health Psychol 3:33–43

Ranson G (2005) No longer "one of the boys": Negotiations with motherhood, as prospect or reality, among women in engineering. Can Rev Sociol Anthropol 42(2):145–166

Robinson JG, McIlwee JS (1991) Men, women, and the culture of engineering. Sociol Q 32:403–21

Ronen S, Ronen A (2008) Gender differences in engineers' burnout. Equal Oppor Int 27(8):677–691

Rubin A, Babbie E (2007) Essential research methods for social work. Wadsworth, Belmont, CA

Rubin HJ, Rubin IS (2005) Qualitative interviewing: The art of hearing data, 2nd edn. Sage, Thousand Oaks, CA

Smith E, Witt SL (1993) A comparative study of occupational stress among African American and White university faculty: A research note. Res Hig Educ 34(2):229–241

Solórzano DG, Yosso TJ (2002) Critical race methodology: Counter-storytelling as an analytical framework for education research. Qualitative Inquiry 8(1):23–44

Swim JK, Cohen LL, Hyers LL (1998) Prejudice: The target's perspective. Academic New York

University of Michigan Advance Program (2007). assessing the academic work environment for science and engineering faculty at the University of Michigan in 2001 and 2006: gender and race in department and university related climate factors. file:///C:Documents%20Settings/

schitraporselvi/Local%20Setting/Temp/SPiCE.htm1#http://www.umich.edu/~advproj/ADV-FacultyClimate-Rpt3-final.pdf. Retrieved 6 Nov 2008

Utsey SO, Giesbrecht N, Hook J, Stanard PM (2008) Cultural, sociofamilial, and psychological resources that inhibit psychological distress in African Americans exposed to stressful life events and race-related stress. J Counsel Psychol 55(1):49–62

Vargas L (2002) Why are we still so few and why has our progress been so slow? In: Vargas L (ed) Women faculty of color in the White classroom. Peter Lang Publishing, New York, pp 23–34

Wing AK (2003) Critical race feminism. New York University Press, New York

Wolcott HF (1994) Transforming qualitative data: description, analysis, and interpretation. Sage, Thousand Oaks

Young, D. (2004). Women vastly underrepresented in academia. Women's eNews. file:/// C:Documents%20Settings/schitraporselvi/Local%20Setting/Temp/SPiCE.htm1#http://www. womensenews.org/artical.cfm/dyn/aid/1672. Retrieved 6 Nov 2008

Chapter 17
Emotions and Social Inequalities: Mobilizing Emotions for Social Justice Education

Michalinos Zembylas and Sharon Chubbuck

Abstract In this chapter we focus on the interplay of emotions with social justice education, with particular attention to how emotions and social justice education can be mutually engaged as both critical and transformational forces to produce better teaching and learning opportunities for marginalized students. We discuss the relevance and complexity of emotions in relation to social justice, through sustaining or remedying social inequalities. We then describe an example of teaching for/about social justice, showing how reflecting on and interrogating emotions can help perpetuate or disrupt historical and local practices that reproduce inequity. This example is grounded in empirical data taken from a case study of a white novice teacher who attempted to teach for/about social justice in an urban school in Midwestern United States. In the last part of the chapter, we argue for the urgent need to reconceptualize the interplay between emotions and social justice education in order to capitalize on the possibilities that lie therein. In particular, we build upon a previous analysis of the notion of *critical emotional praxis*–that is, critical praxis informed by emotion that resists unjust systems and practices as well as emotion that helps create a more fair and just world in our classrooms and our everyday lives–to show how inclusive this notion can be in addressing issues of social justice education.

Keywords Critical emotional praxis · Social inequalities · Social justice education

Concerns about social justice in western thought go back as far as ancient moral philosophers like Plato and Socrates, with various iterations occurring throughout history (Rawls 1971). No matter how social justice has been viewed since its earliest origins (e.g. whether justice is seen a personal virtue and/or as an ideal state of a democratic society), emotions have been identified as pivotal in perceiving and

M. Zembylas (✉)
Program of Educational Studies, Open University of Cyprus, Cyprus
e-mail: m.zembylas@ouc.ac.cy

P.A. Schutz and M. Zembylas (eds.), *Advances in Teacher Emotion Research:*   343
The Impact on Teachers' Lives,
DOI 10.1007/978-1-4419-0564-2_17, © Springer Science+Business Media, LLC 2009

sustaining meanings and practices of justice (Cremer and Bos 2007; Solomon 1989, 1990; Turner 2007). For example, emotions intersect justice because an ideology is not considered "effective" unless people have strong feelings about the ideas embedded in it (Fields et al., 2007), feelings such as love and hope for the creation of a more fair and just world. Indeed, people's very sense of justice–how they perceive whether something is just or unjust–triggers powerful emotions (Jasso 2007), with feelings such as anger and outrage intimately linked to their responses to injustice.

One would expect, then, that emotion also would be seen as integral to social justice in relation to educational practice, yet emotions are frequently marginal to discussions of social justice education (Chubbuck and Zembylas 2008). In this chapter, the term *social justice education* refers to those educational efforts that instigate and enact policies and pedagogical practices that will improve the learning and life opportunities of typically underserved students (Cochran-Smith 2004; Nieto 2000), while equipping and empowering all students to work for social justice in society (Kincheloe and Steinberg 1998; King 2005). Each aspect of this understanding implicates a significant degree of emotion; indeed, social justice education is bound up with the emotional lives of the individuals involved and the social and political circumstances in which those individuals live and express their emotions (Chubbuck and Zembylas 2008; Zembylas 2008b). These emotions play a constitutive role in challenging prevailing social norms about injustice and inequality both in schools and in society. As Ahmed (2004) argues, challenging social norms of injustice or inequity involves having a different affective relation to those norms, partly by feeling their costs as a loss or a gain. Any understanding of socially just education, then, is inextricably linked to analyzing the pivotal role of emotions in reproducing or disrupting existing inequalities. Indeed, engaging emotions in social justice education–such as examining one's feelings in the context of teaching/learning about inequality and injustice–can be a catalyst both to transform educational practices and to problematize perceptions of equity in schools and society (Callahan 2004; O' Brien and Flynn 2007). Ameliorating the educational experiences of marginalized students and empowering all students to be agents of change will have more chances of success as teacher educators, teachers, and administrators understand the tremendous challenges and potential complex relationship of emotions and social justice education.

This chapter, built on this view of emotion as significantly constitutive of justice/injustice, focuses on the interplay of emotions with social justice education, with particular attention to how emotions and social justice education can be mutually engaged as both critical and transformational forces to produce better teaching and learning opportunities for marginalized students. In the first part of the chapter, we discuss how the relevance and complexity of emotions in relation to social justice, through sustaining or remedying social inequalities. In the next section, we describe an example of teaching for/about social justice, showing how reflecting on and interrogating emotions can help perpetuate or disrupt historical and local practices that that reproduce inequity. This example is grounded in empirical data taken from a case study of a white novice teacher who attempted to teach for/about social justice in an urban school in Midwestern United States. In the last part of the chapter, we argue for the urgent need to reconceptualize the interplay between emotions and social justice education in order to capitalize on the possibilities that lie therein. In particular, we build upon a previous analysis of the notion of *critical emotional praxis* (Chubbuck and Zembylas 2008)–that is, critical praxis informed by emotion that resists unjust systems and practices as well as emotion that helps create a more fair and just world in our classrooms and our everyday lives–to show how inclusive this notion can be in addressing issues of social justice education.

Emotions and Social Justice

Solomon (1989) suggests a possible point of departure in addressing the relationship of emotions and social justice with his claim that belief in a just world is a deeply emotional matter, with justice and emotion operating in a reciprocal manner. As he explains: "One cannot develop a theory of justice without a substantial grounding in the empirical knowledge of how people actually feel and behave, but one is in no position to judge how people feel and behave without already presupposing something like a theory (at any rate, a conception) of justice" (1989, p. 354). Yet, with this starting point of the mutual interaction of emotion and social justice, myriad questions about emotions and justice remain. What is the operational relationship between emotions and justice? What emotions are productive and to be encouraged in education for social justice? Once determined, how are those emotions cultivated? These questions do not prompt easy answers; indeed, discussion of these sorts of questions continuously produces both conflicting and complementary perspectives.

Frequently, the fundamental issue in such discussions is whether justice has a rational or a more intuitive basis (Kant 1959). For example, philosophers Hume and Kant debated the role of emotions in social justice issues, with Hume arguing that the basis of justice (and morality) had to be emotion, not reason, because reason cannot motivate action -- only passion can do that. Kant disagreed with this idea, suggesting instead a view of justice that did not depend on the vicissitudes of emotion (Kant 1959). The question goes back even further, however, to Aristotle who opened the door to the role of emotion in justice when he recognized that right emotions were essential to right action, insisting that a just individual was moved by just feelings as well as just thoughts (Solomon 1989). Solomon raised similar arguments aligned with the Aristotelian emphasis on justice as primarily a personal virtue and only derivatively a social one (Kristjánsson 2005). As he wrote: "Justice is 'in us' but it is 'about' the world, as our emotions are (in some purely metaphorical sense) in us but about the world" (1989, p. 359). Solomon further explained:

Justice is, first of all, a set of *personal feelings*, a way of participating in the world. Without the cultivation of those feelings–and some of them are by no means attractive–the principles of justice are nothing but abstract ideals, and the policies that would make us just, however justified, seem overambitious and even irrelevant. (1989, p. 355, added emphasis)

The complex debate over justice as subjective or objective seems unavoidable. Given that an over-personalization of justice implies some degree of depoliticization, Kristjánsson (2005) correctly observed that a balance is needed between the role of social structures (what counts as "political") and personal virtues (what counts as "personal"). Yet, Solomon (1989) was careful to avoid the appearance of an exclusively self-referential relativism, making an important distinction "between subjectivity as the reference point of a phenomenon (the world is neither just nor unjust apart from our conceptions and participation) and subjectivity as a *non disputandum* incorrigibility thesis (whatever I feel is just, is just)" (p. 359).

Several other contemporary treatments of justice continue the debate over the relation of emotion and justice as rational or intuitive when they challenge the way predominant models of social justice have privileged rationalism (as found, for instance, in the theories of John Rawls); this challenge advanced the discussion of the relation of emotion to justice by theorizing emotion as integral to practical reason (as manifested in action, for example). For example, Lyotard and Thébaud's (1985) description of justice focused on the impossibility of a contractual consensus on justice given competing worldviews, and particularly, given the lack of equal participation in the contractual process by those who are marginalized (Dhillon 2000). They called attention to how the very claims about the universality of justice, in fact, have been used to perpetuate oppression against the marginalized. While Lyotard and Thébaud's (1985) problematizing of the so-called universals of justice could be seen as leading to relativism or passivity, this is not the case. Instead, they encouraged reflective judgment to produce emotionally engaged responses to the culpability we all share for social inequalities and injustices. In that response, which elevates engaging emotions about the Other over merely "thinking" or "knowing" about the Other, one comes to understand ethics as action. Indeed, an emotional response acquires its full meaning only when it is accompanied by action.

Lyotard and Thébaud's (1985) description of justice, then, creates ways to conceptualize the relationship of emotions and justice in a more constitutive manner. That is, engaging our emotional attachments and desires becomes a means both to recognize injustice and to respond to injustice with action. The nature of this process, however, by which emotions "show" the effects of injustice while generating openings that position emotion as integral to practical reason, that is action-filled response, raises yet more questions and challenges. As Ahmed asks: "Is a just response to injustice about having more 'just emotions,' or is justice never 'just' about emotions?" (2004, p. 191). Justice/injustice cannot be addressed or even identified by individuals having the "right kind of feelings" (Ahmed 2004, p. 195); indeed, reducing the complexity of how emotions relate to justice by equating the presence of appropriate feelings with either recognizing/naming injustice or rectifying injustice is problematic at a variety of levels.

First, contemporary emotion theory reveals that moral principles and justice claims are not established on the basis of universal emotions; instead, emotions are indicators of moral beliefs–they do not constitute them (Solomon 1990). For example, feelings of anger about the social inequalities experienced by others are indicators of our beliefs about justice, but their presence does not create our beliefs about justice; justice as a circumstance has to be established in its own right, apart from feelings in response to what we perceive as unjust situations (Karstedt 2002). In fact, as Karstedt explains, longitudinal research on the moral development of very young children shows that they understand moral principles but do not attach moral sentiments to them until a later stage, around the age of 10. This finding shows that emotions are linked to antecedent moral judgments but do not constitute them.

Neither does the presence of specific sets of emotions serve as a reliable indicator that just/unjust circumstances do or do not exist. For example, the identification of injustice cannot simply be reduced to having bad feelings. Such reduction of judgment about inequities to an appropriate set of emotions would be deeply problematic at two levels (Berlant 2000). First, such a reduction would essentially make an individual's judgment of what is right or wrong dependent upon the existence of specific emotions; that is, a situation could be identified as unjust if, and only if, specific bad feelings were present, leaving a basis of judgment that is entirely idiosyncratic and without moral basis. Second, this position would render the identification of justice/injustice dependent on a claim of access to the interiority of others' feelings, which is impossible.

Consequently, if injustice is not simply about feeling bad, it is equally important to understand that justice is not simply about feeling good, it is not simply a matter of feeling empathy for those who suffer or for our shared human vulnerability (Butler 2004). The transformation of "bad" feelings into "good" ones does not necessarily repair the damages of injustice. For example, feeling solidarity for poor children is not necessarily an indication of commitment to activism for greater justice in the world. This is particularly evident when we consider that some individuals are constructed as "grievable" (Ahmed 2004, p. 192) to us–that is, deemed worthy of our grief over their suffering, as opposed to others who may be deemed "ungrievable." In this process, the emotion selectively experienced has less to do with a desire for greater justice and more to do with the fact that we sentimentalize loss and assign grief to some but not to others (Butler 2004).

Similarly, feeling bad about social inequalities does not necessarily suggest that injustice is removed. Does feeling bad for children in poverty, as a result of various forms of previous and contemporary colonialisms, repair the injustice of poverty? Is our judgment about what makes an act "bad" dependent upon the other's suffering or our disgust for such an act? Shared vulnerability may be the connective living conception that holds together many manifestations of social justice (Butler 2004), yet the relationship between emotion and (in)justice remains complex.

Nonetheless, these issues do not reduce to simple "either-or" equations. While emotions do not constitute justice identified or addressed, neither are they merely individual, internal side effects of encountering suffering. For example, feelings for others and their suffering provide signs of obligation to others.

Equally, affective relations to social norms that are responsible for social inequalities provide serve to perpetuate those inequities (Ahmed 2004). Challenging injustice, then, implies the interruption of these social norms, which also, then, implicates the subversion of the emotions attached to them. Although injustice cannot be measured by the existence of suffering, as Ahmed emphasizes, some suffering is an effect of injustice. The important idea here is that injustice can be understood, at least in part, as the failure to connect with others and respond to their suffering. Needless to say, this is not all that injustice is; however, this thesis emphasizes a usually neglected aspect–the connection between social norms and the "economies of affect" (i.e. how affects move, circulate and are distributed in society) that maintain such norms (Zembylas 2007a). Feelings of fear, hatred, and resentment, then, are commonly constructed as a result of social and political struggles around injustice and identity claims; similarly, feelings of hope, love and passion develop in relation to conceptions and practices of social justice.

The analysis so far offers two important perspectives in building our argument about emotion and its relation to social justice claims. First, if any attention to emotion is to be an effective force in understanding the ethics and politics of justice claims, that emotion needs to be placed within a particular social and political context (Thrift 2005). Emotions can no longer been seen as simply internal aspects of the mind; instead, positions them as socially and politically formed components of action, serving a crucial role in either addressing injustice or sustaining the status quo (Lutz and Abu-Lughod 1990). For example, emotions (e.g. pride) that are associated with perceptions about meritocracy in the United States make sense if they are understood not only as individual but also as collective responses to specific sociopolitical conditions, both in the past and in the present. In this understanding of emotion, one has to study the socio-political aspects that perpetuate such feelings of pride in the face of pervasive inequalities in gender, race, class, and sexuality.

Second, even though the politics of emotion (Zembylas 2007b) requires grounding in socio-political contexts, this perspective does not preclude a productive and creative engagement with the world through affective interventions rather than through "private bargains with misery" (Thrift, 2004, p. 66). In other words, a politics of emotion can forge a renewed criticality that mobilizes emotional engagement with others in ways that inspire new ways of being in the world such as connection, understanding, appreciation, and love (Zembylas 2007a, 2008a).

In summary, then, emotions may be examined in two ways: first, as contributors to the reproduction of inequality through the suppression or allowance of particular emotional practices and second, as sites of social and political resistance and transformation of such inequality. The following example illustrates this complex interaction of emotion and social justice in one teacher's praxis. Following that example, the last part of this chapter shows how this renewed criticality to mobilize emotional engagement in productive ways may be instigated in everyday pedagogical practices.

Emotions and Social Justice Teaching: Examples from a Case Study

Pedagogies that take into consideration the role of emotions can produce numerous valuable possibilities for educators and students to respond to social justice issues. For example, in the context of social justice teaching, students can learn to understand and live affectively in relation to identity and difference (Zembylas 2007a); equally, issues of social injustice will offer opportunities for students to critique the reproduction of inequality and engage in practices that inspire imagination and emotions such as excitement for a more fair and just world. If educators and students are unaware of the relationship between emotion and the practices that sustain cycles of inequality, they will not be able to disrupt unjust practices and motivate actions that embrace excitement and passion for social justice (O' Brien and Flynn 2007). Our example is drawn from a case study of Sara, a white novice teacher at a large, racially and economically diverse urban school, as she struggled to formulate socially just teaching practices (See Chubbuck and Zembylas 2008 and Chubbuck 2008). In it we highlight both pleasant/positive and unpleasant/negative emotions that operate to impede or motivate action for social justice.

Emotions Related to Social Norms in Larger Context

Sara taught English at Jefferson High School, a large urban/working class school with a relatively balanced racial demographic among the student population, unusual in urban settings, and a predominantly white faculty and administration. While much of the student body was cooperative and engaged in learning, the school experienced frequent threats of and actual gang violence. Sara was pleased to be teaching in an urban setting like Jefferson, expressing a passionate commitment to being "a teacher for social justice," but the overall school culture neither shared nor supported her goals. She described the atmosphere of the school as "very combative, very top down and demand-oriented as opposed to collaborative and creative…like counting down to the hall sweep," a reference to the daily booming interruption over the intercom counting down the remaining seconds before tardy students would be given detentions. This authoritarian, negative view of the students was further evident in the presence of several large, uniformed safety officers stationed in the halls. Sara's vision of a multicultural education, drawing on the rich opportunities afforded by the balanced racial diversity of the school, was not apparent in the overall school ambiance. She was frustrated by "the lack of looking deeply at what our kids are really going through,…a lack of compassion for the kids, a lack of student voice. I feel very angry when I think about how ripe the opportunities at Jefferson are for collaboration and interdisciplinary planning and multi-ethnic and multi-cultural growth and appreciation."

The disconnect between Sara's concern over justice issues and the school culture also created barriers between her and even those colleagues she considered supportive friends, adding to her feelings of alienation and aloneness. "[A fellow teacher] said to me the other day, 'Oh we wouldn't be comfortable having this conversation with you, you're just so moral.' And I kind of probed a little bit and … [my three closest colleagues said], 'It's not that you're moral. You just have so many strong convictions about social justice.' "

Perhaps even more telling was the apparent disconnect between Sara's thoughts that her relationship to students was foundational to any socially just teaching and the prevailing attitude among her colleagues. She wanted to teach in a place with "real human beings with real concern for other human beings, teachers who have real concern for… our students, and not just 'Well, he's in jail, Sara. There's nothing you can do about it.'" Sara desired positive relationships with her students; however, pursuing this goal in a context where both historic and current social norms provoked negative evaluations of the students as "the Other" that, in turn, positioned both students and faculty/administration in oppressive hierarchies of power, provoked myriad emotions in Sara. She described one particularly intense interaction with Chu, a Hmong student whom she described as failing and extremely uncooperative. After Sara had made several calls to his home to work on his struggles, Chu became enraged over a perceived minor slight in class. He threatened her and called her a "racist bitch," describing how he imagined killing Sara multiple times. Though this student had a history of similar episodes with several other teachers, Sara struggled with fears that she had communicated racist attitudes towards him at some point, as seen in this excerpt from her journal.

> And so ends an emotional day. Chu called me a "racist bitch." Ouch…. It is a strange feeling to know that someone else in the world has imagined what it would be like to kill you…–especially someone who I have devoted so much time, energy, and compassion to…. Even though I recognize that this student's anger goes deeper than any interaction I've ever had with him, I still can't help but wonder what I did to provoke him. What does compassion look like in this situation? Should I have been more firm in the get-go? What actions, comments, or behaviors may be perceived as racist? What does it really mean for me to show respect to all of the students in the class?

The emotions of self-doubt, confusion, and disappointment provoked by the encounter with this student then multiplied as Sara struggled to procure psychological support for him in the context of the administration's swift, zero-tolerance approach. Rather than responding in proactive ways to remediate the student's anger problems, the administration merely suspended him from her class for the rest of the semester. Sara felt as if a whirlwind of administrative stonewalling had completely thwarted the sort of socially just response she wanted with Chu.

> It was so troubling…I felt like I had done exactly what I didn't want to do, which was just to pass him off to get suspended again. I made the decision not to have the police called, which the administrator made it clear to me that I could if I wanted to…I didn't feel like that would have helped this kid, this kid is angry and this kid needs somebody to talk to, and…he needs help not punishment….[I feel] disappointment in the whole thing…in him…in me…in the administration. Disappointment in the fact that there was a box for me to check saying, "Do you want the cops to be called?" but there was no box for me to check saying, "No, I want help for him."

Emotions Related to Interactions with Students Around Curriculum

Students' identities were saturated with emotions created through rituals and daily school practices that established certain inclusions and exclusions based on race, color and social class (see Berezin 2001). In other words, emotions were fundamental to students' self-identification and made them feel part of some communities (e.g. based on color) but not others (Suny 2004). Though these emotions existed in the context of larger societal norms, they were also sparked in the daily local exchanges among students and teachers. This interaction of emotions shaped by and shaping of both the local and the larger oppressive hierarchies of societal norms frequently emerged in the curriculum Sara used with her student.

Her semester long curricular focus was to engage students in imagining non-violent rather than violent responses. To do this, she used literature first to lead them in discussions of how stereotyping of the "Other" (based on race, class, gender and tribe) often led to violence. She then asked them to consider a world without violence, which they replied that they could not even imagine it. Sara was startled that they saw non-violence as beyond imagining and asked them for further explanation. In this exchange, some students identified feelings such as hate, fear, anger, humiliation and shame as contributing to the perpetuation of violence in society and then against other students locally. Emotion, and particularly anger, was one of the main sources of violence suggested by students.

> Rachel (African American female): It [violence] all goes back to emotions. People will feel sad or mad.

> Sara: ....So what does that mean? Do we have to stop feeling in order to stop conflict? Would that even be possible? What do you think?

> Esperanza: (Hispanic female): I doubt we could have a world without violence. Anger doesn't just exist on its own. People talk about you and you get mad. I don't think we can even imagine it.

> Carl (White male): I think it is impossible because people have anger. [...]

This discussion–as well as several others we observed–suggests that emotions can serve as vehicles that reinforce differences between privileged and subordinate groups. However, despite the unpleasant emotions in the process, Sara inspired her students to begin acknowledging not only the role of emotion in violence but also its role in political movements (Berezin 2001). Sara added another layer of complexity by challenging her students to consider everyday examples from their own lives in which emotions of anger at injustice are expressed nonviolently.

> Sara: [Ghandi] would never fight back, even in the face of violence. So he's in this [nonviolent] movement that we're talking about, where he has those emotions and you never fight back. So he did that to try to lead the people to a revolution and then somebody else said Martin Luther King, Jr. was another nonviolent resister. So do you have examples of incredible people in history who use nonviolence to make a point?

Sara regularly tried to link the literature curriculum to real life examples. In one extraordinary activity, she had students explore the website of ex-gang leader

"Tookie" Stanley Williams (founder of the Los Angeles gang, the Crips), followed by an assignment to write Williams a letter describing what they had learned about the cycle of violence, inequality and injustice. This assignment allowed her to link themes from their reading, writing instruction, and active engagement with social justice issues. Sara felt satisfaction over this holistic approach to socially just teaching–"I don't need to set up some kind of dichotomy like, 'Today we are going to do social justice. Tomorrow we are going to do writing. The next day we are going to do reading'"–and several students also expressed pleasant emotions such as appreciation and excitement for both the discussions and the activity. In the words of Diedre, an African American student, "She is making us think of our real life with everything we read. Most of the kids in the class have had some trouble with gangs or they've been in rival cliques, so, I mean, I think she is doing a good job of connecting what we're doing in class to our real life."

The final exchange illuminating the levels of emotion evoked in the students' exploration of the issues of violence came in a series of class discussions based on poetry. In these exchanges, various students embraced emotions of hope; others rejected it, drawing from their own experiences and from their view of the larger human experience. Sara first asked students to respond to Langston Hughes' poem, "Harlem Dream," by writing poetry describing their own hopes and dreams. Jonathan (working class White male) commented to Sara "my dream is to have a dream." Similarly, Jake (African American male) first shouted out, "There is no hope! Reality gonna smack you in the head!" and then quietly spoke to himself (picked up on audio-tape but inaudible to Sara): "Don't think your dream will stay alive. I don't have no dreams. I have nightmares…. I'll end up in jail."

Later Sara led a discussion summarizing the ways different groups throughout history have stereotyped, abused, and oppressed others, often resulting in violent exchanges. She then asked students to consider the possibility of nonviolence based on the vision of a shared, common humanity depicted in Maya Angelou's poem, "The Human Family."

Rachel (African American female): [The poem] says that our similarities outweigh the differences. We're all humans.

Sara: And because we're all human, what do we all share?

Jonathan (White male): Emotions. We all feel emotions.

Jake (African American male): Do you believe [the poet, that we are all the same]?

Sara: I do believe her. Do you?

Carl: I don't believe her because she hasn't met everyone….[Some people] laugh and some are serious. That means we're different.

Sophia (White female): We are separated by what we look like on outside, but then we get to know each other and have so much in common. It may be a total stranger, but we can have so much in common.

Lawanda (African American female): I think we all people. We all human.

Emotions Related to Ongoing Reflection on Socially Just Teaching

Sara's strongest emotionality wove throughout the semester as she reflected on her efficacy as a socially just teacher. Many privileged students and teachers do not want to believe that they gain advantage at the expense of others or that their privileges came unearned. As a result, privileges remain largely invisible to those who have them (Fields et al., 2007). As Fields and her colleagues explain:

> The meritocratic ideal allows people to assume that they earned their comforts and advantages. If they came to believe otherwise, they might feel guilty about the benefits they receive. In addition, if privileged people were to recognize their unearned advantages and become allies of subordinates, then they would have to confront their fear about fighting the very system that benefits them. (p. 168)

In this case study, this was vividly seen in Sara's struggle with her white colleagues difficulty in *seeing* the normativity and privileges of whiteness (Chubbuck 2004), and in Sara's feeling that the privilege of her own white experience often tainted even her most sincere efforts at socially just teaching. When discussing gang violence in the literature and related to current events in the local community, Sara struggled with worry that her ignorance as a privileged white woman blinded her to the emotional responses her students might have to the topics. "I also felt uncomfortable and guilty regarding the disparity between my own personal privilege and the general lack of privilege of my students. What does a White girl from [my Midwestern state] know about gangs, and how can I begin that conversation in class in a way that it is meaningful and productive?" This reality struck sharply during a class discussion following a particularly violent week-end in the city. As Sara recounts this discussion: "You know, I come in talking, 'There were 28 shootings over Memorial Day, isn't that sad, this is the cyle of violence, blah, blah, blah,' and one of my students, said, 'I saw one of them.' You know, I don't even know what I'm talking about." Sara's emotional struggle over Chu calling her racist captures similar emotions of doubt and guilt.

Emotions functioned in other ways for Sara, however, as both a product of injustice and a motivation for activism to address injustice. "[M]y interest in becoming a teacher for social justice was that I just became really wrapped up in my emotions about it and I felt a lot of sorrow and frustration early on... that led to my interest in creating awareness in the world or working to end some of those injustice." In addition, Sara equated emotions such as anxiety and distress as evidence of her commitment to social justice. "A part of me feels like if I get rid of my anxiety, then I won't care about social justice any more. Logically, I recognize that you can care without anxiousness, but I think sometimes I equate a lack of anxiety with some kind of complacency. Like 'If you're not pissed off, you're not paying attention.' "

Perhaps her strongest experience of emotion, however, was related to the moral significance Sara assigned to being a socially just teacher. "Teaching for social justice carries a gravity that maybe teaching [by itself] doesn't. I see everything that I do as a political act or philosophical act, so just getting through the day is not just to me. When I have a lesson that I don't think goes well, I equate that with some kind of injustice, which has a greater gravity." Any sense that she was failing in her efforts to be an effective socially just teacher left Sara feeling that she was complicit in a larger system of oppression working against the well-being of her students. The result was a strong mixture of anxiety, guilt, and self-doubt that continually drove her to reflect and adjust her practice to try to reach greater effectiveness.

Reconceptualizing the Interplay Between Emotions and Social Justice Education

Our goals in this last part of the chapter are to transcend some of the complexities and challenges of how emotions and social justice are related in order to provide critical perspectives of social justice education coupled with emotional perspectives. Embracing and enacting a vision of social justice education can evoke a range of emotions, from excitement and passion to anxiety and resentment. Social justice education as a struggle for equitable access to learning and empowered students can leave the teachers feeling overwhelmed by the enormity of the task and the students experiencing tremendous discomfort (Chubbuck and Zembylas 2008). Ellsworth (1989) described vividly the immense emotional challenges of teaching/learning for social justice, emphasizing the emotional ambivalence associated with enacting critical pedagogy. The implied sense of high moral stakes involved in transforming the "iniquitous relations of power" (Giroux 1997, p. 313) existing in society adds yet another layer to the emotionality of social justice education.

To act, then, in opposition to the taken-for-granted social inequalities and to struggle to formulate educational practices that are socially just necessitate the acknowledgement of the interplay between emotions and social justice education. In our previous work (Chubbuck and Zembylas 2008; Zembylas 2008a), we proposed the term *critical emotional praxis* to denote how emotions can be engaged as critical and transformative forces in social justice education. Critical emotional praxis is a "tool" that embodies emotional resistance to the unjust processes and practices that maintain cycles of inequality, in both schools and the larger society. In particular, we have described three important dimensions of critical emotional praxis. First, critical emotional praxis is grounded in and interrogates a historical and political understanding of the role of emotions in power relations within a classroom and the society at large. In other words, critical emotional praxis consists in the ability to question emotionally charged, cherished beliefs, exposing how privileged positions and comfort zones inform the ways in which one recognizes what and how he/she has been taught to see/act (or not to see/act), and empowering different ways of being with/for the other. Second, critical emotional praxis illuminates the transactional role of emotions in local contexts. That is, the specific context produces emotional responses; simultaneously, emotions shape the particulars of the context. This transaction can challenge or sustain just and unjust relations. And third, critical emotional praxis translates these emotional understandings into relationships, pedagogical practices, and policies that benefit social justice education. That is, it is not enough to acknowledge either the politicized terrain of emotion or its local manifestation; rather, social justice education coupled with emotional perspectives ultimately has the goal of transformation. These three dimensions, which operate concurrently rather than linearly, are discussed and further developed below.

First, the important intersection of emotion and social justice education is seen in the constitutive role emotions play in the formation and maintenance of just and unjust structures in society, both historically and currently; in these, emotions work to make various categorizations that include some individuals or groups and exclude others (see Ahmed 2004). Sara demonstrated this understanding by constantly examining the emotional implications of unjust systems and practices such as the relatively indifferent response of faculty and the reactive policy of administrators regarding more problematic students such as Chu. Similarly, during the discussion of anger as inevitably leading to violence, Sara challenged her students to question their interpretations of this dynamic, thus creating an opening to consider how anger at injustice may be instead result in nonviolent activism for greater justice.

This aspect of critical emotional praxis–that is, the acknowledgement of the role of emotion in the unjust systems and practices–suggests that teachers and students need to interrogate how their own emotional investments in core beliefs, derived from unexamined interpretation of historical and current day social norms, may contribute to the perpetuation of social inequalities. Teachers and students can gain a historical and political understanding of the role of emotions in power relationships by constantly reflecting on their core beliefs, emotions, and commitments to various ideas and practices and the *effect* of these beliefs and emotions in their everyday lives. Do emotions work to make various categorizations that include some individuals or groups and exclude others? How are those categorizations linked to personal emotional attachments to ideas and practices and constitute one's ways of seeing (or not seeing) and of being with others? Raising these questions is not a liberator act by itself, yet it begins to challenge students' and teachers' interpretations of emotions (e.g. resentment, hatred, apathy) and the ideologies in which they may be grounded (e.g. nationalism, racism). At the same time, considering how anger can be channeled into activism against inequity and cultivating emotions such as excitement, love and compassion can begin to inspire students and provide them with an alternative "paradigm" of fighting for social justice.

Two implications serve to illustrate the importance of identifying and challenging the ways emotion is linked and sustains historical and political hierarchies of power. First, an education that is grounded on highlighting a society's glory and greatness while failing to appreciate the consequences of sustained social inequalities induces a fictional conception about community and social justice. Focusing almost exclusively on "pleasant" feelings–such as pride for a nation's economic wealth and development on the basis of a meritocratic rhetoric–while ignoring social inequalities, seeks to eradicate past shameful acts via an erasure of certain histories under a veneer of tolerance (Fortier 2005). For example, liberal multiculturalist discourses assume that anybody can adopt "the nation" and be adopted by "the nation", insofar as these individuals "speak the *right* language and do the *right* thing" (ibid., p. 570, added emphasis). Thus pride embraces pleasant emotions (for some) and repels unpleasant ones that mask power relations and sustained inequalities, especially for marginalized groups and communities.

Second, an education which remains fixed on moral polarities ("good-us" vs. "bad-them") that privilege pleasant emotions about one's community and nation, fails to recognize the place of racism, oppression and wrongdoing–and thus unpleasant yet productive feelings for those practices (Zembylas 2008c)–in the historical process of how a modern nation-state has been built (Probyn 2005). The desire for pride and the repulsion of shame in almost all modern nation-states (and their educational systems) since the nineteenth century has become a major mechanism of self-affirmation (Barkan 2000). An opening to gain a renewed sense of passion, excitement and solidarity through questioning existing social inequalities cannot be achieved by good will alone or by declaring that deep down "we are all strangers" (Ahmed 2005). We must acknowledge, insists Ahmed, that we have a shared vulnerability yet at the same time we also need to acknowledge that way some have been systematically marginalized and recognized "as stranger than others, as border objects that have been incorporated and then expelled from the ideal of the community" (p. 109). In order to subvert the moralistic tales that continue to exclude, education must develop critiques of *every* form of belonging and not sanitize some while encouraging others. We need to find new healthier, more just ways of living with others "through the process of speaking about the past, and through exposing the wounds that get concealed by the 'truths' of a certain history" (Ahmed 2004, p. 201). In our case study example, the exchange among students on hope and nonviolence was based on a sense of common humanity (see Butler 2004). Sara was trying to break down the "us-them" thinking and succeeded with the girls, but the boys couldn't get past the despair of their own circumstances.

Third critical emotional praxis illuminates the complex and often contradictory emotions elicited in teachers' and students' enactment of social justice education in the local context. The emotions produced in this transaction can alternately impede or empower the pursuit of justice. In our case study example, Sara constantly pushed herself to reflect on her teaching and to change herself and her practice to make her classroom more democratic and just; that is, her emotions actually served as a vehicle to prompt action for initiating and sustaining changes in her socially just teaching. In fact, both her own and her students' emotions lay at the heart of Sara's struggles for enacting a just teaching practice. Some students' struggled to embrace hope while, simultaneously; others were able to envision the hope of a shared humanity. Sara seemed to understand quite well that if one of her goals was to facilitate social justice through transforming her students, then she had to navigate not only her own emotions but also those of her students and the emotional culture in the classroom and the school. Sara's enactment of socially just teaching fundamentally required personally recognizing and challenging the ways anxiety, disillusionment and hopelessness, both in herself and in her students, were used to reproduce existing structures in the classroom.

Thus, on one hand, the process of engaging in social justice education often incurs feelings of anger, grief, disappointment, and resistance, all of which can reduce efforts to work for a more just learning experience. Teachers who are members of the dominant culture may have to deal with their own emotional demons (Berlak 2004; Dlamini 2002). Among teachers of color, other emotions emerge, including anger, frustration, and discouragement over being marginalized and silenced in school discourse about unjust educational practices (Delpit 1995; Lipman 1997). Also, this process is emotionally discomforting for students. In particular, many privileged students, argues Wang (2005), resort to rational arguments or sentimental reactions and fail to acknowledge how their own emotional attachments affect their knowledge and practices. Some students respond to the discomfort involved "by choosing to reinforce their own identities rather than risk self-transformation, while others feel overwhelmed and depressed by the dark side of history and culture, from which they have been sheltered" (ibid., p. 58). Engaging in critical emotional praxis, then, can easily lead students to emotions of pity for those who suffer or feelings of resentment from the part of those who constantly feel subordinated (Chizhik and Chizhik 2002). Therefore, it is possible that students from dominated groups can be locked in to emotional responses that hamper their ability to embrace greater justice. This is an issue that deserves further investigation in future research.

On the other hand, social justice education can produce passionate emotions that create new openings for critical inquiry and action; developing the capacity for critical inquiry and action regarding the production and construction of differences gives people a tool, which will be useful over their lifetime (Boler and Zembylas 2003; Zembylas 2007b). Critical emotional praxis, as a transformative tool, illuminates how power relations in the classroom and the school are inextricable aspects of how teachers and students feel, and further, that those feelings are linked to larger political and cultural struggles. In their enactment of critical emotional praxis, teachers and students have to deal with "emotional landmines" (Boler, 2001, p. 1) created in the classroom and the community, in order to understand and challenge how they shape and mark one's sense of emotional attachment and identity. Developing the skills and knowledge to analyze how unjust practices teach people to unquestioningly, unwittingly *feel* the world through an ideological lens is an important step in identifying exploitation, alienation, and disparities between the haves and the have-nots.

But things do not stop when identifying alienation and exploitation; it is important that students be provided with *critical hope* (Freire 1994). Critical hope inspires teachers and students to see patterns in their emotional, historical and material lives, to realize how these patterns are made and what their consequences are for maintaining the status quo, and to motivate teachers and students to position themselves critically (Zembylas 2007a). To put it in another way, critical hope entails a willingness to speak with the "language of possibility" in the struggle to initiate transformations in everyday life. This is in fact an eye-opening perspective, if one considers that the notions of hope, possibility and transformation are what emotions are about; our emotions encompass hope, passion and struggle for a transformed life world that rises above injustice, discrimination and healing of past traumas. Pedagogies of critical hope (Zembylas 2007a), then, point to the need to identify how educational discourses and practices are embodied in the day-to-day routines of school life and to recognize possibilities are opened up for interrupting repressive practices. Students and teachers bring different emotional histories with them to school; these histories are embedded in a wider context of sociopolitical forces, needs and interests. Developing pedagogies that offer critical hope would mean developing affective connections and social relations that inspire connection, understanding, appreciation, love and desire, all of which will motivate the creation a more fair and just world.

Finally, critical emotional praxis draws from the above emotional understandings and responds to the particular context in which a school is located, creating and enacting pedagogies that reconceptualize the emotional culture of a classroom/school. In our case study example, a key to sustaining Sara's process of transformation was emotional reflexivity translated into action to initiate changes in her socially just teaching (e.g. through engaging students in real world analysis, embracing justice in all aspects of classroom and school life, and relating with students in a more empathic manner). These pedagogic actions, which essentially re-educate emotions, are important aspects of social justice education because they uncover and problematize the deeply embedded emotional dimensions that frame and shape daily habits, routines, and unconscious complicity with hegemony. Attending to emotional habits as part of social justice education draws attention to the ways teachers and students enact and embody dominant values and assumptions in their daily habits and routines. By closely examining emotional reactions and responses, teachers and students from the dominant culture begin to identify unconscious privileges as well as invisible ways in which they comply with dominant ideology (Boler and Zembylas 2003). Thus, surfacing and interrogating emotions that are prompted by social justice education can also be a critical tool to change those policies and practices that create the cyclical reproduction of injustices and hegemonic relations (Zembylas 2007b; Callahan 2004). Similarly, students from oppressed groups can engage in an interrogation of emotions that may lock them in to responses of violence and postures of despair. In addition, as all students encounter examples of oppression and injustice, the emotions of sorrow and discomfort they experience can pierce apathy and provide the catalyst needed to act for change (Greene 1998).

Critical emotional praxis, therefore, includes the translation of emotions as critical and transformative forces into socially just pedagogies, policies, and action. Education for/about social justice needs to provide opportunities for self-transcendence, passion and imagination to create a more fair and just world. Teachers and students need to be given opportunities to engage in intrapersonal reflection on their emotional understanding of justice related issues (Darling-Hammond 2004). It is important for students to see their teachers enacting just teaching practices in the classroom and be inspired by examples of positive and hopeful possibilities to promote social justice. The analysis of affective relations bound up with stories of (in)justice has important educational implications, and educators need to be able to construct productive and hopeful spaces in which difference and identity can be understood and lived ethically and relationally.

To return to an earlier point we made, there may be no foundational criteria of justice, but this need not rule out provisional agreements for the construction of warranted assertions about what constitutes social inequalities and injustices–that is, the recognition that justice as a response to the Other unavoidably involves the navigation in difficult affective spaces. Social justice is a sign of ethical obligation to others, through the reification of feeling for others and their suffering. This is why injustice may take the form of perpetuating particular kinds of affective relations to social norms. Challenging injustice, then, in the context of social justice education requires the search of practices to interrupt these norms and consequently to subvert normalizing affective relations with respect to the nation, religion, gender or race. Teachers and students must learn how to unpack their cherished beliefs and comfort zones in order to deconstruct the ways in which they have learned to see, feel and act (Boler and Zembylas 2003; Zembylas 2007a). They must recognize in what ways emotions define how and what one chooses to see, and conversely, not to see (e.g. how racial dynamics privilege some groups at the expense of others, and how compassion for the suffering of the underprivileged often involves discomfort for one's own privilege). Justice and identity claims must be constantly interrogated and continually reinvented outside of universal statements that are epistemologically driven. To attend to difference is not to "speak of it" but to offer possibilities to experience the impossibility of responding to others within a set of absolute criteria.

In summary, we need to acknowledge that the disruption of normative politics of emotion around social inequalities is certainly not an easy task for educators. The dispositions of the hegemonic discourses are not easily suspended by a simple effort or will. Affective communities grounded in long-time emotions are not easily undone through an educational program in which ideas of critical emotional praxis are somehow infused. The issue, as Bourdieu asserts, is not "a simple 'conversion of minds'… produced by rational preaching and education" (2000, p. 180). However, it is extremely important for scholars and teacher practitioners to examine the interplay between emotions and social justice education by exploring what emotions *do* in everyday discourses and practices in relation to social justice and by finding ways to translate such analyses into critical emotional praxis. Engaging in critical emotional praxis can evoke public and school pedagogies that provide alternative ways of relating to otherness. A sustained endeavor to recognize social inequalities offers the potential to reinvent pedagogical spaces in which similarities and differences with others may be critically articulated and felt, toward constructing new shared possibilities.

Conclusions

This chapter brings together discussions about the interplay of emotions and social justice education. It has suggested that recognition of emotions is of fundamental significance to social justice education. We hold that social justice education is not simply a cognitive endeavor; emotions are fundamentally significant and constitutive in the process of justice. Therefore, social justice education involves engaging in emotional reflection, finding one's own contextualized relationship to justice, and creating an empowered sense of agency to take action to tackle inequalities in practice. If we ignore the emotional aspects of social justice education or subsume those into cognitive activity, we risk simplifying the complexity of teaching/learning for/about social justice, and in that simplification, we run the risk of missing the openings of possibility where we, as educators, can enact pedagogies that disrupt taken-for-granted knowledge and dispositions.

Giroux (1997, 2004) and McLaren (2003) emphasize the importance of interrogating the politics and meanings of educational practices and discourses as part of a larger project to build democracy and social justice. A task such as this requires the transformation of teachers' and students' dispositions within an affective network of relations. Such a transformation emerges out of the very practices and strategies in which relations operate, that is, by changing the practices enacted in a classroom to produce alterative emotional capital. For example, engaging in inclusive practices rather than exclusive and divisive rituals that divide is an important step towards re-establishing close affective networks; the literature on inclusive, multicultural and anti-racist education is full of practical examples how to accomplish this (Zembylas 2007a). For instance, numerous programs in social, emotional, health and peace education focus specifically on developing social-emotional practices and dispositions (e.g. empathy, multiperspectivity, collaboration, criticality, participation in democracy, and well-being) that help students interrogate the affective ways with which individuals are involved in unequal and unjust social structures (Cohen 2006). Through these programs, students can engage in the critical reflection needed to see how fears are embedded in the absence of care for one another and in the wider social injustices rather than framing the issue of their emotions in individual terms. Engaging and reflecting on the emotions of social justice in education is an important mechanism through which we can advance our understanding of how to tackle the systemic processes that reproduce inequalities in education.

Recognizing the role of emotions in social justice education and enacting critical emotional praxis has strong implications for teachers and students alike. As Callahan (2004) explains, coping with the emotions that occur as a result of critical pedagogies requires more than dialogue. Ellsworth (1989), in fact, emphasizes that, by itself, dialogue that increases awareness of existing power structures in society may simply heighten emotional responses without producing meaningful change. An important implication, then, is that educators need to address the significance of emotion in sustaining or dismantling structures of power, privilege, racism, and colonization. For example, these structures depend upon withholding particular emotional responses (such as grief, remorse, compassion and caring) towards certain groups of people deemed *other*. Teachers and students, then, would benefit if they were given opportunities in to engage in reflection on their emotional understanding of justice related issues.

An analytical focus on emotions in the context of social justice education raises new questions and modifies those that already dominate the field. In what ways can critical emotional praxis further deepen inclusion of marginalized students? How do emotions affect the subjectivities and identities of the teachers and students who are engaged in social justice education? What forms do new openings take when the recognition of emotions in social justice education is used to disrupt educational processes and practices that maintain cycles of inequality? Interrogating the role of emotion in teaching for social justice is an important challenge for critical pedagogues both in terms of policy and practice. Thus explicit attention should be paid to the ways in which the affective politics of social justice intersect with the emotionality of teaching and learning practices.

References

Ahmed S (2004) The cultural politics of emotion. Edinburgh University Press, Edinburgh
Ahmed S (2005) The skin of the community: Affect and boundary formation. In: Chanter T, Ziarek P (eds) Revolt, affect, collectivity: The unstable boundaries of Kristeva's polis (pp. 95 111). Albany. State University of New York Press, NY
Barkan E (2000) The guilt of nations: Restitution and negotiating historical injustices. Norton, New York
Berezin M (2001) Emotions and political identity: mobilizing affection for the polity. In: Goodwin J, Jasper J, Polletta F (eds) Passionate politics: emotions and social movements. The University of Chicago Press, Chicago, pp 83–98
Berlak A (2004) Confrontation and pedagogy: cultural secrets and emotion in antioppressive pedagogies. In: Boler M (ed) Democratic dialogue in education: troubling speech, disturbing silence. Peter Lang, New York, pp 123–144
Berlant L (2000) The subject of true feeling: Pain, privacy and politics. In: Ahmed S, Kilby J, Lury C, McNeil M, Skeggs B (eds) transformations: thinking through feminism. Routledge, London, pp 33–47
Boler, M. (April, 2001). LoveOnLine: *educating eros in digital education.* Paper presented at the annual meeting of the American Educational Research Association.
Boler M, Zembylas M (2003) Discomforting truths: The emotional terrain of understanding differences. In: Tryfonas P (ed) Pedagogies of difference: Rethinking education for social justice. Routledge, New York, pp 110–136
Bourdieu, P. (2000). Pascalian meditations (trans. R. Nice). : Stanford University Press Stanford.
Butler J (2004) Precarious life: the powers of mourning and violence. Verso, London
Callahan JL (2004) Breaking the cult of rationality: Mindful awareness of emotion in the critical theory classroom. New Dir Adult and Conti Educ 102:75–83
Chizhik EW, Chizhik AW (2002) A path to social change: Examining students' responsibility, opportunity, and emotion toward social justice. Edu Urban Soc 34:283–297
Chubbuck SM (2004) Whiteness enacted, Whiteness disrupted: The complexity of personal congruence. American Educational Research Journal 4(2):301–333
Chubbuck SM (2008) A Novice's beliefs about socially just teaching: dialogue of multiple voices. New Educ 4(4):309–329
Chubbuck S, Zembylas M (2008) The emotional ambivalence of socially just teaching: A case study of a novice urban schoolteacher. Am Educ Res J 45(2):274–318
Cochran-Smith M (2004) Walking the road: race, diversity, and social justice in teacher education. Teachers College Press, New York city
Cohen J (2006) Social, emotional, ethical, and academic education: creating a climate for learning, participation in democracy, and well-being. Harv Educ Rev 76(2):201–237

Cremer D, Bos K (2007) Justice and feelings: toward a new era in justice research. Soc Justice Res 20:1–9

Darling-Hammond, L. (2004). Learning to teach for social justice. In L. Darling-Hammond, J. French & S. Garcia-Lopez, S. (Eds.), *Learning to teach for social justice* (pp. 1-7). New York City: Teachers College Press.

Delpit L (1995) Other people's children: cultural conflict in the classroom. New York Press, New York

Dhillon P (2000) The sublime face of just education. In: Dhillon P, Standish P (eds) Lyotard: Just education. Routledge, London, pp 110–124

Dlamini SN (2002) From the other side of the desk: notes on teaching about race when racialized. Race, Ethn Educ 5:51–66

Ellsworth E (1989) Why doesn't this feel empowering? Working through the repressive myths of critical pedagogy. Harv Educ Rev 59:297–324

Fields J, Copp M, Kleinman S (2007) Symbolic interactionism, inequality, and emotions. In: Stets JE, Turner J (eds) Handbook of the sociology of emotions. Springer, Dordrecht, The Netherlands, pp 155–178

Fortier A-M (2005) Pride politics and multiculturalist citizenship. Ethnic Racial Stud 28:559–78

Freire P (1994) Pedagogy of hope: reliving pedagogy of the oppressed. Continuum, New York

Giroux HA (1997) Rewriting the discourse of racial identity: towards a pedagogy and politics of whiteness. Harv Educ Rev 67(2):285–320

Giroux HA (2004) Critical pedagogy and the postmodern/modern divide: towards pedagogy of democratization. Teach Educ Q 31(1):132–153

Greene, M. (1998). Introduction: teaching for social justice. In W. Ayers, J.A. Hunt, & T. Quinn (Eds.) *Teaching for social justice* (pp. xxvii-xlvi). New York: New Press.

Jasso G (2007) Emotion in justice processes. In: Stets JE, Turner J (eds) Handbook of the sociology of emotions. Springer, Dordrecht, The Netherlands, pp 321–346

Kant, I. (1959). *Foundations of the metaphysics of morals* (L. W. Beck, trans.). Indianapolis, IN: Bobbs-Me.

Karstedt S (2002) Emotions and criminal justice. Theor Criminol 6:299–317

Kincheloe JL, Steinberg SR (1998) Addressing the crisis of whiteness: Reconfiguring white identity in a pedagogy of whiteness. In: Kincheloe JL, Steinberg SR, Rodriguez NM, Chennault RE (eds) White reign: Deploying whiteness in America (pp. 3–29). New York: St. Martin's Press

King JE (2005) Black education: A transformative research and action agenda for the new century. Erlbaum, Mahwah, NJ

Kristjánsson K (2005) Justice and desert-based emotions. Philos Explor 8:53–68

Lipman P (1997) Restructuring in context: A case study of teacher participation and the dynamics of ideology, race, and power. Am Educ Res J 34(1):3–38

Lutz C, Abu-Lughod L (eds) (1990) Language and the politics of emotion. Cambridge University Press, Cambridge

Lyotard, J.-F., & Thébaud, J.-L. (1985). *Just gaming* (W. Godzich, Trans.). Minneapolis: University of Minnesota Press.

McLaren P (2003a) Life in schools: an introduction to critical pedagogy in the foundations of education, 4th edn. Allyn and Bacon, Boston

Nieto S (2000) Placing equity front and center. J Teach Educ 51(3):180–187

O' Brien M, Flynn M (2007) Emotions, inequalities and care in education. In: Downes P, Gilligan AL (eds) Beyond educational disadvantage. IPA, Dublin, pp 70–88

Probyn E (2005) Blush: faces of shame. University of Minnesota Press, Minneapolis and London

Rawls J (1971) A theory of justice. Harvard University Press, Cambridge, MA

Solomon R (1989) The emotions of justice. Soc Just Res 3:345–374

Solomon R (1990) A passion for justice: emotions and the origins of the soc contract. Addison-Wesley, Reading, MA

Suny, R. G. (2004). Why we hate you: The passions of national identity and ethnic violence. Berkeley: University of California. http://repositories.cdlib.org/iseees/bps/2004_01-suny

Thrift, N. (2004). Intensities of feeling: Towards a spatial politics of affect. Geografiska Annaler 86:55–76

Thrift N (2005) But malice aforethought: cities and the natural history of hatred. Trans Inst Br Geogr 30:133–150

Turner JH (2007) Justice and emotions. Soc Justice Res 20:288–311

Wang H (2005) Aporias, responsibility, and the im/possibility of teaching multicultural education. Educ Theory 55(1):45–59

Zembylas M (2007a) Five pedagogies, a thousand possibilities: affect, critical hope, transformation. SensePublishers, Rotterdam, The Netherlands

Zembylas, M. (2007b). The power and politics of emotions in teaching. In P. A Schutz & R. Peckrun (Eds.), *Emotions in education* (pp. 293-309). New York: Academic Press.

Zembylas M (2008a) The politics of trauma in education. Palgrave, MacMillan, New York

Zembylas M (2008b) Trauma, justice and the politics of emotion: The violence of sentimentality in education. Discourse Stud Cultur Polit of Educ 29:1–17

Zembylas M (2008c) The politics of shame in intercultural education. Educ, Citizenship Soc Justice 3(3):263–280

Part VI
A Future Agenda for Research on Teachers' Emotions in Education

Chapter 18
Research on Teachers' Emotions in Education: Findings, Practical Implications and Future Agenda

Michalinos Zembylas and Paul A. Schutz

Abstract In this chapter we synthesize the themes that emerge from the other chapters. Additionally, we discuss future directions for inquiry on teachers' emotions, as well as implications for classroom instruction, intervention, teachers' professional development, teachers' lives, and educational policy and leadership. Finally, we use the content of the chapters to discuss the variety, timeliness, and potential for transformation of the field, and the unique contributions of the chapters to our understanding of teachers' emotions in education

Keywords Future research agenda · Teacher emotions · Practical implications

In this book, a variety of scholars have shared a number of important findings on the impact of emotions on teachers' lives, showing what emotions *do* in teachers' everyday practices. These findings suggest that emotions are important to pedagogical practices, to student–teacher relationships, to issues of reform efforts and processes of change, and to an understanding of power relations and social structures in schools and the society. In closing, we synthesize the contributions of these investigations in relation to some relevant themes developed in this book. Additionally, we discuss the practical implications for designing effectively sound classroom instruction for student- and teacher-focused intervention, for teachers' professional development, and for educational policy and leadership and we offer an outline of some future directions for inquiry on teacher emotion in education.

Two important insights are highlighted in the last chapter of this book. First, the subject of practical implications of the research shared here for teachers' lives is addressed. In discussing this subject, we suggest that it is valuable for all researchers in this area to have a critical edge, that is, to address research questions that develop different frameworks and offer mutliperspectival "answers" to questions about the

M. Zembylas (✉)
Program of Educational Studies, Open University of Cyprus, Cyprus
e-mail: m.zembylas@ouc.ac.cy

P.A. Schutz and M. Zembylas (eds.), *Advances in Teacher Emotion Research:*   367
The Impact on Teachers' Lives,
DOI 10.1007/978-1-4419-0564-2_18, © Springer Science+Business Media, LLC 2009

role of emotions in teachers' lives than the responses explored so far. Second, there is the issue of the state of research on teachers' emotions today, the research and intellectual traditions that are followed and the need for further enrichment of this work, in light of the contributing ideas from the present volume. The purpose of this discussion is to indicate aspects of teachers' emotions not fully explored in the past, but which are important to examine in the future. Both of these insights are grounded in an important idea emphasized more or less in almost all of the chapters in this book: the link between micro-perspectives at the level of the "teacher self" and the macroscopic level of social, cultural and political structures of schooling. In concluding this volume, we want to address the importance of keeping both levels in perspective – an idea that is often lost in the effort to investigate how emotions are embedded in teachers' lives and thus to explore the potential transactions among micro and macroscopic perspectives.

Findings and Practical Implications of Research on Teachers' Emotions

Research findings in this book highlight four important implications for teachers' lives, in correspondence to the four major sections in which this book is divided (excluding the introduction and the final chapter). After briefly summarizing each major finding, a discussion of the relevant implication is undertaken. The first major finding is that teacher emotions are inextricably linked to teachers' well being, identity and emotion management in teaching. Evidence from the chapters in the second section shows that teachers' emotional well being is a necessary condition for their sense of effectiveness (Chap. 2: Day and Qing); in particular, beginning teachers struggle emotionally with increasing pressures and accountability demands that have negative effects on their sense of identity and self-efficacy (Chap. 3: Bullough). Emotion management, then, becomes an indispensable process with which teachers deal with professional expectations and leaves a significant mark on teachers' themselves, the culture of teaching and schooling more generally (Chap. 4: Oplatka). As more demands are being made upon teachers, it is important that policy makers, teacher educators and school leaders attend to teachers' own sense of emotional well-being and put in place specific processes that deal with the unpleasant effects of emotion management in teaching. Bullough in Chap. 3, shared one such process; mentoring beginning teachers and offering them emotional support may prove valuable in their struggle to formulate a productive professional identity. Meyer in Chap. 5 emphasizes in particular that there are implications for student teachers' identity and development, if emotions are ignored or adjusted with reason; that is, the kind of emotion management employed on the first stage of professional induction, the student teaching experience, seems to draw particular professional trajectories for new teachers as they enter the emotional practice of teaching. As authors of Chaps. 2–5 suggest, to achieve and sustain a healthy state of well being, teachers (including beginning teachers and student teachers) need to develop specific strategies to manage successfully the cognitive and emotional challenges of working in sometimes difficult conditions and strengthen both relationships with colleagues, students and parents, and their own commitment to educational ideals, sense of efficacy and personal agency. This is an important implication for teachers' professional development and for educational policy and leadership: teachers need ongoing and systematic emotional support in response to the variety of cognitive and emotional challenges of teaching, especially in light of increased performativity demands (addressed in the fourth section).

The second major finding is that teachers' emotions influence and are influenced by student–teacher relationships. These emotions contribute to the formation of particular emotional cultures within classrooms and schools that influence how teachers and students relate emotionally to one another and whether they care for one another or trust each other. There is not yet enough evidence to show the effects of the emotions involved in these relationships on students' learning outcomes (this is certainly an area that needs future investigation) yet there are numerous indications in chapters of the third section that the emotionality of student–teachers relationships is related to both the conditions and the by-products of teaching and learning.

Chang and Davis in Chap. 6 show the pleasant and unpleasant emotional by-products of teachers' relationships with students and the role repeatedly experiencing unpleasant emotions may play in teacher burnout. Chang and Davis also raise the issue of emotion management and teachers' strategies for reframing, rethinking and reinvesting in relationships with students, emphasizing the importance of engaging in critical reflection on the judgments that underlie teachers' emotions. Similarly, Frenzel, Goetz, Stephens and Jacob in Chap. 7 further explain that pleasant and unpleasant teacher emotions have considerable implications for student learning, school climate, and the overall quality of education. Analyzing teachers' resulting emotions from their judgments of perceived success or failure with respect to their classroom goals, Frenzel and her colleagues suggest that attending to teachers' emotional experiences offers great promise for further understanding and optimizing classroom interaction processes; an important educational goal for teachers, then, is to formulate instructional strategies that create and sustain emotionally positive classrooms. The need for emotionally positive classrooms is even more essential in classrooms that have children who experience difficult times such as children living in close proximity to cancer (Chap. 8). The implication of Lasky and Estes's work is that developing school-based, yet community-wide networks of support for teachers and students living with cancer provides the most contextually appropriate resources to deal with the emotional demands of student–teacher relationships under such challenging conditions. Chapters 9 and 10 address several aspects of the ways in which teachers negotiate boundaries in their interactions with their students; while Rosiek in Chap. 9 focuses on the role of emotional scaffolding in advancing student learning, Schutz, Aultman and Williams-Johnson in Chap. 10 emphasize the importance of developing useful emotional climates in the classroom. Rosiek's research has implications in curriculum and instruction processes because it suggests teaching methodologies that place emotional scaffolding at the center. Schutz and his colleagues' research, on the other hand, indicate how teachers feel ill equipped to handle various types of emotional episodes they encounter in the school context.

Therefore, the emotional nature of the classroom provides several implications for the training and professional development of teachers; teacher education courses should provide opportunities for pre- and in-service teachers to examine the individual and social historical influences on their own affective tendencies and reflect upon the ways in which emotional management enhances their ability to anticipate classroom situations with which they may struggle. In general, all of the chapters in the third section draw attention to the idea that teachers need to become aware of the emotions they are experiencing and the ways in which they experience emotional dissonance in their relationships with students; a significant implication from all these findings is that teachers should ultimately seek to be task-focused in their emotion management.

The third major finding is that emotions constitute a key dimension in teachers' lives, especially in times of change – demographic changes; social and cultural changes; large-scale educational reforms – in which emotions are further intensified. Research shared in the fourth section of the book shows that teachers respond emotionally to change in a variety of ways: some teachers are happy to support reforms and welcome change; others experience stress, helplessness or loss, particularly when they face a shift in their student population towards more cultural and ethnic diversity (Chap. 11: Kelchtermans). Particularly, in times of unrelenting social, cultural and political transformations, understanding the emotional aspects of change and the implications for teacher development is essential, if pedagogical and policy initiatives are to be more meaningful and successful. Chapters in the fourth section highlight that teachers' emotional responses toward change are the result of the ways teachers perceive, interpret and evaluate their relationship with the changing environment (Chaps. 12 and 13: van Veen and Turner). For example, when teachers resist externally mandated reforms, it is often because these changes threaten their self-image, their sense of identity, and their emotional bonds with students and colleagues by overloading the curriculum and intensifying teachers' work and control from the outside (van den Berg 2002; Zembylas 2005).

Emotional disappointment with reforms arises not only because of the unwanted imposition of reform demands, but also because of the complex nature of change itself and the changing working conditions. van Veen and Sleegers (Chap. 12) show that even when teachers subscribe to the reform agenda, the complexities of change itself elicit more unpleasant emotions than one would expect on the basis of the teachers' (cognitive) assent. It is not surprising, then, that teachers' emotional responses to change may be negative not only because teachers are excluded rather than included, but also because teachers experience extremely unpleasant emotions about the conditions they have to work in, particularly in an overall climate of increased performativity.

On the other hand, resistance to change is increasingly viewed as part of the process – in fact, it has a modifying influence; thus, teachers' emotional ambivalence towards change can be understood not only on the basis of how individuals respond to change but also in terms of how teachers' emotional responses are embedded in particular social, cultural and political contexts. As Kelchtermans, Ballet and Piot show in their work (Chap. 11), vulnerability is a structural characteristic of the teaching job; this vulnerability triggers intense emotions in times of change. In particular, a careful analysis of the interplay between teacher emotions and micropolitical actions, argue Kelchtermans and his colleagues, and the working conditions in the school can deepen our understanding of how emotions fuel reform efforts and make teachers vulnerable. Kelchtermans and his colleagues analyze the interplay of vulnerability, micropolitics, the changing working conditions, and teachers' coping with them. This research shows how working conditions buffer, modify, and mediate policy demands and thus impact teachers' actions and job experiences.

In Chap. 14, Cross and Hong situate the impact on teachers' emotions as a result of reform efforts in mathematics and science and highlight that changing teaching practices is an emotionally laborious and challenging process, as it involves modifying teachers' existing beliefs about their respective disciplines, teaching and learning, and also reshaping their professional identity as teachers. Understanding the antecedents of these emotional responses, explain Cross and Hong, can allow professional developers and teacher educators to approach reform differently resulting in greater positive effects. Therefore, the first step in accomplishing successful reform implementation is addressing teachers' beliefs about the epistemology of their discipline and teaching and learning within that discipline; furthermore, professional development should take into consideration the psychological factors that influence teachers' decision-making and must also be cognizant of the physical, social and contextual factors that support or impede teachers' efforts to change.

In Chap. 13, Turner, Waugh, Summers and Grove show how social aspects (e.g., teachers' interactions with their principals) interact with teachers' personal characteristics (e.g., their perceptions of personal values and efficacy) in ways that facilitate or hinder their motivation to apply newly-learned skills and content knowledge. According to Turner and her colleagues, understanding factors that affect teachers' implementation of promising ideas presented in high-quality professional development activities as part of educational reform efforts is important because their implementation can ultimately impact students' achievement.

Collectively, Chaps. 11–14 have important implications for teacher education (pre- and in-service). Teacher education and training programs should acknowledge the emotional dimensions of teacher change and help teaching to see the professional relevance and value of teachers' emotional experiences and to support teachers in critically reflecting on those experiences. Professional development could include activities that deliberately aim at making teachers analyze their emotional experience of changes in their working conditions, thus providing ways to disentangle the impact of those changes on their work and on themselves. This "reading" leads to an increased awareness both of the interconnections among teachers' beliefs, identity, goals, and emotions and of the role of social, cultural and political structures in teaching – which is the topic of the fifth section of this book.

The final major finding of this book is that teachers' emotions are embedded in particular social, cultural and political structures. Thus, an emotional culture in a school is held together by a network of socialization practices that are influenced by political, cultural, social and other educational factors. Two important issues are highlighted in the chapters of this section. First, the political aspects of teachers' emotions, especially in light of the power relations involved in social and cultural realities such as diversity and multiculturalism; and the contribution of a critical analysis of teachers' emotions in the context of social and political demands for social justice.

First, the issue of the political aspects of teachers' emotions in light of the power relations involved in social and cultural realities such as diversity and multicultural-ism is raised in Chaps. 16, 17 and 18. Teaching in consideration of diversity and multiculturalism is bound up with the emotional lives of the individuals involved and the social and political circumstances in which those individuals live and express their emotions. These emotions play a constitutive role in how teachers respond to prevailing social norms about diversity and inequality both in schools and the society. For example, Winograd in Chap. 16 suggests that emotions have political implications, which become even more obvious in marginalized teachers' discourses (e.g., African American, Native American and Latino/a American teaches). Teachers' struggles to navigate the emotional ambivalence of teaching in contexts of diversity and/or inequality show both the pleasant and unpleasant emotions that are demanded from coping with school practices and policies under such circumstances. In Chap. 17, DeGuir-Gunby, Long-Mitchell and Grant focus on an exploration of the racist experiences of women professors of color in engineering; how these experiences impact their identities; and the emotions and coping strategies associated with these experiences. The implications of this work emphasize that the best way to help women faculty of color to effectively in the short term is to address and cope with unpleasant emotions in the workplace is to provide them with additional sociofamilial coping resources, particularly more women faculty of color. In Chap. 18, Zembylas and Chubbuck focus on the interplay of emotions with social justice education, and argue that emotions can be engaged as critical and transformational forces to produce better teaching and learning opportunities for marginalized students. There is one important implication in relation to the ways emotion is linked and sustains historical and political hierarchies of power, according to Zembylas and Chubbuck. Teachers need opportunities to engage in critical emotional praxis, that is, critical praxis informed by emotion that resists unjust systems and practices as well as emo-tion that helps create a more fair and just world in our classrooms and our everyday lives. Collectively, the analysis of studies in Chaps. 16–18 suggests that emotions play an important role – essentially a political one – in the context of teaching in/for multicultural societies; therefore, this perspective sets an important agenda for teacher development and teacher education in that teachers should be structurally and emotionally supported in their struggles to cope with the social, cultural and political structures in their work. This brings us to the second issue.

The second issue highlighted by chapters in this section is that understanding teacher development in light of issues of race, gender and power relations is inex-tricably linked to analyzing the pivotal role of emotions and taking action to deal with the impact of social, cultural and political structures. Therefore, engaging teach-ers' and school leaders' emotions in multicultural and social justice education – such as examining one's feelings in the context of teaching for equity and justice – can be a catalyst both to transform educational practices and to problematize perceptions of equity in schools and society. Ameliorating the educational experiences of marginalized students and empowering all students to be agents of change will have more chances of success as teachers understand the tremendous challenges and potential complex relationship of emotions and multicultural and social justice education. If teachers are unaware of the relationship between their own emotional and pedagogical practices, they will be unable to disrupt unjust practices and motivate actions that embrace excitement and passion for social justice.

In this sense, teachers' emotions have profound political dimensions. Once teachers recognize these dimensions, they may engage in a political process of gaining control over how their emotional expressions are interpreted and of changing the meaning of these expressions through participation in practices associated with new meanings. This re-interpretation of the social meanings of teachers' emotional experiences with the creation of positive emotional climate in the classroom and school can be liberatory. The real challenge is to create the space for these meanings to emerge and give rise to new emotional experiences that are personally (and perhaps collectively) more inspiring and evocative.

Future Agenda on Teachers' Emotions

Where do the findings and implications of the research shared in this book leave us? There is undoubtedly a rise of educational interest in teachers' emotions in the last few years. As noted in the edited collection *Emotion in Education* (Schutz and Pekrun 2007), however, the recent rise of interest in emotions in education is not accompanied with the creation of "new" frameworks and constructs but rather the proliferation of frames developed in other related fields (e.g., social psychology, sociology, etc.). The current volume does not completely disassociate itself from this trend as this research area is still young, yet it takes a step further in providing a more focused attention on the emotions of teachers and their implications for teachers' lives. We agree with the claim that it will take some time for researchers in this field to develop contextualized theoretical, conceptual and empirical tools that are relevant to the investigation of teachers' emotions. The issue of developing consensus on the constructs used in this field is important for integrating the findings of studies (Schutz et al.: Chap. 10; Pekrun and Schutz 2007). In other words, it may be useful to develop and use similar concepts or a shared vocabulary for researchers to use while investigating teacher emotion (e.g., see exchanges between Barrett 2006 and Izard 2007). However, it is equally important, in our view, to expand the range of topics and intellectual traditions that are employed to theorize the findings and appreciate their practical implications.

For example, in this volume there are chapters grounded in a variety of scientific paradigms (e.g., experimental research, non-experimental field studies, phenomenological approaches, pragmatism, constructivism, critical race theory, post-structural, feminist, and post-positivist perspectives), and inquiry methods (e.g., quantitative, qualitative, ethnographic, philosophical, historical, autobiographical, and multimethod approaches). It is not uncommon that among these traditions some perspectives might be "incommensurable" on particular grounds, just as it happens in other fields. Without dismissing the problematic grounds of the notion of incommensurability itself, it is important to demonstrate that a "new" approach of researching teachers' emotions requires not only grounding from intellectual resources found in other disciplines (see Barbalet 2001), but also a critical "translation" of those intellectual traditions. Therefore, the stakes are much higher, as researchers of teachers' emotions are unavoidably involved in long-time debates about conceptualizations and theorizations of emotions. The use of experimentalism, pragmatism, constructivism, critical race theory, post-structuralism, feminism or post-positivism, for instance, will have its rewards but it is likely to be limited in a number of ways. Some of these rewards and limitations have been raised in chapters of this volume and thus it is unnecessary to rehearse the arguments. But it is important to suggest that researchers of teachers' emotions should enlarge their theoretical perspectives in the direction of both teacher self and sociopolitical aspects of emotions in teachers' lives as well as the transaction among teacher selves and sociopolitical influences. In this respect, theoretical and methodological approaches need to incorporate multiperspectivity in theorizing and researching teachers' emotions (Schutz et al. 2006).

In a period of increased performativity in teachers' workplace, and under conditions of growing vulnerability and powerlessness, as chapters in the fourth section – "Teachers Emotions in Times of Change" – describe, social, cultural and political changes are experienced as insurmountable obstacles of teachers' capacities to teach. Juxtaposing chapters in the second section – "Teacher Emotions in the Context of Teaching and Teacher Education" – to those in the fourth section, one gets a good impression about the everyday pressures and the emotional intensity in teachers' lives. Although not treated in the frameworks developed in these two sections, there is growing evidence in other fields about the historical development of emotional intensity at the workplace both in North American and European contexts (e.g., see Stearns 1994; Wouters 1986). Emotional labor may involve enhancing, faking, and/or suppressing emotions to modify one's emotional expressions (Hochschild 1983). Emotional labor in teaching and especially the emotional labor demanded in student–teacher relationships in the classroom are areas of research that have not received much attention. Therefore, the chapters of the third section – "Student–teacher Involvement" – shed light on this issue but given its complex dimensions (e.g., emotional self-control strategies; vulnerability) the focus of research on student–teacher relationships needs to broaden to explore, for instance, how student motivation and learning are relevant to emotional labor and self-control. At the same time, the chapters of the fifth section – "Race, Gender and Power Relationships" – show that teachers' emotions are not confined to those emotions constituted by the managed emotions; rather, the social, cultural and political significance of emotion is shown in the experience of teachers struggling to deal with emotional intensity in a wider context.

Given the multiple demands entailed in teachers' work, it is not surprising that much of the current research on teachers' emotions is focused on the implications of emotion management on teachers' lives. The study of teachers' emotions from this perspective informs understanding of how teachers' emotions influence teachers' and students' cognitions, motivation and behavior, but the multiple approaches taken in this book show why such a focus is too limited a perspective. In different chapters in this book the authors focus on different ideas such as the influence of teachers' emotion on one's self-concept, perception, and judgment, the relationship between emotion and teacher identity, how students are influenced by teachers' emotions, and how teachers' emotions are inextricable aspects of curricular decisions and educational reforms. Also, part of the discussion in several chapters – especially those of the fourth and fifth sections – demonstrates the importance of emotion constructs in accounts of social and political structures. The significance of gender and race to power relations and social structures has been indicated in Chap. 15 (Winograd) and Chap. 16 (DeCuir-Gunby et al.); the interplay of emotions with social justice education is understood through an analysis of the politics of emotions in Chap. 17 (Zembylas and Chubbuck). An issue, therefore, that seeks further investigation in the area of research on teachers' emotions is the need to develop research and pedagogical tools that promote teacher and student empowerment and self-development *in light of particular social, cultural and political structures*. Most work so far, even in this collection, has been descriptive in terms of identifying aspects that influence curriculum, teaching and learning outcomes. Central to developing future research methodologies and pedagogies of emotion – that is, pedagogies that take into consideration the role of emotion – are ideas that have largely been ignored or dismissed as irrelevant to an understanding of social, cultural and political structures. On the basis of this notion, for example, teachers' emotions cannot be regarded only in their psychological or interpersonal aspects; instead, they need to be regarded as the very location of the capacity to critique emotional practices implicated in social and political structures.

In the struggles over the questions of how power is exercised, recent theories such as critical, postcolonial and intersectionality theories, along with perspectives in history and anthropology of emotion (e.g., see Lutz and Abu-Lughod 1990; Reddy 2001; Rosaldo 1984), show us how emotions are not constructed from nothing but are controlled, shaped, and challenged in particular ways and for particular purposes. And here is precisely where the political stakes come in (Zembylas 2005, 2007). Our collection here challenges once again the notion that emotions, feelings, and bodies are in opposition to cognition, rationality, and the mind. But more recent theories also enable researchers and educators to question the political motivation behind such dichotomies and the hierarchical control they imply.

Conclusion

Many teachers enter the profession with passion and commitment to give their best to the learning of their students. For some, however, changing working conditions and personal events lead to emotional exhaustion and the erosion of emotional well being. Teachers need to look beyond dominant curricula and the reproduction of existing knowledge and imagine new affective relations with their students. Teachers need to look for alternative resources and to the affective knowledges of themselves and their learners in order to subvert dominant traditions that are limiting to contemporary teaching and learning needs. The affective knowledge of teachers and students needs to be nurtured and thus constituted as a major aspect of creating relevant knowledge. Teachers must be engaged themselves in questioning their own pedagogical assumptions and practices; undoubtedly, this involves a lot of discomfort and risk for teachers and students alike. But acknowledging the power of teachers' emotions lies in its offering of new insights that challenge logocentric discourses, in order to pave the way for recognizing the transformative power of emotion.

The research findings shared in this book and their practical implications for teaching and teachers have the potential to inspire teachers to ask new questions that enrich professional development and encourage alternative expressions of emotions in teaching. How can teachers avoid internalizing certain toxic emotions (fear, guilt, and humiliation) as "appropriate"? How can they find the courage to resist the self-control imposed by an educational environment governed by a strong sense of authority and performativity? How can they create inspiring and effective learning spaces involving emotional depth that are not simply following norms prescribed to them but engage critically with inherited traditions? All these questions call for the need to construct empirical and theoretical accounts of teacher emotion that challenge existing ways of thinking about teachers' lives.

Using some of the ideas and practical tools shared in this book, teachers, teacher educators, policymakers and researchers can further explore in the future how teachers' emotions are "located" in particular educational histories (of institutions and individuals) in visible or invisible ways, and challenge the prevailing social, cultural and political structures. Analyzing and critically reflecting on one's emotions represents a considerable risk of vulnerability yet teachers are constantly challenged in the professional lives to deal with visible of invisible pain and powerlessness. Teachers can be vastly empowered in their lives by developing accounts that recognize emotion as a site of personal transformation, professional development and political resistance.

References

Barbalet JM (2001) Emotion, social theory, and social structure: a macrosociological approach. Cambridge University Press, Cambridge

Barrett LF (2006) Solving the emotion paradox: categorization and the experience of emotion. Pers Soc Psychol Rev 10:20–46

Hochschild AR (1983) The managed heart: commercialization of human feeling. University of California Press, Berkeley

Izard CE (2007) Basic emotions, natural kinds, emotion schemas, and a new paradigm. Perspect Psychol Sci 2:260–280

Lutz CA, Abu-Lughod L (eds) (1990) Language and the politics of emotion. Cambridge University Press, Cambridge

Pekrun R, Schutz PA (2007) Where do we go from here? Implications and future directions for inquiry on emotions in education. In: Schutz PA, Pekrun R (eds) Emotion in education. Elsevier, San Diego, CA, pp 303–321

Reddy WM (2001) The navigation of feeling: a framework for the history of emotions. Cambridge University Press, Cambridge, England

Rosaldo M (1984) Toward an anthropology of self and feeling. In: Shweder R, Levine R (eds) Culture theory: essays on mind, self, and emotion. Cambridge University Press, New York, pp 137–157

Schutz P, Pekrun R (eds) (2007) Emotion in education. Academic, Boston

Schutz PA, Hong JY, Cross DI, Osbon JN (2006) Reflections on investigating emotions among educational contexts. Educ Psychol Rev 18:343–360

Stearns PN (1994) American cool: constructing a twentieth-century emotional style. New York University Press, New York

Van den Berg R (2002) Teachers' meanings regarding educational practice. Rev Educ Res 72:577–625

Wouters C (1986) Formalization and informalization: changing tension balances in civilizing processes. Theory Cult Soc 3:1–18

Zembylas M (2005) Teaching with emotion: a postmodern enactment. Information Age Publishing, Greenwich, CT

Zembylas M (2007) The power and politics of emotions in teaching. In: Schutz PA, Peckrun R (eds) Emotions in education. Academic, New York, pp 293–309

Author Index

Subject Index